RESPECT AND CONSIDERATION

BRITAIN IN JAPAN 1853 - 1868 AND BEYOND

HOW QUEEN VICTORIA'S ROYAL NAVY HELPED TRANSFORM JAPAN
FROM A FEUDAL STATE TO A BENEVOLENT IMPERIAL REPUBLIC

生麦事件

THROUGH MENDACITY, MAYHEM AND MURDER
VIA *NAMAMUGI JIKEN* (THE RICHARDSON AFFAIR)
TO THE MEIJI RESTORATION

明治維新

'Twas yours to dream, to rest,
Self-centred, mute, apart,
While out beyond the West
Strong beat the world's wild heart.
　　　　　Arthur Christopher Benson, *Ode to Japan*, 1909

Copyright © John Denney 2011

All rights reserved. No part of this publication may be reproduced, stored in a retrieval system, or transmitted in any form or by any means, electronic, mechanical, photocopying, recording or otherwise, without the prior permission of the copyright owner

John W Denney hereby asserts and gives notice of his right under s.77 of the Copyright, Designs and Patents Act 1988 to be identified as the author of this work.

ISBN 978-0-9568798-0-6

Photographs and illustrations are either the author's own, used by permission, or are in the public domain and sourced from the Internet.

As far as the text is concerned, I believe I have given a comprehensive bibliography but, doubtless, there are texts I read before this project came to be whose words so impressed me that I have used them without attribution. I have not marked every individual item I have used from my sources because that would have made the book much longer and unwieldy than it already is. If I have quoted too much from my sources, please accept that as a compliment.

If I have inadvertently offended against anyone's copyright, please contact me with details and I will do the right thing. And please forgive me.

John W Denney

Published 2011

35 Laurel Road, Blaby, Leicester LE8 4DL, England

The Monument at Namamugi commemorating the incident of 14 September 1862

Contents

Illustrations: Events, Places, Objects, drawings, photographs, plans		vi
Portraits of People		viii
Tables		x
Thanks and Acknowledgements		xi
Introduction		1
Chapter 1	Summary of the historical background	6
Chapter 2	Relationships with the west before 1853	10
Chapter 3	Collision with the West	15
Chapter 4	Treaties with the West	22
Chapter 5	The Treaties in Practice	30
Chapter 6	Life in Yokohama	38
Chapter 7	Attacks on Westerners	43
Chapter 8	The Japanese Political Climate	54
Chapter 9	Shimazu Saburō, Imperial Envoy	60
Chapter 10	Charles Lenox Richardson	62
Chapter 11	Murder in the Wheatfield: the Clash at Namamugi	68
Chapter 12	The Reaction of the Foreign Community	89
Chapter 13	A Sacredly Secret Meeting	93
Chapter 14	Anglo-Japanese Diplomacy	107
Chapter 15	The Inquest on Richardson's Death	113
Chapter 16	The Obsequies	127
Chapter 17	The British Government's Response to Richardson's Death	134
Chapter 18	The Japanese respond to Britain	143
Chapter 19	Meanwhile, the American Navy chastises Chōshū	152
Chapter 20	The *bakufu* pays up but Satsuma remains Obdurate	159
Chapter 21	The Blazon of our Wrath: the Royal Navy at Kagoshima	166
Chapter 22	Further Outrages, but Satsuma complies at last	203
Chapter 23	Base Customs of former Times are abandoned	215
Chapter 24	Controversy in Britain	221
Chapter 25	The British Squadron in Japan	233
Chapter 26	HMS *Euryalus*	237
Chapter 27	Who won at Kagoshima?	244
Chapter 28	Distribution of the Satsuma compensation	246
Chapter 29	The Allied Chastisement of Chōshū: Shimonoseki	253
Chapter 30	Residual Outrages	273
Chapter 31	Early Japanese Students in Britain	291
Chapter 32	Why did the Tokugawa *shōgunate* fall?	306
Epilogue		311
Appendix 1-1	Ancient and Modern	318

Appendix 1-2	The *shōguns* and the sweep of history	332
Appendix 1-3	First Christian Arrivals from the West	340
Appendix 1-4	Three Leaders	345
Appendix 1-5	Back and Forth to Edo	355
Appendix 1-6	The *samurai*	358
Appendix 1-7	Other Ranks	365
Appendix 1-8	Japanese Religion and Philosophy	367
Appendix 1-9	*Samurai* weapons	378
Appendix 2	Text of President Fillmore's letter to the Emperor of Japan	383
Appendix 3	Biographical notes on various people mentioned in the text.	389
Appendix 4	Dr Willis' Autopsy Report on Richardson's body	448
Appendix 5	A *kyoka* on the arrival of the Black Ships	450
Appendix 6-1	Personnel of the British Legation	452
Appendix 6-2	British Diplomatic and Naval Emoluments, December 1863	457
Appendix 7	The 1860 Japanese Diplomatic Mission to America	460
Appendix 8	Walt Whitman elegiac poem on the Mission	464
Appendix 9	Extracts from surgeon's Log, HMS *Euryalus*, with glossary	469
Appendix 10	Consul Vyse and Aino Bones	482
Appendix 11	All Royal Naval Vessels mentioned	488
Note on conventions used in the text		490
Glossary of Japanese terms, with explanatory notes		492
Select Bibliography		501
Index		509
The Author		528

Illustrations of Places, Events and Objects

Monument to *Namamugi jiken*, at Namamugi	frontispiece
Map of Japan, showing towns mentioned in the text	5
Deshima in the late Seventeenth Century	9
Japanese Print of Perry's Black Ships 1854	14
USS *Susquehanna*	15
USS *Mississippi*, Japanese artist	17
Signature page of English version of Treaty of Kanagawa	18
Complete Picture of the Newly Opened Port of Yokohama, 1859, Sadahide Utagawa	21
Meeting between British and Japanese Plenipotentiaries	26
Plan of Yokohama, 1863	29
55 Stations of the *tōkaidō*. No 4: Kanagawa	30
A silver *ichibu* of 1853	32
Perry's hand reaching in to seize Japan	36
"An enjoyable time over drinks and tea", 1862, by Sadahide Utagawa	39
The English Wharf at Yokohama before the pier was built, Photograph, Kusakabe Kinbei	39
Two *Betto*	40
Panorama of Yokohama from the bluff, August 1864, photographic collage, Felice Beato	41
"General View of Yakuama", 1850, Negretti & Zambra Stereograph	42
The attack on the British Legation 1861	44
Execution of a *samurai* involved in the 1861 attack on the British Legation in Edo	48
British Consulate, Kanagawa, 1860	53
The Namamugi Incident, Woodcut by Hayakawa Shouzan	67
A foreign resident's home in Yokohama, 1861	69
Scene of the Incident 1862	72
Scene of the Incident 1863	73
Spot where Richardson fell, photographed 2006	74
Namamugi Village, 1862	88
Map showing stations on the *tōkaidō*	106
British Consulate building	110
The body of Charles Lenox Richardson lying at Mr Aspinall's house in Yokohama, 15 September 1862	125
A *kago*	126
Basic diplomatic uniform for Her Britannic Majesty's Representative	128
The graves of Richardson, Marshall and Clarke	129
The Foreign Office, Downing Street, London, prior to the completion of the present building in Whitehall in 1868	133
First edition of the Japan Herald, 23 November 1861	142
Japanese Junks, photographed by Ueno Hikoma, early 1860s	151
U.S. Steam Sloop *Wyoming*	155

Captain McDougal's sketch plan of USS *Wyoming's* action at Shimonoseki	158
Discussions on board HIMS *Sémiramis*: Sakai Hida-no-kami, Col Neale, Adm. Kuper, Adm. Jaurès, M. de Bellecourt	160
The Bombardment of Kagoshima, *Le Monde Illustré* 1864	164
Map showing the Bombardment of Kagoshima	165
An Enfield 1853 Rifled Musket	168
Sakurajima: radar image from space	182
British fleet bombarding Kagoshima, Illustrated London News, 7 November 1863	187
Sakurajima, a sailor's-eye view on a calm day	190
A sous-lieutenant of the 3ème Chasseurs d'Afrique	202
Satsuma representatives paying the indemnity	214
In the Hollow of a Wave off the Coast at Kanagawa, Hokusai Katsushika	220
Vice-Admiral's Ensign	235
H.M.S. *Euryalus*, drawn during her sea trials in 1853	238
Kuper's Fleet assembled in Yokohama, preparing to sail to Shimonoseki	254
Victoria Cross	258
Sketch map showing events at Shimonoseki, 1864	259
The Naval Brigade and Marines storming the stockade at Shimonoseki	262
Coehorn Mortar	264
Capture of one of the Shimonoseki batteries, photograph, Felice Beato	265
View near Kamakura where Major Baldwin and Lieutenant Bird were murdered	273
The severed head of Shimazi Seiji, photograph	274
Chōshū students in London	276
The British Legation Building, Yokohama 1865	290
Imperial Japanese Battleship *Fusō*	301
Newly opened Port of Yokohama, 1860 by Sadahide Utagawa	305
"La Courtisane" by Vincent Van Gogh	315
"La princesse du pays de porcelain", by James McNeill Whistler	315
Ukiyo-e by Katsukawa Shunso	315
The *Namamugi jiken* Museum	316
2006 Ceremony at Richardson's graveside: Chairman of Shimazu Corporation, Representative from British Embassy, Asaumi Takeo.	317
A malachite *magatama*, Jōmon period (1000BC-538AD)	320
Three Sacred Treasures	321
Sake Barrels at Itsukushima	322
Kikukamonshō, the Chrysanthemum Crest	323
Cherry blossom	331
A *daimyō's* procession at Namamugi	339
The Shimazu family Crest	343
Panorama of Edo in 1865/6	355
Casket in which Masakado's head was kept	358
Graves of the 47 *rōnin*, Senkakuji	364
A *torii*	368
The *samurai* Suenaga facing the Mongols, c. 1293	378

Parts of a *katana* blade	379
A sheathed *katana*	380
Commodore Perry bringing gifts for the Emperor	384
Great Seal of President of the United States	387
Officer in Royal Regiment of Horse Guards (The Blues), 1865	394
Sakurada Gate, 2006	402
The Oath in Five Articles	403
IJN *kanrin-maru*	406
Waka by Emperor Meiji, in his own hand	413
Tokugawa Crest	437
A Curio Shop	447
Tozen-ji around 1861	454
The 1860 Japanese Mission to the United States	460
Cartoon from *Harper's Weekly*, 26 May 1860	463
Ainu tattoos and Ainu beard	486
An Ainu family, c. 1906	487

PORTRAITS OF PEOPLE

William Adams	11
resident Millard Fillmore	16
Townsend Harris	22
Lieutenant-Colonel Edward St. John Neale	34
Lord Russell	50
Ii Naosuke	54
Princess Kazu-no-miya Chikako	57
Shimazu Saburō	59
Dr. James Curtis Hepburn	74
WE Gladstone. caricature by Carlo Pellegrini	138
Captain David McDougal, U.S.N.	154
Iwashita Sajiemon and the rest of the Satsuma negotiators	216
Sir Austen Henry Layard, GCB	223
Richard Cobden	224
Emperor Meiji on his 21st birthday	277
Sakamoto Ryoma	279
Katsu Kaishu	280
Kondo Isami	281
Enomoto Takeaki	286
Katsuro Kogyo	287
Nishi Amane	291
Professor William Alexander Williamson	292
Itō Hirobumi	293
Inoue Kaoru	293
Yamao Yozo	293
Endo Kinsuke	294
Inoue Masaru	294
Mori Arinori	295

Godai Tomoatsu	296
Terashima Munenori	297
Count Hayashi Tadasu	298
Nagasawa Kanae	298
Kikuchi Dairoku	299
Tōgō Heihachirō	300
Tsuda Omeko	300
Kido Takayoshi	302
Ōkubo Toshimichi	302
Iwakura Tomomi and the heads of the Iwakura Mission	303
Sir William Armstrong	304
Admiral Tōgō in 1904	312
Self portrait of Motoori Norinaga	324
Emperor Go-Daigo	338
Kūkai, or Kōbō Daishi	341
Oda Nobunaga	345
Toyotomi Hideyoshi	348
Buddhist monk Nichiren Daishōnin	372
Zhu Xi	376
Sir (John) Rutherford Alcock	390
Frederick Cornes	392
Earl of Elgin	392
Tokugawa Yoshinobu in French military uniform	393
Ii Naosuke	401
Iwakura Tomomi	403
Amiral Benjamin Jaurès	404
Captain John James Stephens Josling, RN	405
Emperor Kōmei	407
Admiral Augustus Leopold Kuper, RN	409
Lt.-Col. Edward St. John Neale	415
Lord Palmerston	420
Sir Harry Smith Parkes	423
Commodore Matthew Calbraith Perry, USN	424
Saigō Takamori	428
Sir Ernest Mason Satow	429
Takeda Kane, 1870	430
Sir Ernest Mason Satow by "Spy"	431
Shimazu Nariakira	432
Matsudaira Yoshinaga	434
Duke of Somerset	435
Admiral Sir James Stirling	436
Tokugawa Ieyasu	439
Tokugawa Ieyoshi	440
Tokugawa Yoshinobu	440
Tokugawa Yoshinobu	441
Dr William Willis	442

Dr Willis and Ernest Satow, cartoon	444
Commander Edward Wilmot, RN	445

TABLES

Table of details of Satsuma's ships captured, burned and sunk at Kagoshima	180
Captain Brine's table of Satsuma's Guns at each battery round Kagoshima	183
Master Parker's table of Satsuma's Guns at each battery round Kagoshima	183
Captain Brine's table of vessels, guns, shot & shell and casualties at Kagoshima	195
British Casualties at Kagoshima	198
Royal Naval Vessels for Kagoshima, at Yokohama August 1862	236
Gun Poundage, Barrel Length, Barrel Diameter, Calibre relationships	239
Allied Squadrons at the Forcing of the Strait of Shimonoseki, September 1864	260
The landing Party at Shimonoseki	261
Ordnance captured at Shimonoseki	264
Western Casualties at Shimonoseki	266
Percentage of modern Japanese "close to" various religions	373
Diners at the Captain's Table, HMS *Sampson*, 1859	398
Emperor Kōmei's *nengo* (era names)	408
List of Tokugawa *shōguns*	438
Salaries paid to British Legation staff, December 1863	457
Pay of various Royal Naval ranks, December 1863	459
Surgeon's Logbook, HMS *Euryalus*, 1863	470
All Royal Naval Vessels mentioned	488

Thanks and Acknowledgements

I thank my son, Stephen Denney, BA, MA, a long-term resident in Japan, and his wife Nagayama Yasuko for carrying out much remote research on my behalf in Yokohama and Kagoshima, and for translating many Japanese documents and explaining matters Japanese to me. It was on a long holiday in Japan with them that my interest, first in the "Richardson Affair" (Namamugi Incident or *namamugi jiken* as it is known in Japan), then the whole *bakumatsu*, was kindled. See www.denney-net.co.uk for a travelogue of our journeys on and off the beaten tourist track.

I particularly thank Stephen for many constructive comments on the selection and organization of the material I have assembled, and for helping me understand the context of the material. The book is infinitely the better for his contributions.

In matters Japanese, Stephen has been my *sensei*.

I thank my wife Valerie for her draughtsmanship in producing some of the maps and drawings in this book. She has also been a sound and helpful adviser on various aspects of the design and layout of it. And she has been extraordinarily patient with me as I have researched and produced this work.

I thank these three in particular for their encouragement and interest as I have burned much midnight oil. I also thank our friend Sue Hill for the use of her laptop computer on remote research assignments.

I thank the National Archives at Kew for the efficient production of an amazing variety of material from which much of this book has been drawn. It is a privilege to handle precious original documents.

I also thank Leicester University library for allowing me a reader's ticket, and Leicestershire Libraries for arranging several inter-library loans.

And I thank you, dear reader, for buying this book, or causing it to be purchased. Although I do not expect to grow rich from it, the small royalties are in themselves an encouragement and vindication of my effort.

Introduction

In the International Cemetery in Yokohama lie the graves of three Englishmen, side by side. Two died peacefully in their beds. The faint epitaph on the central tombstone reads:

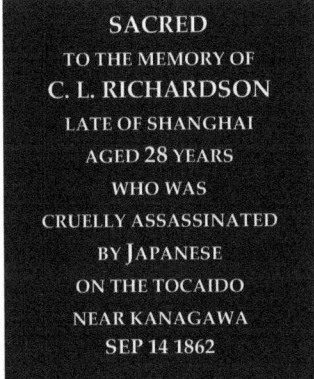

> SACRED
> TO THE MEMORY OF
> C. L. RICHARDSON
> LATE OF SHANGHAI
> AGED 28 YEARS
> WHO WAS
> CRUELLY ASSASSINATED
> BY JAPANESE
> ON THE TOCAIDO
> NEAR KANAGAWA
> SEP 14 1862

In a nutshell, the three Englishmen and a young woman were out for a ride near Yokohama. They stumbled into a procession that was taking the *daimyō* (Lord) of Satsuma, one of the most important Japanese nobles, from the *shōgun's* palace in Edo (now Tōkyō) to the Emperor's palace in Kyōto. His bodyguards drew their swords and laid into the four riders. Three escaped, two of them gravely wounded, but the fourth received fatal injuries.

The British government demanded compensation from the Japanese government and from the *daimyō* concerned. They also

RESPECT AND CONSIDERATION

demanded that the perpetrators of the murder be caught, tried and executed.

The Japanese Government paid up; the *daimyō* refused. So, the following year, the Royal Navy approached Kagoshima, capital of the Satsuma domain. To coerce the Lord of Satsuma to comply with British demands, the Royal Navy seized three of his ships; there was an exchange of gunfire; there was loss of life on both sides; a large part of the town was burned down; both sides claimed a victory.

In parallel, the *daimyō* of Chōshū waged a private war against the westerners in Japan, so the naval and military forces of five nations, under British command, responded robustly. Subsequently, the Lords of Satsuma and Chōshū negotiated settlements with the British; compensation was paid, and friendly commercial relations gradually prevailed, with a supplementary handful of western casualties in the cause of *rapprochement*. Japan came out from its hundreds of years of feudal seclusion and joined the prosperous democracies of the West.

But how did this astonishing story come about? Why was that particular Englishman to die by *samurai* sword on that Sunday afternoon? What historical forces were behind the events? What actually happened that Sunday afternoon? What was the reaction of the small foreign community in Yokohama? What relationship was there between the naval engagements at Kagoshima and Shimonoseki? And what were the consequences of these events?

This account is an attempt to answer these questions and to look at some aspects of Anglo-Japanese relationships during the *bakumatsu*, the fifteen years from 1853 to 1868 - and beyond. The paradigm shift that swept Japan from an introspective, exclusivist, feudal dictatorship to an outgoing western-style trading democracy in fifteen years was unprecedented.

INTRODUCTION

The murder of Charles Richardson and its consequences outlined above does much to shed light on the turbulent events in Japan at the time, and on the Western governments' - particularly the British government's - attitudes towards Japan, in an era when Britain truly ruled the waves. This is as much a story about the era of gunboat diplomacy as about the end of 700 years of a system of Japanese government. The legacy of these events still reverberates in Japanese society today.

And all of this took place in the days before telegraphic communication facilitated contact between the representatives in foreign lands and their government in London. A request from the British Minister Plenipotentiary in Japan for instructions from the Foreign Secretary nearly 10,000 miles away might receive a reply as much as four months later. Thus this was the last period in which the British Minister required truly plenipotentiary powers, for he had to take his own decisions within the general brief he carried. The Minister was always anxious to hear of his government's approval of his actions.

It has proved impossible to retain a strict chronological sequence in this history if we are to make sense of events. If you skip straight to Chapter 11, you'll get the excitement of the events, but won't understand what led up to them, so do start at Chapter 1!

I do not apologise for frequent digressions into secondary areas that I hope the reader will find as curious, informative and entertaining as I do. They fill in the background and explain some of what occurred. Where possible, I have included these things in the main text, but others have to remain as footnotes, or else the narrative would become too complex. But if I have appeared to be applying to enter the ancient Chinese Civil Service, where candidates were locked in a room for three days and two nights and told to write down everything they knew, then that is the way it is. So many threads intertwine in the rich

RESPECT AND CONSIDERATION

tapestry we call "history". I have had to be selective in what I have included; else this would have been a multi-volume work. It has felt at times as if I were trying to pour a quart into a thimble.

I hope this book may serve as an introduction to Japanese thought, history and culture, as an insight into the workings of the Royal Navy, as a record of the successful use of patient diplomacy, and as a reminder of a remarkable period in history, largely neglected, forgotten or ignored, especially in the West.

I trust you find this journey into the ferment of the *bakumatsu* as interesting and rewarding as I have done.

John Denney

April 2011

INTRODUCTION

Map of Japan, showing major locations mentioned in the text

CHAPTER 1
SUMMARY OF THE HISTORICAL BACKGROUND

In order to understand the various Japanese strands that lead up to the murder of poor Charles Richardson detailed in Chapter 11, we need to understand something of Japan's rich mythology and history. I include the bare bones here, but a much fuller treatment is given in Appendixes 1-1 to 1-9.

The Emperors of Japan definitively trace their lineage back historically to Emperor Ōjin in 270 AD. Less certainly, they trace their lineage back mythologically to the first Emperor, Jimmu in 711 BC. Jimmu is said to be the great-great-great-grandson of Amaterasu, the Sun Goddess, herself the daughter of the proto-gods who created the beautiful islands of Japan.

The powerful myth of descent from the gods served to place the Emperors in a unique position and rôle, and for many Japanese, still do. For the first millennium or so, they had the dual rôle of Chief Priest and Temporal Ruler. Over time, though, they ceded more and more of their temporal functions to mortal rulers, and became more and more concerned with religious matters. Eventually, the government was placed into the hands of a succession of dynasties of hereditary military rulers. In 1600 AD, the Tokugawa family took power and remained providers of these *shōguns* until 1868.

The society headed by the *shōguns* always had the Emperor in the background. Theoretically, the power was his, but the

SUMMARY OF THE HISTORICAL BACKGROUND

Tokugawa certainly ran things their own way. Surrounding the Tokugawan Court were other powerful families. Those who had sided with the Tokugawa family in the civil war that ended at the beginning of the seventeenth century were rewarded with lands and influence. Other families had land removed from them and their influence reduced almost to nothing. Each of these clans was headed by a *daimyō* or baron. Some of the *daimyō* headed armies of thousands of *samurai*. The *samurai* developed *bushidō*, a code of ethics and practice that permeated most of their activities. *Bushidō* incorporated *shintō*, *zen* buddhist, and Confucian ideas and ideals, so it served to regulate the conduct of the *samurai*.

In the years following the accession of the Tokugawa family, Japan became closed to foreign trade, and thus foreign influence. This was *sakoku*. Apart from a minor connection through Nagasaki with the Dutch, the only lawful trade and contact was with Korean and Chinese traders. Two and a half centuries of seclusion were rudely ended in 1853 when President Millard Fillmore of the United States commissioned Commodore Matthew Perry to take a letter to the Emperor of Japan. The letter demanded that Japan open herself up to trade with America, and provide friendly haven for her ships.

Japan reluctantly entered into a treaty with the United States, which was rapidly followed up by identical treaties with various European powers. The treaties not only opened up trade, but also gave rights to foreigners that caused much anxiety among the *daimyō*. Apart from the right to travel on various roads, their main bone of contention was extraterritoriality. This was a convention whereby foreigners were subject not to Japanese law, but the law of their own country. The Japanese nobles felt they were not masters within their own land.

Historic privileges for *daimyō* included the right to deference from anyone they encountered on their official travels. Not only

RESPECT AND CONSIDERATION

could they travel unimpeded, but grovelling respect had to be shown to them as their huge processions passed by. Extraterritoriality cut away at this traditional right, because foreigners refusing to show deference within the geographical limits of the Treaties could not be summarily punished according to Japanese customary law. Foreigners could insult the *daimyō* and get away with it. To *daimyō*, used to rigid standards of obsequious behaviour under the law and the code of *bushidō*, this was a source of seething annoyance.

All of this led to the establishment of the *sonnō jōi* movement ("Honour the Emperor, expel the barbarians!") that yearned for a return to *sakoku*.

These factors, and the increasing number of foreign traders and visitors to Japan set the scene for the events recounted in this book.

SUMMARY OF THE HISTORICAL BACKGROUND

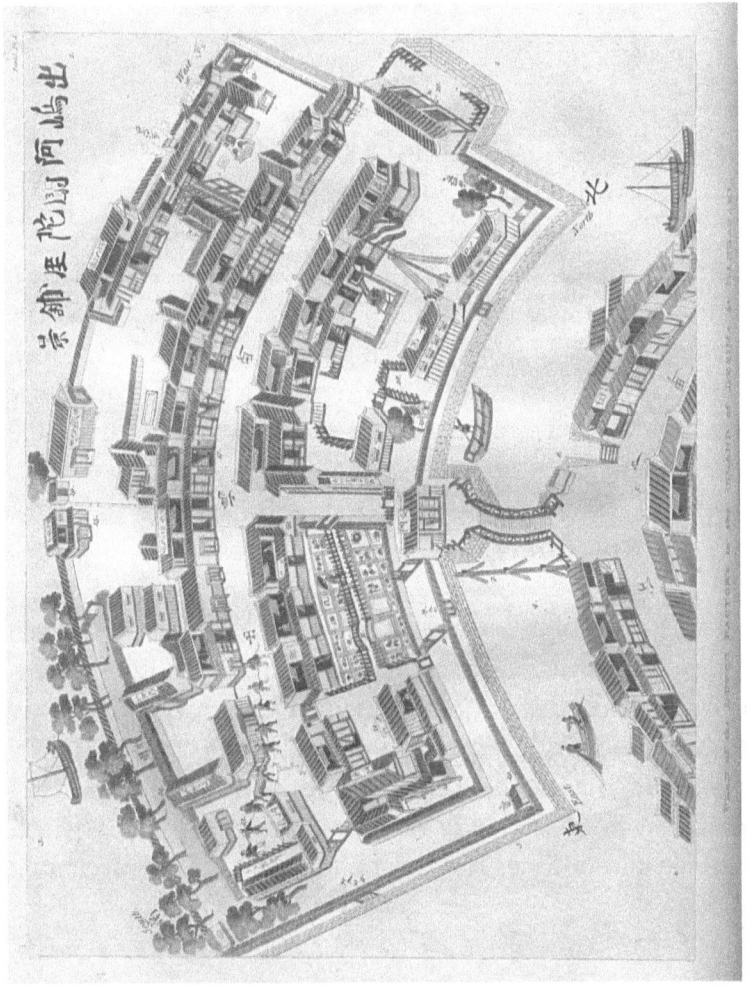

Deshima in the late seventeenth century

CHAPTER 2
RELATIONSHIPS WITH THE WEST BEFORE 1853

From the sixteenth century, there had been a small Dutch trading post at the island of Deshima[1], off Nagasaki. The items imported for the Japanese included woollen broadcloth, which was made on looms much wider than the Japanese variety, and firearms and ammunition. In return, silk, rice and tea were exported.

All foreign trade was conducted through the Japanese government, whose revenues from the taxes accrued to the *shōgun*.

Nagasaki provided a channel of informational communication as well, and it was some surprise to the Western nations in the second half of the nineteenth century, when they first made contact with Japanese intellectuals, to find that they were aware of many scientific developments in Europe. The intellectuals were also aware of current European and world events, at least in outline. The Japanese were horribly fascinated

---

[1] "Deshima" means "protruding island". It was in fact a small artificial island (120 x 75 metres, connected by a bridge to the mainland) constructed in 1634 specifically to service the Dutch traders. About 20 Dutchmen lived on Deshima. Because the island was man-made, it was not formally part of the ancient land of Japan, which was therefore kept unsullied from foreign contact.

RELATIONSHIPS WITH THE WEST BEFORE 1853

by the French Revolution, unable to comprehend how a nation could turn against its ruling class, and depose its monarch.

They did, however, understand and admire the ruthless military driving force of Napoléon Bonaparte. They could see parallels between Napoléon and Tokugawa Ieyasu, the founder of the modern *shōgunate*. Their admiration was carried forward to Napoléon's nephew, Napoléon III, who reigned concurrently with the *bakumatsu*, and called on him for military advice as the later *Boshin* War developed.

William Adams

In 1609, largely through the influence of William Adams[2], the Dutch established a trading post at Hirado, an island just off the coast near Nagasaki. In 1613, Richard Cocks, an agent of the (English) East India Company, established an English trading post there. The English operation lasted until 1623, when the company's "Factory" (what we would call a warehouse today) was closed through unprofitability (not to mention the loss of Adam's influence); notions of future trading with Japan were shelved.

The English trading post at Hirado was closed in 1641, but the Dutch were permitted to retain their small trading post at

---

[2] "Samurai William" - William Adams (1564-1620) - also known in Japanese as *Miura Anjin* (三浦按針: "the pilot of Miura") - was the first English navigator to arrive in Japan, in April 1600. The cargo on board his ship, the *Liefde*, included 19 cannon, which Tokugawa Ieyasu confiscated and used just six months later in his seminal victory at the battle of Sekigahara. Adams rapidly became a key advisor to *shōgun* Ieyasu and built Western-style ships for him. Ieyasu awarded him a 250-*koku* estate at Hemi, next to the harbour at Uraga (where Perry's Black Ships would make their momentous appearance 250 years later). Adams became the key champion for the establishment of trading factories by the Dutch and British. He was a major and prosperous trader with Asian countries, having been given "Red Seal" trading rights by Ieyasu, and made many voyages throughout Southeast Asia.

RESPECT AND CONSIDERATION

Deshima. The Chinese, more favoured, were permitted to operate a small trading post in Nagasaki. The Portuguese were forbidden to trade in 1638. Japan's external contact was solely with the handful of Dutch and Chinese merchants they dealt with.

Apart from this limited commerce, the Tokugawa governments shunned any contact with other countries. The policy became known as *sakoku* ("chained country") or "closed nation". In 1624, Spaniards had been specifically banned from entering Japan. The Japanese government was concerned that Spanish priests had brought Christianity to the country, which they saw as "un-Japanese" and a destabilising influence. Throughout the seventeenth century, many thousands of Christians, both Japanese converts and foreign priests, were martyred. In 1639, the policy of *sakoku* was extended and strengthened to become *sakoku rei* - "total exclusion" of foreigners. For some time, visiting foreigners - even shipwrecked mariners - were automatically put to death. A Portuguese diplomatic mission was sent from Macau[3] to Japan in 1640 to request re-opening of trade. Sixty-one of its delegates were executed, though the thirteen Chinese crew members were allowed to go.

In 1641, it became a capital offence for any Japanese to travel abroad. There was still limited contact, though, through trade via Deshima and minimal dealings with Korean sailors. For this reason, it has become fashionable in recent years for academics to refer to the policy of exclusion as *kaikin* 海禁, "maritime restrictions". During the *bakumatsu*, however, the *sonnō jōi* brigade was more robust and hankered after a return to *sakoku rei*, not *kaikin*. The whole period from the arrival of Pinto in 1543 to the imposition of almost total isolation around 1650 is known

---

[3] Sometimes spelt "Macao"

RELATIONSHIPS WITH THE WEST BEFORE 1853

as *nanban-bōeki-jidai,* 南蛮貿易時代, "Southern barbarian trade period".

Since the early seventeenth century, foreign books had been banned. The prohibition on these was lifted in 1720, with the exception of books promoting Christianity, which the government still viewed with suspicion.

The Dutch merchants trading from Deshima provided a conduit between Japan and Europe. The flow of information was largely towards Japan. In 1771, following diagrams in a Dutch anatomy textbook, the body of an executed criminal was dissected. This was the start of modern medical understanding in Japan, and excited a thirst for other European knowledge. Dutch textbooks on medicine, economics and botany were avidly sought. In fact, at the time of Perry's first mission, the Japanese knew more about the West than the West knew about Japan, including matters political and military. The Japanese expert *élite* who studied these things were called *rangakusha*[4] - "Scholars of Dutch knowledge".

In 1839, the "Opium Wars" waged by Britain against China came to the attention of the Japanese. They were impressed by the evident military superiority of the British military and naval forces, in arms, techniques, discipline, strategy and leadership. From that time, the Japanese added matters military to their quest for knowledge. Thus, as Japanese horizons widened, *rangaku* was gradually replaced by *yogaku* - "Western knowledge".

Western humanitarian ideas started to have some impact. In 1842, the *sakoku rei* order to drive off all foreign ships was

---

[4] Japanese lesson: the country of Holland is 阿 蘭 陀 *o-ran-da* in Japanese. It sounds somewhat like "Holland" if you think about it. "Study" or "Learning" is 学 *gaku*. The *ran* is combined with *gaku* to produce 蘭学 *rangaku*. And *sha* are scholars.

relaxed, allowing ships that were "storm-damaged or shipwrecked, come seeking food, fuel, or water" to enter port.

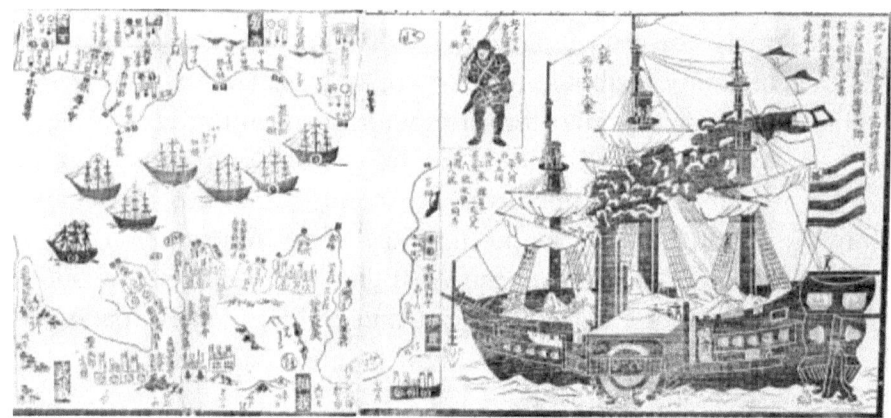
Japanese print of Commodore Perry's Black Ships

CHAPTER 3
COLLISION WITH THE WEST

In 1853, the United States Navy interrupted Japan's 250 years of self-imposed near-isolation. Commodore Matthew Calbraith Perry, with his four black[5] ships, sailed into Uraga Harbour, near Edo. The sidewheel[6] steamers USS *Mississippi* (Perry's flagship) and USS *Susquehanna*, the steam sloops of war USS *Plymouth* and USS *Saratoga* were all equipped with large guns.

USS *Susquehanna*

Perry proceeded ashore at Kurihama (near present Yokosuka) on the 14th July. He made sure that his sailors and marines were immaculately turned out, and had them perform intricate drill manoeuvres, accompanied by the ship's band. Crowds of Japanese flocked to enjoy the impressive spectacle. In discussion

---

[5] "Black" from the black smoke that poured from their funnels to the alarm of the Japanese, who had no idea that such power could be generated. The tar that waterproofed their hulls was also black. The Japanese term for the "black ships" was 黒船, *kurofune*, meaning, er, "black ships".
[6] American term for paddlewheel.

RESPECT AND CONSIDERATION

with Japanese officials, Perry boasted of being able to marshal fifty warships, or even a hundred, if need be. He reminded the Japanese of the recent victorious U.S. war against Mexico and his own part in it — which, among other things, had added California to the United States, thus providing home ports for the warships that could threaten any nation sitting in the Pacific Ocean. Perry's object was to impress the Japanese and instil in them the certainty that in any conflict, the Japanese would lose.

President Millard Fillmore

He got his point across.

Perry's arrival caused great anxiety among the *daimyō*, the *bakufu* and the Imperial Court, as they realised that such a display of force could not be ignored. They ordered him to take his flotilla to Nagasaki, the only port that they permitted foreign vessels to use, but Perry refused. This caused even greater alarm to the *bakufu*, who had no force strong enough to compel Perry to comply. The ordinary people of Japan, though, were more excited than fearful. Perry brought an insistent letter[7] for the *shōgun* (who was mistakenly thought to be equivalent to the King of Japan, in western terms) from the 13th President of the United States of America, Millard Fillmore[8]. The letter includes this summary:

---

[7] See the text of the letter and the pomp and ceremony attending its presentation, in Appendix 2.

[8] Fillmore, a Whig and later (failed) presidential candidate for the anti-Catholic "Know Nothing" Party ("I know nothing but my country, my whole country, and nothing but my country") left office in 1853, before Perry made contact. He was succeeded as President by the Democrat Franklin Pierce (1804-1869), who had risen to the rank of Brigadier-General in the war with Mexico. Pierce was a "doughface", a Northerner with Southern sympathies. Among a number of

COLLISION WITH THE WEST

> These are the only objects for which I have sent Commodore Perry, with a powerful squadron[9], to pay a visit to your Imperial majesty's renowned city of Yedo: friendship, commerce, a supply of coal and provisions, and protection for our shipwrecked people.

The Japanese no doubt took special notice of the "powerful squadron".

Perry promised (or in *bakufu* terms, threatened) to return the following year for a reply, bringing with him a larger squadron of ships, and retired to over-winter in Okinawa.

As soon as Perry's ships disappeared over the horizon, Abe Masahiro (Chief Magistrate

USS *Mississippi*, Japanese artist

---

illiberal policies, he favoured the expansion of slavery. Pierce was disowned by the Democratic Party, and was not renominated for a second term. He is widely thought to have been one of the least successful American Presidents, in the company of his own successor in 1856, Democrat James Buchanan. (Current and recent Presidents may well overtake them in the list of notoriety, but we are yet too close to see clearly.) Buchanan was another "doughface" and is still the only unmarried man to have held office as President. He had been Ambassador to Britain from 1853 to 1856. He proposed in his "Ostend Manifesto" that the USA should purchase Cuba from Spain for $130 million (or failing a purchase, it should be "wrested" from Spain) in order to strengthen the institution of slavery. This policy (the "Manifesto of Brigands", according to its opponents) was espoused by Pierce and brought about his downfall. Buchanan's greatest mistake - perhaps the greatest mistake of any American President - was to fail to deal with the Confederate secessionists. His inaction directly led to the Civil War that *his* successor in 1861, the Republican Abraham Lincoln, had to deal with.

[9] Technically, this was a "flotilla", commanded by a Commodore. A "squadron" is larger, led by a Vice-Admiral. But usage is variable, and who is to countermand the "Commander-in-Chief of the Army and Navy of the United States, and of the Militia of the several States, when called into the actual Service of the United States"?

RESPECT AND CONSIDERATION

and convener of the *gorogio* or Council of Elders) wrote to all the *daimyō* asking their opinion. Unusually, Abe included the *shinpan* and *tozama* in his survey (which indicated a relative weakening of the *fudai* position). The majority favoured rejection of Fillmore's requests, but then, they had not all seen the military might displayed by Perry's force. Others wanted, as always, to temporise, in the hope that Perry would give up and go away. Nariaki and seven others recommended preparation for war. Only Ii Naosuke and one other were for opening up to foreign trade. The Council decided that they had no option but to treat with America.

In 1854, Perry returned with a force now grown to eight ships. The Japanese had prepared a draft of a Treaty incorporating virtually all of the terms of President Fillmore's letter. Even then thinking that he was dealing with the Emperor, Perry signed the Treaty of Kanagawa - the Treaty of Peace and Amity - on 31st March 1854.

It gave America some limited trading rights, hospitality for shipwrecked mariners, and access to the second-rate and distant ports of Shimoda and Hakodate. And extraterritoriality.

But the most significant provision in the Treaty was for the establishment of an American consulate in beautiful Shimoda in September 1855. In time, this would cement commercial relationships between Japan and the rest of the outside world. *Sakoku* ("closed country") had gone forever, to be replaced by *kaikoku* ("open country").

Signature page of English version of Treaty of Kanagawa, with Perry's signature
(General Records of the United States Government, RG 11)

Extraterritoriality at this time meant that foreign subjects were to be dealt with under the law of their native land, not the

COLLISION WITH THE WEST

country where they were residing. This concept had a precedent in relations between England and Japan. In 1616, Richard Cocks, controller of the East India Company's factory in Hirado, deflected the threat of capital punishment being inflicted on William Eaton, one of his company. Eaton had killed a Japanese timber merchant in a fight, and the local *daimyō* had him in custody. Cocks informed the *daimyō* that he had special privileges granted by *shōgun* Tokugawa Ieyasu, whereby only he, Cocks, had jurisdiction over Englishmen in Japan. The *daimyō*, not wishing to offend the *shōgun*, willingly consented to Eaton's release.

The extraterritoriality provisions of the 1850s were one of the main reasons why the Japanese referred to the various "Amity and Commerce" treaties with Western countries as "Unequal Treaties". The British maintained their treaty rights to extraterritoriality until they signed the Anglo-Japanese Treaty of Commerce and Navigation (日英通商航海条約 *Nichi-Ei Tsūshō Kōkai Jōyaku*) on 16th July 1894. Other countries soon followed suit, and the separate laws that governed the foreign residents of the treaty ports were abolished.

The *samurai* classes throughout Japan were incensed at what they regarded as the humiliation brought by the treaties. Katsu Kaishū, a key statesman within the *bakufu*, later wrote[10]

> At that time, the *bakufu* decided to open the country, and gradually did so. There were many people, including the *daimyō*, who resented this. They said the *bakufu* was forced by the barbarians to open the country because of its cowardice and weakness, and that this was why the *bakufu* submitted to this humiliation. They no longer believed in the *bakufu*. There was heated argument everywhere. People were killing foreigners, and assassinating government officials.

---

[10] In *bakufu shimatsu*, vol. 11, p256.

RESPECT AND CONSIDERATION

The overriding hot issue with those opposed to the treaties was the inclusion of extraterritoriality provisions. It was as if Japan were treated as a colony, not a proud sovereign nation created by the gods. Extraterritoriality was the fuel and a focus for the *sonnō jōi* movement.

Despite their resentment at extraterritoriality, the Japanese put an extraterritoriality clause into the Kangwha Treaty it enforced - by gunboat diplomacy - on Korea in 1876. They had learned their lessons well.

There *is* a Japanese word for irony: 皮肉 (*hiniku*[11]).

---

[11] Enigmatic fact: the two *kanji* characters are for "skin" and "meat" respectively. How this translates to "irony" is perhaps something only the Japanese can understand.

COLLISION WITH THE WEST

Complete Picture of the Newly Opened Port of Yokohama, 1859
Sadahide Utagawa

CHAPTER 4
TREATIES WITH THE WEST

Although the Kanagawa treaty was formulated to American satisfaction, the Japanese governmental bureaucracy did everything in its power to delay, prevent and make difficult any transactions under the treaty. This persisted until March 1857, when Townsend Harris, the American Legate, insisted that the treaty should be implemented freely. The memory of Perry's powerful fleet visit in 1854 caused the *bakufu* to remove bureaucratic obstacles. In 1857, the treaty provisions were extended to allow trading from Nagasaki.

Townsend Harris
Detail from portrait by James Bogle, 1855
City College, New York

One of Harris's negotiating ploys for the extension was to say that it would be better for Japan to conclude negotiations with the Americans than to wait until the British turned up to negotiate. Britain, he pointed out, was much more aggressive commercially than America. There is a note in the Japanese transcripts of the discussions where Harris is quoted as saying

> ...the English Government hopes to hold the same kind of intercourse with Japan as she holds with other nations, and is ready to make war on Japan.

LIFE IN YOKOHAMA

Harris went on to talk of
> British desires to take possession of Yezo (present-day Hokkaidō), as a buffer against Russia

and also warned of the evils of the opium trade that the British had forced on China:
> If a man use opium once he cannot stop it, and it becomes a life-long habit to use opium; hence the English want to introduce it into Japan.

These were duplicitous assertions that rather over-stated the case, but they had their effect on the *bakufu*: they would deal with the Americans.

In December that year, the *shōgun*, for the first time, met a Western Legate - Townsend Harris - in person. This voluntary indignity indicated a painful acknowledgement that the Japanese had to pursue friendly relations with the foreigners.

In 1853, the *Illustrated London News* had commented,
> The opening of Japan has become a necessity, which is recognized in the commercial adventure of all Christian nations, and by every owner of an American whale-ship, and every voyager between California and China."

That statement held true for all time, at least for the West.

The Harris Treaty of 1858 went much further than the Japanese initially appreciated when negotiations opened. Key provisions in the final agreement included:
- The exchange of diplomatic representatives.
- The opening of five ports (Kanagawa, Nagasaki, Hakodate, Niigata, and Hyōgo [present day Kobe]) to unimpeded trade. American citizens were granted the right to reside in and around those designated ports. In fact, the Japanese presciently chose to develop Yokohama, on the other side of the bay, rather than Kanagawa. Kanagawa was too close to the *tōkaidō*, with the danger of clashes between hostile *daimyō* and

westerners. Yokohama, a small fishing village, was a better anchorage, and not too far from Edo.
- Extraterritorial privileges continued for American citizens.
- A low fixed scale of duties on imports. This prevented Japan from erecting high tariff barriers to protect their own industries. Though rates varied over the years, by 1866, the duties had became fixed at 5% *ad valorem* for almost all foreign items, with no clear provisions for when these exceedingly low rates would be terminated. To compound the matter, currency exchange rates were artificially fixed at disadvantageous rates, as far as the Japanese were concerned.
- Commerce in opium was specifically prohibited. This was an American strike against Britain, who had shaefully forced China to accept imports of the debilitating drug by defeating China in the first Opium War of 1839-1842.
- Christianity was permitted to be practised by foreign residents, though native Japanese were still under restriction in this regard. From the earliest approaches to Japan by the West, there was a strong religious desire to evangelize Japan with the Christian faith. "Trade", an American magazine opined as Perry prepared to sail to Japan, "is but a vehicle for opening a highway for the chariot of the Lord Jesus Christ."[12]
- The Japanese were permitted to "purchase or construct in the United States ships of war, steamers, merchant ships, whale ships, cannon, munitions of war, arms of all kinds"

---

[12] Website www.blackshipsandsamurai.com/yokohama

LIFE IN YOKOHAMA

- The Japanese were permitted to employ "scientific, naval and military men, artisans of all kinds, and mariners to enter its service."

Within a few months, the Netherlands, Russia, Britain, and France swooped in to extract similar bilateral treaties. The Japanese called these four countries along with the United States the "people of the five nations." In 1861, Prussia was a *Johannes*-come-lately number six to the commercial feeding frenzy that developed, but the "five nations" rubric remained.

It was noted by the Japanese that on Britain's part, there were no demands of the sort that Harris had deviously suggested would be made. American statements were henceforth viewed with some scepticism by the *bakufu*, and Britain was viewed as being straightforward in her diplomatic statements.

The Anglo-Japanese Friendship Treaty (日英和親条約 *Nichi-Ei Washin Jōyaku*) was signed on 14th October 1854 at Nagasaki. The British signatory was Admiral Sir James Stirling, who acted on his own initiative and negotiated the Treaty without instruction from his government. The *bugyō* (governors) of Nagasaki signed on behalf of the *bakufu*. It provided for safe haven for shipwrecked mariners, and access to supplies and provisions for British ships. Stirling's main aim was to prevent the Russians from disrupting British Trade with China, and to prevent the Russians gaining access to Japanese ports, for the Crimean War was being waged at that very time. Stirling's independent Treaty was, in the event, ratified by the British Government, and Stirling was commended for it. Some bellicose factions in the Royal Navy, however, castigated Stirling for preferring the niceties of diplomacy over pugnacious action - attacking the Russian Eastern Fleet that cruised the China Sea with impunity.

The subsequent Anglo-Japanese Treaty of Amity and Commerce (日英修好通商条約 *Nichi-Ei Shūkō Tsūshō Jōyaku*) was negotiated by Lord Elgin on a special visit from his base in Shanghai, and signed on 26th August 1858.

Among other provisions, the Treaty with Britain provided for
- A British representative to live in Edo.
- Minimal import duties on British goods imported to Japan.
- British subjects' rights to travel unimpeded within 25 miles of Kanagawa, Hakodate and Nagasaki.
- Extraterritoriality.

Meeting between British and Japanese Plenipotentiaries
from *The Earl of Elgin's mission to China and Japan*

After signature, Elgin unilaterally inserted a clause to the effect that any concessions later granted to other countries would apply also to the British.

All of this was traumatic for Japanese society, used to its hundreds of years of isolation, consoling itself with the idea that its unique values gave it a superior way of life. The treaties were regarded by the Japanese government as having been signed under duress. They were always referred to as the "Unequal Treaties" within the *bakufu*, but many Japanese xenophobes

LIFE IN YOKOHAMA

blamed the *bakufu* for failing in its duty to inflict a painful rebuke to Perry and his successors and then send them away.

Another factor that caused rumblings of discontent among the warrior classes against the western merchants was the economic impact of the treaties. Unemployment rose. The domestic prices of many staple commodities such as rice and other cereals, silk and silkworms, tea, and *sake* soared astronomically. So precipitous was the inflation that in 1862 a city magistrate in Edo reported that living costs had increased by 50 percent in just one year. In the mid-1860s there were several consecutive bad harvests; famine was widespread, and was blamed, unsurprisingly, on the five nations. By 1867, the price of rice - the most vital of staples - had increased twelvefold in some areas over the price that had held steady for the entire two centuries before 1858.

The exchange rates between silver and gold bullion were so skewed as to be disastrous for the Japanese economy. This precipitated an enormous drain of gold from Japan, leading to a heavy devaluation of the Japanese currency in 1860. The domestic exchange ratio within Japan was five units of silver to one of gold. The international rate, however, was 15 units of silver to one of gold. Traders could take, say, 100 pounds of gold to India and exchange it for 1500 pounds of silver. Bringing that back to Japan enabled them to exchange the silver for 300 pounds of gold. This could be done repeatedly, multiplying the gold's value by three each time. The westerners who latched onto this opportunity for arbitrage rapidly became rich. But this was no magic egg-laying goose. The multiple had to be acquired from somewhere. It was of course obtained from the Japanese nation, whose economy was restricted as a result, and the people were impoverished.

There was a culture shock for the British, too. Japan was sophisticated in cultural, social and even industrial matters.

RESPECT AND CONSIDERATION

They were surprised that Japan had a literacy rate of some 70%, when in Britain it was only 40%. *Imari-yaki* pottery[13] was superior in quality even to highly prized British Wedgwood. The Japanese used discarded ukiyo-e orints to wrap pottery sent to the west, much as one might use old newspaper. Opening the parcels, Britain was astonished that such high-quality art could be so discarded. This fuelled the great upsurge of *Japonisme* in the art world of the later nineteenth century. And some of those discarded prints, carefully pressed, are still hanging in art galleries in Europe today.

Consequently, the British approach to Japan differed from their approach to China or India. Japan was regarded as a recognisable 'nation' in the western sense. Perhaps this is one unspoken reason why Britain demanded such a high indemnity for the Richardson murder - £25,000 - from the most powerful of the *daimyō*: as a test to see how easily Satsuma would give in, and therefore how soft future trading negotiations with him and the other *daimyō* would be.

The *bakufu* sought to keep the Western trading communities confined to closely defined areas. The main trading port authorised by the Treaties was Kanagawa, today part of Yokohama. Shimoda and Hakodate as well as Nagasaki were also ports of entry. There were separate treaties that provided for foreign Legations to be established in Edo, close to the *bakufu* headquarters. Kanagawa (more so its neighbour Yokohama) thus became a large and thriving Western settlement.

---

[13] Imari was simply the port of export of the pottery. The fine porcelain was made in fact in Arita in northwest Kyūshū.

LIFE IN YOKOHAMA

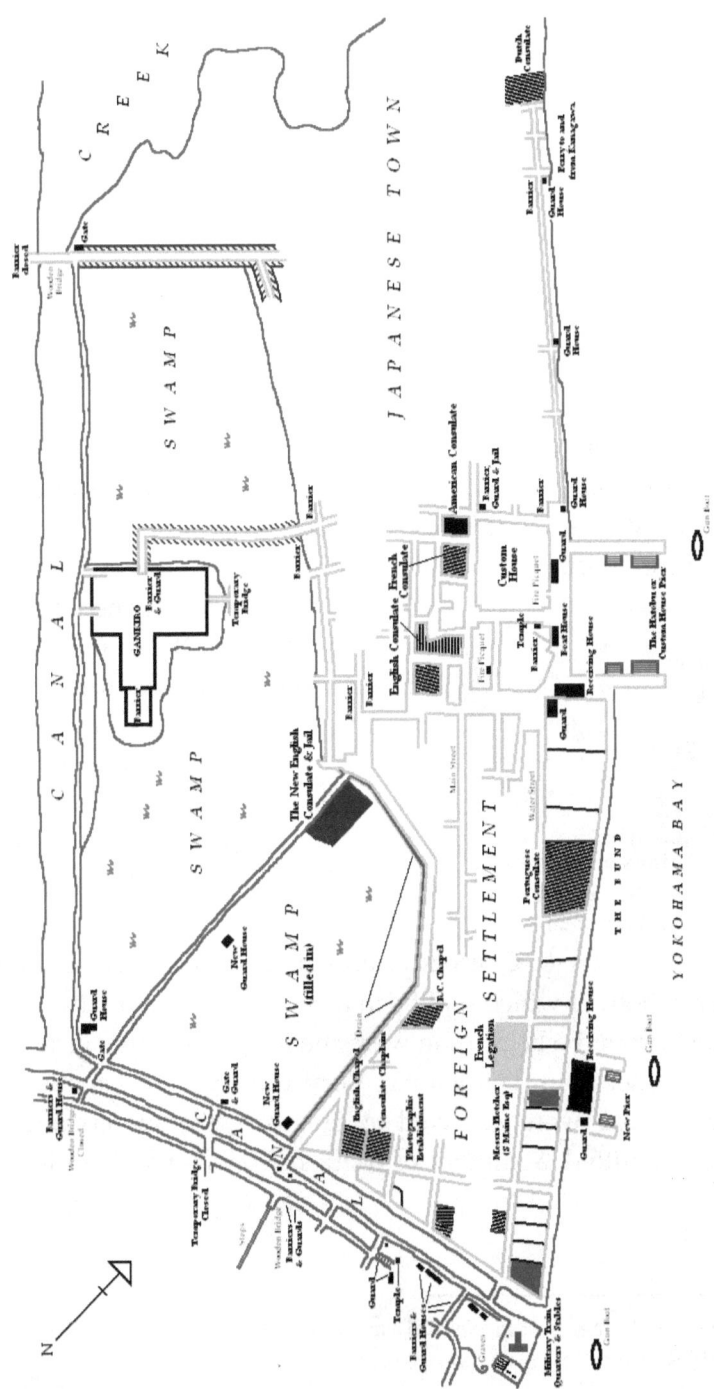

Yokohama in 1863. Valerie Denney, after Capt. F. Brine R.E.

Chapter 5
The Treaties in Practice

As part of the treaties, the *tōkaidō*, the road from Edo (seat of the *shōgun*) to Kyoto (seat of the *tennō*[14]) was open to Westerners within 25 miles of the treaty ports without the need for special permit. Travel elsewhere required a licence from the *bakufu*. The *tōkaidō* passed through the outskirts of Kanagawa. This was important, as later events would show.

The 55 stations of the *tōkaidō*:
No. 4. Kanagawa
Hiroshige Ando

The new opportunities thus obtained were quickly exploited by entrepreneurs and opportunists from the western nations. Led by the firms of Jardine Matheson & Company, and their bitter rivals Dent & Company, both of which had been active in China's treaty ports, the British from the beginning were the largest national group of foreign residents in Yokohama. Very quickly, the established Trading Houses were followed by chancers, freebooters and, it has to be admitted, a number of rogues. They met and started to

---

[14] The reigning Emperor of Japan is always referred to as *tennō heika* ("reigning heavenly sovereign"). Foreign monarchs are called *kotei*.

THE TREATIES IN PRACTICE

trade with equally rapacious Japanese merchants. Sir Ernest Satow[15] says,

> The Japanese traders were a class of adventurers, destitute of capital and ignorant of commerce. Broken contracts and fraud were by no means uncommon ... Raw silk was adulterated with sand or fastened with heavy paper ties, and every separate skein had to be carefully inspected before payment, while the tea could not be trusted to be as good as the sample ... The Custom House officials were in the highest degree corrupt, and demanded ever-increasing bribes from the foreigners who sought to elude the import duties ... (on) wines, beer, spirits and stores, for which exemption from the payment of duty was claimed as goods intended for 'personal use'.

Indeed, in 1861, the visiting bishop of Victoria (Hong Kong) reported that he had heard complaints from a Japanese silk-dealer that the Japanese customs officials were charging a completely unauthorised tariff of three percent "secret" duty on his bales of silk destined for export to Britain. The bishop was in no doubt as to the destiny of that three percent.

There were a number of cases where the Western traders cheated their Japanese counterparts, some of them brought before the consular courts. Formalities apart, there was something of the Wild West about the life of Yokohama. The *Yoshiwara*[16], or brothel quarter, was a popular resort for the many unattached men of the port. Satow says,

> The foreign community was somewhat extravagantly described by an English diplomat as 'the scum of Europe'. No doubt, some men, relieved of the

---

[15] Pronounced to rhyme with "tomato" in the British pronunciation of the word.
[16] *Yoshiwara* (吉原) means "Good Luck Meadow", and housed up to 3000 prostitutes.

pressures of society and family they experienced at home ... did not conduct themselves with the strict propriety of students at a theological college.[17]

The number of foreigners who took up residence in 1858-1859 was around one hundred. By mid-1861, it had risen to some 250, and around 400 by 1866. The British were the single largest national contingent, with about 70% of the population of Yokohama being British. According to historian Foster Rhea Dulles, in 1866 there were "five hotels, twenty-five grog shops, and an unrecorded number of brothels in the foreign settlement" of Yokohama.

Silver *ichibu* of 1853

In 1861, trade was only just starting to build up. Around 100 ships docked at Yokohama that year, about half of them British. The value of legitimate goods (excluding bullion) imported into Japan was about $300,000, and exports were about $700,000. The bulk of the export trade was still "edibles for the Chinese market"; but during 1861, tea and silk became significant.

Even the diplomatic corps was prone to self-interest and standards of financial conduct that would not be acceptable today. Satow explains,

---

[17] Satow, in his published memoirs, repeatedly comments on the prettiness of the young Japanese maids and serving-women he met in tea-houses, restaurants and other places of resort. There is an air of dalliance - even flirting - in the way he expresses himself on the matter, though, of course, no suggestion that he ever descended from theological college standards of behaviour. He did, however, have a Japanese "common-law wife" (marriage with a foreigner was unthinkable for an ambitious British diplomat of the period), Takeda Kane, by whom he had two sons, Eitaro and Hisayoshi.

THE TREATIES IN PRACTICE

The merchant had to buy his *ichibu*[18] in the open market, while Ministers and Consuls and their staff, and sailors and soldiers, obtained the equivalent of their salary, and often much more, in native coin nearly weight for weight of his "Mexicans", which was to the minds of all unprejudiced persons a far greater scandal. The "scandal" worked like this: in September 1862, the actual rate of exchange was 214 *ichibu* for 100 Mexican dollars[19], though the Treaty stipulated an exchange rate of 311 *ichibu* to the dollar. Each diplomatic or consular establishment was allowed to exchange a certain number of dollars each month, calculated to represent the establishment's expenses and the total salaries of the staff. So a diplomat or military man whose salary was $100 a month received 311 *ichibu* less a standard 13-ichibu commission on each $100. Thus he had 298 *ichibu* in his hand. He could then reconvert this back to Mexican dollars at 214 *ichibu* to the dollar. His 298 *ichibu* thus converted to $139.25. For no effort, his salary was increased by 39.25%.

---

[18] The *mon* 文 was a coin used in Japan until just after the Meiji restoration. Coins denominated in *mon* were of copper or iron and had a hole in the centre: they were usually strung together. For higher values there were cast silver and gold ingots denominated in *shu, bu* and *ryō* 両 . 16 *shu* = 4 *bu* = 1 *ryō*. *Ichibu* means "one *bu*".

[19] Strictly speaking, the Mexican "dollar" was a *peso* (= 8 silver *reales*), but it was universally referred to as the Mexican dollar. It varied in value, but at the time of the events described here, it was worth around 1s.9d. The exchange rate for the American dollar at this time was around 4s.2d. to the $ ($4·80 = £1).

RESPECT AND CONSIDERATION

Lt.-Col. Edward St. John Neale

Lieutenant-Colonel Neale, the British Chargé d'Affaires, had an annual salary of £800 in 1863, and a further £1095 as Acting Consul General, a total of £1895. By dint of the exchange rate rip-off scheme, he could make an extra £743 a year.[20]

Not only that, but the total establishment monthly amount permitted to be exchanged, after expenses had been met and the salaries had been paid to the staff, was put through the same process, and the profit distributed pro-rata to their salaries. Satow comments,

> on a nominally small income, it was consequently possible to live well, keep a pony and drink champagne.

but he laments, twenty-four years later,

> I cannot look back on that period without shame, and my only excuse, which is perhaps of little worth in the court of history, is that I was at the bottom of the ladder, and received the proportion paid to me by those who were in charge of the business.

The westerners' attitude to non-westerners in general was one of a superior to an inferior. The subjugation of India in the eighteenth century and of China in the 19th had given the British (and by association, the European and American trading nations) a conviction that they were indeed the natural superiors

---

[20] See Appendix 6 for a note on the salaries paid to the members and retainers of the British Legation and the Royal Navy personnel of the same period.

THE TREATIES IN PRACTICE

of the Asian peoples. At the diplomatic, educated and gentry levels of society, this was expressed in genteel ways. The conceit of the westerners became more pronounced and widespread the lower down the social strata it emanated. His grace the Right Reverend Dr. George Smith[21], the Lord Bishop of Victoria (Hong Kong), a pioneer missionary in Asia, had visited "Lewchew" (the Ryūkyū Islands) in 1850 and toured Japan in 1860. He expressed concern about the behaviour of some of the foreign residents in Japan:

> I have seen Englishmen and others of my acquaintance in different parts of Japan riding at a rapid pace through the villages and suburbs of cities amid crowds of people, who had to scamper in hurried movement from side to side to avoid being knocked down, and who may doubtless be supposed to view with no kind feelings the presence of such equestrians ... Such scenes entail annoyance of the native population and may bring danger on foreigners themselves ...

And a French visitor complained of

> the insolent arrogance and swagger, the still more insolent familiarity, or the besotted violence, of many a European resident or visitor[22].

Prophetic words, perhaps.

Britain's long association with India, and the fact that Indian ports were often the immediate staging-posts for the sea voyage to Japan brought an unfortunate side-effect of trade: cholera. Despite their high standards of public and personal hygiene, certainly tens, and possibly hundreds, of thousands of Japanese died from cholera over the first 20 years of commercial relations

---

[21] George Smith, D.D. (1815-1871) was the energetic first Anglican bishop of Victoria (Hong Kong) from 1849 to 1865. He was also founder-warden of St Paul's Missionary College from 1850. He learned Mandarin and conducted services in that language.

[22] www.blackshipsandsamurai.com/yokohama.

RESPECT AND CONSIDERATION

with the West. Sir Rutherford Alcock says that in 1861 there were 200,000 deaths in Edo alone. The Japanese were firmly of the belief that the 1861 outbreak was occasioned by the visit of the USS *Mississippi*. An alternative scapegoat was the introduction of the watermelon, which Commodore Perry had brought seven or eight years previously, along with potatoes. Perhaps the plants had been fertilised with cholera-infected human waste[23], and not properly washed before consumption of its delightful and refreshing flesh.

There were, of course, many beneficial results of the treaties. One of them was the despatch of a Japanese diplomatic mission to the United States when 76 emissaries visited America to enthusiastic acclaim and welcome in 1860. The New York *Times*

Perry's hand reaching in to seize Japan
Woodcut c. 1855

---

[23] Human manure was, apart from occasional use of seaweed, the only fertiliser known to, and used by, the Japanese at that time. There were few domestic animals.

THE TREATIES IN PRACTICE

of 18th June 1860 reported on the official parade in enthusiastic terms. The poet Walt Whitman composed a poem on the occasion. See Appendixes 7 and 8.

Satow's comments on the quality of trade between Japan and the west are echoed in a later comical ditty from "Residential Rhymes" by Osman Edwards. Launched in 1899, this was
> Published for the hapless foreigners who (un)fortunately lived through the humorous side of their endeavors in the land of the rising sun in Meiji era. 8 poems for the Merchant at Yokohama.

THE GLOBE-TROTTER AT KAMAKURA[24]
Air: "Yankee Doodle"

Doodle *san* will leave Japan
With several tons of cargo;
Folk will stare, when all his ware
Is poured into Chicago.

    There's silk, cut velvet, old brocade,
    And everything, that's *"joto,"*
    And ancient bronzes, newly made
    For dealers in Kyoto.

        His tones entice with accent nice:
        "Ikoorah?" and *"Ikutsu?"*
        A million dollars is the price
        For mammoth *Daibutsu*.

            Doodle *san* will leave Japan,
            A happier man, though poorer;
            Unpurchased yet, the god, you bet,
            Will stay at Kamakura.

---

[24] *Joto* is "first class, the best"; *Ikoorah?* and *Ikutsu?* are "How much?" and "How many?" The *Daibutsu* is the huge bronze statue of Buddha at Kamakura, still one of the great sights of Japan.

CHAPTER 6
LIFE IN YOKOHAMA

After Yokohama became an open port in 1859, foreigners began steadily arriving in Japan. It was difficult, initially, to find food acceptable to the European palate. The Japanese peasant diet was predominantly rice, with small quantities of fish and even smaller quantities of meat, enlivened by an occasional pickle, and on high days and holidays, fruit. The *samurai* and *daimyō* had perhaps a little more fish and meat, but the essence of the daily diet was similar. This nutritional règime was not congenial to the average westerner, used to richer fare.

In 1878, Isabella L. Bird complained in her book that in Japan
> bread, butter, milk, meat, poultry, coffee, wine, and beer, are unattainable, that fresh fish is rare, and that unless one can live on rice, tea, and eggs, with the addition now and then of some tasteless fresh vegetables, food must be taken (on travels), as the fishy and vegetable abominations known as 'Japanese food' can only be swallowed and digested by a few, and that after long practice.

LIFE IN YOKOHAMA

The English Wharf at Yokohama before the pier was built
Ships were unloaded onto small boats by stevedores.
Photograph by Kusakabe Kinbei

As late as 1893, Amy Carmichael, an English missionary not given to complaint about conditions, says, in a semi-jocular letter home, that Japanese food consisted of

> native fish paste, pale mud colour and nasty; semi-boiled animal, nature unknown; eggs young and old; perfectly raw fish; brown seaweed; black beans in a liquid like senna tea; chicken (usually a fowl of much experience) in sugary juice; leathery scraps floating around in some terribly fishy liquid; sliced bamboo, lily roots, odoriferous radish, sea-weed, sea-ears, sea-slugs, plus pickle, plus rice.

"An enjoyable time over drinks and tea"
1862, by Sadahide Utagawa

RESPECT AND CONSIDERATION

Occasional treats were obtained from trading ships' larders, and the trading companies received irregular shipments of western comestibles. It was not long, then, before entrepreneurs started to open simple dining establishments.

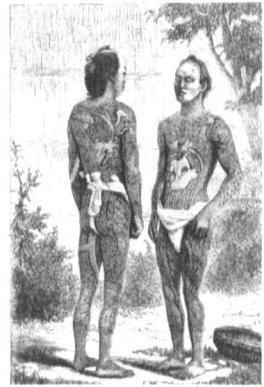
Betto
from Harper's magazine

In December 1862, the first true western restaurant in Japan - the Golden Gate Restaurant - opened for business at lot no. 49 in the Yokohama foreign settlement. It was founded by C. George & Co. to serve the Europeans and Americans living at the foreign settlement, as well as foreigners putting in at Yokohama. It had no fixed opening hours, but provided meals and drinks "at reasonable prices" at all hours. It later moved to lot 130, and became an inn with a fine dining room.

In 1863, a restaurant called *Au Trois Frères Provencaux* advertised its opening in the *Japan Herald*. The partners, Messieurs Pellet et Debez, declared it was the first to provide an *à la carte* selection as well as the more usual *table d'hôte*, and it became famous for its range of pastries and confectioneries. Their advertisement proclaimed that their staff would give

> close and individual attention to the alimentary requirements of every patron, who would be welcomed between 10 a.m. and 7 p.m.

M. Debez soon dropped out of the establishment, and M. Pellet recruited a renowned chef from Shanghai. The business prospered.

In response, on 30th July 1864, the Yokohama Restaurant opened for business at the Yokohama Hotel, at No. 70 in the foreign settlement. Their unique selling point was

> a French chef, from one of the finest restaurants of Paris.

LIFE IN YOKOHAMA

Such was the admiration for his skills, that the Yokohama Hotel became the favoured place for official banquets, which were a staple of diplomatic entertainment.

The prospering foreign community had time for leisure pursuits. A favourite Sunday's excursion was to ride along the *tōkaidō* to Kawasaki for tiffin, a light meal that might include small sandwiches and cakes as well as tea or coffee, followed by a return to Yokohama as evening fell, champagne being consumed along the way. Riding was popular, and many foreigners employed *betto* or running grooms to look after their horses and ponies. There was even a pack of hounds imported from Shanghai, and a large and enthusiastic (not to say drunken) hunt crashed through the countryside — and rice fields — hunting boar, deer, and particularly foxes, to the disapproval and dismay of the Japanese. In 1866, the Japanese Government commissioned an English architect to build a horse-racing track and wooden grandstand on a site in Negishi near Yokohama. The *bakufu* was responding to requests by the foreign community for a place where they could enjoy equestrian pursuits in safety, having been deeply disturbed by the Namamugi Incident. The racetrack is still in use today.

Stitched panorama of Yokohama from the bluff in August, 1864.   Felice Beato

RESPECT AND CONSIDERATION

Kawasaki has a fine temple known as the *Daishi*[25], established in 1128AD, a favoured tourist destination. Charles Richardson and his party were going there when the events described in this book took place. Longer outings were to Kanazawa, Kamakura or Enoshima; but anyone who had ventured as far as Hachiōji or Hakone, which were beyond the Treaty limits, was regarded as a bold, adventurous, not to say, reckless, spirit.

General view of Yakuama, 1859
No. 72 in "Views in Japan" Stereograph series published by Negretti and Zambra.
Probably photographed by Swiss photographer Pierre Rossier.
The caption on the reverse of the stereograph says
> Yakuama is a city built only in the last twelve months. The Houses in the foreground of the picture, beyond the rice fields, are the Government offices, the city is seen in the distance across the water.

---

[25] Or *Taishi*. Its official name is *Kongozan Kinjo-in Heiken-ji*, and has a site occupying 33000 square metres (a little over 8 acres). It was almost entirely destroyed by a bombing raid in April 1945, and has been completely rebuilt, largely to the original design, since. In 1862, its particularly elegant roof, which housed vast numbers of doves, was regarded as a marvellous construction. In its twenty-first century incarnation, the temple has a prayer hall specializing in motor accidents and good driving.

Chapter 7
Attacks on Westerners

In reaction to the unwelcome end of *sakoku*, there was much angry dissent among many Japanese who did not wish to be tainted by contact with the outside world. There were, ominously, assassination attempts by roving bands of *rōnin* (masterless *samurai*) on Westerners, some of them successful.

- On the evening of 26th August 1859, just six weeks after the establishment at Yedo of the British and American Representatives, an officer and a seaman belonging to a Russian man-of-war were - literally - cut to pieces in the streets of Yokohama, where they had landed to buy provisions;
- In November 1859, a Chinese servant working for the French vice-consul was attacked and killed in the foreign settlement at Yokohama;
- On 30th January 1860, Sir Rutherford Alcock's native Japanese interpreter, Dankichi, was stabbed from behind[26] as he was standing in the gateway of the British Legation in Yedo;

---

[26] Being stabbed from behind was an ignominious assault. Under the code of *bushidō*, a *samurai* wounded from behind, even in a surprise ambush, was strictly required to commit *seppuku*, since the direction of the attack meant that

RESPECT AND CONSIDERATION

- In February 1860, two Dutch merchant captains were slaughtered in the high street at Yokohama;
- In October 1860, the French Minister's Japanese servant was cut at and badly wounded as he was standing at the gate of the Legation near Shinagawa, Yedo.
- The First Secretary of the American Legation, Henry Heusken, was stabbed and killed on the 14th January 1861, as he was riding home after a dinner-party at the Prussian Legation[27].

On the night of 5th July 1861 the boldest attempt yet made on the life of foreigners took place, when the British Legation in the Buddhist Temple of *tozen-ji* was attacked by a band of armed men and the guard provided by the *bakufu* initially ran from their posts. The would-be assassins intended to take the life of the British Minister, Sir Rutherford Alcock.

The attack on the British Legation, from the Illustrated London News 12 October 1861

The Minister's secretary, Laurence Oliphant, and the British Consul at Nagasaki, George S Morrison, who were both staying in the Legation, were severely wounded. Morrison was the only one to have a pistol at readiness, and he loosed off two shots, killing one of the assailants. After Morrison had fired his two shots, the majority of the Japanese guard returned and killed a

---

the *samurai* might be thought to have been running away. *Samurai* were not averse to <u>attacking</u> from the rear, though.

[27] In the light of subsequent events, it is interesting to note that the *bakufu* readily conceded $10,000 Mexican as compensation for Heusken's death, to be given to his widowed mother. The *bakufu* subsequently said they would have paid much more than this, had Townsend Harris demanded it.

ATTACKS ON WESTERNERS

number of the assassins.

Morrison went home on leave after the attack on the British Legation to recuperate from his wounds. He only returned to Nagasaki in the spring of 1863, nearly two years later. However, he never really recovered. In September 1863, he was sent home again on sick leave, having submitted a report to Col. Neale concerning what he believed was a plot against himself, the object being to assassinate him. Neale, judging by the eloquent silence of his response, thought Morrison had developed paranoia, or at least had lost his stiff-upper-lip nerve. Oliphant had had to be repatriated[28,29], so serious were his wounds.

Oliphant had arrived as Secretary to Lord Elgin at the Legation in Edo at the end of June 1861. The official British account of the attack by the Mitō *samurai* reveals that Oliphant rushed out with the only weapon to hand, a hunting-whip, and was attacked by a Japanese with a heavy two-handed *katana* or sword. A wooden beam, invisible in the darkness, interfered with the *samurai's* sword-strokes, but Oliphant was severely wounded and had to be evacuated to a hospital berth on a ship.

The *daimyō* of Mitō had been furnished, it was said, with a secret document from the Emperor, commanding him to induce the *shōgun* to exterminate the barbarians, so he had moral

---

[28] Oliphant returned via China to England, where he resigned from the Foreign Office, pursuing initially a career as Member of Parliament for Stirling (1865-1868). He was also an author and journalist. He became a member of a religious commune, the "Brotherhood of the New Life" led by Thomas Lake Harris. When the Japanese students from Chōshū arrived in London in the 1860's, Oliphant befriended them and several of them later joined the commune.

[29] Eventually, the *bakufu* paid £2458.12.3d as compensation, which Lord Russell decreed should be paid as to £500 to Morrison with his "minor" injuries (minor, despite medical certificates showing that he was unfit to return to Japan for almost two years), and £1958.12.3d to Oliphant, who had suffered permanent loss of use of a hand. This equates to some £29,000 and £113,000 in 2008 values respectively

authority for his action at the Legation. Whether or not this is true, sword and bullet marks can still be seen in the woodwork of the rooms of *tozen-ji* where the attack took place.

Sir Rutherford Alcock, the British Minister in Japan, was understandably concerned about the frequent assassinations of Europeans in Japan. Triggered by this latest attack, he wrote to Admiral Hope (Rear-Admiral Kuper's predecessor as commander-in-chief of the East Indies and China Station of the Royal Navy) on 8th July 1861, saying there were "but one or two alternatives open to the Western Powers, either to withdraw their diplomatic agents, and cease all intercourse with the Japanese; or to maintain them in security by calling the Japanese rulers to account, and making them responsible for the lawless acts of their subjects."

Rear-Admiral Hope in distant Shanghai, whose resources were spread very thinly[30], tried to belittle the dangers experienced by the British in Japan. It was evident he lacked sympathy for their perceived plight. However, mindful that the Foreign Office was bent on Britain becoming a dominant trading partner with Japan, he had little alternative but to provide Alcock with at least a stronger British guard. Royal Naval policy throughout this time was to remain an instrument of government policy, not to be the maker of policy, and Hope did not want to escalate the situation unduly, since ultimately he might be forced to wage warfare on his own authority. Alcock (and later, Neale) continued to press for stronger naval forces to be stationed in Japanese waters for the security of the British diplomats, consular officials and traders.

---

[30] The China Station extended from the Bering Sea to the Red Sea, and took in all of the East Indies, Singapore, Malaya, Siam, Korea, China and of course Japan. Until 1859, the station had also been responsible for New Zealand, Australia, and the islands of the Pacific Ocean. In 1863, the station had 47 warships, but only the steam-frigate HMS *Euryalus* and the steam-corvettes *Encounter*, *Pearl* and *Scout* were heavily armed.

ATTACKS ON WESTERNERS

The *samurai* from Mitō who had attacked the British Legation were eventually arrested and, after a brief trial, executed in June 1862. WL Clowes reports that such was the weakness of the *bakufu* that the culprits, it was announced, were punished, not for the assault on the British Legation, but for a trumped-up charge of highway robbery. The *bakufu* dared not announce that they had been unable to protect the representatives of a foreign power.

An insight as to the motives of the Mitō *samurai* may be gleaned from the contents of a declaration found on one of them when arrested. It said,

> I, though I am a person of low standing, have no patience to stand by and see the sacred empire defiled by the foreigner. If this thing from time to time may cause the foreigner to retire, and partly tranquillize the manes[31] of departed Emperors and *shōguns*, I shall take to myself the highest praise. Regardless of my own life, I am determined to set out.

The letter bore fourteen signatures.

---

[31] The *manes* were, in Roman mythology, the spirits or souls of deceased loved ones and ancestors. The thought is to appease or give rest to the spirits of dead Emperors and *shōguns* that would otherwise be roaming the country, distraught at the intrusion of the foreigners. The anonymous translator of the note obviously had a classical education and assumed his readers were also versed in Roman mythology.

RESPECT AND CONSIDERATION

Execution of a *samurai* involved in the 1861 attack on the British Legation in Edo
Detail from Charles Wirgman's drawing, *Illustrated London News*, 25 February 1865

- On the morning of the 27th June 1862, another assault was made on the British Legation. Two British servicemen, Sweet and Crimp, were killed. Following the 1861 attack, when the Japanese guard appointed by the Government for the British diplomats turned away from conflict with the Mitō *samurai*, the British Government had provided a military detachment to guard the Legation and its staff. At this time, the complement guarding the Legation consisted of 80 British men and 500 Japanese, made up as follows:
    - 12 soldiers from the Military Train under Lieut. Applin;

ATTACKS ON WESTERNERS

- 68 marines and sailors from H.M.S. *Renard*, under Captain Bingham and Lieuts. Edwards and Warren;
- 500 Japanese men, not one of whom was wounded in the attack. It was inferred that once again, they had sided with their compatriots, or at least turned a blind eye.

Corporal Richard Crimp, a Marine from HMS *Renard*, was going his rounds, when he was suddenly attacked and stabbed nine times. He managed to stagger to Colonel Neale's door, where he fell and died. The other victim was Ordinary Seaman Charles Sweet, a sailor from the same steam-driven screw sloop, on sentry duty at the door, who received sixteen "desperate" lance and sword wounds. So sudden and unheralded was the attack that the assailant was able to make his escape undetected. The next morning one of the Japanese guard, Itō Gunbei of the Matsumoto *han*, was missed at roll-call. Enquiries were made, and he was traced to his own house, where he was said to have committed *seppuku*. Colonel Neale asked to be permitted to examine the body of the murderer but in the event was not shown it. The embassy doctor, though, was shown it and confirmed that *seppuku* had been committed. The Japanese asserted that on examination, the body was found to have at least one ball through the chest, though not a single shot was heard during the murder of Crimp and Sweet. It was put about by the murderer's comrades that he had been mightily affronted by a thoughtless insult by the youngest employee of the Legation, and was seeking vengeance in accordance with the code of *bushidō*. However, secret sources said that in truth the

RESPECT AND CONSIDERATION

attack had been made to avenge the executions of the Mitō *samurai* in respect of the June 1861 attack.

The French, American and Dutch ministers in Japan were almost as outraged as Alcock. They complained in strong terms to the Japanese Foreign Ministers, who in similar replies, expressed their regrets to all the foreign representatives. The Japanese asked for sympathy: it was a difficult thing for the *daimyō* to come to terms with the West after all those years of *sakoku*. This was not regarded by anyone in the foreign community as a satisfactory response.

Lord Russell

Lord Russell, the Secretary of State for Foreign Affairs, instructed the British Legation to demand compensation of £10,000 for the families[32] of Sweet and Crimp. Russell's instructions were criticized by the Duke of Somerset, the First Lord of the Admiralty. He wrote

> It seems to me that the amount of compensation which you have instructed Col. Neale to demand is too large. I should have said if you had obtained 2000£ that is 1000£ for the family of each marine who was killed it would be sufficient. The demand of 10,000£ would be quite just if the Japanese Govt could raise it from the Daimio who was responsible for the guard, but I believe the

---

[32] Sweet's mother was the landlady of the "Coach and Horses" in Fan Street, Aldersgate, London; Crimp was estranged from his wife due to her "bad behaviour". Crimp's parents, though, were living, and it was the parents who received the eventual compensation, worth some £290,000 each in 2008 terms.

ATTACKS ON WESTERNERS

> Japanese Govt cannot compel these Daimios to pay.

Thus it was well understood by the British Government that there was a tension between the *bakufu* and the *daimyō*, to the extent that the *bakufu* did not entirely control the country.

- In February 1863, as the new British Legation building in Edo neared completion, Chōshū loyalists attacked it and burned it down. No British lives were lost, nor injuries suffered, on this occasion. But the arsonists shot and killed some Japanese who tried to extinguish the flames. *The Times* reported

> Fire and gunpowder were the means employed, and the incendiaries beyond a doubt were the Government of the Tycoon. It is asserted that the site had been ceded by the Tycoon with great reluctance, and it is now certain that its cession was viewed by the Mikado with great displeasure. It appears that some Japanese officers of high rank lately had an interview with the British Minister at Yokohama on the subject of relinquishing the position; but little time was allowed for consideration, for before the required answer could be given the difficulty had been solved by the Japanese in their own peculiar fashion. This act confirms the reported haughty bearing of the Mikado's latest ambassador, and reveals the inability of the Tycoon to resist the reviving power of the central authority.

The Times mistakenly blamed the *bakufu*, when it was Chōshū, but there was no doubt considerable satisfaction among the supporters of *sonnō jōi* at the destruction of the building.

RESPECT AND CONSIDERATION

There were other attacks on traders and soldiers based in Kanagawa, and there were deaths among the Dutch and the French. The official policy of the *bakufu* was *kaikoku* 開国 - "open the country!" By contrast, the growing movement for expulsion of the foreigners rallied under the cry: "*sonnō jōi!*" – "Honour the Emperor, expel the barbarians!" Four domains were in the forefront of the *sonno jōi* movement: Chōshū, Mitō, Satsuma and Tosa. The Mōri family of Chōshū and the Shimazu family of Satsuma had a history of antagonism, but shelved their differences in what they saw as the national interest. They were a formidable pairing, though Mitō, as close relatives of the Tokugawa dynasty of *shōguns*, could not contemplate open opposition to the *bakufu*. The three other clans grew into a xenophobic, nationalistic, anti-Tokugawa movement. *Sonnō jōi* was gradually transformed into "*kinnō tōbaku*" - "Loyalty to the Emperor and down with the *bakufu*!"

There was considerable nervousness on the part of all the westerners. Almost everyone wore a pistol when venturing beyond the limits of the foreign settlement, and constantly slept with one under his pillow. There was a substantial trade in small arms, powder and shot. That Charles Richardson and the others were unarmed on the *tōkaidō* on that Sunday afternoon in September 1862 shows that they felt confident in their treaty rights. Had they been armed, who can say what the consequences might have been? Perhaps they would have driven off the attack; perhaps they would have wounded and killed a handful of assailants before being overwhelmed.

ATTACKS ON WESTERNERS

British Consulate, Kanagawa, 1860
Lithograph from *Niphon and Pe–che–li*
by Edward Barrington de Fonblanque

CHAPTER 8
THE JAPANESE POLITICAL CLIMATE

In April 1858, Ii Naosuke (*daimyō* of Hikone, the largest of the *han*) had been appointed *tairō*. This was a very powerful office in itself, but made even more so by the feeble health and unstable mental state of the *shōgun* Tokugawa Iesada. Ii planned to open the country to western nations only until the Japanese had learnt enough to wage successful warfare against them and thus oust them from Japan. To facilitate this, Ii began unprecedented face-to-face negotiations with Townsend Harris, the American Minister. The Treaty of Amity and Commerce was signed in July 1858, followed within a month with similar treaties with the other western nations.

Ii Naosuke

In addition to trading issues, the treaty allowed for freedom of worship for foreigners, and the provision of a cemetery for them. The original cemetery is in Yokohama. Christian clergy from the west started to arrive in 1859, many of them hoping to carry out covert missionary activity among the Japanese (which was still forbidden by Japanese law), as well as ministering to the western community.

THE JAPANESE POLITICAL CLIMATE

After 1865, when the restriction on Japanese becoming Christians was removed, as many as 60,000[33] *kakure kirishitan* 隠れ クリスチャン "secret Christians" emerged: they had kept a version of Roman Catholic practice through over 2½ centuries of lethal persecution. Their faith was heavily adulterated with Buddhist and *shintō* elements, and they had neither bible nor ministers. Their liturgy had degenerated into incomprehensible chanting. But they retained a faith in salvation through Christ, and they continued to baptize their infants - in secret, of course. They are still a separate religious community to this day. In 1867, the *bakufu* reimposed restrictions on, and sanctions against, Japanese Christians. These were lessened and finally rescinded by the Meiji government, following sustained pressure from Western countries, particularly Protestant Britain.

The *bakufu* came under internal political attack because of what the Japanese called the Unequal Treaties. Ii was bitterly opposed by Tokugawa Nariaki, the *daimyō* of Mitō, who unconditionally opposed the opening of the country, and saw Ii's policies as traitorous. Many influential people in the *bakufu* and Imperial courts, together with many of the *daimyō* supported Tokugawa Nariaki. To compound the rift between Ii's faction - the pragmatists - and the traditionalists, Ii unilaterally appointed Tokugawa Iemochi as *shōgun* in succession to Tokugawa Iesada, who died suddenly in August 1858. This appointment was a breach of precedent, for Iemochi was not the best-qualified candidate. He was only 12 years old, so his regent - unsurprisingly, Ii - would hold all the power. Ii's opponents had agitated to appoint Hitotsubashi Keiki, although Hitotsubashi had publicly declared that he did not wish to become *shōgun*. Tokugawa Nariaki, who was by merest coincidence the father of Hitotsubashi and not at all looking

---

[33] The number varies between sources. 60,000 is at the top end; the lowest number I have so far encountered is 12,000.

after his own interests, together with the rest of the traditionalists, would never forgive Ii for out-manoeuvring them.

Ii responded to the intense opposition by firm, not to say high-handed, treatment of his opponents. Mitō *daimyō* Tokugawa Nariaki and his heir Hitotsubashi[34] were placed under house arrest, incensing the Mitō *samurai*. The *daimyō* of Owari and Fukui were forced to retire from their positions and Ii appointed their successors. The pretext for these punishments was that they had caused the death of Iesada by foul play, though this was never proven. This further enraged Ii's opponents clustered round Tokugawa Nariaki, and they started to plot the overthrow of Ii's *bakufu*.

Murderous attacks by Ii's opponents were made against the *bakufu* and, in retaliation, by *bakufu* loyalists against the anti-*bakufu* factions. The anti-*bakufu* movement was centred around the Imperial Court in Kyotō. How far the Emperor himself was behind this is uncertain. (Later, in 1863, he was persuaded to issue an Imperial Edict to "expel the barbarians" (攘夷実行の勅命). The Chōshū clan was the most enthusiastic supporter of the Edict and agitated for its armed enforcement.)

In March 1860, Ii Naosuke was assassinated at the Sakurada Gate of the *shōgun's* palace in Edo by young anti-*bakufu* Mitō *samurai* led by Sano Takenosuke and Oseki Washichiro. Ii had not been a popular *tairō*. It was said in the streets, "Ii deserved to be assassinated a hundred times".

Ando Nobumasa replaced Ii Naosuke as chief adviser to the young *shōgun*. In 1861, he devised a scheme to unite the *bakufu* and the Imperial court by arranging the marriage of *shōgun* Tokugawa Iemochi and the Emperor's half-sister Princess Kazu-

---

[34] With a change of name to Tokugawa Yoshinobu, he was to become the 15th and last Tokugawa *shōgun*, retiring in 1868, having handed power to the Emperor.

THE JAPANESE POLITICAL CLIMATE

no-miya Chikako (和宮 親子内親王 *kazu-no-miya chikako naishinnō*). This policy was known as *kobu gattai* - "shaking the Emperor's hand".

Shimazu Saburō, the *daimyō* of Satsuma, was a strong proponent of *kobu gattai*, which he saw as a solution to the rift between traditionalists and pragmatists in the ruling classes. Shimazu was the most influential and powerful among the *daimyō* at the Imperial court in Kyotō and was used by the Emperor as a go-between with the *bakufu*.

The anti-*bakufu* faction immediately saw that if the marriage were to happen, they could not overthrow the *bakufu* without indirectly attacking the Imperial family, to whom they had pledged absolute loyalty. They sought by any means to prevent the marriage. In January 1862, Ando survived an assassination attempt by Imperial loyalists in Edo, though he was too badly injured to continue his duties. This was a time of rumour, and wild conspiracy theories circulated among the courtiers, among them that Tokugawa Iemochi intended to depose Emperor Kōmei and replace him with someone who could be manipulated by the *shōgun*.

Princess Kazu–no–miya Chikako
和宮 親子内親王

The Tokugawa *mon* is visible on her *kimono*

15-year-old Tokugawa Iemochi did indeed marry 15-year-old Kazu-no-miya Chikako on 11 March 1862.

In March 1863, following Shimazu Saburō's mission in September 1862, Tokugawa Iemochi obeyed the Imperial

RESPECT AND CONSIDERATION

summons and went to Kyotō, the first *shōgun* to do so for over two hundred years. There, he argued against the Imperial Edict that all foreigners be expelled from the country and all ports be closed with effect from 24th July. But eventually, in the face of an implacable Emperor, Iemochi gave nominal consent to the Edict.

Iemochi died on 29 August 1866, aged 21. It was officially declared that he died of beriberi[35], but many believed that he had been poisoned by the opponents of *kobu gattai*. He was prone to sucking his calligraphy brush, and may have been poisoned by that route. Several members of the *gorogio* and *wakadoshiyori* were dismissed from their offices, including Matsudaira Idzu-no-kami, Itakura Suwo-no-kami, and Sakai Wota-no-kami. Two physicians came under suspicion in connection with His Highness' death, and were arrested.

---

[35] Beriberi is caused by a deficiency of vitamin B_1 (thiamine). Symptoms include appetite loss, weakness, irritability, muscle aches, limb pains, swollen joints, and paralysis of hands and feet. Some of these are also symptoms of various forms of poisoning. Beriberi was very common in Japan at this time, occasioned by the diet high in polished white rice and deficient in fresh meat, legumes, green vegetables, fruit, and milk.

THE JAPANESE POLITICAL CLIMATE

Shimazu Saburō
© 2004 National Diet Library, Japan

CHAPTER 9
SHIMAZU SABURŌ, IMPERIAL ENVOY

Shimazu Saburō, the father and regent of the young Shimazu Tadayoshi, the *daimyō* of the rich and powerful *han* of Satsuma, had become the most powerful and therefore influential of the *daimyō* at the Imperial court in Kyotō. In June 1862, Shimazu Saburō arranged to be appointed by the Emperor as escort to an Imperial messenger. The message to the *shōgun* in Edo that the messenger carried was an unprecedented summons to come to Kyotō for consultations with the Emperor.

While waiting for a reply from the *shōgun* in Edo, Shimazu Saburō took time in August 1862 to buy an English steamer, the S.S. *Fiery Cross*, on behalf of his son-nephew, the Prince of Satsuma. The purchase was strongly opposed by the *bakufu*, but Satsuma was too powerful to be thwarted. Satsuma's chief Engineer and Artillery Officer, Nakahara Naosuke, had to be smuggled off the *Fiery Cross* in disguise as a common coolie after examining her engines, to avoid arrest. Satsuma needed reliable transport to deal with its Ryūkyū Islands possessions, and to carry out a little illicit trade with the Chinese through its port in Okinawa. In the local language, Ryūkyū was pronounced "Luchu" or Loochoo. Hence the references to "Lewchew", "Loochoo", and "Loochoo junks" elsewhere in this narrative. Shimazu Saburō visited his new ship in Yokohama and took her for a trial trip, and was reported to have been on very friendly terms with the British vendor and crew of the vessel. There was no hint in his demeanour of any anti-western sentiment.

To the consternation of the pro-*bakufu daimyō* in Edo, *shōgun* Tokugawa Iemochi agreed to go to see the Emperor in Kyotō, which visit, we have seen, would take place in March 1863. No *shōgun* had gone to Kyotō since Tokugawa Iemitsu went there in 1634 - and *he* took 300,000 troops with him. Shimazu's military might - he brought 800 *samurai* in his retinue to Edo - was a deciding factor in Iemochi's decision to accept the summons.

Shimazu set off to return to Kyotō on 14th September 1862[36] to carry the news of Iemochi's unprecedented agreement to go to see the Emperor. There was a suggestion that before leaving Edo on his return to Kyotō, he made a direct threat in front of the *bakufu*, that, should opportunity arise, he would assault foreigners. This was universally believed in the foreign community as an indisputable fact, though there is no known Japanese record to back this up. The account of the purchase of the *Fiery Cross* also militates against this. If there was any truth in the story, the threat may have been made as a means to create a situation to force the supine *bakufu* to act to drive foreigners out.

Shimazu left half of his train at Edo, and travelled with a reduced complement of 300 two-sworded *samurai*, some of whom bore lances, and some bows and arrows in addition to the *daishō*. There were perhaps 100 servants and bearers as well. Travelling in a south-westerly direction along the *tōkaidō*, the impressive procession came to the sleepy village of Namamugi, just outside Yokohama.

---

[36] Upon his eventual arrival back in Kyotō, Shimazu found that his influence at the Imperial court had been severely reduced. The Imperial Court now listened attentively to the more radical Chōshū *han*.

Chapter 10
Charles Lenox Richardson

Charles Richardson senior, the father of the murdered man, was born in Rotherhithe, Surrey, in 1796. His wife Louisa Ann was born in Hoxton, Middlesex in 1801, and they married in the 1820s. Their first child, their daughter Georgihana, was born in 1829. Then came Louisa Grace in 1830, followed by their only son Charles Lenox[37] in 1833. Finally, Mavis Flossie was born in 1835.

Charles senior was described in the 1831 and 1841 censuses as a "merchant". The 1839 Pigot directory shows him as trading from 145 Leadenhall Street in London. In 1851, he was a "merchant and dealer in glass", and in 1861, he had become a director of a public company. The name of the company is virtually illegible on the census return, but appears to be something like Barton Vasy Market Limited.

His rise to prosperity was mirrored by the location of the family home. In 1831, the family lived at Lansdown Place, London Fields, in "St John at Hackney" parish, together with three female servants. In 1841 and 1851, it was Dalston Place[38],

---

[37] In a number of published accounts, the spelling is given as "Lennox". However, in manuscript documents penned by his father, and in the census returns, the spelling is clearly given as "Lenox".
[38] Now Nos. 128-146 Dalston Lane.

CHARLES LENOX RICHARDSON

Hackney (there was a convenient horse-drawn omnibus service linking Dalston Place with Leadenhall Street). Between 1851 and 1861, they moved to Duppas Hill, Croydon, where they employed a cook and a housemaid. By 1864, after the murder, their ever-prospering household had moved to Belle Vue[39], Tunbridge Wells.

Georgihana Richardson went on to marry Mr F Searle, who was general manager of the Crystal Palace[40]. The Palace was a wonder of the Victorian age, and Searle was well known in London. Georgihana's sisters Louisa and Mavis remained unmarried at the 1861 census. One of them presumably married before 5th December 1862, because Mr Richardson senior wrote to Lord Russell, speaking of "the loss my wife my fond daughter and I have sustained". Which daughter married and which remained at home is not known. Young Charles, aged 18 in the 1851 census, was still living with his parents at Dalston Place. He was described as a merchant's clerk, and we might speculate that he worked for his father, although there is no evidence for this.

At some point, young Charles moved to Shanghai. From this time on until the Incident itself, the facts are hazy. According to his uncle, young Charles had set up a trading business in Shanghai in 1858. His uncle gives us a tantalising glimpse of the young man's character:

---

[39] Richardson senior wrote to Earl Russell, 3 February 1864 from that address (see Chapter 28). During the 1840s, Belle Vue had been the residence of Aretas Akers, the grandfather of Sir Aretas Akers-Douglas GBE, 1st Viscount Chilston (1851-1926), Conservative Home Secretary under Balfour 1902-1905.

[40] The Great Exhibition hall built for the Hyde Park Exhibition of 1851 was dismantled and re-erected at Sydenham, and, renamed the "Crystal Palace", constituted the world's first Theme Park (lifesize model dinosaurs a speciality), immensely popular with Londoners and Royalty alike. It also housed the eponymous football team, whose ground was used for F.A. Cup Finals until 1914.

RESPECT AND CONSIDERATION

> Charles was incredibly reckless and stubborn. He had to leave England because of his crazy stunts.

What had the youngster been up to? What was the disgrace that forced him to flee the country? Whatever the reason for his departure, he prospered in trade.

This was some twenty years after the time of the Opium Wars, and not all the trade would meet modern ethical standards. Indeed, Shanghai was known as late as the 1930s as "the Whore of the Orient", such was its shady reputation. However, the 1842 Treaty of Nanking had opened up five cities, including Shanghai, for western access (and ceded Hong Kong to Britain in the process). Trade had prospered, and many a fortune was made. The Hong Kong and Shanghai Bank was founded to facilitate trading (silver bullion being gradually replaced by the Mexican dollar as the trading currency of choice). What goods young Charles traded in, we do not know, but silk and tea were the predominant exports from Shanghai, while manufactured goods and raw cotton from India were slowly replacing opium as the major imports through western hands.

By 1862, young Charles, now aged 28, was due to return to spend Christmas with his parents in Croydon[41]. One newspaper[42] suggested that he had made his fortune and was retiring home permanently. Dr Willis said that Richardson "had made his fortune in China. I believe he was possessed of some thousands a year".

Travel in those days was not a rapid business. Townsend Harris said, "By means of steam one can go from California to Japan in eighteen days", but this was a one-leg journey of a little over 5000 miles. Charles set out from Shanghai for Hong Kong and thence for Yokohama, where he expected to travel to

---

[41] Letter from Charles Richardson senior to Earl Russell 5 December 1862.
[42] Japan Herald *Extra*, 16 September 1862.

CHARLES LENOX RICHARDSON

Nagasaki to pick up another passage on the next leg of his journey, perhaps to Singapore or Colombo or some port in India. One account says that he had booked passage on a merchant vessel, possibly the SS *St Louis*[43], which was due to have sailed on the 13th. It had developed boiler trouble, and so Charles Richardson was forced to stay in Japan for two further days while it was mended. Instead of meeting his death that Sunday, he might have been on the high seas but for a mechanical malfunction.

Charles had made a good impression on the people he met in Japan. Vice Admiral Kuper calls him "a gentleman held in high estimation by the community" in a letter to Vice Admiral Hope, 20th September 1862. If true, that implies that he had been at Yokohama for some time, in order to make the acquaintance of the community. Or perhaps Kuper was passing on what he had been told by someone who would not speak ill of the dead.

The *Japan Herald*, unlike his uncle, described him in fulsome terms:

> ... a fine and manly specimen of a young Englishman. He had just left Shanghai where he had been resident for several years, and was in Japan on a visit. His excellent qualities both of head and of heart, with his gentle manner and chivalrous disposition were concealed under a quiet exterior, but we know that in many cases when many would have thought it manly to resent, he preferred the more godlike of forgiving and forgetting, and only a few days before his death he told a friend that it was a great gratification to him to think, that he had left Shanghai without leaving a single

---

[43] Another account suggests it was HMS *Renard*, but the commercial *St Louis* is more likely. Richardson had no official status. The *St Louis* seems to have plied between Yokohama and Nagasaki, where ships bound for India could be found.

RESPECT AND CONSIDERATION

disagreeable reminiscence with any member of the community.

A visitor from Hong Kong was Mrs Margaret Borradaile, whose purpose was to visit her older sister, the wife of William Marshall. He was a principal of the Yokohama traders Marshall & Hart[44] Ltd. Margaret Borradaile was a keen horsewoman.

Woodthorpe Charles Clarke, a silk inspector[45] of the American trading house Augustine Heard & Co., was an old friend of Richardson. Clarke had worked for over ten years in Shanghai, where the two had struck up a friendship during Richardson's four years there. Clarke introduced Marshall and Richardson to each other.

The four of them - Richardson, Marshall, Clarke and Mrs. Borradaile - decided to make an excursion by boat to Kanagawa and thence on horseback to the Daishi Temple[46] at Kawasaki, about four miles further on, that pleasant Sunday afternoon. It was an excursion commonly taken by visitors, and doubtless Marshall and Clarke had made the trip on previous occasions.

---

[44] The name appears variously as Marshall & Hard, and Marshall & Heard.
[45] See Satow's remarks on adulteration (Page 26). Inspectors were necessary to prevent fraud.
[46] This huge Buddhist temple complex specializes in protection against misfortunes, and attracts large attendances at the New Year festival. It has a small but beautiful Chinese garden, the *shinsu-en*.

CHARLES LENOX RICHARDSON

The Namamugi Incident

as depicted in a nineteenth Century Japanese woodcut print by Hayakawa Shouzan (signature 図山松川早 right-to-left in the central cartouche at the bottom of the print, last character modernized). Charles Lenox Richardson is at the centre of the scene.

The label above the characters 川早 of Hayakawa says 英国人 "*ei–koku–jin*" ("The Englishman" i.e. Richardson). The label on the right of this says "*go–kin–shin*" 御近臣 (personal attendant / trusted vassal). To the right of this is a samurai leg with hooped stockings. The label to the right of the leg says "*chuu–shou–sei*" 中小姓 (a 'middle- to low-ranking page/valet'). The white label above this next to the important looking man grasping the hilt of his sword says "*shima–zu sa–buro hisa–mitsu–kou*" (嶋図三郎久光公 – 公 *kou* is a title honorific for a man) – Shimazu Saburō (Hisamitsu) himself.

The label on the left of Richardson (as you look at it – under the samurai with black leggings) says "*satsu–han shi*" 薩藩士 ("a retainer/samurai of the clan Satsu")

The flag/sign まるや at left top says "*maruya*" which is probably a shop name. The white sign dangling down just the other side of the wooden column says 大山講 "*oo–yama–kou*", the Ōyama ("holy mountain") religious group.

Chapter 11
Murder in the Wheatfield: The Clash at Namamugi
生麦事件

Sunday 14th September was a fine day. It was warm and not too humid; a good day for a leisurely visit by boat and on horseback to see the famous temple of Daishi at Kawasaki, or so William Marshall, Woodthorpe Clarke, Charles Richardson and Mrs Margaret Borradaile thought. Charles Richardson was, willy-nilly, a tourist. He was *en route* back to his parents in England[47], and was impatiently waiting for his ship - the *St Louis* - to effect some boiler repairs before leaving Yokohama for the next stage of his journey. William Marshall was married to Mrs. Borradaile's older sister. Perhaps Marshall proposed to show the visitors the temple, and to bring along his friend Woodthorpe Clarke.

Sunday mornings, for the respectable elements of the British community, would have been spent at a service conducted by the Rev. M. Buckworth Bailey, chaplain to the Anglicans in Yokohama, meeting in the British Consul's commodious house. Just how many of the British community actually attended is not known, but given Satow's strictures on the lax morals of many

---

[47] The *Japan Herald* said that he had retired from business in Shanghai and was on his way back home with the fortune he had made.

MURDER IN THE WHEATFIELD:
THE CLASH AT NAMAMUGI

of the traders, it was perhaps only the senior men and their womenfolk who attended. The French had already opened a church dedicated to "The Sacred Heart of Jesus" on 12th January 1862 partly funded by the Catholic "mission", and partly by the subscriptions of "all sects and denominations". Just four days after its dedication, on 16th January, a solemn mass was celebrated for the repose of the soul of Mr. Heusken, murdered on the 14th.

The pillars of the British traders were mainly protestants, and they did not want to have to rely on the French Catholics to provide Christian ministry to them. So, in 1861, a successful effort had been made to obtain funds for a building in connection with the English Church establishment, and the community petitioned the Foreign Office for the provision of a Consular Chaplain. The Rev. M. Buckworth Bailey was appointed to the office in early 1862 at a stipend of £600 per annum, of which half would be

A foreign resident's home in Yokohama, 1861.

guaranteed by the trustees of the new church. The putative trustees had also raised nearly £350 to pay for the new Chaplain's passage to Japan and his outfit. The Rev. Michael Buckworth Bailey, formerly of 31 St. Mary's Road, Canonbury, petitioned Earl Russell for his stipend to commence on embarkation at Southampton rather than on arrival in Yokohama. He was unsuccessful.

RESPECT AND CONSIDERATION

The erection of an Anglican church building in the English style was started at the same time. Captain Vyse donated a stove, Mr Eusden the font, Marcus Flowers the lectern, and two visitors to Yokohama the harmonium. William Marshall would be appointed one of the trustees of the new church in 1863, alongside Mr IJ Miller. Pending the completion of the church building, services were held at the spacious house of the British Consul. So we might speculate that the four who would ride to the temple had attended Matins - the Anglican morning Service - at Captain Vyse's house that fateful 14th Sunday after Trinity. Would the words of Psalm 71, from that morning's liturgy, cross poor Richardson's mind as he lay dying in agony only a few hours later?

> Deliver me, O my God, out of the hand of the ungodly; out of the hand of the unrighteous and cruel man ... Go not far from me, O God: my God, haste thee to help me.

Doubtless, the party would have lunched together, before setting out around 2 o'clock in a boat to cross to Kanagawa. Richardson carried a bottle of champagne with him to enliven the planned visit to a tea-house[48]. At Kanagawa, they met the *betto*, who had travelled ahead with their horses. They mounted and rode up to the *tōkaidō*, the high road from Edo to Kyotō. They turned towards Kawasaki, riding two by two, Richardson on a chestnut horse with Mrs. Borradaile beside him, leading. Marshall and Clarke were ten yards or so behind. Margaret Borradaile would have turned heads as she rode, for in feudal Japan, only warriors had horses. And perhaps she rode side-saddle, in the lady-like fashion demanded of European ladies of breeding at the time.

---

[48] Many "tea-houses" were, in fact, gracious brothels. This may account for the frequent westerners' documentary references to the attractiveness of the waitresses.

MURDER IN THE WHEATFIELD:
THE CLASH AT NAMAMUGI

Because of his exalted status, it was not permissible by Japanese customary law for anyone to overtake a *daimyō's* procession. Japanese people in the vicinity would, if possible, get well out of the way. If they could not get away before the procession arrived, they had to kneel on the ground with their foreheads touching the ground before them until the procession had passed, sometimes for lengthy periods. Failure to show this level of respect meant instant execution by one of the *daimyō's* bodyguard.

Unaware, or heedless, of this, was Charles Richardson, leading the party with Mrs Borradaile by his side. It was significant that Richardson was a stranger to Japan. Marshall and Clarke, some distance behind them, would have known the protocol in these circumstances. But Richardson only knew the Chinese customs and usages. In China, the natives were treated by the Westerners as inferiors. Indeed, the Chinese at that time were in effect a subjugated people, and western - particularly British - military might and main meant that deference was shown by the Chinese to the Westerners and expected from the Chinese by them. Richardson certainly carried these attitudes with him, failing to recognise the fact that Japan was not subjugated by military force as China had been, but was an ostensibly equal partner in their relationships with the west. Three and a half miles or so along the *tōkaidō*, they rode into Shimazu Saburō's procession.

At this point in the narrative, we have to acknowledge that there are conflicting accounts of what actually occurred. This is not surprising: it is well known that adjacent eye-witnesses notice different details of what has occurred (or even convince themselves they have seen something they haven't!), so we should not be taken aback if the accounts of the assault at Namamugi vary in detail. The incontestable points are that Shimazu Saburō's *samurai* killed Richardson and severely wounded Marshall and Clarke, and Mrs Borradaile narrowly evaded injury but received an enormous fright from which she took several days to recover.

Scene of the Incident, 1862
Unknown photographer, but recognizably the same place as photographed by Beato

The official facts were first given at the inquest, the principal eye-witnesses giving evidence being Marshall and Clarke. Both had been severely wounded. In Marshall's case, there was grave concern that he too might die. Nonetheless, he gave evidence in person at the inquest, which started on Monday morning, was adjourned for Richardson's funeral in the afternoon, and resumed afterwards at about 5.30 p.m. So we can say that Marshall, though critically injured, was well enough to give evidence 24 hours or so after being grievously wounded. Despite nearly losing his arm at the shoulder, Marshall's evidence, as minuted, is clear. Clarke, too, had been gravely wounded, but he too was well enough to give clear evidence.

According to Marshall, he had observed some *samurai* along the road, but did not realise they were part of a *daimyō's* retinue. They had been riding slowly because of the large number of Japanese they encountered and did not want to run the risk of forcing them out of the way. Immediately the four riders had turned a corner and found they were twelve men deep into the procession and close to the *daimyō's norimon*, he realised that they were in a hazardous situation. However, none of the party had shouted or gesticulated at the Japanese in front of them, so he was confident that no hostile moves would be made by the *samurai*. A hefty *samurai* stepped forward in front of Richardson

MURDER IN THE WHEATFIELD:
THE CLASH AT NAMAMUGI

and Mrs. Borradaile and barred their way. Richardson turned in his saddle and called to Marshall and Clarke "We are stopped." Clarke called back, "Don't go on. We can turn into a side road", and Marshall shouted, "For God's sake, let us have no row." All four of them were turning their horses so they could go into a side road out of the way, when Marshall saw the same man who had barred their way throw off the clothes from his upper body and swing his large sword at Richardson. Marshall shouted "Away!", but before they could spur their horses to a gallop, Richardson received a huge sword wound under his left arm. The *samurai* who did this immediately turned on Marshall, and inflicted a similar, but as it transpired, lesser, wound on him.

The four horses, perhaps startled by the commotion, started to a gallop, and they ran through the crowd of retainers. Half a dozen of them drew their swords and attempted to bar the way, but failed to do so. Two *samurai* were knocked over by the headlong rush of the four on horseback. As the four Britons

Scene of the Incident
taken c.1863 by Felice Beato

raced through the retinue, the *samurai* struck at them with their swords, inflicting further injury on Richardson, and wounds upon the horses. Mrs. Borradaile's hat was sliced off her head, but by a miracle, she was not hurt, though her face and clothes were sprayed with Richardson's blood. Once they had escaped the initial onslaught of the *samurai*, no one else attempted violence against them.

Clearing the armed assailants, they came to a tea-house[49] by the entrance to the "Avenue". Clarke says he reined in his horse,

---

[49] Probably it was "Black-eyed Susan's" tea-room, which is mentioned later in the narrative.

RESPECT AND CONSIDERATION

The spot where Richardson fell, spilling his intestines, is by the barrier outside the present-day timber yard.
This is looking towards Kanagawa and away from the samurai – the direction they were fleeing
Photo by Stephen Denney

and Richardson came up and said, "Oh! Clarke, they have killed me!" Clarke replied that he, too, had been wounded and they must keep moving as their only hope of safety. Marshall called to Clarke and Mrs. Borradaile to go on apace, and that he would look after Richardson. Richardson's horse was weakening from its wounds and the extraordinary effort it had made to escape the attack.

As Marshall drew alongside Richardson, whose horse had by now almost stopped, he asked Richardson if he were hurt. There was no reply, and Marshall could see that he was almost dead. As the horse came to a halt, Richardson fell onto the ground, with his intestines falling through a gaping wound. Marshall believed him dead, and so could be no further help to him.

Marshall spurred his own horse on, and at the entrance to Kanagawa, he overtook the other two. Waiting for them were

Dr. James Curtis Hepburn

his *betto* and that of Mr. Aspinall, from whom, we may surmise, Richardson and Mrs. Borradaile had borrowed horses. Sending one groom to guard Richardson's body and the other back to Yokohama with Richardson's injured horse, he and Clarke went on until they arrived at the American Consulate at Kanagawa. There they received medical attention from J.C. Hepburn, the Legation doctor. The American Consul sent a messenger to

MURDER IN THE WHEATFIELD:
THE CLASH AT NAMAMUGI

Colonel Neale, the British Chargé d'Affaires, to inform him of what had occurred.

Rev. Dr. James Curtis Hepburn (1815 - 1911) was the Legation doctor and a Presbyterian medical missionary to Japan. He is best remembered as the inventor of the Hepburn romanization ("*romaji*") system for writing Japanese in the western Roman alphabet, used to this day, with modifications. He was the first person to translate the entire Bible into Japanese, a copy of which, momentously, he personally placed into the hands of the Emperor in 1872. He also published several Japanese-English dictionaries.

Mrs. Borradaile, perhaps because (according to the *Japan Herald*) she was "fearfully shattered in nerves and in body", did not give evidence at the inquest. However, John Black, the editor of the *Herald*, published an interview with her, where she described what had occurred. She said that about four miles from Kanagawa, the four of them had encountered part of a *daimyō's* train consisting of a large body of two-sworded men coming from Yedo, some of whom signed to them to move aside, which they did. They drew up their horses at the side of the road, but the *samurai* indicated that they should turn back. They duly turned their horses to return towards Kanagawa.

But there were other reports that Mrs. Borradaile had become concerned that the retinue were exhibiting signs of hostility to the party. Accordingly, they said, she begged Richardson to be prudent to avoid a row when they realised something was wrong. But Richardson replied. "Let me alone. I have lived for fourteen years in China. I know how to manage these people".

Without a word, or the slightest further notice, some of the retainers drew their swords and fiercely attacked them. A cut was aimed at Mrs. Borradaile's head, which she fortunately avoided by quickly stooping, though her hat was cut away by the blow. The three gentlemen were badly wounded, and the four of them were entirely surrounded by men with drawn swords. Unarmed themselves, their only course was to charge through the crowd of *samurai*, which they did. Mrs. Borradaile saw Richardson fall from his horse, and believed him dead.

Marshall called to her to ride for her life and save herself; he and the other two would not be able to keep up, because of their wounds. Thereafter, such was her understandable agitation, she could not remember clearly what happened. At one point, her horse rode into the sea, but then regained the road to Yokohama and galloped on. Twice, the horse fell, but she remounted and continued until, her hands, face and clothes bespattered with Richardson's blood, and her skirts soaked in seawater, she reached safety at Abel Gower's[50] house in Yokohama.

Dr. Jenkins of the British Legation took care of her, administering a "restorative". She begged Samuel J. Gower[51], Abel's brother, to get help to recover the bodies of her three companions, whom she thought had been killed. Samuel Gower went off and reported to Captain Vyse. According to Lieutenant-Colonel Neale, he (Neale) went to Abel Gower's house and escorted Mrs. Borradaile to her temporary residence, hearing from her, first-hand, what she had experienced. It is not clear how Neale was informed that Mrs. Borradaile had arrived in disarray after her escapade. It is likely that there was a general commotion at Gower's house, and he went to investigate the cause of it.

Marshall and Clarke rode on, wounded but alive. They made their way to the American Consulate in Kanagawa. Frank Schoyer, the 14-year-old son of an American merchant, ran a

---

[50] Abel AJ Gower was the First Secretary and *de facto* Accountant of the British Legation.
[51] SJ Gower was a senior manager for Jardine, Matheson & Co., was a pallbearer at Richardson's funeral, and a signatory to the minutes of the secret residents' meeting of Sunday night.

MURDER IN THE WHEATFIELD:
THE CLASH AT NAMAMUGI

quarter of a mile from the Consulate, through a crowd of agitated *samurai*, to ask Dr Hepburn to attend them.

When Marshall and Clarke had first arrived at the Consulate, the American flag was hoisted, Union down, as a signal to the various western ships in harbour. The American Consul despatched Mr JOP Stearns and Mr Ayrton Mann to the British and French Ministers, respectively, to inform them of the outrage. Stearns returned in the company of Dr Hepburn. On their journey, swords were drawn by some of the *samurai* who had spread out from Shimazu Saburō's *gyoretsu*. They were only prevented from attacking the Americans by Mr Stearns' determined attitude, who pointed his loaded and cocked revolver at potential assailants.

Until 1875, there was no other account but those of Mrs. Borradaile and Messrs. Marshall and Clarke. But in that year, a pamphlet, written by an American, E.H. House[52], was published, giving, for the first time for western eyes, the Satsuma version of the affair. As might be expected, there is a different slant on the events when viewed from the Satsuma point of view.

In the version given by what was described as a "leading *samurai*"[53], House stated that Richardson was notorious for his violent dealings with Chinese people during his residency in Shanghai, and his reputation preceded him. Mrs. Borradaile, too, was a visitor from China - at least from Hong Kong. It was

---

[52] E.H. House was a campaigning journalist, author and playwright. He successfully sued Mark Twain for plagiarising the stage play of *The Prince and the Pauper*. House wrote *A Yankee in Meiji Japan* based on his lengthy visit in the early 1870s.

[53] The pamphlet says that he has "since attained a high position in the Japanese service". It is not known for certain who, among the many distinguished Satsuma *samurai*, was meant. It may well have been Kukimura Rikyū, who rose to become a *chujo* 中将 (Lieutenant General) in the Japanese Army, though he was but a 19-year-old messenger at the time of the incident.

RESPECT AND CONSIDERATION

unfortunate, says the "leading *samurai*", that Richardson was with Mrs. Borradaile ahead of Marshall and Clarke, who understood and respected Japanese ways.

The English party, on their way along the *tōkaidō*, had spoken with various Japanese people with whom they were acquainted[54], asking why they had dismounted from their horses, but not taking notice of their reply. The dismount was, of course, in preparation for the passing of the *daimyō*, according to Japanese custom. One of the inexorable regulations of Japanese etiquette was that no casual passenger should continue to ride, either upon his horse or in any conveyance, during the occupancy of the road by a dignitary of high station. The Satsuma people felt that the courtesy should have been offered by the English party, saying that most visitors in strange lands recognize the expediency, if not the propriety, of conforming to the established public customs. Was it not true that a traveller who refused to lift his hat at the approach of a European monarch would receive uncomfortable treatment despite his plea that he came from a distance and owed no allegiance to the sovereign in question?

What is certain is that no Japanese would have been suffered to pass unmolested had they ridden through the procession as the English had done. As long as the English party gave no other offence other than that which might have proceeded from ignorance, they had not been harmed. This was on the express orders of Shimazu Saburō, quelling the desire of his bodyguard to avenge the perceived slight upon their chief. The commander of the bodyguard remarked that he had no regrets concerning the whole episode, save that he should have been the one to inflict justice on Richardson for his insolence. It was only the fact that he had a direct order not to do so that had restrained him.

---

[54] Presumably the interpreter(s) from the Custom house.

MURDER IN THE WHEATFIELD:
THE CLASH AT NAMAMUGI

Even after the behaviour of one of the English had become distinctly objectionable, they were allowed to proceed unmolested. After what the Japanese retrospectively called the "catastrophe", Mrs. Borradaile admitted that she had repeatedly begged Richardson to be more careful in his conduct, and that he had given no heed to her remonstrances, but had continued to push his horse in and out of the groups forming the *cortège*, reckless of menacing glances and gestures. Finally, at or near the village of Namamugi, a more compact and regular body of attendants came in view, preceding, in two long files, the *norimon* in which Shimazu Saburō was seated. The commander turned to the left, in obedience to instructions, and drew his men to the side of the road.

He is positive in declaring that if the strangers had done likewise, and moved in single file, they could have passed uninjured, as others had done before them, and as others did after. They themselves, at least the three survivors, invariably declared that they had kept well to the left, but two abreast. The Japanese agreed that Mrs. Borradaile, and Marshall and Clarke had indeed kept to the left, but that Richardson persisted in holding to the centre of the road, forcing the procession, to their great irritation, to move to the side.

Richardson had hardly passed the head of the column when the signs of dissatisfaction became so ominous that Clarke, who was some distance in the rear, felt it necessary to interpose: "Don't go on", he called, "we can turn into a side road." Marshall chimed in: "For God's sake, let us have no row". "Let me alone", answered Richardson; "I have lived in China four[55] years, and know how to manage these people". Richardson's uncle had spoken truly, when he said young Charles was "incredibly reckless and stubborn" (Chapter 10).

---

[55] House's account says fourteen years, but that is impossible.

RESPECT AND CONSIDERATION

At that point, the commander of the Satsuma bodyguard realised that Richardson was not going to give way, and that he plainly expected the *norimon* to give way to him[56]. The affront, in Japanese eyes, had become unendurable. According to House, a young *samurai* drew his short sword and swung at Richardson, but failed to wound him. Another *samurai*[57] sprang from the ranks, and made an imperative sign to Richardson to move out of the way, calling *"modore! Modore!"* (Get back! Get back!)

The party headed by Richardson had by now passed the *norimon*. The warning was now taken, but it was too late. At this point, the *tōkaidō* was a narrow, tree-lined road, and it is clear that there was not much room to manoeuvre. The party managed to turn their horses round and went to pass close by the *norimon* a second time, as they retraced their route. They clattered into the ranks of the Shimazu retainers, and the head of the Japanese column closed upon them.

Kukimura Rikyū confessed in 1936 that he had been the first to seek to attack Richardson, who was now at the rear of the party of four. The young Kukimura went to draw his *katana*, but it was so tightly bound by his sash that, in his inexperience, he could not free it. So he drew his *wakizashi* and swung at Richardson. The sword struck Richardson's steel stirrup and, such was the force of the blow, the *wakizashi* was bent.

---

[56] A letter from Robert Pruyn, the American Minister in Japan, tends to confirm that this was widely believed. He wrote, "it is supposed that the horse of one of the party forced itself between the *norimono* and the retainers who marched as a guard beside it".

[57] Said by a Satsuma source to be Narahara Kizaemon. His brother, Arimura Jizaemon, had assassinated Ii Naosuke (virtual dictator of Japan 1858-60 as *Tairō*) in 1860, with seventeen *samurai* from Mitō. Another brother, Kaeda Noboyushi (a.k.a. Kaeda Takeji and Arimura Shunsei) went on to become governor of Nara in the Meiji period, and Chairman of the Council of Elders. Narahara committed *seppuku* in 1865 at the Satsuma estate in Kyotō, for reasons not connected with this incident.

MURDER IN THE WHEATFIELD: THE CLASH AT NAMAMUGI

Narahara Kizaemon was now ready to attack, his *katana* successfully drawn. He slashed at Richardson, and simultaneously others rained blows with their weapons on Marshall and Clarke. The three men were wounded almost at the same moment, Richardson fatally. Mrs. Borradaile was not hurt, though blows were aimed at her. The group spurred their horses to a gallop and broke through the group of guards, and rode back at full speed toward Yokohama.

According to the version of events published by Kukimura when he was 94 years old, the Satsuma retinue was sworn to secrecy concerning these events, which accounts for the fact that the killers of Richardson were never brought to justice. Indeed, once the *gyoretsu* (procession) had reached the rest station at Hodogaya, Shimazu Saburō sent a messenger back to Kawasaki to report the incident to the authorities. The message he gave to pass on to the bakufu was false and misleading in every particular:

Shimazu Saburō's Statements	The Truth
"There were three people involved in the assault."	There were many more.
"One had run away."	They had stood their ground.
"The one who ran away was Ōkano Shinsuke."	This was a fake name provided by Shimazu Saburō.
"Shimazu Saburō and his chief retainers were unsure of the names of the other perpetrators."	Everyone knew very well who had perpetrated the attack - and on whose orders.
"When they were caught, Shimazu Saburō would hand the perpetrators over to the authorities."	Under no circumstances would Shimazu Saburō break faith with any of his retainers, nor they with him.

Far from there being unknown assassins who had run away, Shimazu Saburō lauded those who had acted decisively against the foreigners. Shimazu Saburō had himself clandestinely received the thanks of the Emperor for giving the foreigners a severe lesson. Satsuma demanded secrecy among the 400 witnesses within the *gyoretsu*, because they would not give up any of these loyal, obedient retainers who had been involved, and especially not Kukimura, a rising star in the Satsuma firmament. Furthermore, the shame of the incident might well cause the *shōgun* to require Shimazu Saburō to commit *seppuku*.

At Hodogaya, Narahara Kizaemon was asked why he had drawn his *katana* against unarmed foreigners. He replied that it had been his duty, as a personal guard to Shimazu Saburō, to ensure that due respect was always accorded to him. Had the foreigners actually harmed the procession, Narahara would have taken responsibility by committing *seppuku*. As it was, he had been able to forestall any such eventuality by cutting one of them down before they could inflict any harm to his Lord.

Wild rumours immediately began to circulate in the Foreign Community in Yokohama.

- The least horrifying one was that a young woman, wife of the farmer and village carpenter, and keeper of the small roadside tea-house where Richardson fell, brought him, at some risk to herself from vengeful *samurai*, water in response to his pitiful calls for help. She dabbed his brow with a cloth, and covered him over to keep the flies away. With a woman's gentle sympathetic nature (went the story), she wished she could do more. This noble legend appealed to the Westerners, who were sentimental on the inside, if hard and indomitable on the outside. So they took to frequenting "Black-eyed Susan's tea-room" which underwent a period of prosperity as her trade temporarily rocketed. Susan[58] was half-Spanish, half-Japanese, and her *kissaten* (tea room), the *kiri-ya*, was famous for its *kasutera* (カステラ) or castella cake. This is an Iberian sponge cake introduced by the Portuguese

---

[58] She was wife of the farmer (*hyakusho*) Jingoro, and was known to the Japanese as Ofuji-san ("Miss Fuji"). Perhaps "Susan" was a verbal corruption of Ofuji-san.

MURDER IN THE WHEATFIELD:
THE CLASH AT NAMAMUGI

who arrived in Japan in the early seventeenth century. To this day, it is a speciality of Nagasaki, where those early traders had been required to reside. It is akin to Madeira cake.

- This had been a deliberately-planned assassination of the first available westerners, as a terrible warning to foreigners to go away.
- Worst of all, though, was the rumour, universally believed by the western community at the time, to the effect that Richardson had lain, alive and suffering, by the side of the road for ten minutes or so, surrounded by a small crowd of country people, when the *norimon* of Shimazu Saburō came up. Seeing the crowd, Shimazu Saburō asked his attendants what was the cause of it. On being informed, he ordered them to put Richardson to death at once; which they did, cutting his throat and stabbing him repeatedly.

Captain Vyse, the British vice-Consul, was concerned to discover the truth of these things. If true, they would as a minimum partially vindicate his actions. If false, at least knowledge of the facts would calm the populace. A fortnight after the events, he set out on a mission of inquiry. In the statement he forwarded to the British Foreign Secretary, he reported on his findings. He found "Black-eyed Susan", who recollected seeing a foreigner fall from his horse, on the afternoon of the 14th of September. The foreigner had a large wound in his stomach; and she went up to him, and he immediately asked for water, but she took him none, because she was too much afraid of retribution. Afterwards, she saw Richardson drinking from a bottle. Vyse says that it was known that Richardson had taken a bottle of champagne on the ill-fated expedition, slung upon his arm. Susan pressed Richardson to crawl off the *tōkaidō*, because, on looking up the road, she saw that the cortège of a *daimyō* was approaching.

Susan saw one of the advance guard of the train draw his sword and attempt to cut the wounded foreigner's throat, but Richardson prevented this by putting up both his hands. One of his hands was then cut away; more men came up, drew their swords, and hacked him. Finally, one of them caught him by the beard and cut his throat; they then covered up the body with straw and moved off.

Vyse questioned Susan further and she stated that she did not recollect any orders being given by any person in a *norimon*; she recognized that the train was composed of Satsuma's men, but did not know the name of the chief personage in the procession. Her final piece of information was that an interval of about ten minutes or a quarter of an hour elapsed from the time the foreigner fell until the men came up and cut his throat.

How much we can rely on Susan's evidence is not clear. That she did not know it was Shimazu Saburō's procession, even two weeks after the startling events, is scarcely credible: it must have been the talk of the whole region, let alone the village, and the tea-room was a focal point of community life. It is likely that, like most Japanese at the time, she lived in constant fear of her feudal superiors and their retainers. The slightest offence to a *daimyō* would likely result in summary retribution from his *samurai*: better to keep quiet. But what she says is awful enough.

The Satsuma account given above says nothing of finally putting Richardson to death. However, under the *bushidō* code, it was regarded as an act of mercy to save a wounded adversary from unnecessary pain by the act of *todome*, which westerners would recognise as the *coup de grâce*. A later Japanese source says that Kaeda Takeji (or Kaeda Noboyushi), who later went on to become Governor of Nara, administered *todome* to

MURDER IN THE WHEATFIELD:
THE CLASH AT NAMAMUGI

Richardson. Perhaps an honourable death was what the Satsuma *samurai* were offering Richardson.

On the other hand, baser motives could have been at work. Maybe they wanted their piece of the action: to have put a foreigner to death was a badge of honour among the extreme supporters of *sonnō jōi*. The brutality of the assault on the helpless Richardson points to the latter view: his hand was almost severed as he tried to prevent his throat being cut.

The western community was aghast at what had happened. The *Japan Herald* of 20th September 1862 fulminated:

> A coolie belonging to Yokohama who happened to be passing near the body, stopped with others, when the retinue again came up, and Shimadzoo Saburo asked what was the matter. On being told it was a Foreigner, he directed them to cut his throat, and they accordingly nearly severed the head from the lifeless body. Could there be greater brutality and cowardice in a human being? Thus was murdered Charles Lenox Richardson, a young Englishman, in coolest blood and in the most fiendish way, by creatures calling themselves his fellow creatures, but who by such actions shew that their courage is only the cunning of a tiger, and their courtesy the slime of a snake.

The Japanese resident magistrate in Kanagawa, Abe Masato, led the Japanese inquiry into the incident. He was outraged that Shimazu Saburō had acted in such a cavalier fashion. It was a serious matter, and yet he had nonchalantly continued on his way, as if nothing untoward had occurred. Abe went immediately to the British Legation to offer condolences, then inspected the scene of the incident and ordered his subordinates to investigate. He reported to his superiors in Edo, ending his report:

> Odawara domain should immediately be ordered to close the Hakone checkpoint [on the *tōkaidō*]. I also

RESPECT AND CONSIDERATION

>think it expedient that Hisamitsu [Shimazu Saburō] be prevented from journeying any further west.

According to his own diary, *shōgun* Tokugawa Yoshinobu had himself suggested that Satsuma should arrest the murderer after arriving in Kyoto. It is not clear whether his suggestion was conveyed to Satsuma. In any case, the *bakufu* was a toothless government as far as controlling the *daimyō* was concerned, and dare not confront Satsuma directly.

A statement was given to Abe on behalf of Shimazu Saburō that the initial assailant had been a *rōnin* with no connection to Satsuma; and in any case, the arrogant behaviour of Richardson meant that he had brought it on himself. Shimazu also complained that the English party had failed to do what other foreigners did - show appropriate deference to a *daimyō*. They cited the example of Mr Eugene van Reed[59], who is said to have fallen in with the train of Shimazu Saburō on the same day as the incident, and to have immediately and without reservation conformed to the native custom. Satow castigated van Reed for submitting to this "indignity". He went on to say that it was normal, though, for the Japanese to show deference to him and other Legation officials.

>In many towns the people knelt down by the side of the street as we passed along, being invited to assume that posture by the municipal officers who preceded us beadle-fashion, crying out *shitaniro, shitaniro* ("down, down"). This honour used in those days to be rendered to every *daimyō*, no matter

---

[59] Eugene Miller van Reed was an American businessman and Hawaiian Consul-General in Japan, who in 1868 was the first to recruit Japanese people to work, under slave-like conditions, on Hawaiian sugar plantations. Recruitment for overseas work was subsequently forbidden until 1885 due to van Reed's mistreatment of the Japanese workers. Van Reed was 24 years old in 1862. Four years later, van Reed was shipwrecked at Wake Island on the *Libelle*, and took part in an arduous and celebrated 1400-mile journey in a small boat to Guam.

MURDER IN THE WHEATFIELD: THE CLASH AT NAMAMUGI

whether travelling in his own dominions or those of another nobleman, and also to the high officials of the *shōgun's* government, as, for example, the governor of Kanagawa, to the great indignation of the European residents. The practice had its origin, perhaps, in the necessity of protecting the nobles from sudden attack, combined with the rule of Japanese etiquette which considers that a standing posture implies disrespect.

Abe was unsatisfied by the Satsuma version of events, and demanded that the perpetrators should be punished by the Satsuma clan. Their failure to comply caused him to recommend to his superiors that the *bakufu* should penalise Satsuma for their irresponsible behaviour.

However, Shimazu Saburō, on his arrival in Kyōto after the murder of Richardson, told his own tale, saying that foreigners had insulted him, and he had ordered them to be slain. Instead of being rebuked, it was known in both the *shōgun's* and the Emperor's Courts that the Emperor approved of Shimazu's anti-western actions and so silently commended him.

A celebratory poem from the cloistered Prince Kashuji[60] written the evening of the incident speaks of the Emperor's approval:

> Satsuma's veteran chief, hair rising through his headgear,
> Has saved the Son of Heaven[61] and his court from peril;
> The Namamugi action shows his hero's mettle,
> While cold the moonlight gleams along the ten-league shore.

---

[60] At least, according to Shiba Ryōtarō.
[61] A poetic reference to the Emperor, descendant of Amaterasu.

RESPECT AND CONSIDERATION

No wonder, then, that Abe's recommendation was permanently placed in the "Pending" file. This was another indication of the waning power of the *bakufu*: Abe was their appointee as magistrate, but the Emperor had made it impossible for the *bakufu* to act on their official's recommendations.

Namamugi Village, 1862

Chapter 12
The Reaction of the Foreign Community

The news of the outrage reached the settlement within minutes. Great excitement was generated. Immediately, all the men put themselves on a war footing. Revolvers were taken out and loaded, and several parties of residents mounted their ponies, riding off as fast as they could to Namamugi. The French Minister, M. de Bellecourt, was particularly zealous, ordering the immediate landing at Kanagawa of a large detachment of sailors and marines with sabres, muskets and field pieces from the French frigate *Le Monge*. He hastened there himself with his mounted and foot guards. Colonel Neale ordered the British seven-man mounted Escort to hold themselves at once in readiness to start for the scene of the outrage. However, learning that Richardson was actually dead and that his companions were alive and not in danger of further assault, he decided not to send the Escort to the *tōkaidō*, where they would probably run the gauntlet through hundreds of armed *samurai*, fresh from the blood-letting and thus in a dangerous mood. Furthermore, Lieutenant Applin, their commander, was not present, and it was not to be expected that a troop corporal would be able to give the leadership required in a sticky situation.

RESPECT AND CONSIDERATION

Indeed, there were several sticky confrontations between parties of residents and detachments of Satsuma *samurai*. When a posse of five or six residents was threatened by a group of *samurai* led by a senior government officer, the westerners promptly drew their pistols, and pointed them at the head man in his *norimon*, who sensibly ordered his men not to draw their swords. Further death and injury was thereby averted.

Now, Namamugi, where Richardson's body lay, was directly over the bay from Yokohama. Accordingly, Neale was rowed to the anchorage of HMS *Centaur*, and requested her captain to send an armed cutter and sufficient men across the bay to bring back Richardson's body.

Neale returned to the place where he had ordered the Escort to await his return. To his consternation, he found them gone. He was told that H.B.M.'s Consul, Captain Vyse, had ordered them to accompany him *en route* to Kanagawa. Vyse had obtained a horse from Mr Gower's *betto*, and set off at the head of the leaderless troop. This clearly angered Neale. At that moment, Lieutenant Applin arrived, and Colonel Neale informed him that the Escort had gone without authority on a wild-goose chase.

Applin set off at a gallop to retrieve his men. About half way to Namamugi along the *tōkaidō*, Applin caught up with Vyse and the Escort, accompanied by a large company of residents on horseback. Among them was Dr William Willis from the Legation, who hoped to render aid to any injured people he might find. Applin ordered his men to halt, and informed Vyse that Colonel Neale was extremely incensed that the guard should have been taken out of Yokohama without his express order. Vyse, however, contended that in his role as British Consul, it was his duty at all hazards to recover and identify his missing countryman. He had found the guard in the saddle ready to start, but without any orders, and, though Colonel

THE REACTION OF THE FOREIGN COMMUNITY

Neale had rejected Vyse's urgent demand for assistance, he had thought it his duty to order the Escort at once to follow him. Applin was persuaded by Vyse's justification, and ordered his troop to advance.

The party now continued along the road until they arrived at the half-way house between Kanagawa and Kawasaki. There they were joined by the French mounted guard, who had received orders from M. Duchesne de Bellecourt, the French representative, to act in concert with Captain Vyse and his *ad hoc* militia.

At Namamugi, a young boy directed them to the spot where Richardson's body lay. They found his corpse lying a little off the roadside, dreadfully mangled with sword-cuts and spear-wounds. The body was decently laid out on a straw mat, and covered with another. A third mat lay, tent-like, over them both. A swift search of Richardson's clothing showed that none of his belongings had been removed. On enquiry it appeared that he could not have been actually dead when Marshall had left him. A Japanese bystander said that, despite his appalling wounds, Richardson had managed to drag himself to the bank at the roadside, and to raise himself to a sitting posture. He had called for water, but no Japanese dared to approach him for fear of the nearby *samurai*.

A litter was constructed and the party returned with the body to Kanagawa. Richardson's body had been so dreadfully mutilated that Dr. Willis had to sew it together before it could be moved. At Kanagawa, Dr. Hepburn of the American Mission handed Marshall and Clarke over to the care of Dr. Willis. They were joined there by the detachment from HMS *Centaur* and a French contingent under the command of *Capitaine le Comte* d'Harcourt, together with M. De Bellecourt and his personal bodyguard. D'Harcourt told them that some two-sworded men had, a moment or two previously, drawn their weapons upon the French guard.

There was great uproar within the foreign community, and the sense of outrage and indignation was extraordinarily high. It was the immediate expectation of the inhabitants of the Settlement that the British Chargé d'Affaires - a decorated military man, no less - would lead a charge to the location of the errant *daimyō*, arrest him, and administer sufficient punishment on his troops to make it impossible for such an outrage to occur again. A contemporary account says, "one word from Colonel Neale would have put every available man in motion to avenge the murder, and to seize upon the chief culprit". But Neale kept his counsel. He was the only one to remain cool in that febrile atmosphere.

Neale had the long-term interests of his country at heart. He was not beholden to the local community, and thought of what would have been likely to follow any retributive action by them, or on their behalf. He foresaw that there would be the certain death of many of that community. He anticipated an inevitable attack on the settlement by Satsuma's men - and others - if Shimazu were captured. Worst of all, he could see that a state of war between Britain (and of the Western nations generally) and Japan, would *de facto* be declared. That would bring an end to all the treaties of Amity and Commerce that had so painfully been negotiated over the previous nine years. War with Japan was against the policy of the British government, and in no one's interest.

Chapter 13
A Sacredly Secret Meeting

A hastily-convened and well-attended meeting of the foreign residents of Yokohama was held that evening at ten o'clock at the House of Mr. Edward Clarke, of Dent & Co. The chair was taken by Captain Vyse, who had just returned from an interview with Rear-Admiral Kuper, who had himself arrived only that evening aboard HMS *Euryalus*, accompanied by the *Ringdove*. Vyse had informed the Admiral about the outrage, and understood that Kuper intended to discuss the matter with Neale at noon the next day.

The meeting resolved:

1. That the British, French, Dutch, American and Portuguese authorities be requested to take such immediate steps as seem to them best calculated to prevent the recurrence of such a deplorable event as has occurred this evening, and that ample reparation be demanded of the Japanese Government for the murderous attack on unarmed British subjects peacefully travelling within treaty limits.

A proposition from a French resident, M. Jaquemot, to request the foreign authorities to land 1,000 men with sufficient *matériel* for the purpose of arresting the guilty parties at once, and to take possession of Kanagawa, was rejected. The meeting was persuaded by Samuel Gower that this would be an improper attempt to dictate to the western authorities what steps they ought to take.

2. That in consequence of the explanation given by Her Britannic Majesty's Consul of his interview with the British Admiral, it is earnestly desired by this meeting that the commanders of the foreign forces may be at once conferred with, so that immediate steps may be taken to secure, if possible, the person of the *daimyō* whose retainers have committed the murder, or of some of his high officers, in order to guarantee speedy reparation for the horrible outrage.

3. That a deputation be appointed to wait on the naval and other authorities.

The appointed deputation shows the international flavour of this meeting. SJ Gower (British), Captain White (American), Edward Clarke (British), HJ Hooper (British), L. Bourret (French), Mr. Plate (probably British or American), A. Schultz (Prussian), RB Smith (British) and Dr. CHD Visscher (Dutch) would be introduced to the authorities by Captain Vyse.

Finally, the meeting took on a conspiratorial air. They resolved:

4. That these proceedings be for the present kept sacredly secret amongst ourselves, lest the Japanese gain any information as to the course of action proposed to be pursued.

The usual sentiments of such a meeting were then resolved:

5. That we cannot part, this night, without expressing our deep and hearty sympathy with Mrs. Borradaile, Mr. Marshall, and Mr. Clarke, and the families of those who have suffered from this infamous and cowardly outrage.

6. That the cordial thanks of this meeting be tendered to M. de Bellecourt and M. le Commandant le Comte d'Harcourt for the prompt and active steps

A SACREDLY SECRET MEETING

> which they took on hearing of this painful occurrence.

And the final act of business:

> 7. That this meeting be now adjourned till 3 o'clock a.m., when the Committee appointed to confer with the Commanders of the Forces will be able to lay before the community that which has transpired, and such measures can be adopted as may then be thought necessary.

An extraordinary postscript to the meeting now occurred. It shows the emotive depths of the feeling that decisive military action was what the community desired. Mr FH Bell (of WR Adamson & Co) addressed the meeting.

> Gentlemen, it is usual, before a meeting disperses, to propose a formal motion of thanks to the Chairman for his able conduct in the Chair. But we have something more than this to do; we have to return our special and sincere thanks to Captain Vyse, not only for attending at and presiding over this meeting, but for the noble and spirited manner in which he has acted throughout this affair, and the way in which he has gone hand in hand with the community. And I would wish to associate, with his name those of several others, officers of Her Majesty's ships, members of the Legation and Consulate, all of whom have given such prompt and valuable assistance; and would especially mention Mr. Applin, who took upon himself the responsibility of sending out his troop to assist and guard us in recovering the body of our poor friend, which would have now lain rotting in the road had he awaited orders.

Samuel Gower intervened to correct what Bell had said:

> It was Captain Vyse who ordered the troop out, as Lieutenant Applin was not at home at the time.

And this was corroborated by Applin himself:

> Captain Vyse had led the troop out, but that on myself Colonel Neale's displeasure had fallen, and that certainly the responsibility did now rest on me, as I had immediately followed up the party and resumed the command.

The meeting then resolved (as in all resolutions, unanimously):

> 8. That the special and sincere thanks of the meeting be tendered to Captain Vyse for the noble and spirited manner in which he has acted throughout this affair; and that with his name be associated those of several of Her Majesty's servants who gave their aid in recovering the body of our poor friend, especially those upon whom the responsibility fell of leading, put the guard to seek for the body, which would have laid rotting in the road had they awaited orders of a superior.

So ended that meeting. Pressure would be put on the naval and military commanders of all the nations present to act to achieve retribution on Shimazu and his retainers. Vyse was the noble and spirited hero of the hour, and Neale had failed the community.

For "noble and spirited", though, we might read "hot-headed and excitable". Colonel Neale did. He subsequently complained to Earl Russell that Vyse had taken a

> highly improper course … throughout the proceedings … which I can assure your Lordship has embarrassed me in the discharge of my duties during the difficult circumstances in which I have been placed, to a degree more than I am enabled to express. It is my duty, nevertheless, to direct your Lordship's notice to the fact that the whole proceedings of the meetings of the community, of whom one-half were foreigners, were presided over, as your Lordship will observe, by Captain Vyse and that he accompanied as spokesman, the deputation

A SACREDLY SECRET MEETING

> which waited upon all the civil and naval foreign authorities.

In other words, Vyse had acted outside the scope of a Consul's remit, involving himself in matters of foreign policy that were Neale's diplomatic prerogative. Neale went on,

> Admiral Kuper informs me that Captain Vyse more especially urged upon him the adoption of immediate coercive measures, while I was in total ignorance of the whole of his proceedings.

Vyse had overstepped the mark entirely.

Vyse saw to it that the international deputation wasted no time in doing their work. Around midnight, when the meeting adjourned, they left and boarded HMS *Euryalus*. Admiral Kuper rose from his bed to receive them. Kuper had, of course only arrived in Japan that day, and had no first-hand experience of the local political and diplomatic climate. Wisely, he refused to take any action until he had had the chance to discuss the matter with Neale. It was therefore arranged that a meeting should be held at 6 o'clock the next morning at the residence of the French Minister. The deputation then went on board the French and Dutch flagships, to speak with Captain d'Harcourt and Commodore Buys, who agreed to attend the early morning meeting. Finally, after all was cut and dried, they called upon Colonel Neale.

At 3.00 am, the deputation met with Neale and later gave an account to the adjourned meeting of Neale's reaction to their visit. Colonel Neale did not, they reported, having heard their statement, appear either to approve of the steps that had been agreed by the meeting, or concur in what was proposed to be done. However, Neale had said that he would attend the 6.00 am meeting, since the French Minister, the English Admiral, and other foreign officials would be present. Nonetheless, he considered it a most unusual proceeding, and was considerably annoyed that any unauthorised meeting had been held by the community at large.

At the 6 o'clock meeting, Colonel Neale dismissed the community meeting's proposals. They were impracticable, "Quixotic", even. Even if they could be carried out with any chance of success, they would be tantamount to a sudden commencement of hostilities with Japan, and likely result, by forcing the hand of the British government, in the waging of unwanted open warfare. Trade, the principal reason why the west was in Japan, would come to a stop. Furthermore, he had received no official report of the murder and assaults, and requested Captain Vyse to prepare one prior to any further action being taken. This may have been a ploy to delay things further so that feelings might cool down. The French Minister concurred, though the firebrands in the community hardly noticed.

Neale added an infelicitous remark that incensed the foreign community when it was reported to them at their twice-adjourned meeting at 8 o'clock that morning. Neale said,
> However distressing the outrage, it was not as significant in national terms as the premeditated attacks[62], accompanied by bloodshed and murder, on the British Minister (i.e. himself), Her Majesty's Representative in Japan, which even more loudly called for reparation than the murder of a merchant.

The traders who made up the bulk of the community distinctly heard the silent "mere" before "merchant".

The meeting was also incredulous that Neale had asked for an official report on the outrage before he would authorise any action. It was well known in the community that he

---

[62] Neale was referring to the attacks on the British Legation itself on 5 July 1861 and 27 June 1862. See Chapter 7.

A SACREDLY SECRET MEETING

- had met Mrs. Borradaile and heard her account of the attack;
- had himself seen Richardson's frightfully mutilated dead body;
- had received a visit from the Governor of Yokohama at about 10 o'clock in the evening; and
- had been waited on by the Committee at 3.00 a.m. upon the subject.

That he was ignorant of the events was beyond belief. That he was *officially* ignorant was irrelevant. Right must be done! Neale and the rest of the Legation, they thought, were falling short of their duty: to carry out the wishes of the community. That Neale was the servant of Her Majesty's government in London and not the servant of the inhabitants of Yokohama was beyond their understanding at that heated moment. It was this misconception that led to their low opinion of Neale and their calls for his replacement.

In his despatch to Earl Russell on these matters, Neale wrote in these terms:

> A crisis has arisen on the present occasion arising out of the effervescence and irritation of the community, the disastrous tendency of which I may say I have single-handed opposed myself to stem. I have not done so without incurring obloquy. Much pressure was brought to bear upon me, but I have been sustained by a strong sentiment of duty which dictated the urgency of resisting a precipitate and ill-advised course of action, suggested by the tempting though accidental presence of several ships of war, but which, if it had been entered into, would, as the least of its consequences, have instantly awakened into activity the civil strife which lies beneath the surface of events in this country.
>
> I now await your Lordship's instructions respecting the accumulated grievances for which

> reparation is due to the British nation and to British subjects by the Rulers of Japan. Until I am in receipt of those instructions no pressure from without or popular displeasure shall influence my course of action, founded upon national interests, and supported, as I earnestly trust it may be, by the approval of Her Majesty's Government.

The meeting of residents indeed regarded Neale with obloquy. They had requested him to forward a copy of the minutes of their meetings to Earl Russell. In a covering letter, they said,

> the general opinion amongst the foreign officials and naval authorities, as well as the mercantile community, who certainly are the most interested in the maintenance of peace, was, that immediate action, and a severe lesson inflicted on the spot, would have been the best means of preventing a recurrence of a similar crime, and would probably have prevented future international complications, which now appear to be only too imminent.

On the original document, there is a handwritten annotation: "Directly opposed to the facts. E.N."

When they later received the meeting's slanted version of events, the English press, which was as prone to hasty and unthinking judgement then as it so often is today, vilified Neale. He was accused of cowardice in the more lurid English newspapers, a grave affront to a distinguished military man who had been decorated for bravery in the field. The *Japan Herald* of Yokohama republished extracts from the home papers and opined that doubtless Neale himself would demand an enquiry, to clear himself of the charge of cowardice, and to prove that certain statements of Captain Vyse and Lieutenant Applin were false, expecting, of course, that he would be unable to do so. The Hong Kong and Shanghai newspapers, writing from over 1000 miles away, repeatedly demanded that Neale be

A SACREDLY SECRET MEETING

recalled, as he had shown himself unfit for his post. Neale was largely isolated. He was shunned by the British community, even being denied entrance to the British Club. He must have felt great resentment at his unfair treatment at the hands of the community.

Charles Richardson senior only had the press reports and communications from Earl Russell to go on. He wrote a letter to Captain Vyse:

Duppas Hill, Croydon. 10th Dec 1862

Dear Sir

I feel assured that no apology is necessary from me, for addressing you on behalf of my broken hearted family & myself, to return you our warmest thanks for your noble, & truly Christian conduct, in recovering the body of my only & most dearly loved son Mr. Charles Lenox Richardson, after he had been so cruelly & wantonly murdered by a party of Japanese, in the neighbourhood of Yokohama; but for your gallant & truly philanthropic perseverance, it is quite evident that our dear Boy would have been thrown ignominiously into some ditch or river, & we should not have had even the melancholy satisfaction of knowing where his cherished remains lie.

A more gross outrage on [one] so amiable & unoffending was never perpetrated, & I trust H.M.'s Government will not pass it over with indifference - I have been honored with one or two communications from Earl Russell and have reason to hope that he will not allow the subject to go without serious notice.

I observe that Lieut. Applin and other gentlemen, most kindly exerted themselves to aid in effecting the object you had in view; and to all (especially to Mr. Aspinall, if in Yokohama) I beg you will please to tender our heartfelt grateful acknowledgements.

      I have the honor to be
       Dear Sir
      Yours most faithfully
       Sd.) C. Richardson

Captain Vyse
 &c. &c. &c.
  Yokohama

It was not until early 1863, when a despatch from Earl Russell was received, that Neale could consider himself vindicated. Russell wrote:

> Colonel Neale's conduct seems to have been severely but unjustly attacked. It was right to send out the escort to bring back the body of Mr. Richardson, but it was for Colonel Neale, and not for Vyse to decide that point. The further and more important question whether an attempt should be made at once to capture the murderers and bring them to trial, seems to have been rightly decided by Colonel Neale. Sending out eight men to take ten or twelve from among a body of 300 armed Japanese must have led to further bloodshed, and probably to the loss of the whole body of the escort. The other proposition of landing 1000 men might have been effectual as far as the capture of the Daimio's men, or some of them, was concerned, but even this is doubtful. What is certain is that it would have been an act of war, and Colonel Neale is not authorized to make war. Colonel Neale should therefore be approved.

That approval was evidenced by the subsequent appointment of Neale as a Companion of the Most Honourable Order of the Bath. The inappropriate behaviour of Vyse resulted in his posting - for "posting" read "banishment" - to remote Hakodate three months after the incident. Lieutenant Applin disappears

A SACREDLY SECRET MEETING

from the records, and we might surmise that he, too, had been posted away. And in time, even those who were most bitter against him admitted that Neale had been right. War would have been in no one's interest.

Interestingly, Admiral Kuper concurred with Neale's desire to keep the British response as low-key as possible. In a despatch to the Admiralty on 20th September, referring to the meeting on board *Euryalus* on the 15th, he explained why it was unwise to send a raiding party to arrest Shimazu Saburō:

> This meeting was attended by the French Minister, the British Chargé d'Affaires, myself, the Commanders of the British, French and Dutch Vessels of War, and the British Dutch and Portuguese Consuls. It was decided that although it was necessary to take steps to secure the lives of foreigners within the limits in which they had by treaty a right to move; & to prevent the possibility of a recurrence of such barbarous murders as that which had been committed on the previous day, it would be inexpedient to land a large force for the purpose of making a prisoner of the Prince of Satsuma.
>
> I was induced to coincide in this decision for various reasons amongst which were:
>
> 1st - The small chance of success in securing the right man in the midst of a mob of some 800 or 1000 followers, all probably prepared to sacrifice their own lives to ensure the escape of their Chief;
>
> 2nd - The probable result, in the event either of success or failure, of immediate hostilities with Japan, for which we are not prepared;
>
> 3rd - The questionable right of landing a large force, for an aggressive purpose in a country, with the Government of which we are at amity and under treaty;

> 4th - The danger such an act would entail upon the lives and property of the whole European Community in Japan;
> and
> 5th - The Difficulty that would arise in the event of success, as to the disposal of the Prince when taken.

These were very much the same sentiments as Neale had put forward.

But back to our narrative. Irrespective of his desire not to commit an act of war, Neale was not insensible of the threat to the community's security posed by the proponents of *sonnō jōi*. He had briefed Admiral Kuper about the circumstances surrounding Richardson's murder, and reminded him of other outrages committed against the western - particularly the British - community. On 15th September, he wrote to Admiral Kuper about the attack at Namamugi and the high levels of anxiety that it had engendered. He asked Kuper to land guards on shore, or to take other military measures that would serve to calm the community.

Kuper informed Neale that the Captains of the British, French and Dutch ships of war at Yokohama had already met with him that same day on board the *Euryalus* to consider the best measures to be adopted to protect the lives and property of the European community. It was Kuper's assessment that the danger of a further murderous incident was small. On the 20th September, he wrote to the Admiralty:

> The feeling of alarm has now considerably subsided; and I do not myself see any reason for supposing that the murderous assault committed on the 14th will be followed up by any aggressive act, on the part of the Japanese at Yokohama; the parties concerned in that murder passed on their way, & are probably many miles from this place.

Nevertheless, as a matter of prudence and to placate the feelings of the community, the naval commanders had agreed:

A SACREDLY SECRET MEETING

1. That the force at each of the Legations should be strengthened during the night, so that they could send small detachments to patrol the Settlement.
2. Guard-boats should patrol along the beach at each country's "station", to be in readiness to communicate with the military patrols in the event of an alarm.
3. Any boat receiving notice of a disturbance or alarm should go to the gun-boat *Kestrel*, which would fire two shots as a signal for naval detachments to go to the various landing-stages in readiness for orders to land.
4. All personnel sent to strengthen the Legation forces at sunset would be re-embarked at dawn the following morning.

And Neale was active on the diplomatic front. He was renowned for doing everything calmly and in order. He already had before the *shōgun's* Government the unsettled case of the murders of Sweet and Crimp, the two servicemen killed defending the Legation in July. He now had another murder and woundings for which to seek atonement. He had already ordered Vyse to make a formal report to him concerning the incident. So, the very day after the murder, he put himself in communication with the *gorogio*.

RESPECT AND CONSIDERATION

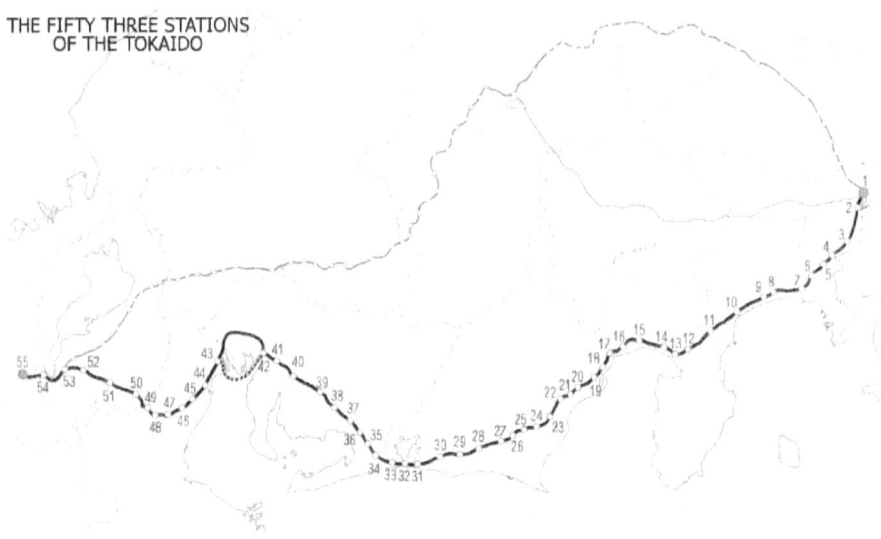

THE FIFTY THREE STATIONS OF THE TOKAIDO

Stations on the *tōkaidō*
from Nihonbashi 日本橋 in Edo to Sanjō Ōhashi 京都 in Kyoto

1. Shinagawa 品川
2. Kawasaki 川崎
3. Kanagawa 神奈川
4. Hodogaya 程ヶ谷,保土ヶ谷
5. Totsuka 戸塚
6. Fujisawa 藤沢
7. Hiratsuka 平塚
8. Ōiso 大磯
9. Odawara 小田原
10. Hakone 箱根 Checkpoint.
11. Mishima 三島
12. Numazu 沼津
13. Hara 原
14. Yoshiwara 吉原
15. Kanbara 蒲原
16. Yui 由井,由比
17. Okitsu 興津
18. Ejiri 江尻
19. Fuchū 府中 / Sunpu 駿府
20. Mariko / Maruko 鞠子,丸子
21. Okabe 岡部
22. Fujieda 藤枝
23. Shimada 島田
24. Kanaya 金屋,金谷
25. Nissaka 日坂
26. Kakegawa 掛川
27. Fukuroi 袋井
28. Mitsuke 見附
29. Hamamatsu 浜松
30. Maisaka 舞阪
31. Arai 荒井,新居 Checkpoint.
32. Shirasuga 白須賀
33. Futakawa 二川
34. Yoshida 吉田
35. Goyu 御油
36. Akasaka 赤坂
37. Fujikawa 藤川
38. Okazaki 岡崎
39. Chiryū 知立 /Chirifu 地鯉鮒
40. Narumi 鳴海
41. Miya 宮 Optional ferry boat service from Miya to Kuwana
42. Kuwana 桑名 Ferry
43. Yokkaichi 四日市
44. Ishiyakushi 石薬師
45. Shōno 庄野
46. Kameyama 亀山
47. Seki 関
48. Sakanoshita 坂ノ下
49. Tsuchiyama 土山
50. Minakuchi 水口
51. Ishibe 石部
52. Kusatsu 草津
53. Ōtsu 大津

CHAPTER 14
ANGLO-JAPANESE DIPLOMACY

The failing *bakufu* was running out of ideas as to how to deal with the truculent, not to say rebellious *daimyō*. Behind their diplomatic discussions lay an oblique request for western support in dealing with the disaffected clan chiefs. They frankly confessed their inability to deal with Shimazu Saburō in the peremptory way that was demanded of them by the British. They undertook to do all in their power (which was lessening by the month) to bring the real culprits, whoever they might be, to justice. They also agreed to give better protection to western visitors on the *tōkaidō*.

This they did by establishing guard-houses, each manned by five armed men, every 550 metres or so, all the way from Hodogaya to Kawasaki (just over 14½ kilometres), the limit that foreigners were allowed to visit in the Edo direction under the Treaty provisions. The *bakufu* proposed to keep westerners and *daimyō* well separated. They partially constructed a new road for the *daimyō* and other officials to travel, as a replacement for the *tōkaidō* within the treaty limits, and foreigners agreed not to use this new road.

On the day before Richardson's murder, the Japanese ministers for foreign affairs had written to Colonel Neale:

RESPECT AND CONSIDERATION

> We send you the following communication.
> Ohohara Sayamon no Kami, the Mikado's Envoy, who has been staying here, as we informed you some time ago, intends to leave Edo on (September 15th) and to take up his lodgings for the night at Kawasaki; on (September 16th) he will pass through Kanagawa on his way to Kyotō.
> As we informed you at his arrival, a great number of his retainers accompany him, travelling promiscuously along the *tōkaidō*.
> Now these latter, not knowing the ways and customs of foreigners, we fear some misunderstanding might arise, and therefore we request you to make known to your Consul at Kanagawa, that we do not wish British subjects to pass along the road the said Envoy will take on the said 15th and 16th. We intend furthermore to instruct the Governor of Kanagawa to settle this matter with your Consul.
> With respect and consideration.

Neale instantly replied.

> This day I have received your letter announcing to me that the Envoy of the Mikado, who has been for some time residing at Edo, was returning to Miako[63] to-morrow, and requesting that I would signify to the British Consul at this port to prohibit British subjects from going on the *tōkaidō* on that and on the following day, lest any misadventure might arise in consequence of the Envoy's adherents and attendants being unacquainted with the usages of foreigners.
> I have to express to your Excellencies my extreme surprise at receiving this communication at a time so close upon the Envoy's departure that the necessary time is not afforded to consider or reply to your communication before he is actually on the *tōkaidō* himself.

---

[63] Miako, sometimes Miyako, (都, "capital") was an alternative name for Kyōto.

ANGLO-JAPANESE DIPLOMACY

I have to state to your Excellencies that it is not so light a matter to prohibit British subjects from proceeding where they will, within the limits assigned to them by Treaty.
Her Majesty's Representative in this country is charged with securing the rights acquired by that Treaty to British subjects, and not to set them aside, or suspend any portion of them, unless for most urgent and pressing reasons which have been submitted for consideration by the Japanese Government, and found to be sufficient and satisfactory.
The reasons assigned by your Excellencies on the present occasion are inadmissible and unsatisfactory. The Envoy's attendants, I am informed, are not so formidable and numerous that no check can be placed by the Tycoon's Government upon the order and propriety of their march, which, indeed, might and ought to be imposed upon them by the Envoy himself. If they are under no control, guards amounting to twice their number might accompany them along the short distance on the *tōkaidō* frequented by foreigners, rather than that a whole community of foreign subjects should, during two days, be deprived of recreation on the road, which they are in the habit of frequenting.
The chief object of this communication is to remind your Excellencies that I have undoubted right, for all the reasons above stated, to decline to accede to the wish signified in your letter, but I shall abstain from causing any interruption to your arrangements on the present occasion and shall instruct the Consul to request British subjects not to frequent the *tōkaidō* on the days in question.
But I have distinctly to acquaint your Excellencies that it will be my duty on all future occasions to decline acting upon any similar communications,

RESPECT AND CONSIDERATION

leaving the responsibility of whatever may occur upon the Japanese Government, unless it has been addressed to me at a period affording sufficient time for consideration, discussion, and correspondence with your Excellencies.

On 12th October, a month after the murder of Richardson, a notification was issued from the British Consulate on instruction from Colonel Neale. It referred to that given on 15th September in pursuance of the above letter from the Japanese foreign Ministers, cautioning British subjects to be careful when walking or riding on the *tōkaidō* until the Japanese precautions had been effected. Neale now issued a special notification that the Japanese Government had "earnestly requested" him to caution British subjects that a high personage, the son of a former Emperor, would pass along the road from Miako to Yedo, accompanied by a numerous retinue, on the 15th, 16th, and 17th of October. It gave the locations and date where he would be staying. It was

The British Consulate Building

> advisable that this special communication should be made known to British subjects, the Japanese Government having pressed their great fear lest any recurrence of the recent lamentable event should take place.

Similar communications had been sent to the French, Dutch, American and Portuguese Ministers. The residents received the news of these intimations from their Ministers with intense indignation. The French residents swept up the French Minister and took him to the Japanese Ministry for Foreign Affairs to protest face-to-face to the Japanese authorities. The British portion of the community also protested to Neale, principally to give him moral support in resisting such detestable demands to abrogate the Treaties.

It seems that no notice had been given by the Japanese authorities to the foreign community that Shimazu Saburō and his retinue would pass along the *tōkaidō* within the Treaty limits on 14th September. Their appearance there was a surprise for Richardson and his party. Admiral Kuper, in his despatch to the Admiralty on 20th September concerning notice given by the Japanese authorities, said

> A notice of this description appears to have been given for the 15th and 16th Instant but not for the 14th, consequently no apprehension was entertained of falling in with any of these great processions on that day.

We have seen that the later Japanese justification for the cutting down of Richardson was that he and his party neither dismounted nor moved to the side of the road, as every Japanese of rank inferior to the personage whose procession it was, was bound to do. As the English seemed to act contemptuously to the proud man whose cortège they met, they were justly cut down. At the time, however, these views were not expressed by the Japanese in regular contact with the foreign community in Yokohama. They were as much horrified – or expressed themselves as being so – as foreigners themselves were. Indeed, the *bakufu* expressed

> extreme regret at the deplorable event that had occurred

and went on,

> we have been thoroughly informed of all the circumstances, and sincerely thank H.M. Chargé d'Affaires for the course which has been adopted. We are fully aware of the excitement which prevailed at Yokohama, and the coercive measures against the *daimyō* and his cortège which have been so urgently pressed in many quarters.

RESPECT AND CONSIDERATION

As early as 16th September, the Japanese Ministers[64] for Foreign Affairs had written to Neale,

> All this has caused us great grief. In the answer which this Shimazu Saburō gave to the officer officially inquiring into the matter, there is something very improper; therefore we will have the whole state of the case more accurately inquired into, and inform you of the result afterwards.

Whether these statements were a true expression of the sentiment of the Japanese people and government is an open question. As we will repeatedly see, it was a standard tactic for the Japanese authorities to prevaricate. Buying time would allow calmer reactions to unfortunate events, or so they hoped. But attempts by the Japanese authorities to avoid dealing with unpleasant issues merely served to make the British (and the western nations generally) the more determined to have matters resolved to their satisfaction. Playing for time was a dangerous game.

---

[64] As with most Japanese government posts in the *bakufu*, there were three co-equal incumbents. It was a saying among the *bugyō* themselves, only half in jest, that one made policy, the second ensured it was in accordance with central policy, and the third reported the failings of the other two to the central authorities.

Chapter 15
The Inquest on Richardson's Death

The inquest was convened under Consul Vyse. There was a Coroner's Jury of six "good and lawful men of the settlement of Kanagawa, duly chosen, and duly sworn and charged to inquire for the Lady the Queen when, how and by what means Charles Lennox (sic) Richardson came to his death". They were John Hughes (foreman of the jury), Henry Edward Hoey, Gilbert Henderson, John Hudson, William M. Strachan and John W. Broadbent, only one of whom makes any other particular appearance in the annals of the Foreign Settlement at this period. Hoey owned a substantial Yokohama house in which the British Legation had installed itself in early 1862. Hoey was himself murdered in his bed in 1870, by a Japanese for personal revenge. It was never ascertained what grudge the Japanese murderer bore against Hoey.

The inquest was held on 15th September, the day after the incident at Namamugi. It was held at the home of Mr W.G. Aspinall, business partner of the Mr Cornes mentioned in the first deposition. Richardson's body was lying in a room at Mr Aspinall's residence on 15th September prior to the funeral that afternoon.

The inquest extended over two days. Ellis Elias and Dr Willis gave evidence on the Monday, and Woodthorpe Clarke and William Marshall gave evidence on Tuesday 16th, when the jury

RESPECT AND CONSIDERATION

delivered its verdict. The inquest was adjourned at 5.30 pm on the Monday, to allow the funeral to take place that evening.

Francis Howard-Vyse, Her Britannic Majesty's Consul in Kanagawa, was sitting in the rôle of Coroner, despite having been involved in the immediate aftermath of the discovery of Richardson's body. The full inquest need not have taken place so soon after the death, for all that was needed for the interment of the body was for the cause of death to be established, which it was, by Dr Willis's evidence. And there were no Japanese witnesses called.

But one gets the impression that the Incident was Captain Vyse's Hour, the event for which his life, experience and military training had equipped him. Or at least Francis Howard-Vyse, - the passed-over Captain with no decorations, no campaign history, and nothing so far to tell his grandchildren - thought so. So keen was Vyse to make this *his* Incident, that he acted not only as (a thwarted) avenger, nor only as Coroner, but as pallbearer too. Vyse's hot-headed actions on the Sunday brought him into sharp conflict with the cooler, more experienced, more diplomatic stance of Colonel Neale.

The first to give evidence under oath was Ellis Elias:

> I was going out for a ride with Mr Cornes, yesterday afternoon on the 14th and met the chestnut horse on which the deceased Mr Richardson went out riding. The horse was covered with blood. We asked the person who was leading it[65] what was the cause of it. He said, the *'hia-kfoo-ban danasan'* (meaning the master of the house No. 100 in foreign Settlement, and by whom we thought at first was meant Mr Marshall or Mr Macpherson[66])[67] had been cut down

---

[65] Mr Aspinall's *betto* (see Marshall's evidence)
[66] The literal translation of the Japanese appears to be "Number 100 master of household". Macpherson was a business partner of Marshall, but makes no further appearance in this story.

THE INQUEST

in Kanagawa; and added, as we were going off, that a large *daimyō's* train was passing through. We went on as fast as possible to see if we could render any assistance.

We had got as far as the gate at the foot of Kanagawa Hill, which we found shut, a large body of men (coolies) bearing large baskets, apparently the luggage of the *daimyō*. Inside the gate, that is to say, on the Yeddo side of it, there were a great many two-sworded men (*samurai*) coming down the hill. We asked the gate-keeper whether it was true that any one had been cut down. He said, 'Yes, two;' and added that they (Marshall and Clarke) had been carried back to Yokohama, in a boat. We then came back to give the alarm at Yokohama, and again went back with the guard[68]. When we came as far as where the body was, we found it lying in a little garden close to a tea-house, about half-way between Kanagawa and Kawasaki.

I recognised the body at once as that of Charles Lennox[69] Richardson. It was dreadfully mutilated and quite dead. The wounds were evidently inflicted by a sword and spear. So far as I could see, there was nothing stolen from his person. The body was then conveyed to Yokohama. When I first saw the body it was about 5.30 pm. I identify the body now lying dead here as the body of Charles Lennox Richardson, which is the same that I saw dead in the garden between Kanagawa and Kawasaki.

---

[67] The statements and remarks in (parentheses) appear to be explanatory notes added at a later stage. Whose additions they are is not known, but it is likely they are Vyse's editorial to explain points of detail to his masters in Whitehall.
[68] This was Lieut. Applin's Mounted Guard, which Captain Vyse had, unauthorised, ordered out.
[69] As stated elsewhere, the correct spelling is Lenox; but the note-taker could not be expected to know this.

RESPECT AND CONSIDERATION

William Willis M.D. then gave evidence[70].

> Yesterday evening, about 5.30 pm, I saw the deceased lying quite dead by the roadside about four miles on the other or Yeddo side of Kanagawa. On examination, I discovered several very extensive wounds, each of which was of a mortal character. Deceased's death was caused by these wounds. I identify the body now lying here dead to be the same that I saw by the road about four miles on the Yeddo side of Kanagawa. The wounds which caused the death of the deceased were evidently produced by a sharp-cutting weapon, except two in the abdomen, which appeared to have been produced by a weapon of the nature of a lance.
>
> I am of the opinion there is no danger to the inmates of this house to be apprehended from keeping the body of the deceased uninterred until tomorrow; but I would recommend its being interred as soon as convenient.

The following day, Woodthrope[71] Charles Clarke, described as "a silk inspector of Yokohama", gave his evidence:

> About 2.30 pm on Sunday, the 14th instant, a party, consisting of Mrs Borradaile, Mr Richardson, Mr Marshall and myself, left Yokohama for Kanagawa in a boat. Our horses were sent round to Kanagawa before us, and meeting them at the landing-place at Kanagawa, there we mounted and rode on towards Kawasaki. Along the road we passed several *norimon*[72], surrounded each by a few attendants, each armed with two swords, and occasionally a few spears. Those *norimon* and

---

[70] See details of the autopsy conducted by Willis, in Appendix 4.
[71] His name appears variously as Woodthrope and Woodthorpe. I believe the latter to be the correct name, but I have left it as recorded in official papers.
[72] Palanquins, variously *kago* (baskets), in which important people were conveyed.

THE INQUEST

attendants formed a continuous but irregular train, broken at intervals. When these people were passing we walked our horses at a steady pace, and cantered during the intervals when no people were passing.

This continued for about three and a half to four miles of the road from Kanagawa to Kawasaki, when we met a regular procession preceded by about a hundred men in single file on either side of the road. We kept well to the near side of the road, going at a walking pace, until we arrived at the main body, which was then occupying the whole of the road, which at that place had, I think, a rather wide Japanese bridge across it. Mrs Borradaile and Mr Richardson were about ten yards in advance, Mr Richardson riding on the off-side[73] of Mrs Borradaile. I observed that on nearing the main body, Mrs Borradaile and Mr Richardson halted, and Mr Marshall and myself immediately did the same. As we did so, I observed a man of large stature issue from the main body, at the same time raising both his arms making some gesture, whereupon both Mrs Borradaile and Mr Richardson instantly turned their horses round towards Kanagawa, Mr Marshall and myself doing likewise. As I was in the act of turning round, I saw a Japanese, whom I think was the same big man I saw at first issuing from the main body, cut with a sword at Mr Richardson.

Upon this I observed also that a portion of the advanced guard, namely, those referred to before as advancing in single file, closed in upon us as to the number of about thirty. On seeing this, I immediately put my horse to a hand gallop and went through them. While doing so, I received a wound on the left shoulder and my horse received another on the near hip. I saw several swords drawn and blows aimed at

---

[73] On Mrs Borradaile's right.

RESPECT AND CONSIDERATION

me, which I escaped perhaps by bending forward and on account of the rapid pace at which my horse moved. As soon as I had cleared the advanced guard, I checked my horse somewhat. Then Mr Richardson came up with me and begged me to pull up, saying at the same time, "Oh, Clarke, they have killed me."

I replied that I was wounded, and I further begged him to endeavour to keep his seat, and to move on as quickly as possible as the only chance of safety. At the same time Mrs Borradaile and Mr Marshall came up, and I then moved on at a hand gallop with Mrs Borradaile - she keeping a little ahead. I think Mr Marshall stopped a moment or two with Mr Richardson, and that was the last I saw of Mr Richardson.

Mrs Borradaile and myself kept on and were joined by Mr Marshall at Kanagawa just immediately before we came to the bridge at Kanagawa. We had then slackened our pace; but, seeing Mr Marshall coming on all right, and feeling myself becoming somewhat faint, I pushed on with Mrs Borradaile, agreeing among ourselves to go to the American Consulate, at Kanagawa. I rode on some distance until arriving at the landing-place at Kanagawa, and again telling Mrs Borradaile to go to the American Consulate, I became dizzy and lost my sight from loss of blood, and I remember nothing more until I found the American Consul and someone helping me into a chair. I then fainted, and came to my senses as Mr Marshall was brought in. I was then kindly attended to by the family of the American Consul, and later in the evening we were removed to Yokohama.

Very shortly before meeting the compact train by which we were attacked, I noticed in a house by the wayside two of the Japanese interpreters belonging

THE INQUEST

to the Custom-House[74] at Yokohama, and who were personally known to Mr Marshall and spoken to by him.

I think I could recognize one of those interpreters on seeing him again. I can also recognize the uniform and crest of the advanced guard. They were dressed in dark blue, and I saw on the sleeves of nearly the whole of the advanced guard a crest similar to the sketch I now give in pencil, consisting of two broad white lines placed parallel[75].

The final witness was William Marshall, of Yokohama, "merchant".

On the afternoon of Sunday 14th instant, Mrs Borradaile, Mr Richardson, Mr Woodthrope C Clarke, and myself rode along the *tōkaidō*, or high road from Kanagawa, in the direction of Kawasaki. When we got to that part of the road which is called by foreigners here "the Avenue," I saw a Japanese interpreter, whom I knew, and two other Japanese.

That interpreter I know as one belonging to the Custom House at Yokohama. I said to the interpreter, "What are you doing so far away from Yokohama?"
He made no reply. We proceeded about quarter of a mile farther, when, on turning a corner, I perceived a large procession coming towards us along the road.

We did not stop, but went on, taking the left-hand side of the road. There was apparently no

---

[74] The Custom-house was formerly the building erected by the Japanese for the negotiations that resulted in Townsend Harris's Treaty of Kanagawa. Next to it was the only two-storeyed building in Yokohama at that time, the merchant house of Jardine Matheson & Co.

[75] This description presents a mystery. So far, no crest resembling the description has been identified. There are several crests with two horizontal parallel lines but within a circle, and at least one where the lines are vertical within a circle. But none without a circle, although this may be implied by the very word "crest". It is certainly not the Shimazu crest, which is a "plus" cross within a circle.

RESPECT AND CONSIDERATION

opposition until we had got about twelve men deep in the procession.

By this time our horses had fairly started. The greater number of the people remained stationary, but about half a dozen drew their swords, and, barring our passage, struck at us as we passed. Clarke rode over one man, and I rode over another. We galloped on – no person attempting to obstruct our passage until we reached the tea-house, just before the entrance to the avenue, when I saw Richardson's horse begin to flag. I shouted to Mrs Borradaile and Clarke who were leading, to go on, and that I would look after Richardson. I drew alongside, his horse and said "Richardson, are you badly hurt?" He made no reply. I looked into his face and saw that he was all but dead, if not quite so. His horse stopped, and he fell to the ground. I saw then that he was quite dead, his bowels protruding, and that I could do him no good. I put my horse into a gallop, and just at the entrance of Kanagawa overtook Mrs Borradaile and Mr Clarke.

Here also I met my own *betto* and Mr Aspinall's *betto*. The one I sent back to look after Mr Richardson's body, and mounting the other on Mr Richardson's horse sent him on to Yokohama. I felt very faint from loss of blood, and feeling comparatively safe in Kanagawa rode quietly until I reached the American Consulate, where I received every kindness and attention. There were a great number of people coming along the road and formed, I believe, the advanced part of the procession. I observed on the dresses of most of them one or other of the three crests which I can describe, the crest prevailing most being that of Satsuma.

We did not go faster than a walking pace for at least a quarter of a mile before we came up to the

THE INQUEST

procession; in fact we tried to get out of the way to avoid it.

As far as I could see, every man belonging to or forming the procession which attacked us was armed each with two swords, and some with long lances, and I observed in front two men carrying bows and bundles of arrows.

The jury brought in its verdict:

That certain Japanese men (whose names are to the jurors unknown), armed with swords, lances, and other arms after the fashion of their country, and bearing the same by authority, being officials or officers in either the civil or military service of Japan[76], marching in large bodies from Yeddo, on the 14th day of the present month of September, in the year of our Lord 1862, between the hours of 2 and 4 o'clock in the afternoon, with force and arms, at a place about four miles from Kanagawa, on the high road between Kanagawa and Kawasaki, the same being within the Consular district of Kanagawa aforesaid, the said Charles Lennox Richardson, in the peace of God and our Lady the Queen, then and there being, feloniously, wilfully, and of their malice aforethought[77], did kill and murder, against the peace of our Lady the Queen[78], her crown and dignity.

---

[76] They were in fact in the service of the *daimyō* of Satsuma. Whether the jurors were unable to understand the difference between *han* and *bakufu* forces, can only be speculated about. Perhaps this is indicative of a careless attitude of the Foreign Settlement towards Japanese culture.

[77] "Malice aforethought" by the perpetrator was (and is), in English law, the distinguishing condition between murder and other forms of homicide such as manslaughter or accident. It does not have to be very much "afore": it can arise in the heat of the moment, but it must be deliberate.

[78] This is an interesting extension of the concept of extraterritoriality. Extraterritoriality is normally confined to the perpetration of a crime *by* a foreign subject, not of a perpetration *against* him. Whether the Queen's "peace"

RESPECT AND CONSIDERATION

The verdict refers to evidence that was not recorded from the evidence of the witnesses. The death occurred between 2 and 4 o'clock, said the jurors, but no evidence was given for this[79]. Given that there were no independent western witnesses, no Japanese witnesses and even Mrs Borradaile was not called to give evidence, one wonders whether the full story had been told. Certainly, Richardson had been killed by sword and spear, but can it be said that he was murdered? Had there been Japanese evidence, perhaps the verdict might have been other than murder, for the Satsuma men would doubtless claim that they were acting in accordance with established Japanese law and custom: anyone interfering with the procession of a *daimyō*, especially on Imperial business, was liable to summary execution.

Some of the evidence given by Clarke concerned what happened to him after he had lost sight of Richardson. It was therefore irrelevant to the inquest on Richardson's death, and served only to confirm the shock content of the events. Neither Clarke's nor Marshall's evidence follow the timeline of events. The main story is followed by details related to occurrences before the attack. It looks very much as if they were responding to Howard-Vyse's questions, which were themselves omitted from the transcript of evidence. Perhaps this was to avoid cluttering the record and keep a clean story.

---

can be said to run under extraterritorial provisions of a treaty is dubious. That is a question for international lawyers; however, Richardson was still dead, and it was by Japanese subjects that he met his death.

[79] Clarke said they set out at 2.30. Allowing half an hour for the boat trip, the death could not have occurred before 3.00pm. Willis said he saw the corpse at 5.30pm. Those, strictly speaking are the time limits according to the evidence. The evidence implies that Dr Willis set out from Kanagawa on hearing the alarm given by Aspinall's *betto*. This perhaps gives Richardson's death as occurring before 4.45pm. The evidence cannot be stretched further than this: death was between 3.00pm and 4.45pm.

THE INQUEST

However, there are some loose ends. Both Clarke and Marshall refer to encountering some Japanese people before the Incident. Clarke says they were "two of the Japanese interpreters belonging to the Custom-House at Yokohama, and who were personally known to Mr Marshall and spoken to by him. I think I could recognize one of those interpreters on seeing him again." But Marshall says he "saw a Japanese interpreter, whom I knew, and two other Japanese. That interpreter I know as one belonging to the Custom House at Yokohama. I said to the interpreter, 'What are you doing so far away from Yokohama?' He made no reply." Marshall's evidence is strangely emphatic about his one-sided conversation with the Japanese interpreter.

There are mysteries here:
- One Japanese interpreter, or two?
- Who were the other two Japanese that Marshall speaks of?
- Why were these Japanese mentioned in evidence when they seem to have played no part in the events? Or did they?
- Was there some sinister purpose in their presence four miles from Kanagawa?
- Were they in fact associated with the xenophobes?
- Did they suspect the danger the English party would be in, and chose not to tell of it in the hope an attack would occur?
- Did they suspect the danger the English party would be in, but were too afraid to warn them?

Or ...
- Did Clarke and Marshall suggest by their evidence that there was some information withheld from the jury that should have been considered by them - evidence from the one or two Japanese interpreters whom Marshall could identify and who could therefore be interviewed?

RESPECT AND CONSIDERATION

- Why were the Japanese, according to Marshall, a long way from where he expected them to be? – and suspiciously close to the great procession[80]? Might they be look-outs? Was the Incident a planned ambush?
- And if there was evidence not to be brought before the jury, why did Consul Vyse, sitting as Coroner, not wish to have it brought out in Court? Would it have spoiled a heroic tale?

We must draw our own conclusions. And these should perhaps take into account the improper, inadequate and possibly corrupt conduct of a criminal trial by Consul Vyse in Hakodate in 1866 (see page 482). On that occasion his actions caused a scandal. Perhaps it should have this time, too.

---

[80] The ordinary Japanese were well advised to stay well away from a *daimyō's* procession. If they encountered one, they had to abase themselves by kneeling with their foreheads touching the ground, and not look up until the procession had passed by, on pain of instant death. A procession of eight hundred men, *norimono* and additional baggage handlers might take half an hour or longer to pass, and might even stop to make use of wayside facilities. However long it took, the position of abasement had to be maintained. Sensible Japanese stayed away from a *daimyō's gyoretsu*.

THE INQUEST

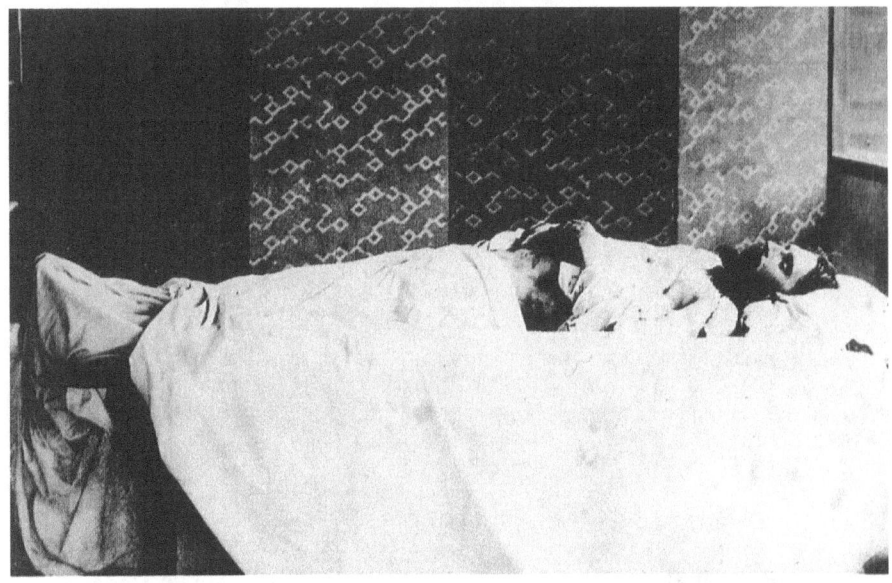

The body of Charles Lenox Richardson lying at Mr Aspinall's house in Yokohama, 15 September 1862
Wounds to his upper arm, upper chest and abdomen are visible, as is a stab wound to his middle chest

RESPECT AND CONSIDERATION

A *kago* ("basket"), or palanquin, drawn by William Heine (1827–1885) c. 1856, from Matthew Calbraith Perry's official Narrative of his expedition to Japan. He says,

> The roads, which by–the–bye, are provided with roadside conveniences answering to the French *cabinets d'aisances*, are excellent throughout the country, and are occasionally wide and paved, though most frequently they are mere bridle paths, but kept in good order for the horsemen, the pack animals, and the sedans or kagos. These latter are most generally used for traveling, and consist of small wooden boxes, supported by poles, which are carried upon the shoulders of the bearers. They are adorned and enriched according to the distinction of the proprietors, but are never very comfortable conveyances.

CHAPTER 16
THE OBSEQUIES

It was a magnificent occasion, that funeral. The inquest on Richardson's death was adjourned for the ceremonial at about 5.30 pm, after Dr Willis had indicated there was no impediment to his burial, and indeed that it was desirable that the interment should take place before his corpse started to decay in the hot and humid climate.

The procession was led by the band of His Imperial Majesty's[81] ship *Le Monge*[82], playing slow funeral marches. The band was followed by a number of British soldiers slow-marching with "reversed arms" - their rifles held upside-down. The Rev. M. Buckworth Bailey[83] (Anglican chaplain to the British Legation and Vicar Of Christ Church, the Church of England congregation in Yokohama) preceded the coffin, which had four pallbearers. Wearing his full consular uniform with cocked hat, tunic and sword, and taking a break from his duties as Her Majesty's Coroner in Yokohama, was the chief pallbearer and

---

[81] Napoléon III of France.

[82] It is strange that it was the band of *Le Monge* that was playing, and not the band of HMS *Euryalus*. Too newly arrived, perhaps?

[83] Rev. Michael Buckworth Bailey appears to have been active in the secret meetings of the community. In any event, he was the first signatory of the minutes, and had spoken in those meetings. EH House says that M Buckworth Bailey was a "minister-editor known as much for his feuds with church organists as for his writing".

RESPECT AND CONSIDERATION

hero of the hour, Captain Francis Howard-Vyse. The other pallbearers were Messrs. SJ Gower, WG Aspinall[84] and FH Bell.

It is interesting to recall the part each of the pallbearers played in the events. Samuel Gower had summoned Vyse when Mrs Borradaile arrived at his brother's house, and had been prominent - but relatively cool-headed - in the meeting of residents. Bell also spoke at the meeting, and signed its minutes along with SJ Gower. Richardson's body had been lying in Aspinall's house, and the post-mortem examination and the inquest were held there. Moreover, Aspinall had almost certainly lent horses to Richardson and Mrs Borradaile for their jaunt to Kawasaki. And then there was Francis Howard-Vyse. Vyse was the Coroner, and Vyse was the temporary commander of the guard, and Vyse was the prime mover in attempting to involve the military in retribution, and Vyse chaired the community meetings. And the Rev. M. Buckworth Bailey was the first signatory of the minutes, and had spoken in those meetings as an advocate of decisive retributive action.

Basic diplomatic uniform for Her Britannic Majesty's Representative

As a guard of honour, there were also files of French and English soldiers with their arms reversed on either side of the coffin. Then followed in solemn procession and in full navy blue diplomatic uniform trimmed with gold brocade with sword,

---

[84] At this time, William Gregson Aspinall was a tea inspector and textile & general merchant in Yokohama, in partnership with Frederick Cornes. They were the first trading house to open in Yokohama. They formed Aspinall, Cornes & Co. with share capital of £100 in 1861, becoming Cornes & Co. in 1878 after Aspinall pulled out. They were agents for P&O shipping, Lloyds etc., and still operate today.

THE OBSEQUIES

splendid Spanish decorations and a gilded cocked hat complete with white ostrich feathers, the British Chargé d'Affaires. By his side, and similarly attired, was his French counterpart. Next was Admiral Kuper in full dress uniform, his badge as a Companion of the Most Honourable Order of the Bath around his neck on its crimson ribbon. By his side marched *L'Amiral* de Barcourt of the French screw frigate *Le Monge* and Commodore[85] Buys of HNMS *Vice-Admiral Koopman*, then the consular and diplomatic officers of the various western governments represented in Japan. Finally, there were hundreds of the foreign community, in their best suits. At the rear of the procession was the English mounted guard led by the always magnificently attired Lieutenant Applin. Everyone moved in silent procession, apart from the funeral marches provided by the French band and the sound of the massed boots and horses' hooves on gravel. At the graveside, at the bottom of the hill near the gate of the new foreign cemetery in Yokohama, the Church of England burial service was solemnly intoned by the Rev. M. Buckworth Bailey in the open air.

Both Marshall and Clarke are also buried there, on either side of Richardson. They died relatively young, perhaps weakened by their severe injuries, Clarke aged 33 in 1867, and Marshall in 1873 aged 46. Their graves were moved next to Richardson's in 2002, at the instigation of Asaumi Takeo, founder and curator of the little museum in Namamugi

---

[85] A Royal Naval commodore ranks immediately below a Rear Admiral. The Dutch rank of commodore at this period was held equal to that of a British Rear Admiral.

RESPECT AND CONSIDERATION

devoted to *Namamugi jiken*. Margaret Borradaile died in 1869 in England.

In the graveyard, the headstones of Marshall's and Clarke's graves are at the rear; Richardson's monument is the granite slab in front of them. (Photo: Stephen Denney)

So it was that Charles Lenox Richardson was interred, eleven thousand miles from his home and family. His parents and sisters would remain unaware of the terrible events that had befallen him until they read a short but devastating "telegram" published in *The Times* of 21st November. What terrible distress they must have felt.

Charles' father, with Victorian restraint, wrote immediately to Earl Russell:

> We have had the deep sorrow to see by a telegram in the Times newspaper, that my only and fondly loved son has been murdered in Japan.
>
> Beyond this we are without all particulars and can know not that we shall receive any further, when the Mail arrives.
>
> Should then the next dispatch from the English Minister in Japan refer at all to the dreadful event or give any details, may I ask, as a great kindness, that you will allow me the great privilege, if not of having a copy, at least of hearing what the dispatch may say on this, to us, heart rending subject?

Russell's secretary replied by return:

> I am directed by Earl Russell to acknowledge the receipt of your letter of yesterday's date enquiring whether any Despatch has been received at this office from Japan respecting the Murder of your son announced by telegraph in the "Times".
>
> I am to state to you, in reply, that Lord Russell has not received any report respecting this melancholy occurrence, but that you shall be informed as soon as

THE OBSEQUIES

any intelligence on the subject is received at this office.

The community, once it had got over the initial shock and outrage at Richardson's murder, and even more the severe wounding of two of their own community, started to lay plans to better protect themselves. On the 24th September, just ten days after the incident, a public meeting was held at the house of Mr Edward Clarke of the trading house of Dent & Co, with a view to forming a Volunteer Corps. The first resolution, passed *nem con*, was proposed by SJ Gower of Jardine, Matheson & Co., Richardson's erstwhile pallbearer. It said, "That any of the Foreign community willing to join, should form themselves into a Rifle Corps for the defence of our life and property". Gower was elected its Captain and Woodthorpe Clarke its Lieutenant, as he had previously served when a junior merchant in Shanghai.

RESPECT AND CONSIDERATION

On Tuesday 16th September, the *Japan Herald* printed an "Extra" devoted entirely to detailing the outrage. The newspaper was a weekly, published on Sundays, and the community couldn't wait. They concluded with an effusive elegy by "S.C.L." of Yokohama (it reads as if an earlier verse has not been printed):

    -And that brave gentlewoman -
    Bloodstained, rode for life, bringing
    To us th'alarm! - though overtolled
    By that day's awful violence, every
    Nerve o'er strained! Let her name
    Have place midst England's Heroines!"
        Minutes, an age -
            But in scarce longer time
            Than at flood the full-tided
            river
        Turns to fall seaward -
    She stood aside to wait the issue,
    Not daring watch the unequal strife,
    Only breathe low words of prayer -
    Shook all her pulses, when those
    Craven wretches bore down upon her
    friends -
        * * * * * * * * *
        Buried he is -
    Not as the unknown, nor meanly -
    But with those obsequies we give
    To those our Country mourn
    With prayer and solemn music.
    And when they lay him in the grave
    All hearts spake! - Let his tomb
    Be the blazon of our wrath to come.
    The stern remembrancer of our just
    Revenge - not in golden letter
    Thereon inscribed - but slumb'ring only
    In our inmost hearts!

THE OBSEQUIES

The Foreign Office, Downing Street, London
Prior to the completion of the present building in Whitehall in 1868

Chapter 17
The British Government's Reaction to Richardson's Death

In response to the information received from Japan, Lord Russell wrote to Colonel Neale concerning action to be taken. After commending Neale for his cool response to the events surrounding the murder and its immediate aftermath, Russell wrote on 28th November as follows.

> I propose that we should make the following demands:-
> 1. The degradation of the Daimio who permitted the murder.
> 2. The capital punishment of not less than five of the chief murderers among the Daimio's retinue.
> 3. The payment of 100,000*l.*, by the Daimio or the Government, as a fine for the outrage on an unarmed English party.
> The Admiral and General on the China Station to employ the forces under their command to obtain these terms.

This was uprated by Russell in a further letter to Neale on 24th December. This time his proposal was an *instruction* to Neale to demand from the Government of Japan:

> 1. An ample and formal apology for the offence of permitting a murderous attack on British subjects passing on a road open by treaty to them.

THE BRITISH GOVERNMENT'S REACTION TO RICHARDSON'S DEATH

> 2. The payment of £100,000 as a penalty on Japan for this offence.

and went on:

> Next you will demand from the Daimio Prince of Satsuma:-
> 1. The immediate trial and capital execution, in the presence of one or more of Her Majesty's naval officers, of the chief perpetrators of the murder of Mr. Richardson, and of the murderous assault upon the lady and gentlemen who accompanied him.
> 2. The payment of 25,000£, to be distributed to the relations of the murdered man, and to those who escaped with their lives the swords of the assassins on that occasion.
> If the Japanese Government should refuse the redress you are thus instructed to demand, you will inform thereof the Admiral or Senior Naval Officer on the station, and you will call upon him to adopt such measures of reprisal or blockade, or of both, as he may judge best calculated to attain the end proposed. You will at the same time communicate the substance of your instructions to the Envoys and Naval Commanders in Japan of other European Powers; and you will concert with the British Admiral, and the naval officers of those Powers, arrangements for the safety of foreigners during coercive operations.
> If the Daimio Satsuma should not immediately agree to and carry into effect the terms demanded of him, the Admiral should go with his own ship, and with such others as he may think fit to take with him, or he should send a sufficient force to the territory of the Prince, which I have been informed is a peninsula on the most southerly point of the island. He has a port, I am told, at the south-west end of the Island of Kiu-siu. The Admiral or Senior Naval Officer will be better able to judge than Her Majesty's Government

> can be, whether it will be most expedient to blockade this port, or whether it will be possible or advisable to shell the residence of the Prince.
>
> I have also been informed that the Prince of Satsuma has steam-ships brought from Europe of considerable value; these might be seized or detained till redress is obtained.
>
> During these operations, whether against the Government of Japan or the Prince of Satsuma, care must be taken by the Admiral to protect the ports where British persons and property may be in jeopardy.
>
> The distinction between the Government and the Daimios is one that must be kept in view. The Prince of Satsuma is said by one of the Japanese Ministers to be a powerful Daimio, who could not easily be coerced by the Japanese Government. He must not, nor must the other Daimios, escape, on that account, the penalty of their misdeeds.

Russell was under much pressure from within the government and from Charles Richardson's father. It doubtless served to strengthen his own resolve in the matter.

The Duke of Somerset, the First Lord of the Admiralty, had interviewed some officers who had recently been in Japan. On 5th December 1862, he had written in his own hand to Lord Russell with ideas how the British should act "in order to convince the Japanese that outrages on British subjects cannot be committed with impunity". He went on,

> Our object should be to punish the Daimios who encourage hostility to foreigners, and especially the Prince Satsuma, who according to Lieut Col Neale's letter dated 19th September is the Daimio to whom the assassins belonged, and of whom the Japanese minister said he was 'a powerful Daimio who could not easily be coerced'. These daimios have, as I am informed, ports exclusively their own; and Satsuma

THE BRITISH GOVERNMENT'S REACTION
TO RICHARDSON'S DEATH

who was previously known as most hostile to foreigners, has a port at the South-west point of the island of Kiu-su. It would, I am told, be easy to blockade his port, and probably to shell his capital; the blockade of his port would be a serious inconvenience to him, because the country inland is very steep, and all the trade and communications of that place are carried on by junks or other coastal vessels.

This measure would embarrass Satsuma and his people, while it would not interfere with our Japanese trade, and it seems to me that if that Government cannot or will not afford us redress, we should convince these Daimios that they will personally suffer for their misdeeds. I have now a chart of the Japanese islands on which the properties of several principal Daimios are marked. They can be attacked by ships and gun-boats. An example should be made of one and Satsuma is specially pointed out as deserving of this distinction unless satisfaction shall have been made before the next mail reaches China.

Russell made a scrawled note for himself, setting out his view on Somerset's suggestion. It read, as far as it can be deciphered,

> The method pointed out by the Duke of Somerset is the true one for putting an end to these atrocities. The central Government is weak and unable to control or punish these Daimio chiefs. If their Residences are accessible to Raiders landed from our ships, or if they have an Interest in Ports which can be blockaded or knocked about their ears without disturbing these Gentlemen [indecipherable] - one of their residences should share the fate of the Summer Palace in China[86]. JR ??-12-62

---

[86] The Summer Palace in Beijing had been razed to the ground in 1860 by British troops on the orders of Lord Elgin, in retaliation for the imprisonment,

RESPECT AND CONSIDERATION

Gladstone by Carlo Pellegrini

Even William Ewart Gladstone, Chancellor of the Exchequer at the time, tendered his advice in a handwritten note dated 9th December 1862:

> It seems to me that if we cannot obtain from the government of Japan, on the score of inability or otherwise, the satisfaction of our demands, it would be wise to confine any measures of force that may be adopted to the territory ports & property of the Daimio Satsuma - to levy off them a compensation in money or money's worth - to carry away for trial any persons reasonably suspected of participation in the murder - to make, above all, a <u>short</u> operation - and to avoid as well as disclaim hostility not only to the nation, but even, all things considered, to the State.

On 5th December 1862, Charles Richardson senior had written to Lord Russell from his home at Duppas Hill, Croydon, as follows:

> My Lord, I am indeed very sensible of your kindness in having favoured me with such particulars respecting the death of my beloved and only son in Japan, as it was in your power to afford me.
>
> If my dear Boy had offered the slightest offence to the persons by whom he was so barbarously murdered[87], or had provoked his fate in any possible way, there might be a shadow of excuse for this dreadful deed; and but there can be none, and I humbly hope that your Lordship will be of opinion that there ought to be none, if you bear in mind that

---

torture, and execution of several British diplomatic envoys who had been promised safe conduct by the Qing government. This was during the Second Opium War.

[87] The Japanese who attacked the party of four indeed *did* perceive grave offence, particularly from Richardson. Japanese customs were not understood at all outside the country.

THE BRITISH GOVERNMENT'S REACTION TO RICHARDSON'S DEATH

he was unexpectedly killed in cold blood, and that he had done nothing whatever, to bring upon him so terrible an end.

I feel assured I need not tell your Lordship, that the loss my wife my fond daughter and I have sustained was overwhelming. My dear Son was indeed our chief earthly stay & hope, and the very joy of our hearts! and your Lordship can imagine with what intense delight we were looking forward to his return at the approaching Christmas.

My Son, just before leaving Shanghai, for Japan, had made a will[88] with a view to benefiting his Mother and Sister; but as it appears probable from the terms of it, that the property will have to be immediately realized, we are afraid that a great sacrifice of the Estate will inevitably ensue. There is also a question whether a Policy of Insurance and effected on his life, with permission to reside in Shanghai on the payment of an extra premium, may now be forfeited, in consequence of his having left that place for a visit to Japan, and there meeting his death.

Under all the circumstances then, I would respectfully ask your Lordship, whether the case is one in which you may feel at liberty to interfere, and to require of the Japanese Government such adequate compensation on my behalf, as the deplorable event may in your opinion justify?

There is a handwritten note on the back of the letter:

Mr Richardson 5 Dec 1862

Requests compensation for his son's murder.

Instructions will be so sent to Japan to demand reparation. R.

Actioned Dec. 13

Thus it was that the letter of 24th December was sent to Neale. It arrived in March 1863, and Col. Neale saw he was to demand

---

[88] The will has not been traced in any of the relevant registries or archives.

compensation for the murder of Richardson from both the *bakufu* and the Prince of Satsuma. So on the 6th April, Neale sent Eusden, the Japanese Secretary of the Legation, up to Edo on board the gunboat *Havoc*[89] to deliver a formal note. The note demanded several things:
- payment of £10,000 in gold for the wives and families of Sweet and Crimp, the two marines who had been killed at the incident at the British Legation in July 1861, and whose unsatisfied compensation claim had become a festering sore in the relations between the British Legation and the *bakufu*;
- ample apology for that transgression of diplomatic rights;
- the payment of £100,000 as a penalty on the *bakufu* for allowing Richardson to be murdered in his territory in open daylight without making any effort to arrest the murderers.

Neale gave them twenty days to consider their reply, but told them
- if the *bakufu* refused to accede to these demands, that refusal would be attended with very deplorable consequences to their country;
- if, after twenty days had elapsed no satisfactory response had been made by the *bakufu*, or if an unsatisfactory one was given, coercive measures would at once be taken.

In delivering the note, Eusden had formally requested that the *bakufu* should send a messenger down to Kagoshima to advise the Prince of Satsuma to comply with the demands that Britain would shortly make on him.

---

[89] Her name is spelt "Havock" in a number of documents, but I have consistently used the spelling from the Ship's Book and Ship's Log.

THE BRITISH GOVERNMENT'S REACTION TO RICHARDSON'S DEATH

In parallel, plans were made to send HMS *Pearl* to Kagoshima as soon as *Havoc* returned from Edo with Eusden on board. *Pearl* was to carry the following demands to the Prince of Satsuma:
- the trial and execution of the murderers of Richardson in the presence of one or more English officers;
- the payment of £25,000 to be distributed to the relatives of Richardson, to Marshall, to Clarke and to Mrs. Borradaile.

Eusden returned from Edo on the 10th, bringing a receipt for the note and a refusal on the part of the Council to send an officer down to Kagoshima. He could not say whether the *bakufu* would comply with the demands he had delivered to them.

So the idea of despatching *Pearl* to Kagoshima was put to one side for the moment. If the *bakufu* proved obstinate, the full force of Royal Naval power might be needed to inflict the threatened coercive measures against it. Satsuma would have to wait.

Thus Neale waited until the 26th. The British navy started to amass a mighty fleet in harbour. *Euryalus*, *Pearl*, *Encounter*, *Rattler*, *Argus* and *Centaur*, carrying a total of 99 heavy guns, were supplemented by three gunboats, and *Coquette* was on its way from Hong Kong. The despatch boats *Racehorse* and *Ringdove* were travelling backwards and forwards between Yokohama and Shanghai as fast as they could go with the mails.

RESPECT AND CONSIDERATION

Front Page, first edition of the Japan Herald, 23 November 1861
Note its status as Official Organ with the British, French, Portuguese and Dutch Legations

Chapter 18
The Japanese respond to Britain

As so often, the *bakufu* temporised. Their consistent tactic was to ask for more time, and then more, and more still, hoping that the problem would simply go away as events overtook them. They asked for thirty days more before they could reply to the British note brought by Eusden. Colonel Neale gave them fifteen.

Taking their lead from the more fearful of the *daimyō*, the residents of Edo began to move their valuables out of the city to the countryside, expecting imminent war between Britain and Japan. By contrast, the British residents of Yokohama declared that they would not leave the Settlement unless specially called on to do so by Colonel Neale. Their motives, however, had more to do with wealth preservation than solidarity with their government: they believed that if they deserted their property without an official order from the British representative, no compensation for its loss would be forthcoming from any public source.

On the 1st May, the *bakufu* asked for a further delay of fifteen days. Eusden was sent up to Edo with a message to them that before the Colonel could grant their request they must send an official envoy to him to receive an important communication which he had to make to them. The native population now

RESPECT AND CONSIDERATION

began to be seriously alarmed, and the Japanese shopkeepers in Kanagawa removed their effects to Hodogaya to be out of reach of the bombardment they expected. The *bakufu*, responding to Neale's demand, sent Takemoto Kai-no-Kami and Takemoto Hayato-no-Sho, two senior negotiators. On the 4th and 5th May, long meetings took place. They explained that for political reasons, the *bakufu* could not be seen to accede to the British demands for punitive compensation. However, they might be able to pay the indemnity, disguising it as payment for a (fictitious) warship purchased from Britain but wrecked on its journey to Japan. Neale held firm, but conceded a further extension of time until the 23rd of May, so that the personal consent of the *shōgun*, who was expected to return by that date, might be obtained. This was now 47 days since the British demands were issued, and 27 days after the original deadline before sanctions were applied.

During the night of the 5th May, Satow recounts, there was a "sudden and secret exodus" of most of the Japanese servants employed by the western community. Satow recalled that

> many of them took advantage of the occasion to 'spoil the Egyptians'[90].

Satow and Willis's servants and cook had gone off, carrying with them a revolver, a Japanese sword, and several spoons and forks that they doubtless, though mistakenly, imagined to be

---

[90] Exodus 3:22 (KJV):
> But every woman shall borrow of her neighbour, and of her that sojourneth in her house, jewels of silver, and jewels of gold, and raiment: and ye shall put them upon your sons, and upon your daughters; and ye shall **spoil the Egyptian.**

The Israelites demanded - and were given - jewellery, gold and silver from their erstwhile captors before the flight from Egypt. The suggestion here (note Satow's "exodus" earlier in the paragraph, tee hee) is that the Japanese took valuables from their European masters without permission.

THE JAPANESE RESPOND

silver. Satow thought this remarkable, since the day before he had entrusted his servant with a large quantity of *ichibu* and *ryō* to change into Mexican dollars, which had faithfully been done. However, the servants had asked to be paid up to date, and Satow had complied. Not every servant took to his heels. Satow was gratified that his teacher and his *betto* remained with him, as did his messenger. Satow and Willis, though, had an immediate problem: breakfast! They managed to procure some eggs and castella cake, and provided for themselves. They reported the theft of the various items to the Japanese authorities at the custom house. The officials, of course, promised to find the thieves, but nothing more was ever heard of the thieves or the property.

On the 11[th,] an undercover envoy contacted Satow's Japanese teacher, who, as had happened frequently before, passed on a private message from the *bakufu*. Was Colonel Neale disposed to await the return of the Tycoon, which would not be for three or four months, before taking hostile measures? If so, the envoy, a high personage of superior rank to the *bakufu*, would agree to issue a proclamation that a delay of a thousand days had been agreed on, which would have the effect of restoring tranquillity in Yokohama. Sadly, were the Colonel, tired of these repeated delays, to change the seat of the negotiations to Osaka, the "high personage" would have to perform *seppuku*, which he rather wished to avoid, as a penalty for failing to induce the foreigner to listen to his representations. Satow duly passed this on to Colonel Neale, who replied *sotto voce* that he would not consent to waiting so long as three months, let alone a thousand days.

The *bakufu* had previously announced that the *shōgun* would return on 24th May, so Neale replied to their request for delay that under the circumstances he would give time for the *shōgun* to settle down again at home. But on 16th May a note was received from the *bakufu* stating that circumstances had arisen which prevented their fixing any date whatever for his arrival at Yedo. This seemed to point to an indefinite postponement of a settlement, despite the threatened coercive measures. Colonel Neale, exercised exemplary forbearance yet again, and continued to wait. The "high personage" turned out to be the Prince of Owari. Satow's teacher, Takaoka, now said that having transmitted Colonel Neale's answer to Kyōto, the Prince would no longer be under the necessity of committing suicide, as he had been able to show that he was not responsible for "the foreigner's" obstinacy.

Eventually, on 14th June, Kikuchi Iyo-no-Kami and Shibata Sadataro, Commissioners for Foreign Affairs, appeared at the British Legation to complete arrangements for paying $440,000[91] in seven instalments extending over six weeks, the first to be delivered on the 18th. But on that day came a note of excuse from one of the Council stating that unavoidable circumstances had arisen which prevented the agreement being carried out, and that he himself would in a day or two arrive at Yokohama to discuss matters with the English Chargé d'Affaires. Colonel Neale announced that in view of their gross prevarication, he refused to hold any more communications with the *shōgun's* ministers. After a couple of days' consideration, Neale finally placed the matter into the hands of Admiral Kuper. Kuper was to prepare to chastise the Japanese government.

On learning this, there was great alarm inside the *bakufu*. They had temporized as long as possible, and had finally worn out the patience of the British Chargé d'Affaires. But they left no stone unturned to avoid the shame of openly giving way, and

---

[91] £100000 in respect of the Richardson murder and £10000 compensation for the families of Sweet and Crimp - a total of £110000 at $4 (Mexican) to the £ sterling. The *bakufu's* coffers were lightened by 264000 *ryō*.

THE JAPANESE RESPOND

Ogasawara Nagamichi[92] came down to Yokohama to urge the French - the *Ministre* and *L'Amiral* - to intercede with Britain on behalf of the *bakufu*. France had assiduously ploughed its own furrow and cultivated its own relationship with the *bakufu*. But the French were nothing if not pragmatic, and recognised an implacable force when they saw it. They told Ogasawara that there would be no help from the French. There was no choice but to satisfy the just demands of the British.

Ogasawara had just returned from Kyōto. The *shōgun*, on his unprecedented visit to the Emperor's Court, had argued insistently for *sonnō jōi* to be put aside. There had been furious debate about the matter, but eventually the Emperor resolved the arguments by issuing an Imperial Edict to expel the barbarians and close the ports. Ogasawara had been among those opposing the order, but he had no choice: when the Emperor issued an Edict, his command must be obeyed. So when Ogasawara came to ask for French help to ameliorate the British resolve for action, he carried with him a document addressed to each representative of the western governments. It said:

> I communicate with you by a despatch.
> The orders of the *shōgun*, received from Kyōto, are to the effect that the ports are to be closed and the foreigners driven out, because the people of the country do not desire intercourse with foreign countries. The discussion of this has been entirely entrusted to me by His Majesty. I therefore send you this communication first, before holding a Conference as to the details.
> Respectful and humble communication.

---

[92] Ogasawara Dzusho-no-Kami was the *daimyō* of Karatsu and one of the most senior and influential councillors in the *bakufu*. He was a signatory of the *bakufu*'s letter of apology dated 3 July 1863 (see Chapter 20).

However, when informing the various Legations of this order, Ogasawara gave nod-and-a-wink verbal assurances in "Conference" that the *bakufu* would not enforce the Edict. He even suggested forms of words for the Western governments' replies.

The Settlement was utterly astonished and outraged at the terms of the Edict when they were made public. The traders were, however, reassured by the presence of the combined squadrons in the harbour. The naval and military power they evidenced would enable the foreign Legations to reject the Edict without fear of effective Japanese enforcement.

Neale prepared an instant rejection of Ogosawara's despatch. It read:

> The undersigned, Her Britannic Majesty's Chargé d'Affaires, has received, in common with his colleagues, and with extreme amazement, the extraordinary announcement which, under instructions from His Majesty the Tycoon, His Excellency has addressed to him.
>
> Apart from the audacious nature of this announcement, which is unaccompanied by any explanations whatever, the Undersigned is bound to believe that both the Spiritual and Temporal[93] sovereigns of this country are totally unaware of the disastrous consequences which must arise to Japan by their determinations thus conveyed through you to close the opened ports, and to remove therefrom the subjects of the Treaty Powers.
>
> For himself, as Representative of Her Britannic Majesty, the Undersigned has to observe, in the first instance, that the Rulers of this country may perhaps still have it in their power to modify and soften the severe and irresistible measures which will, without

---

[93] The "Spiritual Sovereign" was the Emperor, the "Temporal Sovereign" the *shōgun*, in the imperfect understanding of the West.

THE JAPANESE RESPOND

the least doubt, be adopted by Great Britain most effectually to maintain and enforce its Treaty obligations with this country, and, more than this, to place them on a far more satisfactory and solid footing than heretofore, by speedily making known and developing any rational and acceptable plans directed to this end, which may be at present concealed by His Majesty the *shōgun* or the Emperor, or by both, to the great and imminent peril of Japan.

It is therefore the duty of the Undersigned solemnly to warn the Rulers of this country that when the decision of Her Majesty's Government, consequent upon the receipt of Your Excellency's announcement, shall have in due course been taken, the development of all ulterior determinations now kept back will be of no avail.

The Undersigned has in the meantime to inform Your Excellency, with a view that you may bring the same to the knowledge of His Majesty the *shōgun*, who will doubtless make the same known to the Emperor, that the indiscreet communication now made through Your Excellency is unparalleled in the history of all nations, civilized or uncivilized; that it is, in fact, a declaration of war by Japan itself against the whole of the Treaty Powers, and the consequences of which, if not at once arrested, it will have to expiate by the severest and most merited chastisement.

With Respect and Consideration.

                        EDWD. ST. JOHN NEALE.

Neale wrote this in one session, and, with the might of the British fleet at his back, expressed most clearly the consequences of the *bakufu's* prevarication. It elegantly indicated the iron fist that could so easily be discovered within the velvet glove. It is a masterpiece of diplomatic menace.

RESPECT AND CONSIDERATION

So Ogasawara reported to the *bakufu* that far from being assuaged, the British were the more determined to enforce their demands. Furthermore, the French had refused point-blank to assist, particularly once they had received their copy of the Edict. One can imagine the fearful realisation that dawned on the *shōgun* and his cohort: their bluff had been called, and they had lost the moral battle with Britain.

So a messenger arrived at the British Legation at 1.00 am on 24th June, having earlier again sought, unsuccessfully, the assistance of the French Minister in interceding on their behalf. The message was simply that the *bakufu* would now pay the full demand for $440000: when would Colonel Neale be ready to accept the instalments?

Neale, roused from his bed, instantly pressed his advantage. The original agreement to pay in instalments, having been broken by the Japanese Government, was now null and void, he announced. Every last silver dollar must be delivered in the course of that day.

THE JAPANESE RESPOND

Japanese Junks
Photographed by Ueno Hikoma, early 1860s

Chapter 19
Meanwhile, The American Navy chastises Chōshū for the closure of the Kanmon Straits at Shimonoseki

On 25th June 1863, in pursuit of the Imperial Edict, Mori Takachika, the *daimyō* of Chōshū (also known as the Prince of Nagato), ordered his fierce and powerful forces at his castle town of Shimonoseki to open fire on foreign ships passing through the Kanmon Straits, between the major land masses of Honshu and Kyūshū. At one o'clock in the morning of the 26th, two armed Chōshū vessels - the brig *Lanrick* and the barque *Daniel Webster* - masquerading as *bakufu* ships, attacked the American merchant ship *Pembroke*, flying an American ensign. *Pembroke* was bound from Yokohama for Shanghai via Nagasaki, and was anchored for the night off Shimonoseki.

The shore batteries of 10-inch and 32-pounder guns also opened up on her. Although struck by several shots, *Pembroke* suffered no casualties or significant damage and hastily got underway. She quickly moved out of danger, and escaped via the Bungo Strait with all speed for Shanghai, dropping Nagasaki from her itinerary.

It was important to the foreign traders that the sea route through the Kanmon Straits was available to them, because it was the quickest route from the Western trading settlements at

The American Navy chastises Chōshū

Nagasaki to Edo via Ōsaka. It was also the shortest route from Edo to Shanghai via Nagasaki. Shimonoseki had been a safe anchorage hitherto, providing shelter from storms, and provisions for the journey.

News of the attack on *Pembroke* reached Nagasaki the following day and caused much concern among the western community. On the 28th of June, the chartered French mailboat *Kienchiang*, unaware of what had happened to *Pembroke* the previous day, steamed into the Kanmon Straits and dropped anchor off Shimonoseki. Barely had the anchor been let go when several shots from the shore struck her. She had to cut her lines and make all speed to escape from the guns.

On 11th July, the 16-gun Dutch corvette *Medusa* set out from Nagasaki for Yokohama, in the hope that her captain could achieve an armistice with Chōshū. The Dutch Consul-General, Dirk de Graef van Polsbroek, was on board, ready to negotiate. Also on board was a Japanese pilot, sent by the Governor of Nagasaki, who was disturbed by Chōshū's belligerence.

Again, Mori Takachika ordered his batteries and his two gunships to fire on *Medusa*. As she came parallel to the Chōshū anchorage, where several of Mori's ships lay, large calibre shots started to strike *Medusa*, killing four and wounding five of her crew. However, *Medusa*, unlike *Pembroke* and *Kienchiang*, was not a defenceless merchant vessel, but a powerful corvette. She ran the straits at full steam, returning rapid and heavy fire for an hour and a half. Two days later, when *Medusa* reached Yokohama and brought the news of the attacks, it was found that thirty-one shots had found their mark on her (van Polsbroek, in an unofficial account, says it was twenty-one). *Kapitein* François de Casembroot was later knighted for his gallantry on his return to Holland, and every crew member was decorated.

RESPECT AND CONSIDERATION

On 10th July, formal news of the 26th June attack on *Pembroke* had been received by the American Minister in Japan, Robert Pruyn. He immediately demanded action by the *bakufu* on the insult to the American flag, but was not assuaged by the *bakufu's* temporising over the matter. Commander (later Captain) McDougal of the *USS Wyoming* conferred with Pruyn. McDougal announced that he had decided to seize and, if necessary, to destroy, the two Chōshū ships that had fired on *Pembroke*. Pruyn assented. The prevailing sentiment was that inaction by the western community would only encourage further assaults by Japanese xenophobes. They had to be taught a sharp lesson.

Captain David McDougal, U.S.N., photographed in 1860

There was only one American warship in Japan at this time. The *USS Wyoming* was a steam sloop, skippered by Commander McDougal. She was armed with six powerful guns: two 11" Dahlgren smoothbore pivot guns, one 60-pdr. Parrot Rifle, and three 32-pdrs. America was in the throes of her Civil War. Wyoming was scouring the Pacific in pursuit of Confederate warships, and was engaged in particular on an abortive search for the Confederate cruiser *Alabama*.

Calling into Yokohama for provisions in May 1863, *Wyoming* had remained to protect the American community, and possibly to evacuate them had the Imperial Edict been enforced. She eventually left Japan in the autumn of 1863 in further pursuit of *Alabama*. *Alabama* was finally sunk by gunfire from USS *Kearsarge* off the coast of France on 10th June 1864.

On 16th July 1863, *Wyoming* steamed toward the eastern end of the Straits of Shimonoseki, with vengeance in the minds of the crew. As she approached Shimonoseki on 24th July, she was concealed by a rocky promontory on the southern shoreline. She steamed at full speed directly toward Shimonoseki and the three armed Chōshū vessels moored there: a 6-gun barque (the *Daniel Webster*), a 10-gun brig (the *Lanrick*, now *Kosei*) and a 4-gun steamer (the *Lancefield*, now *Koshin*), all purchased from America.

The Shimonoseki batteries opened intense fire on the intruder from the top of the hillsides, and a number of shots passed through *Wyoming's* rigging. Had she remained in mid-channel, the shot and shell would have struck her hull and sunk her. Ironically, Chōshū's most accurate guns were five 8-in Dahlgren[94] guns, recently presented to Japan by America, which had found their way to Shimonoseki. McDougal surprised the Japanese by leaving the normal channel and audaciously driving between the barque and the brig on the starboard and the steamer on the port, with just 20 feet of clear water on either side. McDougal intended to capture the *Lancefield*. But this objective was stymied as *Wyoming* temporarily grounded on a mudbank in the unfamiliar waters.

U.S. Steam Sloop Wyoming

The *Lancefield* approached *Wyoming* at high speed, intending to board her. At that moment, *Wyoming* freed herself from the

---

[94] The Dahlgren Gun, named after its designer John A Dahlgren, was a muzzle-loading cannon of varying bore that was very thick at the breech, but thin at the muzzle. Made of cast iron, it was relatively cheap and easy to manufacture. It was nicknamed the "bottle cannon" because it looked like a beer bottle. The 11-inch fired both shot and shell, and was regarded as a powerful weapon, though no navy other than the American Navy adopted it. It was generally pivot-mounted on warships, so that it could cover a wide arc of fire from its fixed mounting point.

RESPECT AND CONSIDERATION

mud. McDougal ordered his forward pivot gun to fire, but nothing happened. Three times more, McDougal ordered the gun to fire, but it was only after the fourth command that the gun fired. The captain of the gun had been taking his time to sight exactly on the waterline - possibly the most difficult target for him to aim at - and his shot penetrated *Lancefield* at that precise spot. The shell failed to explode, but burst through one side of the hull, ripped through her boilers, and then passed through the other side of the hull and lodged on shore. But this was enough. Her boilers exploded spectacularly, she heeled over, and within a minute, sank, to the cheers of the American sailors. Then the barque and the brig came under the eyes of *Wyoming's* gunners. They turned their guns on the two ships and inflicted severe damage on them.

A few of their shots passed over or through the two ships and landed in Shimonoseki, causing some damage to buildings.

McDougal then systematically destroyed the shore batteries, but sustained some further damage before they were silenced. After an engagement lasting one hour and ten minutes, *Wyoming* retired to Yokohama, nursing damage to her funnel and rigging, having plugged the damage from the eleven Chōshū shots that had pierced her hull. Four of her men had been killed[95], and seven men wounded (one of whom would later die of wounds). Chōshū later revealed that they had suffered 40 casualties.

On 7th August, two French ships joined in. The *Tancrède* and the *Dupleix*, under *Vice-Amiral* Benjamin Jaurès, sailed through

---

[95] Two gunners were killed and four wounded when a shot from one of the two starboard Chōshū ships struck *Wyoming's* forward pivot gun. During the engagement, a sailor and a Marine were fatally struck by shrapnel. One of the seven men wounded in the engagement later died from his injuries, making five deaths in all.

The American Navy chastises Chōshū

the Kanmon Straits and shelled a village on the coast, destroying an artillery emplacement, and receiving no damage themselves.

The retribution served as a warning to the *daimyō* and the *bakufu* that the western powers were not to be trifled with. However, it did not extinguish the hatred towards the west felt by those who yearned to revert to full-blooded *sakoku rei*. On August 8th, the Kanagawa authorities had discovered a bloody human head in a wayside public lavatory on the *tōkaidō*, with this notice attached to it in Japanese:

> This is the head of a Pilot who went on the American Ship-of-war to Shimonoseki on the 13th July and fought against his own countrymen on the 16th of the same month. There are five more men at large who are to be served in the same fashion.

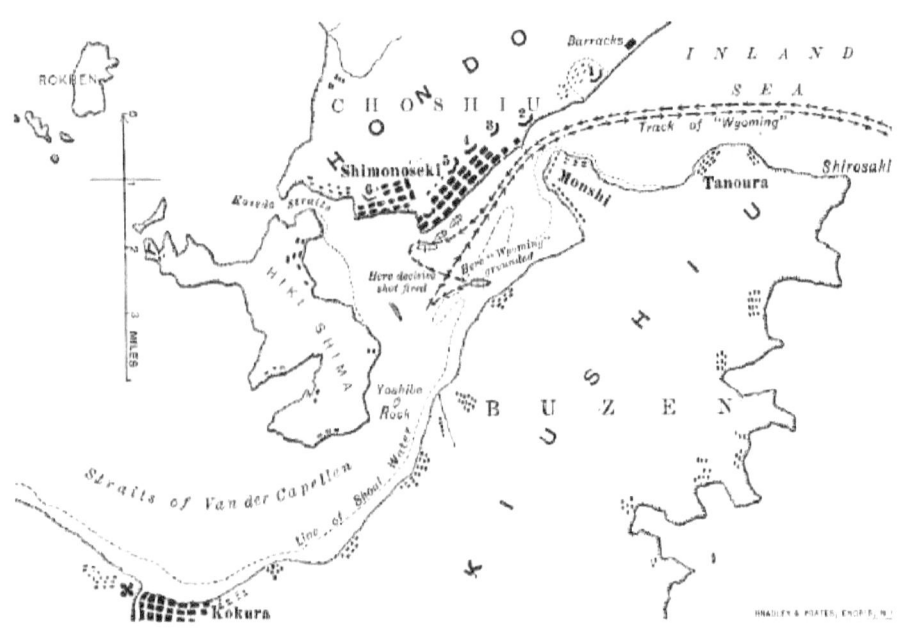

McDougal's Sketch plan of *Wyoming's* action

CHAPTER 20
THE *BAKUFU* PAYS UP BUT SATSUMA REMAINS OBDURATE

Fearful of a military response that would certainly lead to the *bakufu's* defeat and disgrace, the *bakufu* instantly complied with Neale's demand for full payment. During the hours of darkness of 23 June 1863, carts laden with boxes of silver coin started to arrive at the Legation building. The *bakufu* did not want the Japanese population to see that it had capitulated to Britain, and the deliveries were completed by dawn. Each box contained some $2000, and 2000 troy ounces of silver adds up to over 62 kilograms. So heavy were the boxes that the *bakufu* had to hire *sumō rikishi* (wrestlers) from a local *heya* (training stable) to heave the 220 boxes into the Legation building.

For its part, the British legation was presented with the problem of how to handle, prove and count the coins. Neale sent for every available shroff to test and count the coins. Shroffs were men employed by merchants and bankers throughout south Asia to examine coin to see whether it is genuine. They were mainly Chinese, and had a reputation for impartiality, honesty and sharp-mindedness. The chancery was crowded with the shroffs busily employed in clinking one coin against another, stacking and packing them into parcels, and putting them back in the boxes. Marines mounted an armed guard for the sailors who ferried them out to HMS *Euryalus* for safe

RESPECT AND CONSIDERATION

Saikai Hida–No–Kami, vice–Minister of the *bakufu*, in discussion with the western representatives on board the French ship *Sémiramis* on 2nd July 1863. By his right hand, M. Gustave Duchesne de Bellecourt, French minister; to his left, Admiral Augustus Kuper, RN, French *Amiral* Benjamin Jaurès and Lt. Col Neale, British Chargé d'Affaires.   *Le Monde Illustré, 26 Septembre 1863*

keeping and ultimate transmission to London. The shroffing occupied three whole days.

On 24th June 1863, as dawn broke and even before the shroffing had started, Colonel Neale wrote to Admiral Kuper on board *Euryalus*. As the Japanese had given in to the British demands, the Colonel was pleased to relieve Admiral Kuper of the need to prepare imminent coercive operations against the *bakufu*. He also wrote a despatch to Lord Russell that day, saying

> I HASTEN to announce to your Lordship that I have received within the walls of Her Majesty's Legation the whole amount of the indemnities demanded by Her Majesty's Government from the Government at Yeddo, amounting to 110,000*l*. sterling, represented

The Bakufu Pays Up; Satsuma Remains Obdurate

by 440,000 Mexican dollars; the reparation affixed for the families of the guards murdered at Her Majesty's Legation on the 26th June is comprised in this amount.

The diplomatic and naval authorities breathed a sigh of relief. Conflict with the *bakufu*, with all that such action would entail, had been averted.

On 13th July, Neale was able to transmit to Lord Russell the formal apology from the *bakufu* that had been demanded. Two previous apologies had been rejected by Neale because they were worded ambiguously, but he now felt able to accept this:

WE communicate with you by a despatch.

Last year at the British Legation in Yeddo a wicked and murderous act took place. Again, on the *tōkaidō* a British subject was murdered. Such unfortunate affairs were for us highly to be regretted. Thus we hope that affairs likely to break off the intercourse between the two countries may not again arise. We desire to inform you thus much.

Respectful and humble communication.

3rd July 1863

MATSUDAIRA BUZEN-NO-KAMI.

INOUYE KAWACHI-NO-KAMI.

OGASAWARA DZUSHO-NO-KAMI

The Japanese version had been accompanied by a version in Dutch, still the preferred diplomatic language by the Japanese at the time. Translated more readily into English, it was rather more fulsome:

WE have the honour to send you the following communication.

Last year an outrage and murder was committed at the British Legation at Yeddo, and again on the *tōkaidō*, when a British subject was murdered, and others wounded.

RESPECT AND CONSIDERATION

> We are extremely sorry for these occurrences, and hope such events may not again occur to interrupt the friendly relations between the two Governments.
> With respect and consideration.

Neale's report to Russell continued

> Thus the demands I have been instructed to make upon the Government at Yeddo have been happily brought to a satisfactory and successful issue, not, however, without the most persistent efforts on my part to resist all difficulties and obstructions opposed by the distracted Government of this country at so serious a crisis.
>
> In respect to the apology, however expedient I had deemed it to abstain from being over-exacting as to the terms in which it should be expressed, especially as the payment at last, without comment, of the indemnity was of itself an acknowledgment of the justice of the reparation demanded, - still I was under the necessity of twice declining to accept two other written apologies tendered to me, as in translation they were obscure and undefined.
>
> The third I conceive to be clear and acceptable; and it remains for me to trust it will be found sufficiently satisfactory by Her Majesty's Government.

Indeed it was.

There remained, though, the problem of Satsuma. The British Government's demand transmitted to them had been for the apprehension, trial and execution of the perpetrators of Richardson's murder, and compensation of £25000 to be shared between Richardson's family and the three other victims of the assault. Ogasawara had intimated to Neale that the *bakufu* was impotent on the matter of enforcing the demand. It was a clear indication of the waning power of the *bakufu* and the strengthening of the *han*.

Satsuma's defence to the matter was that they had only been upholding long-standing Japanese custom and practice in the

The bakufu pays up; Satsuma remains obdurate

protection of *daimyō* from harm and the showing of appropriate respect. They conveniently ignored the Treaties, which they regarded as nullified by the Edict. Furthermore, said Satsuma, it was the *bakufu's* fault for not forcing the British to keep away from the *gyoretsu*: they should have warned all foreigners that the entourage would be passing that day. Normal procedure was for Edo to inform foreign legations when a *daimyō's* entourage was scheduled to travel the *tōkaidō*. Foreigners would then be advised by their legations to stay away on those days. Thanks to the *bakufu's* inefficiency, said Satsuma, the British, and hence Richardson, had not been informed of Shimazu Saburō's travels and that is why they happened to cross paths.

Neale was having none of this. A British subject had been murdered while peacefully exercising his right under the Treaties to proceed along the *tōkaidō*. The perpetrators, whoever they were, must be punished. Compensation must be paid to the victims. The whole of the foreign community concurred with Neale's stance. So Neale requested Admiral Kuper to prepare to convey him and his staff to Kagoshima, in order to present the British Government's demands directly to the Prince of Satsuma. By 6th August, Admiral Kuper had assembled his squadron.

Neale, as a diplomatic courtesy, informed the *bakufu* that they were about to set sail for Kagoshima. An urgent reply by return begged the British to postpone the expedition. Within minutes of the message being received, a Vice-minister of the *bakufu*, no less, arrived hot-foot to say that they did not wish to prevent the expedition, but would like to send a *bakufu* steamship with a high official on board, to accompany the squadron. True to form, the *bakufu* failed to follow this up. It had been another delaying tactic, but one that did not work.

So seven and a half months after Russell's letter of demand of 24th December 1862, Her Majesty's Ships *Euryalus*, *Pearl*, *Perseus*, *Argus*, *Coquette*, *Racehorse* and *Havoc* with their ninety heavy guns prepared for the expedition. The entire Japanese-speaking staff of the Legation was taken on board the various ships. Neale himself, fittingly, occupied the Admiral's cabin on board the flagship *Euryalus*, and the powerful squadron set off for Kagoshima. They sailed for five days through pleasant seas, arriving on the afternoon of the 11th in the uncharted waters of Kinko Bay. They remained far out, and rode through the night before proceeding towards Kagoshima.

The Bombardment of Kagoshima *Le Monde Illustré* 1864

THE BAKUFU PAYS UP; SATSUMA REMAINS OBDURATE

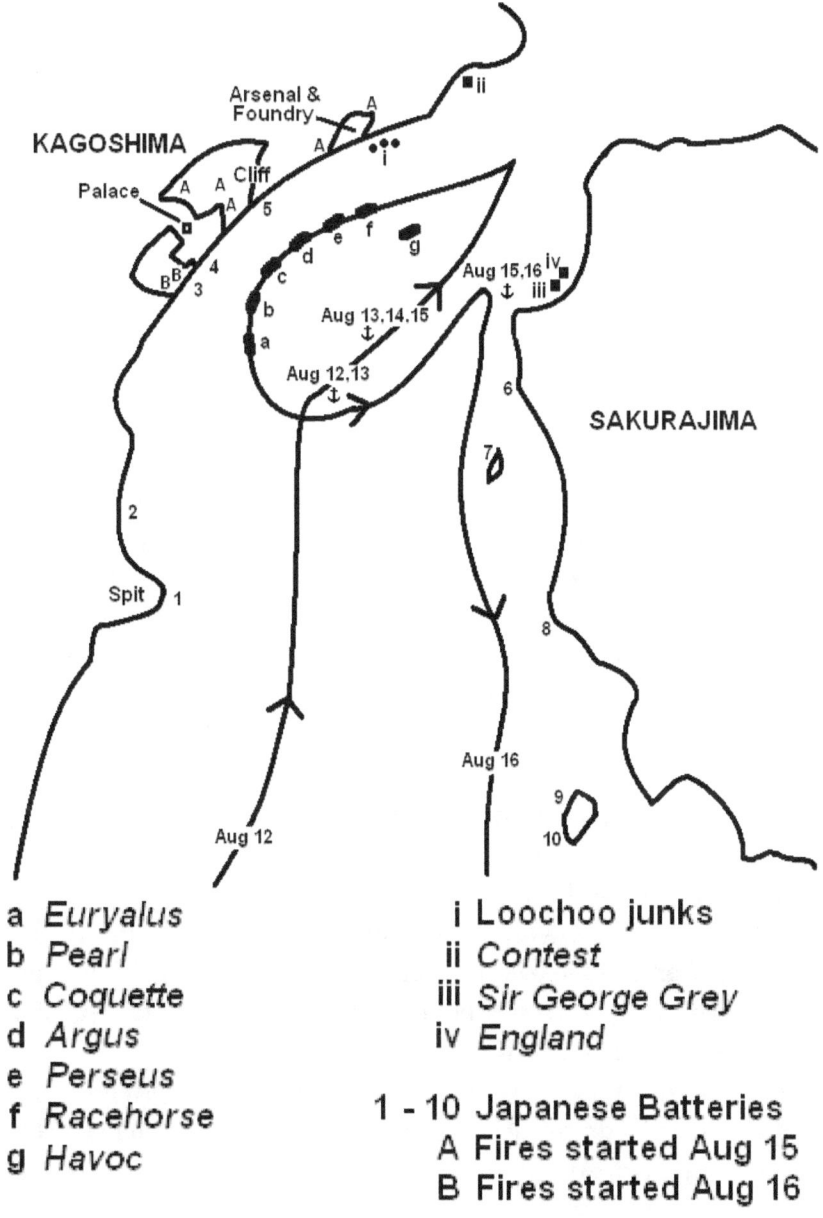

a *Euryalus*
b *Pearl*
c *Coquette*
d *Argus*
e *Perseus*
f *Racehorse*
g *Havoc*

i *Loochoo junks*
ii *Contest*
iii *Sir George Grey*
iv *England*

1 - 10 Japanese Batteries
A Fires started Aug 15
B Fires started Aug 16

The Royal Naval Expedition to Kagoshima, 12-16 August 1863
Sketched by Valerie Denney after the original plan by Capt. Brine, R.E.

Chapter 22
The Blazon of Our Wrath:
The Royal Navy at Kagoshima

The naval squadron arrived in Kinko Bay on the evening of the 11th August. It took time to find a suitable place in the deep waters, but by ten o'clock in the evening, they were safely anchored. On the morning of the 12th, at 6.00 am, a small boat rowed out from the harbour and two Satsuma officials came aboard *Euryalus*. They enquired the nationality of the ships, whether it was the intention of the squadron to proceed further into the bay, whether a native pilot was on board, how many guns *Euryalus* carried and other such questions. The manner of the Japanese officials was unconciliatory and assertive. To ensure that the Satsuma intelligence officers were impressed with the power the British wielded, frank replies were given to the two *samurai*. They were also told that there would be a letter for the Prince of Satsuma. The officers returned to Kagoshima.

For the most part, as the ships assembled off Kagoshima, Royal Naval domestic routine continued as usual. On Wednesday 12th August, for example, *Pearl's* log records that they "scrubbed and washed clothes". The next day they slaughtered a bullock weighing 217½ pounds[96], and various casks of supplies were opened - rum, sugar, raisins, pork and preserved beef. No special preparations were recorded: the Royal Navy was prepared for anything, anywhere, anytime.

A few hours later, the squadron weighed anchor and sailed closer to Kagoshima. They anchored again. As they did so, another boat with four other officials came off immediately to *Euryalus* from the port, and said they understood there was a letter to be received. The letter, which had been prepared previously stating the British demands, was presented to them.

They took it away, and nothing more was heard until the following afternoon, when different officials led by Ijichi Shogi and a large company of forty men came aboard. Among them were Narahara Kizaemon and Kaeda Noboyushi, who between them had killed Charles Lenox Richardson. They presented a receipt for the letter, but informed Neale that the Prince of Satsuma was not at Kagoshima, but at his residence in Kirishima, 20 *ri* (about 50 miles or three days' travel) away[97]. They also stated that they had been ordered by the Prince's Council to request that Admiral Kuper and Col. Neale would go ashore, where a building for the reception of foreigners had been specially arranged. They were very anxious to persuade Neale and Kuper to go ashore to negotiate verbally, but the British suspected that they would be assassinated once they were off *Euryalus*. Neale and Kuper told the officials that the only business that had brought them to Kagoshima was fully set forth in the letter, conveyed in three languages - English,

---

[96] This is very small. Slaughter weights of bullocks in the twenty-first century are typically in the region of 660 lbs, so the bullock was about ⅓ the weight of a modern equivalent.

[97] This was very likely true as far as the titular *daimyō*, Shimazu Tadayoshi, was concerned, but it was Shimazu Saburō who wielded the power, and he was in the Kagoshima area.

RESPECT AND CONSIDERATION

Japanese, and Dutch. The officials were very disconcerted that their entreaties had failed.

Some thirty years later, Ijichi admitted what had been planned:

> ... Since we were unable to convince them to land, we came up with the daring plan to board their flagship, immediately kill all of their officers, cut down everyone else on board, and seize the ship.

The forty warriors had shared a parting cup of *sake* with Shimazu Saburō, and set off for the fleet, accompanied by another fifty-eight *samurai*, disguised as fruit-sellers bringing watermelons and peaches for sale. However, the British officers had been very suspicious of the Japanese, and took precautions against any such action. They only permitted two or three Japanese access to the Admiral's cabin at any time, and the Marines on board, with their loaded rifles[98] and fixed bayonets, maintained a watchful eye on those who remained on deck. Ijichi, through an attendant, said that he had brought a reply to Neale's letter, but that he had serious matters to add to it.

A further Japanese boat arrived from the shore, waving a flag. None of this party was granted permission to board *Euryalus*. Ijichi spoke with them and then announced that he and his men must return to shore, because a mistake had been discovered in the reply he had brought. No British officer caught sight of any

---

[98] The Marines were equipped with the Enfield 1853 Rifled Musket (illustrated above, with bayonet), a .577 calibre muzzle-loaded rifled musket, 53 inches (134.6 cm) from stock to muzzle, weighing 9lb 5 oz. (4.22 kg). It used the Minie conical bullet, of which between 2 and 3 per minute could be fired. It was very popular, for it was well-engineered, reliable, and allowed great accuracy. A good rifleman could hit a man-sized target at 650 yards, and an average rifleman at 300 yards: this compared to the Brown Bess muskets it replaced, which were only accurate at 100 yards, and that in skilled hands. It was this rifle - or its greased cartridges - that was a major factor in the outbreak of the Indian Mutiny of 1857.

document setting this out, despite requesting sight of it. Ijichi departed, announcing that it was impossible to say when a response to the British letter would be given. With the benefit of thirty years' hindsight, Ijichi concluded,

> Since we thought it would be useless to kill common sailors, we left without accomplishing our purpose. When I look back upon it now, it seems like so much child's play.

The naval officers had observed that throughout the time of this abortive parley, the batteries on shore were constantly manned, and their guns diligently trained and pointed at the ships of the squadron, and especially on the flagship. The whole squadron was within easy range of the shore. Kuper gave prudent orders for the squadron to move further out to sea. Even as the Japanese officials were descending the ship's side, the anchors of the squadron were being weighed.

In the evening of the 13th, a written reply from Shimazu Saburō was received. A verbatim transcript of the meeting with the envoys survives, and it shows the tenor of the discussions:

Colonel Neale	Your arrival at this hour is quite unexpected, what is the object of it?
Japanese	We have brought the reply of the Prince's Government, and come to explain that we misinformed you today in stating that we were recalled on shore to correct an error in the despatch; we were apparently only required to return immediately after having delivered it.
Neale	Do you desire to state anything verbally to me before delivering the despatch?
Japanese	Nothing.
Neale	Why is there no Dutch or English translation? We know you have Interpreters on shore.
Japanese	We do not know why this is so.
Neale	We have the means of translating, but I wish you to state to your Government that if this reply is not satisfactory I shall consider it as a refusal and act accordingly. It is now eleven

	months since your Prince became aware of what occurred. When lately I told the Tycoon's Government that perhaps your Prince had not been officially informed of the demands to be preferred upon him, they assured me that they had even sent him copies of every conference which had taken place on the subject.
Japanese	We know nothing about this.
Neale	I have come here to settle the question amicably, if possible; we have not therefore entered upon any hostilities, but this matter can no longer be left undetermined.
Japanese	We will communicate what you now state.
Neale	That is what I wish you to do.
Admiral Kuper	The settlement of this matter can no longer be delayed. Kagoshima is at my mercy; hostilities once commenced, your town would be destroyed, and I shall stop your trade both here and at the Loo-chew Islands.
Neale	Such is not our wish; but if you compel us to do so, it will be your own fault.
Japanese	We will report all this.
Kuper	You must remember that we are one of the first nations in the world, who, instead of meeting civilized people as you think yourselves, in reality encounter barbarians.
Japanese	We cannot discuss these subjects but we will report all this to our Government.
Neale	Evasion or delay can no longer be submitted to.
	(Japanese rise to leave.)
Neale	You had better listen to what we state for the sake of your Government, that it may be thoroughly informed of our determination.
Japanese	We know nothing of these matters.
Neale	I will then inform you that when this murder was committed, the Tycoon's Government declared to me that they could not arrest anyone in Satsuma's territory, or assure me that any satisfaction could be obtained; at the time, the foreign community wished that Shimazu Saburō and his cortège should be attacked, but this was averted by the authorities, with a view that full redress might be

THE BLAZON OF OUR WRATH

obtained through the proper channels. The *gorogio* replied that they had written to your Prince, and would write urgently and constantly until your Prince sent the murderers to Yeddo for trial. Your Prince has not done so.

In the meanwhile, instructions have reached me from my Government to the effect that specific demands should be preferred:-

>1st. Upon the Tycoon's Government, which has fully satisfied those demands.
>
>2nd. Upon the Prince of Satsuma, whose adherents had actually perpetrated the murder.

The Tycoon has suffered severely by the acts of your Prince's adherents, for the Tycoon's ministers had really nothing to do with Shimazu Saburō's orders to murder British subjects.

Japanese	We know nothing, of all these matters.
Neale	But I wish to inform you respecting them, that you may report what I say to your Prince.
Kuper	Colonel Neale wishes to settle the question with you amicably; but if by tomorrow at ten o'clock a.m. you do not do so, the matter will be handed over into my hands, when I shall commence by not allowing a single boat to pass.
	(The Japanese officials rise to leave).
Neale	Your reply, which may be a refusal, having been delivered, do you propose further to communicate with us?
Kuper	We wish you to communicate with us again to-morrow before ten a.m., your boat flying a white flag.
Japanese	Perhaps we will send before ten to-morrow morning.
Kuper	That would be better.
Neale	Your envoys and boats will not be molested whatever may be the nature of your despatch.
	(The Japanese then left).

Colonel Neale's letter had read:

>To His Highness MATSUDAIRA SHIURI-NO-DAIBU, the daimio prince of Satsuma, or in his absence to the regent or other High Officer for the

RESPECT AND CONSIDERATION

time being administering the Government of the prince of Satsuma, Fiuga, Ohosumi, and the Loo Choo Islands.

H.B.M.'s Legation in Japan,
    August 12th 1863.
Your Highness,
    It is well known to you that a barbarous murder of an unarmed and unoffending British subject and Merchant was perpetrated on the 14th of the month of September last, 21st day of 8th month of 2nd year of Bung-kew of Japanese reckoning, upon the Tokaido near Kanagawa, by persons attending the procession and surrounding the norimon of SHIMADZU SABURO, whom I am informed is the father of your Highness.
    It is equally known to you that a murderous assault was made at the same time by the same retinue, upon a lady and two other gentlemen, British subjects, by whom he was accompanied, the two gentlemen having been severely and seriously wounded, and the lady escaping by a miracle.
    The names of the British subjects here referred to are as follows:
CHARLES LENOX RICHARDSON, murdered,
Mrs. BORRODAILE.
Mr. WOODTHORPE CLARKE, severely wounded.
Mr. WILLIAM MARSHALL, severely wounded.
    This event filled with great and just indignation the British Government and people, and excited the sympathy of, and produced a painful impression upon, all civilized countries.
    Impressed with friendly and considerate feelings towards the Government of the Tycoon, with whom the Queen of Great Britain, my august Sovereign, is in relations by treaty of peace and amity, I acted with proper consideration for the

THE BLAZON OF OUR WRATH

Tycoon's Government by leaving in its hands the legitimate means of speedily arresting and bringing to capital punishment the murderers from among SHIMADZU SABURO's retinue.

This necessary forbearance on my part has been entirely approved of by my Government, and appreciated and acknowledged by the Government of the Tycoon.

A different course proposed at the moment to be adopted in the excitement attending this barbarous outrage might have resulted in the capture and perhaps death by summary retribution of SHIMADZU SABURO himself.

Ten months have now elapsed since the perpetration of this unprovoked outrage, during which period my Government has been duly informed by me of the circumstances attending it, while the Tycoon's Ministers have held out to me from time to time assurances and hopes that the murderers would be given up by your Highness and sent to Yedo for trial and execution.

But I have had occasion to report to my Government that, removed in your distant domain from the direct influence of the supreme Government, and shielded also by certain privileges and immunities which belong to daimios of this Empire, you had utterly disregarded all orders or decrees of the Japanese Government, calling upon you to afford justice by sending the real criminals to Yedo. They have not been arrested nor sent; and no redress has consequently been afforded by the Tycoon's Government, however desirous it may be of doing so.

In the meanwhile I have received the explicit instructions of my own Government how to act in the matter.

RESPECT AND CONSIDERATION

The Tycoon's Government may be impeded by the laws of the country, and more especially by political embarrassments from enforcing its desires upon daimios of the Empire in regard to criminal acts committed by their adherents. But when British subjects are the victims of those acts, Japan as a Nation must through its Government pay a penalty and disavow the misdeeds of its subjects, to whatever rank they may belong.

Under instructions from my Government I demanded from the Tycoon's Government an apology, and the payment of a considerable penalty for permitting the murderous attack made by your retainers on British subjects passing on a road open to them by treaty. Both these demands have been acceded to.

But the British Government has also decided that those circumstances constitute no reason why the real delinquents and actual murderers should be shielded by your Highness, or by any means escape the condign punishment which they merit, and which they would be subjected to for great crimes such as they have committed, in all other parts of the world.

It has therefore been determined by the Government, and I am instructed to demand of your Highness as follows:-

- First: The immediate trial and capital execution in the presence of one or more of Her Majesty's Naval Officers of the chief perpetrators of the murder of Mr. RICHARDSON, and of the murderous assault of the lady and gentlemen who accompanied him.
- Secondly: The payment of twenty-five thousand pounds (25,000) sterling to be distributed to the relations of the murdered

man, and to those who escaped with their lives the swords of the assassins on that occasion.

These demands are required by Her Majesty's Government to be acceded to by your Highness immediately upon their being made known to you. And upon your refusing, neglecting or evading to do so, the Admiral commanding the British Forces in these seas will adopt such coercive measures, increasing in their severity, as he may deem expedient to obtain the required satisfaction and redress.

The Commander of Her Majesty's Ship of War charged with the delivery of this letter is made acquainted with the specific demands which I have the honour to communicate to you in this letter, and according as they are accepted or refused he has received instructions either to carry out and witness their execution, within a period of days which will be named, or in the event of a refusal, to commence at once coercive operations, pending the arrival of additional forces.

Your Highness is therefore earnestly requested seriously to consider the course you will adopt on the receipt of this communication, the terms of which it is not in my power to modify, alter or discuss.

I avail myself of this occasion to offer to your Highness the assurance of my respect and consideration.

(Signed)   EDWD. ST. JOHN NEALE
H.B.M.'s Chargé d'Affaires in Japan

Once the Satsuma reply had been translated, it was, as suspected, found to be very unsatisfactory from the British point of view. The translated letter said, in full:

RESPECT AND CONSIDERATION

IT is just that a man who has killed another should be arrested and punished by death, as there is nothing more sacred than human life, and although we should like to secure them [the murderers], as we have endeavoured to do since last year, it is impossible for us to do so, owing to the political differences at present existing between the Daimios of Japan; some of whom even hide and protect such people; besides this, the murderers are not one, but several persons, and therefore find easier means of escape.

The journey to Yeddo [undertaken by Shimazu Saburō] was not with the object of committing murders, but to conciliate the two Courts of Yeddo and Kyōto; and you will easily, therefore, believe that our master [Shimazu] could not have ordered it [the murder]. Great offenders against the laws of their Country [Japan], who escape, are liable to capital punishment. If, therefore, we can detect those in question, and, after examination, find them to be guilty, they shall be punished and we will then inform the Commanders of your men-of-war at Nagasaki, or at Yokohama, in order that they may come to witness their execution. You must, therefore, consent to the unavoidable delay which is necessary to carry out these measures. If we were to execute criminals condemned for other offences, and told you that they were the offenders [above referred to] you would not be able to recognize them; and this would be deceiving you, and not acting in accordance with the spirit of our ancestors.

The [Provincial] Governments of Japan are subordinate to the Yeddo Government, and, as you aware, are subservient to the orders received from it. We have heard something about a Treaty having been negotiated in which a certain limit was assigned to, foreigners to move about in; but we have not

THE BLAZON OF OUR WRATH

heard of any stipulation by which they are authorized to impede the passage of a road.

Supposing this happened in your country, travelling with a large number of retainers as we do here, would you not push out of the way and beat any one thus disregarding and breaking the existing laws of the country? If this were neglected princes could no longer travel. We repeat that we agree with you that the taking of human life is a very grave matter. On the other hand, the insufficiency of the Yeddo Government, who govern and direct everything, is shown by their neglecting to insert in the treaty [with foreigners] the laws of the country [in respect to these matters] which have existed from ancient times. You will, therefore, be able to judge yourself whether the Yeddo Government [for not inserting these laws] or my master [for carrying them out] is to be blamed.

To decide on this important matter, a high official of the Yeddo Government, and one of our Government, ought to discuss it before you, and find out who is in the right.

After the above question has thus been judged and settled, the money indemnity shall be arranged.

We have not received from the Tycoon any orders or communications by steamer that your men-of-war were coming here. Such statements are probably made with the object of representing us in a bad light. If it were not with this object you would certainly have them in writing from the *gorogio*; and if so we request you to let us see them.

In consequence of such mis-statements great misunderstandings are caused.

All this surprises us much. Does it not surprise you?

Our Government acts in everything according to the orders of the Yeddo Government.

RESPECT AND CONSIDERATION

> This is our open-hearted reply to the different subjects mentioned in your despatch.
> 29th day of the 6th month of the 3rd year of *Bung-kew*. (13th August, 1861)
> (Signed) KAWAKAMI TAJIMA. *SHISSEI* (Minister of MATSUDAIRA SHIURINO-DAIBU, prince of Satsuma &c.).

So, then, in summary:
- the murderers could not be found;
- according to the laws of Japan, a *daimyō*, travelling with his retinue, should be fully justified in beating or thrusting off the road all persons who encounter him on the highway;
- the *bakufu* was to blame for making faulty treaties that failed to preserve the rights of the *daimyō* to travel unimpeded;
- until the murderers were found - which would take an indefinite time - no discussions could take place concerning compensation;
- and the British government should in any case be looking to the *bakufu*, not Satsuma, for redress.

Not a single acceptance in meaningful terms of the justice of the British demands! Neale summed it up as a communication

> ... in every respect evasive of the point at issue, as confirming rather than repudiating the outrage for which redress has been long sought, and in short a virtual refusal and setting aside of the demands.

Neale discussed the matter with Admiral Kuper, and asked him immediately to prepare to take preliminary measures of coercion, by reprisals or otherwise, as he thought most expedient and best calculated to make the prince of Satsuma realise the serious and implacable nature of their mission.

On the morning of the 14th, the messenger duly returned by boat, under a white flag, at 9 o'clock. He was told that Satsuma's response was unsatisfactory, and that no further discussions would be held except under a flag of truce. Hostilities had therefore been declared.

Admiral Kuper readied himself for action. At 10:30, he personally boarded *Havoc* with Master Parker, and for five hours, they reconnoitred the waters of Kinko Bay, taking depth soundings as they went. They found an average of fifty fathoms (300 feet, 91·4 metres) at 100 yards (300 feet, 91·4 metres) from shore, which promised safe sailing. Returning on board Euryalus at 3:30, he summoned the commanding officers of the squadron on board *Euryalus*, and briefed them as to his plans.

Kuper ordered Captain Borlase of *Pearl*

> to proceed at daylight on the following morning with *Coquette, Argus* and *Racehorse*, to a bay to the northward
> of Kagoshima, to seize and bring back to the anchorage three steamers, the property of the Prince, which had been previously ascertained to be lying there.

These were the British-origin screw propelled steam/sail ships *England* (759 tons), bought for $125000 in 1861; *Contest* (350 tons), bought for $95000 in May 1863; and *Sir George Grey* (492 tons), bought for $85000. Their Japanese names were *Tenyū-maru, Hakuo-maru* and *Seiyō-maru*, respectively. The ships plied a significant secret trade with China and the Ryūkyū Islands (Loochoo), against the rules of the central government. At this moment, they were all laden with sugar. Kuper's objective was to detain the ships until Satsuma complied with the demands made upon him. Capt. Borlase was also

> desired to avoid, as much as possible, all unnecessary bloodshed or active hostility.

RESPECT AND CONSIDERATION

Return of iron-clad screw Steamers purchased by Prince Satsuma from foreigners since opening of the PORTS and both captured and burnt at SICETOMI and KAGOSIMA respectively on the 15th August 1863. Fired by their respective captors + sunk by HMS Havoc.

Name Originally Japanese	Nationality	Where Built	Year	Horse-power	Tons	Price $,000	Date of Purchase	Where Delivered	Previous Owner	Captured by HMS
Contest Seiyô-maru	American	Boston	Not known	Not known	522	95	Apr-63	Nagasaki	Russell & Co.+ Chinese	Coquette
Sir George Grey Hakuo-maru	British	Hamburg	1860	Not known	492	85	May-63	Nagasaki	Siemssen and Son	Argus
England Tenyû-maru	British	Glasgow	1860	100	949	128	Jan-61	Nagasaki	W.S. Lyndsay	Racehorse

180

THE BLAZON OF OUR WRATH

Captain Borlase, furnished with Master Parker's new charts, executed a textbook mission. At 4:00 am, the four ships slipped their moorings and steamed to the North-East, where the three Satsuma steamers lay. As *Argus* came alongside *Sir George Grey*, all but two of the crew of the Satsuma vessel dived over the side and made for shore. These two remaining identified themselves as "Godai" and "Matsugi Kowan". Later, they were transferred to *Euryalus*, when they said their real names were Captain Otani and Doctor Kashiwa. Kashiwa had just returned from the first Japanese diplomatic visit to Europe. "Kashiwa" was in fact Terashima Munenori, who became Foreign Minister in the Meiji government. "Otani" was Godai Tomoatsu (1836-1885), who went on to become a wealthy businessman, and later founded the Osaka Stock Exchange.

With their three prizes lashed alongside, the ships returned to their sheltered anchorage under Sakurajima.[99] *Coquette* anchored with *Conquest* lashed alongside at 9:00, and at 9:45, *Argus* brought *Sir George Grey*, and *Racehorse* brought *England*. Not to be outdone, *Havoc* had brought three Satsuma-owned thirty-five foot junks in tow.

Their anchorage was calculated to be out of the range of Satsuma's nine shore batteries.

---

[99] In 1863, Sakurajima ("Cherry Blossom Island") lay in the middle of Kinko Bay, on which sits Kagoshima. The bay was the result of an enormous volcanic explosion 22,000 years ago. Sakurajima has been one of Japan's most active volcanoes, but dormant for 100 years until 1914. On January 11 that year, and lasting for several months, the enormous "Taishō" eruption occurred. Taishō was the name of the Emperor at the time of the eruption. Volcanic debris covered the island to a depth of four metres, and so much lava was deposited into the sea that it permanently linked the island to the mainland opposite Kagoshima. Enough magma was ejected to deepen the Bay by over half a metre, and tides rose by a similar height. The new, post-Taishō Kinko bay bears a close resemblance to Pearl Harbor in Hawaii, and the Japanese Navy practised its aerial manoeuvres there prior to the attack in 1941.

RESPECT AND CONSIDERATION

Euryalus and *Pearl*, with their formidable firepower, were between the rest of the squadron and Kagoshima, around mid-channel. The weather worsened, and by late morning, a force 8 gale[100] was lashing the area. The mid-day meal was being served on board, with none but the look-outs, doubtless cursing the foul weather, on deck.

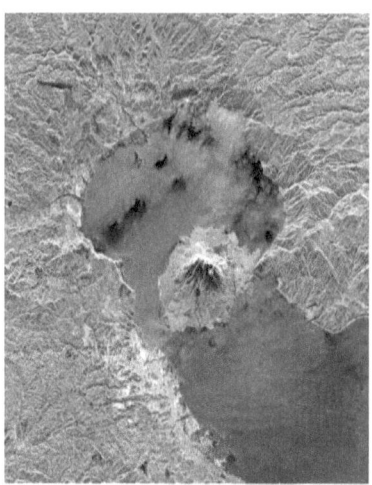

Sakurajima: radar image from space. It was not joined to the mainland until the 1914 Taishō eruption. NASA photograph.

Kuper's aggressive but bloodless intentions were suddenly and unexpectedly set aside by an unheralded attack by Satsuma. Shimazu Saburō had equipped his town with European-style gun batteries, with about 81 guns and mortars, including at least three 10-in. and two 8-in. guns, and forty 32- and 24-pdrs.

---

[100] Force 8 on the Beaufort wind speed scale is between 34 and 40 knots and is classified as a gale. There are moderately high waves (up to 5½ metres high) with breaking crests forming spindrift, and there are streaks of foam on the water. Such a wind speed will break twigs from trees and cause cars to swerve on roads.

THE BLAZON OF OUR WRATH

No	Captain Fred. Brine's Table of the Kagoshima Batteries			Total	Remarks
	Armament				
	Siege	Field	Mortars		
1	8	2	1	11	
2	3		1	4	
3	11	3	3	17	
4	7	2	4	13	Most of the Guns of "Bronze"
5	7		1	8	SIEGE Guns 18, 24, 32 Prs & 8 Inch
6	4			4	FIELD Guns 3, 6, 9 & 12 Prs
7		3		3	MORTARS 8 & 10 Inch - Masked
8	5	1		6	
9	4		1	5	
10	5		1	6	- " -
11	4			4	Entrance of Bay
TOTAL	58	11	12	81	

Table of guns from Parker's Chart						
Batteries	10 Inch Guns	8 Inch Guns	32 & 24 pors	18 pors, fl pcs	Mortars	Remarks
No. 1 * (Spit Battery)		8			2	7 or 8 fp between
No. 2		3			2	
No. 3					3	
No. 4						
No. 5		2	9			3 field pieces
No. 6				3		
No. 7	2		5			
No. 8	1		5		1	2 Do.
No. 9				1		
No. 10			4			
No. 11		2	4	3		
No. 12			15			
						3 W face 12 E
Total 88 guns and Mortars	3	4	49	11	8	12 to 13 field pieces

RESPECT AND CONSIDERATION

As can be seen, there are some discrepancies between the assessments of Satsuma weaponry by Capt. Brine of the Royal Engineers and Master Parker of *Euralyus*.

Almost every gun was pointed towards *Euryalus*, the only ship in reach. John Reddie Black records that Satsuma later admitted they had taken advantage of the typhoon.

> Satsuma believed that no ships could stand the combined forces of nature and science - the raging elements and the deadly hail of the forts. There was a certain amount of ignorance displayed on their part; and perhaps Admiral Kuper ought to have taken some pains to explain the truth to them. All he wanted was to enforce the rendition of the murderers of Richardson, that they might meet the justice due to them; and the payment of £25,000 as indemnity to the relatives of Mr. Richardson and of his companions. The Admiral's object in taking the three ships was to hold them until these demands were satisfactorily complied with.
>
> ... it might have been reasonably supposed that they would gladly have redeemed the ships by the payment of the $100,000 - the equivalent of the required amount ... But it does not appear that they understood this. They saw their ship taken possession of, and doubtless felt the most natural indignation at such a proceeding on the part of the English. They opened upon the fleet with shot and shell ... The damage suffered by Satsuma was - the destruction of the town - very much to be regretted, though most of the populace had fled in anticipation of the fight ... It was a terrible retribution; but as, in order to secure the safety of her Majesty's ships, not from the effects of the guns in the forts but from the severity of the weather, the British Admiral, considering he had administered punishment enough, withdrew to a safe anchorage, the Satsuma

people professed to believe that they had gained the victory.

Euryalus was taken entirely by surprise. But we see a splendid example of British *insouciance*, and a wonderfully ironic response to the situation. Sir Alfred Jephson, then a lieutenant on board *Euryalus*, later recalled that
> she hastily weighed, while her band played, "Oh dear, what can the matter be?"

It was subsequently rumoured that Admiral Kuper's first thought was to move out of range, and wait for the storm to abate. Naval gunnery through extreme wind and high wave could not possibly be accurate. However, Captain Josling urged him to fight, advising that here was an opportunity to coerce Satsuma by demonstrating what devastating firepower the Royal Navy wielded.

Whether Admiral Kuper needed to be persuaded is a matter of conjecture, but in any case, he issued immediate orders to engage the shore batteries. As it was impossible for the small squadron to carry out the requisite retaliation and at the same time to retain possession of the three steamers, Kuper signalled to the ships "Burn prizes". This was a blow to the sailors' expectations. Prize money would not now be received, and the three steamers alone were conservatively worth £300,000. The commanders of the naval vessels allowed officers and men to board the Japanese steamers and plunder whatever they could find. Some officers found silver and gold coins, but most found minor and personal items like decanters, furniture, small arms and telescopes. Ernest Satow reported that he took a black war-helmet (*jingasa*) and a Japanese matchlock firearm[101]. By 12:45, the captured vessels were ablaze.

Ten minutes later, steam was fully up, the squadron weighed anchor and formed into line of battle. They headed towards

---

[101] Our old friend the arquebus.

RESPECT AND CONSIDERATION

Kagoshima, *Euryalus* in the van. A long period elapsed before *Euryalus* opened fire. It took her an hour and twenty-five minutes to clear for action. She was unable to deploy her guns until the door and passageways to the ammunition magazine had been opened. But they were blocked with the scores of heavy boxes of coin received at the Legation in compensation from the *bakufu*, which had been stored on board. This is a further indication that it was not Admiral Kuper's intention to open fire on the shore batteries, for otherwise the route for the ammunition from the magazine to the guns would have been kept clear. But Kuper should surely have had the passageways cleared beforehand, given the tension that had built up between the antagonists.

Perseus had difficulty in weighing anchor, and eventually had to slip her cable. The anchor was later dredged up by fishermen and returned ceremoniously to her, as a demonstration of renewed feelings of friendship by Satsuma in November 1864. Because of the delay, she took last place in the line of battle.

At 2:10, the line of ships, headed by *Euryalus*, started to sail about quarter of a mile off and parallel to the shore, from North to South, pouring broadside after broadside into the forts. Master William Hennessey Parker, of *Euryalus*, steered his vessel with great judgment, taking her at times within 400 yards of the batteries; yet Kuper was heard continually spurring him on with: "Go in closer, Parker; go in closer!" Owing to the heavy sea in which the action was fought, the decks were awash, adding to the difficulties of maintaining a course that would enable the guns to bear on their intended targets.

Nonetheless, many shots were seen to find their mark on buildings and batteries on shore. At five minutes before three, *Euryalus* unwittingly placed herself in a perilous location. Shore battery No. 7 had habitually practiced firing on targets floating in the bay at a particular point.

THE BLAZON OF OUR WRATH

Euryalus rode at that exact spot, and the shore battery ranged precisely as it had practised many times before, and fired a roundshot at her. The projectile tore through *Euryalus'* narrow bridge, smashing the heads of Captain Josling and Commander Wilmot. The ship's surgeon noted[102], of Captain Josling's death,
> Head shattered by a round shot from a field piece. Frontal, Parietal and Occipital bones smashed, and the Brain scattered about the Deck. Struck by the same shot as Commander Wilmot.

At that moment, Captain and Commander were in conference with Admiral Kuper and Master Parker. Miraculously, the Admiral and Master Parker escaped unscathed. The Admiral was, unsurprisingly, rather shaken by the sudden, bloody and shocking deaths of the senior officers at his side. He and Captain Josling had served together for many years, and they were close friends.

At about the same time as Captain Josling and Commander Wilmot were killed, the 10-inch Armstrong No. 3 gun on the main deck misfired, and the explosion of the shell killed six men

Detail of British fleet bombarding Kagoshima (*Euryalus* leading)
Illustrated London News 7th **November 1863 by our Special Artist**
This picture was denounced in the House of Commons as being faked, which, indeed it was. The Special Artist, Charles Wirgman, copied from a sailor's sketch. It was not an eye-witness' accurate drawing, as claimed by the publication.

---

[102] See Appendix 9

instantaneously[103]. This calamity put back the further introduction of breech-loaders by the British Admiralty by nearly 20 years[104]. A 10-inch shell from the shore came through the starboard waist bulwark and burst under the starboard launch. Three men died subsequently, each of them horribly wounded, and Lieutenant Jephson was injured, though not critically. And on board *Coquette*, Gunner Thomas Finn was killed by a shot from the shore. Several others were wounded seriously enough to merit the Admiral's notice:

Euryalus   Assistant-Paymaster George Washington Jones
             Gunner W. Sale
Pearl   Carpenter M. Armstrong
Coquette   Lieutenant D'Arcy Anthony Denny
             Gunner W. Harris
Perseus   Lieutenant Francis Joseph Pitt
             Master Robert Gilpin
             Midshipman John Robert Aylen

The atrocious weather meant that the ships of the squadron could not maintain their stations. *Racehorse's* engines broke

---

[103] This one incident caused a major re-think on the Admiralty's part about using the Armstrong breech-loaders. The fact was, that the closure of the breech mechanism had no fail/safe device to prevent detonation while the breech was open. For fifteen years, the Navy reverted to muzzle-loaders until Armstrong and others devised breech safety mechanisms.

[104] One of Euryalus' officers later wrote, concerning the Armstrong guns, "We had on our main-deck 32-pr. 56 cwt. muzzle-loaders; and they, of course, gave no trouble. On our quarter-deck we had four 40-pr. Armstrongs, and we got two or three from the port side over to the spare ports on the starboard side to make a larger battery. These all worked well. But in the forecastle we had a 7-in. Breech Loading 110-pr. Armstrong. Whether the men in the heat of the action became hurried I cannot say; but certain it is that the breech piece of this gun blew out with tremendous effect, the concussion knocking down the whole gun's crew, and apparently paralysing the men, until Webster, captain of the forecastle and of the gun, roused them by shouting: 'Well; is there ere a b----- of you will go and get the spare vent piece?" The men, as well as their officers, had little confidence in the Armstrong gun.

THE BLAZON OF OUR WRATH

down at this moment, and consequently, out of direct control, she ran aground within the arc of fire of one of the batteries, but Commander Boxer set up such a rate of fire from her carronades that not a single shot from shore came anywhere near her. Indeed, he silenced No. 8 battery completely. *Coquette* and *Argus* bravely went back to tow her off. At one point, when it seemed she was stuck fast, plans were laid to set fire to her, to prevent her falling into Satsuma's hands. After about an hour, though, *Argus* finally managed to drag her off the shoal on which she had been caught.

The squadron had been instructed to fire on a distinctive large white building, Admiral Kuper being under the impression that it was the Shimazu palace. In fact, the building they fired at was a temple, and Shimazu Saburō and his senior advisers were well out of reach at the time of the bombardment. Rockets were fired upon the town, and the wood-and-paper buildings burned fiercely, the more so because of the high winds from the storm. By twenty past four, firing from the shore batteries had ceased. At seven o'clock, *Havoc* was sent to burn five Loochoo[105] junks lying close onshore, near Satsuma's warehouses. By eight o'clock, sparks from the junks had ignited the wooden warehouses. On all sides, the sky was filled with a cloud of smoke lit up from below by the pointed masses of pale fire, which continued all night. Many guns were observed to be dismounted, the batteries had been cleared several times, and the explosion of various magazines gave evidence of the destructive effects of the Armstrong shells. Half of the town was

---

[105] The Loochoo Islands (variously spelt Lew-Chew at the time) is, as previously noted, an alternative name for the Ryukyu Islands. The most populous island, then as now, is Okinawa. The Ryukyu island chain is half way between Kyūshū and China / Korea, and was thus an ideal staging post for trade between the two. The Satsuma clan invaded the islands in 1609, and thereafter used them (illegally) for such trade. The Loochoo junks were junks used for that illicit foreign trade.

RESPECT AND CONSIDERATION

in flames and entirely destroyed, it was reported, as well as a very extensive arsenal and gun foundry.

After the squadron had sailed past the southernmost battery, Kuper ordered the squadron to disengage and seek anchorage. The weather, already at gale force, was worsening, and night was approaching. The safety of Her Majesty's ships had to be secured. So the fleet returned to the anchorage under Sakurajima.

Sunday 16th August dawned, with a full-blown storm raging. Winds peaked at 55 knots, and the waves rose to 9 metres. It was impossible to see the shore. On land, trees were uprooted, and some of the buildings on shore that had escaped the fire were damaged by the wind.

Sakurajima, a sailor's-eye view on a calm day, half way between Kagoshima and the former island.
Author's photograph

Gradually, though, the storm abated, and by nightfall, there was hardly any breeze at all. Waves fell to a mere ten centimetres. At 11 o'clock, Captain Josling, Commander Wilmot and seven men were committed to the deep, buried at sea, in the periphery of Kinko Bay[106].

At quarter past twelve, Kuper gave orders to move to a shallower anchorage than the deep waters under Sakurajima. Furthermore, the navy could see the Japanese at work erecting batteries on the hill immediately above the little bay where the small vessels were at anchor. Engines were fired up, anchors

---

[106] Each body was sewn into a bag made from sailcloth, and weighed down with two cannonballs at the feet. It was customary for the last stitch forming the bag to be sewn through the nose of the deceased, as a final proof that he was, in fact, dead. The ship rode motionless in the water; the Anglican service for burial at sea was read by the naval chaplain, in the presence of the entire ship's company, save those on duty or injured; and the bodies were released into the sea.

THE BLAZON OF OUR WRATH

were weighed, and the squadron manoeuvred to the west, aiming to anchor southward of Sakurajima. Turning back on itself, and running in the middle of the bay, the squadron steamed slowly past the still-smoking city of Kagoshima. The opportunity was taken to shell the batteries on the Sakurajima side, which had not been previously engaged, and also the white temple, mistakenly thought to be the palace of the Prince, on the Kagoshima side. Several direct hits were observed on land, but some of the shore batteries were still able to return fire, though without any further damage to the squadron. *Perseus*, at the rear of the squadron, carried on firing rockets into the town, even after the Kagoshima guns fell silent, until she, too, was out of range.

The Bombardment of Kagoshima was over. Kuper wrote to Neale

> Thus having accomplished every act of retribution and punishment within the scope of operations of a small naval force, and having received from yourself the verbal expression of your satisfaction with the extent of those operations, I purpose returning with the squadron to Yokohama, immediately the partial refit which is now in progress shall admit of our putting to sea.

The squadron anchored for the night far out of range of Satsuma's guns, and on the morning of the 17th started back for Yokohama. There was a feeling of anti-climax throughout the squadron. Could they fairly say that their objects had been achieved? No compensation had been collected. No prizes had been carried away, save for the trivial possessions looted from the Japanese vessels. Thirteen British personnel were dead, and fifty lay in the sick bays, wounded. The Japanese batteries had not been completely silenced, though indeed some had been dismounted. Opinion on board was that they had disengaged too soon, that they should have continued until every gun on

RESPECT AND CONSIDERATION

shore was suppressed. Then, they might have exacted their demands on Satsuma.

It was rumoured that Colonel Neale had urged the Admiral to send raiding-parties on shore to seize some guns as trophies of war and as proof of British success, but Kuper had refused, being demoralized and in shock following the gruesome deaths of the Captain and Commander in his presence. Ernest Satow, who, though junior, was within the inner circle, did not believe the rumours. He thought that differences had arisen between the Neale the diplomat and Kuper the sailor, and Neale had interfered too much with the conduct of operations. Indeed, Kuper said as much in a mild complaint in his despatches. The protocol demanded that Neale should stand back after he had placed matters in the Admiral's hands, but his military background and his affinity for action had stirred within him a desire to influence command decisions. But Kuper stood firm, for *his* masters were the Lords of the Admiralty, not the Foreign Secretary, and their Lordships would hold *him* to account for his actions.

1399 rounds had been fired. The boilers of the ships had been burning coal at maximum rate for four days. Supplies were not limitless. The city of Kagoshima had been extensively and visibly damaged. The British assessment of damage was that perhaps 20% of Kagoshima's buildings had been destroyed and as many as 30,000 people made homeless. A million pounds worth of damage had been done to the city (£65m in twenty-first century terms). One report later said that 1500 townspeople had perished, though only a handful of these (variously seven or nine) were *samurai*. One Japanese report says that only one died and 6 were wounded. Another says that nearly ten percent of the town was burnt to the ground. Yet another says that only 500 houses were destroyed. Kuper himself said that 1000 Japanese townspeople must have died, such was the devastation[107]. It had never been his intention to fire upon Kagoshima, only being forced to retaliate after Satsuma opened fire on the squadron. Coercive measures were one thing, punitive ones another. Discretion and human decency called for him to cease inflicting retribution on a largely innocent populace. It was right for him to end the action.

Neale was in any case appreciative of the exemplary action that the squadron had fought under Kuper's command in response to the attack by the shore batteries, made without warning. He wrote in his concluding despatch of 26th August, from Yokohama, to Lord Russell:

> It would be unbecoming in me to indulge in expressions of admiration at the able and gallant manner in which the operations, suddenly rendered necessary, were determined upon, and immediately carried out by the ships of Her Majesty's Squadron, under the immediate command and direction of Vice-Admiral Kuper, upon whom it devolves to bring to the knowledge of Her Majesty's Government, the spirited incidents and all sufficient results, which attended the combat at Kagoshima. The strength of the batteries, mounting 81 guns, the gale blowing during the action, the comparatively severe loss sustained by us, especially in the untimely fate of those brilliant and deplored Officers, Captains Josling and Wilmot, of the flag-ship, will be duly appreciated by Her Majesty's Government.
>
> I did not hesitate to convey to Admiral Kuper my unqualified opinion that enough had been effected to vindicate the outrage committed upon British subjects by the adherents of Satsuma, at least until I had the honor (*sic*) to receive your Lordship's further instructions.

---

[107] Satsuma itself admitted to just five deaths.

RESPECT AND CONSIDERATION

The chief agent of that outrage is generally understood to have been Shimazu Saburō, the father of the Prince: his guards but obeyed his instructions. No power as yet brought to bear upon Japan by Her Majesty's Government is calculated to coerce the Prince of Satsuma to deliver up his father to condign punishment, as the principal perpetrator of the outrage committed.

It was determined upon this to return to Yokohama, when, after a series of severe gales and typhoons prevailing at this season on this dangerous coast, the squadron returned to this anchorage on the 24th instant.

Thus I have the satisfaction to report to your Lordship, that the instructions with which I have been charged, onerous as they were palpably and in fact, and having reference to the outrage of last September, have been carried out in letter and in spirit. The indemnities demanded of the Tycoon's Government are afloat on board Her Majesty's Ships. I have had the honor to transmit to your Lordship the written apology of the Government of Yeddo; and in respect to the Prince of Satsuma having illadvisedly sought to evade the specific demands which Her Majesty's Government deemed it advisable to direct me to make upon him, after due consideration of all the circumstances, and after long forbearance, his capital is in ashes, his foundries destroyed and his steamers burnt.

It remains for me to trust that Her Majesty's Government may deem that my instructions have been thus fulfilled in a manner best adapted to the difficult circumstances with which I have been, and still continue to be, surrounded.

In conclusion, I trust your Lordship will pardon me if I do not resist the natural impulse of desiring to bring under your Lordship's notice the special and

THE BLAZON OF OUR WRATH

RETURN giving the Armament, Tonnage etc. of Seven Men of War under Vice Adm. Kuper CB engaged on the 15 + 16 August 63 with the No. of Rounds Fired + No. killed and Wounded.   Sd. Fred. Brine, Capt., R.E

Ship: HMS	Tons	Guns/Fired	Rounds Day 1 Shot	Rounds Day 1 Shell	Rounds Day 2 Shot	Rounds Day 2 Shell	TOTAL	Casualties Killed Off.	Casualties Killed Men	Casualties Wounded Off.	Casualties Wounded Men
Euryalus	2371	35/18	47	71	48	95	261	2	8	2	19
Pearl	1469	21/11	71	97	5	80	253				7
Coquette	677	4/4	82	36	39	20	177		2	1	3
Argus	981	6/4	0	35	18	37	90				6
Perseus	955	17/9	100	60	97	84	359			4	6
Racehorse	695	4/4	42	30	80	46	198				3
Havoc	233	3/2	19	25	0	17	61				
TOTALS		90/52	361	354	287	379	1399	2	10	7	44

In addition to the above, Persus fired 18 Rockets. Argus was a Paddlewheel ship; all the others were Screw propelled.

unlooked for services rendered on the occasion of the expedition to Satsuma of Messrs. Eusden, Gower, Macdonald, Willis, Fletcher, Von Siebold[108], and Satow, of this Legation. In their absence all communications with the shore at Kagoshima must have failed. Interpreters from the shore were held back and never appeared; an attempt to impede all explanations rendered nugatory by a ready knowledge of their own language, which they found on board, nor shall I have accomplished my duty were I to omit to solicit your Lordships favourable notice to the devotion with which these members of Her Majesty's Civil Service exposed themselves to the anticipated perils of

naval combat, unaccompanied by any ostensible prospect of the ordinary honours and rewards attending the exposure of life in the profession of arms.

Kuper was not dilatory in rewarding some of his officers with promotions based on their actions at Kagoshima.

Commander to Captain

>John Hobhouse Inglis Alexander, to replace Captain Josling of *Euryalus*
>
>Lewis James Moore of *Argus*

Lieutenant to Commander

>James Edward Hunter, to replace Commander Wilmot of *Euryalus*
>
>Arthur George Robertson Roe, to replace Commander Alexander of *Coquette*
>
>James Augustus Poland of *Pearl*
>
>George Poole to command *Coromandel*

Lieutenant to Flag-Lieutenant

---

[108] This is Mr A. von Siebold, not to be confused with the renowned German physician and botanist Philipp Franz Balthasar von Siebold who had spent much time in Japan.

THE BLAZON OF OUR WRATH

Robert Peel Denistoun of *Coromandel* now to serve Adm. Kuper on *Euryalus*

Sub-Lieutenant to Lieutenant

Mr Morris (replacing Hunter)

Mr Wickham (replacing Roe)

Assistant Surgeon to Surgeon

Charles Richard Godfrey

So ended the hostilities in what the British would call the "Bombardment of Kagoshima" and the Japanese the "Anglo-Satsuma War" 薩英戦争 *satsu-ei sensō*.

On their return to Yokohama, life resumed its normal course. The *bakufu* had cornered the market in silk, and were refusing to sell to western traders except at considerably higher prices, in an attempt to recoup the fortune they had paid in indemnity to the British. Colonel Neale protested loudly and firmly, and, having heard of what Britain was capable of at Kagoshima, the *bakufu* relented, and trade went on at the former prices.

RESPECT AND CONSIDERATION

Table of British casualties at Kagoshima					
HMS *Euryalus*					
Josling, JJS	Captain, RN	37	Killed		Skull shot away
Wilmot, E	Commander	30	Killed		Back part of skull shot away
Hegarty, Michael	AB	22	Killed		Compnd fracture of skull and jaws
Fleming, Patrick	Private, RM	23	Killed		Fracture of base of skull
Lindsey, William	AB	21	Killed		Fracture of base of skull
Warren, John	Ordinary	19	Killed		compnd fracture of skull
Smith, John	AB	22	Killed		compnd fracture skull and pelvis
Yardeley, William	AB	24	Killed		compnd fracture of skull
Hawkins, John	Ordinary	19	Mortally wounded		compnd fracture of pelvis and upper third of femur
Harding, Thomas	1st class Boy	17	Mortally wounded		Right side of chest torn away by shell, ribs fractured, lungs lacerated, compnd fracture of arm
Jephson, Alfred	Lieut., RN	22	Slightly		Contused wound from shell on right shoulder, face burnt by explosion, various minor contusions
Jones, George W	Asst. Paymaster 1st class	26	Slightly		contused splinter wound, right leg
Kennett, James	Ordinary	28	Slightly		Face & arms burnt by explosion of shell
Pittman, John	Ordinary	20	Slightly		Splinter scalp wound, face burnt by explosion of shell
Abbott, Sylvanus	AB	22	Slightly		Splinter wound back both forearms, contusion inside left thigh

THE BLAZON OF OUR WRATH

Skinner, John	Ordinary	19	Slightly	Face scorched with powder
Mitchell, W	Ordinary	22	Slightly	Scalp wound (splinter)
Reader, George	L/Seamn	23	Slightly	Contusion of right arm (splinter)
Fox, Samuel	AB	22	Slightly	Contusion both arms, right groin, leg
Oram, Henry	Ordinary	19	Slightly	Contused wound of left leg (splinter)
Newberry, Isaac	Ordinary	19	Slightly	Wound of scalp and left foot by splinters
Badcock, William	Wardrm. Cook	40	Slightly	Contusion of left side and arm (splinter)
Huggett, William	Ordinary	19	Slightly	Contusion of right leg (splinter)
Howden, W	Private, RMLI	26	Dangerously	Right side of face shattered by shell, right half of lower jaw excised
Leary, Daniel	Private, RMLI	21	Severely	Shell wound of right thigh; eyes, face and arms scorched by explosion
Sale, William	Gunner, RMA	27	Slightly	Contusion of chest from splinter
Neil, Eugene	Leading Seaman	24	Slightly	Contusion of left arm, fingers and face scorched by explosion of shell
Stiff, John	AB	23	Slightly	Lacerated wound of left foot by splinter
Bartlett, George	Ordinary	19	Slightly	Face burnt by explosion
Alexander, George	Ordinary	19	Slightly	Contusion of right thigh (splinter)
Mitchell, Thomas	AB	22	Slightly	Splinter wound of foot, face scorched by explosion of shell
HMS *Pearl*				
Armstrong	Carp'ter 2nd class	38	Slightly	Splinter wound of forehead and ankle

RESPECT AND CONSIDERATION

Name	Rank	Age	Severity	Wound
Friend, James	Quartermaster	44	Dangerously	Splinter wounds of face and left thigh
Farrell, William	Drummer RMLI	18	Severely	Splinter wounds of buttocks, thighs and feet
Mercer, H	AB	26	Slightly	Splinter wounds of ankles
Kimmins, George	Ordinary	21	Slightly	Splinter wound of calf of leg
Dobson, F	Blacksmith	32	Slightly	Splinter wound of finger
Mitchell, James	2nd class Boy	16	Slightly	Splinter wound of calf of leg
HMS *Coquette*				
Finn, Thomas	Gunner, RMA	27	Killed	compnd fracture of pelvis and upper third of femur
Gale, Henry	Captain maintop	29	Mortally wounded	compnd fracture of upper third of right thigh
Denny, DA	Lieut., RN	20	Dangerously	Gunshot wound of left knee
Harris, William	Gunner, RMA	30	Dangerously	Gunshot wound of left leg
Mumford, William	Private, RM	35	Severely	Contused wound of right thigh
Vernon, William	1st class Boy	17	Slightly	Contused wound of left side
HMS *Perseus*				
Head, George	3rd class Boy	16	Mortally wounded	compnd fracture of both legs
Pitt, Francis J	Lieut., RN	22	Slightly	Incised wound on left leg and contusion of right leg
Gilpin, Robert	Master	33	Slightly	Burn rt hand from effects of a shell
Cook, Henry	Act. Chief Engineer	40	Slightly	Incised wound of third finger of right hand from splinter
Aylen, John R	Midshipman	17	Slightly	Contusion and punctured wound under right scapula from splinter

THE BLAZON OF OUR WRATH

Biggs, Thomas	2nd Captain foretop	29	Slightly	Lacerated wound of right arm
Knight, William	Cooper	25	Slightly	Incised wound of left arm from splinter
Suitors, Charles	AB	27	Slightly	Lacerated wound of left ankle from splinter
Gibson, William	Ordinary	21	Severely	Lacerated and contused wound of both arms from splinter
Gale, Charles	Private, RMLI	??	Dangerously	compnd fracture of right arm and wound of right thigh from splinter
HMS Argus				
Barnes, William	Captain, afterguard	31	Slightly	Splinter wound of leg
Fountain, John	AB	29	Slightly	Splinter wound of face
Hemett, John	Ordinary	20	Slightly	Splinter wound of leg
Lardner, Thomas	Private RMLI	27	Slightly	Splinter wound of leg
Doyne, George	Gunner's Mate	30	Slightly	Splinter wound of arm
Cooper, William	Captain Fo'c's'le	41	Slightly	Splinter wound of face
HMS *Racehorse*				
Chilton, William	AB	28	Dangerously	Amputation of left arm
Keenan, James	2nd Captain Foretop	23	Slightly	Laceration of thumb on right hand
Purr, James	1st class Boy	19	Slightly	Contusion of right arm

A *sous-lieutenant* in the 3ème *Chasseurs d'Afrique*

CHAPTER 22
FURTHER OUTRAGES, BUT SATSUMA COMPLIES AT LAST

At Kyōto, the Chōshū clan attempted a *coup d'état* at the end of May 1864, including an attempt to kidnap the Emperor. But a Chōshū insider loyal to the Emperor had disclosed the plot to Nakagawa-no-miya, the Emperor's uncle. Forewarned, the imperial troops fought and defeated Chōshū. An angry Emperor had several Chōshū retainers who had survived the fighting executed. Every remaining Chōshū man, including seven who had been Court nobles, was banished to their domain, their status as guardians of the Imperial Court stripped from them. These seven had been among the most vociferous in the *sonnō jōi* movement. Their disgrace and removal allowed the *bakufu* to rescind the Edict brought by Ogasawara for the closure of the ports. Tokugawa undertook to subjugate and punish the rebellious Chōshū. *Sonnō jōi* was emasculated. The western trading community breathed a sigh of relief. Normal relations were back.

But anti-western feeling had been a long time a-dying around the country. Around 8 o'clock in the evening on the 3rd March 1864, at Nagasaki, Charles Sutton, an Englishman, had been attacked. The American Consul's report reads:

> The victim is ... well known to every one as a sober peaceable, inoffensive man. He received a severe sword cut on the neck, and two on the left arm-one

of the latter severing the bones. The blow at the neck was evidently intended to take the head off, and only failed in its object by coming in contact with a thick coat collar.

Sutton still lives, and there are good hopes of his recovery, although the wounds are severe. The ruffian who made the assault escaped and has not yet been arrested. The British consul informed me yesterday that the local authorities express much regret at the occurrence, and profess the greatest desire to arrest the perpetrator, saying they were making the greatest efforts to do so.

Sutton's arm had to be amputated. He went on to live an active life in Yokohama as proprietor of a stevedore's business, a general contractor, and the English language newspaper *Rising Sun and Nagasaki Express*. The perpetrator of the attack was never discovered, and the western commercial and diplomatic community believed, indignantly, that the Japanese authorities had no true desire to deliver the attacker to justice.

On 14th October 1864, French *sous-Lieutenant* Camus of the 3rd *Chasseurs d'Afriqu*[109]*e* was murdered at Idogaya, a village a little way off the *tōkaidō*, some three miles from Yokohama. He had been riding alone, and had been killed by sword. His right arm was found at a little distance from his body, still clutching the bridle of his pony. There were cuts across and down his face, and he had nearly been decapitated. His left arm was hanging

---

[109] Les Chasseurs d'Afrique was a light cavalry corps in the French army, recruited from Frenchmen resident in Africa. In 1859, the Chasseurs d'Afrique wore a sky blue tunic with pleated skirt, the red trousers bearing a darker blue stripe up the seam, and a cap (shako) with silver braiding. In 1862, the officers of the 3ème Chasseurs d'Afrique were issued a ceremonial sky blue hussars' jacket with yellow facings and braids, worn over the shoulder. They were an élite corps, and sought to cut a dash. They had served with distinction in the Crimean War, and had protected the British flank during the Charge of the Light Brigade.

BASE CUSTOMS OF FORMER TIMES
ARE ABANDONED

on by a piece of skin and his left side was cut through as far as the heart. Every wound was a clean slice, the *katana* having been wielded by a skilled swordsman. Despite enquiry, the perpetrator was never found.

There was a grand funeral on the 15th, attended by all the Foreign Ministers and Consuls, the Admirals, Marines, almost all the foreign residents, and a considerable number of Japanese.

The Camus incident caused renewed alarm in the Settlement. Memories of the murder of Richardson were rekindled, even though Richardson's murder, alone of all the outrages, had been unpremeditated. Everyone carried a revolver, but it was generally conceded that a firearm was of limited use against a planned attack by a skilled swordsman. The only real defence was by travelling in numbers, when one of the party might be able to shoot an assailant before all had been killed; so people travelled in threes and fours in vulnerable locations, even for short journeys.

An agreement was struck between all the diplomatic representatives in Yokohama to protect the foreign community from acts of violence. Armed patrols of from 10 to 30 men with an officer were established for the safety of those who went outside the settlement. The patrols were to choose their own roads from day to day, according to circumstances. Their duty was to protect foreign pedestrians and riders and to arrest any suspicious-looking Japanese, bring them into town and deliver them to the duty Consul for examination. The English and the French furnished a patrol on two days of the week each, the Americans, the Dutch and the Prussians one patrol each week, respectively.

The violence was not confined to foreigners, however. In September that year, a head, apparently just cut off, was found stuck on a wooden pole at the Western end of the *Sanjo* bridge[110]

---

[110] This was the final station on the *tōkaidō*.

in Kyōto. As dawn broke, the grisly object was recognised as the head of Yamatoya Wohe, a leading merchant. Below the head, the following notice was affixed to the pole:

> Genjiro, Hikotaro, Ichi-jiro and Shobé; these four persons were not at home when this occurrence took place, but the Emperor's punishment which they have merited shall be meted out to them hereafter. A few years ago, the *shōgun* made treaties with outside nations without the consent of the Emperor. And these people, taking advantage of these treaties, have been dealing largely with foreigners and made much profit, without considering or caring how much others suffered by reason of their conduct. They have trafficked in copper cash, silk, wax, oil, salt, tea, - in fact in all the staples of the land, in articles necessary for the use of the people of the country. They have bought them up and sent them to Nagasaki, and Kanagawa or Yokohama, and there sold them to foreigners for their own gain. By so doing they have enhanced the price of all articles and all but themselves suffer. Many in the interior are pinched as in time of famine; families can no longer live in one place together; households are broken up and scattered; many have died from sheer want of food. On account of all this, we can no longer remain blind to the sufferings of the people.
>
> It may be asked why we wish to punish people who traded with foreigners under licence from the *shogun's* Government. We make answer that it is because they have forgotten their obligations to their country and to their Sovereign—because of their selfishness and indifference to the welfare of Japan—because, instead of regarding the suffering of their fellow-countrymen and giving heed to the warning of the Emperor, they have associated with the *shōgun's* officers and traded with foreign

BASE CUSTOMS OF FORMER TIMES ARE ABANDONED

barbarians. The *bakufu* officials are below the brute beasts, and the mischief they have compassed is more than we can tell of. We, in our persons, represent the suffering people of *dai nippon* [Great Japan], and in their names we have put Yamatoya Wohe to death. 23rd of 7th moon.

N.B. Take note all those who may disregard the above warning in Osaka, Nagasaki, Joshu, Ida, Nagahama, Oshu, Woji, and in all places, East and West—We the *rōnin* shall watch and investigate the conduct of all merchants, and shall exterminate all those who deal with foreigners. Those who show even the smallest liking for foreign people shall be dealt with even as this Yamatoya Wohe has been dealt with. Whoever owes money to this Yamatoya need not take the trouble of repaying it. Should the Governor of Kyōto make any stir in the matter, debtors ought to make the fact known to us by putting a written notice in this place. And as for the Governor and his minions, they shall be served after the fashion of this Yamatoya Wohe.

Some *rōnin* were less political in their public utterances. In August 1864, it was reported that at Yashu[111], *rōnin* posted placards:

These lands belong to the gods, and are given to men. Whoever tills them is under no obligation to pay any tax to the so-called owners. But for the protection we afford them, the tillers shall pay to us (rōnin) one-half of the customary tax they have hitherto paid.

They were running a naked protection racket.

As a result of the hostilities, Shimazu Saburō had become convinced of the superiority of Western military technology. In November, Iwashita Sajiemon, the Satsuma representative in Edo, went to the British to start negotiations. Discussions

---

[111] Near Tochigi in present-day Japan.

RESPECT AND CONSIDERATION

commenced on 9th November and reached their conclusion, after several interim meetings, on 11th December 1863.

Iwashita opened by saying that Shimazu Saburō believed that he had been harshly dealt with in the seizure and destruction of his steamers at Kagoshima without due notice of the intention of the Admiral to destroy them.

Colonel Neale replied by recounting the whole Kagoshima episode, pointing out that

- the British squadron had proceeded to Kagoshima to negotiate upon the matter of satisfaction required for the murder of Mr. Richardson and the attack upon his companions;
- that during the long delay that had elapsed before sending any reply the squadron had had occasion to shift its anchorage;
- that the reply to his demands, when it eventually arrived, was so unsatisfactory that it rendered some pledge or hostage necessary during further negotiations;
- that with this view, and for this purpose alone, the steamers had been taken. There had not been any intention of either destroying them or of taking them away;
- that the Prince's people had themselves commenced the hostilities by firing upon the British ships without warning.

Therefore the destruction of the steamers was a consequence of their own act at the time.

Iwashita replied that he quite appreciated, after the explanation given, the patience and moderation exercised by Col. Neale and Admiral Kuper on the occasion. This exceedingly polite and moderate response to Col. Neale's remarks, in direct contrast to his own opening statement, perhaps indicates that his instructions were to get the matter settled at any cost.

BASE CUSTOMS OF FORMER TIMES
ARE ABANDONED

The final written statement from Satsuma read as follows:
The agents of the Prince of Satsuma
to Lieutenant-Colonel NEALE.
Yokohama, December 11th, 1863
The money demanded by the British Government having been paid by the officers Of SHIMADZU AWAJI-NO-KAMI, a branch of the family of Satsuma, we hereby promise as follows:
The persons who last autumn, in the eighth month, killed and wounded your countrymen at Namamugi, on the Tokaido, have escaped from that place, and although we have diligently searched for them, their place of abode has not been found out.
And as also some time has passed, it is not possible to state with certainty whether they are still alive, but we will use every diligence in searching for them, and as soon as arrested punish the same with death in the presence of your country's officers.
As a promise for the future we sign this.
(Signed)   SHIKENO KONOSHO
Diplomatic Agent of the Prince of Satsuma
IWASHITA SAJIEMON,
Acting Minister of Satsuma
Countersigned as witnesses to the above promise.
(Signed)   UKAI TAICHI,
Officer of Department for Foreign Affairs of Tycoon's Government
SAITO KINGO,
Assistant Ometsky[112].

The £25,000 had been paid on 11th December, at noon. On his part, Col. Neale agreed in these terms:
British Legation in Japan,

---

[112] Properly, *ometsuke*. This translates as "supervisor", but in the governmental context referred to an official who reported back to the *bakufu* that nothing had been done outside their remit. Akin to the communist commissars of the Soviet Union.

RESPECT AND CONSIDERATION

December 11th, 1863.
The basis of good will and amity being established by the settlement of the demands preferred on the Prince of Satsuma; and the Prince of Satsuma having preferred to the undersigned, her Majesty's Chargé d'Affaires, a request in presence of Officers of the Tycoon, and as a token of friendly feeling re-established, that he would facilitate the desire of the Prince of Satsuma to purchase a ship of war in England, her Britannic Majesty's Chargé d'Affaires does hereby engage to represent such request when formally and specifically preferred to her Majesty's Government, provided that at the period when such request is made or in course of examination, the relations of the Tycoon's Government with Great Britain in general, and the proceedings and disposition of the Prince of Satsuma in particular, are not inimical or directed against the rights acquired by treaties now existing between the Tycoon of Japan, Great Britain, and other friendly States.
Given at Yokohama, this 11th day of Dec., 1863.
(Signed)   " EDWD. ST. JOHN NEALE,
Her Majesty's Chargé d'Affaires

To pay the indemnity, Satsuma borrowed £25,000 from the *bakufu* (which he never repaid since the *bakufu* was shortly to be abolished in the Meiji restoration).

The *bakufu* was relieved that the matter was now settled. They wrote in these terms to Col. Neale:

The Japanese Ministers for Foreign Affairs
to Lieutenant-Colonel NEALE.
Yedo, December 13th, 1863.
We beg to make the following communication to your Excellency.
With respect to the murder which was committed last year upon a British merchant at Namamugi on the Tokaido, the subjects Of MATSUDAIRA SHIURI-

BASE CUSTOMS OF FORMER TIMES ARE ABANDONED

NO-DAIBU and SHIMADZU AWAJI-NO-KAMI, of the family of Satsuma, have lately had an interview with you, and the negotiation was of a peaceful nature, thus affording a proof that the subjects of SHIURI-NO-DAIBU (Satsuma) will search for and punish the murderer, as by their written engagement. The indemnity money was moreover handed over by the subjects of AWAJI-NO-KAMI of the family of Satsuma, and also as a proof of peace, the engagement entered into by you to facilitate the purchase of a man-of-war in terms of the writing was given, and everything ended satisfactorily, which we have fully understood from the communication received from our Government officers who were present.

It gives us great pleasure, as it is a sign of the continuance of a lasting friendship between the two countries.

With respect and consideration.

The 3rd day of the 11th month of the 3rd year of Bunkiu (December 13th, 1863).

(Signed) MIDZUNO IDZUMI-NO-KAMI.
(Signed) ITAKURA SUWO-NO-KAMI.
(Signed) ARIMA TOTOMI-NO-KAMI."

None at the British Legation believed that the perpetrators of the crime would in fact be brought to justice, since it was generally held that Shimazu Saburō himself had given the order to attack Richardson's party. The British would not be wholly satisfied if the swordsmen involved were handed over, for they were merely following orders, or so the British thought. It would be against the British tenets of fair play that the subordinates would forfeit their lives when the principal culprit went scot-free.

The Satsuma envoys handed over their borrowed £25,000 worth of Mexican dollars, and Colonel Neale agreed to make peace once it had been paid, even though the other demands had not been met. Enough destruction was enough, and though it was within British resources to bring British soldiers over from China and, with the naval resources in hand, invade Satsuma and fight their way to Shimazu Saburō, there would be many casualties. It might even provoke the remainder of the *daimyō* to believe that this was a war against Japan, and so enter the fray. If that occurred, trade would end for the foreseeable future.

Satsuma had borrowed the £25,000 from the *bakufu* to hand over to the British. In fact, they never repaid the loan, for they prevaricated repeatedly, and then the *bakufu* fell, and the Emperor took control. All such debts were wiped clean. Thus Satsuma met not a single one of the British demands. They had paid a heavy price, though, in the destruction of a large number of the buildings of Kagoshima.

The British, meanwhile, had correctly assessed that the future rulers of the Japanese nation did not reside within the *shōgun's* stronghold at Edo, but in the remote castle towns of Satsuma and Chōshū, and with the Emperor himself. An alliance, to the benefit of all parties, was thus forged between the British government, the Shimazu clan of Satsuma, and the Mōri clan of Chōshū. Shimazu Saburō negotiated the purchase of metal-clad steam-powered warships from the British, which formed the foundation for the formidable Japanese Navy of later years.

In December that year, eight whole companies of Royal Marines[113] sailed from Plymouth for Japan, aboard HMS *Conqueror*. A contemporary Japanese record says of 25th May:

> This morning the native population of Kanagawa and Yokohama became greatly excited over the appearance in the Bay of a huge three-decked ship with painted ports and a great swarm of men on

---

[113] Properly, the Royal Marine Light Infantry

BASE CUSTOMS OF FORMER TIMES ARE ABANDONED

board. It turned out to be the English transport *Conqueror*, which brings 530 marines to be stationed in Yokohama.

The marines marched crisply through Yokohama, led by the regimental band. This was a show of strength that led many of the *shōgun's* supporters to realise that the days of the *shōgunate* were drawing to a close. Thus was the scene set for the Meiji restoration.

Satsuma representatives paying the indemnity
Illustrated London News 20 Feb. 1864

Chapter 23
Base Customs of Former Times are Abandoned

The bombardment of Kagoshima, subsequently reinforced by the punitive bombardment of Shimonoseki, had a salutary effect on the Japanese ruling classes. The *daimyō* had been exposed as weak in the face of western military and naval power. The Emperor, in dismal mood, wrote to the *shōgun*, saying

> I held a council the other day with my military nobility, but unfortunately inured to the habits of peace, which for more than two hundred years has existed in our country, we are unable to exclude and subdue our foreign enemies by the forcible means of war ... If we compare our Japanese ships of war and cannon to those of the barbarians, we feel certain that they are not sufficient to inflict terror upon the foreign barbarians, and are also insufficient to make the splendour of Japan shine in foreign countries. I should think that we only should make ourselves ridiculous in the eyes of the barbarians[114].

---

[114] American Executive Document, Diplomatic Correspondence, Part 3, 1864-65, p. 502, 2nd Sess. 38th Cong.

RESPECT AND CONSIDERATION

This photograph was taken by Felice Beato in 1864. It shows the two samurai envoys (the chief was Iwashita Sajiemon, possibly the central figure) and their assistants sent by the Satsuma *daimyō* to negotiate a settlement with the British Chargé d'Affaires. The original is a hand–coloured albumen print.

The two swords (the *katana* and the smaller *wakizashi*) of the *samurai* are clearly visible. The envoy at the left is holding a *tantō*.

BASE CUSTOMS OF FORMER TIMES ARE ABANDONED

A later Japanese governmental memorandum said
> Satsuma's eyes were opened since the fight of Kagoshima, and affairs appeared to him in a new light; he changed in favour of foreigners, and thought now of making his country powerful and completing his armaments[115]

It was not long before Satsuma was calling on Colonel Neale to implement his avowed best endeavours to promote appropriate trade between Satsuma and Britain.

The military elite, the *daimyō* and the Imperial and *shōgunate* courts, or at least the thinkers among them, realised that a united front had to be presented to the outside world, in order to deal adequately with it. The bombardments had shaken the Japanese national confidence, leaving them with a realisation that something had to be done. The whole constitution would need to be reformed. In particular, it became evident that:

- The nation needed a centralised form of taxation that was acceptable to the whole population, in place of the arbitrary local taxes that had hitherto applied. A fair, impartial, and thus properly remunerated civil service, responsible to the central Government, would be needed.
- A national police force had to be formed, with common application of common laws throughout the nation. Arbitrary local justice had to be wrested from the hands of the *daimyō*.
- The power of the *han* had to be reduced, to be replaced by a strong central government. This could only be achieved with the cooperation of the *daimyō*, who would have to be given power either regionally or in the central government.

---

[115] American Executive Document, Diplomatic Correspondence, Part 3, 1865-66, p. 233, 1st Sess. 39th Cong.

RESPECT AND CONSIDERATION

Thus it was in March 1868 that delegates from all the *han* met, and within a month they agreed to the following charter oath, drafted by Yuri Kimimasa, Fukuoka Kotei, and Kido Koin:

> A widely-based assembly shall be established, and all matters of state shall be decided by public discussion.
>
> All classes high and low shall unite in vigorously promoting the economy and welfare of the nation.
>
> All civil and military officials as well as the common people shall be permitted to fulfill their aspirations so that there may be no discontent among them.
>
> Base customs of former times shall be abandoned, and all actions shall conform to the principles of international justice.
>
> Knowledge shall be sought throughout the world, and thus shall be strengthened the foundation of the imperial polity.

The constitution based on these ideas was drafted and promulgated by June 1868. The central organ of government was called the *dajokan*, with legislative, executive, and judicial branches. A Justice Department was established for the separation of powers, and the Legislative Department was bicameral with an upper Council and an (ultimately ineffective) lower Assembly made up of *han* representatives. The other departments were Education, Executive, Finance, Foreign Affairs, Public Works, Shinto, and (inevitably) War. All officials were to hold office for no more than four years, and they were subject to income tax at one thirtieth of their earnings.

Within a surprisingly short time, these reforms had been achieved, along with the greatest reform of them all - the Restoration of the Emperor as the fount of government, and the abolition of the *shōgunate*.

The foundations of modern Japan had been set. And the driver for this lay in the chance encounter between a young English merchant and a Japanese nobleman in the sleepy village

BASE CUSTOMS OF FORMER TIMES
ARE ABANDONED

of Namamugi on the *tōkaidō*, on a warm Sunday afternoon in 1862.

But lest we run away with the idea that there was a sudden, complete and wholehearted embracing of the West, here is a popular song from around 1880, translated by English historian George Sansom:

> In the West there is England,
> In the North, Russia.
> My countrymen, be careful!
> Outwardly they make treaties,
> But you cannot tell
> What is at the bottom of their hearts.
> There is a Law of Nations, it is true,
> But when the moment comes, remember,
> The Strong eat up the Weak.

RESPECT AND CONSIDERATION

In the Hollow of a Wave off the Coast at Kanagawa
Hokusai Katsushika (葛飾北斎), (1760-1849)
No. 1 in Hokusai's *ukiyo–e* series "Views of Fuji" 1827

This well–known print received great acclaim when copies first arrived in Europe in the late 1850s. Hokusai created the 'Thirty-Six Views' both as a response to a domestic travel boom and as part of a personal obsession with Mount Fuji.

Chapter 24
Controversy in Britain

Because of the typhoon, and the rolling of the ships, much of the shot intended for Kagoshima's batteries fell in the wood-and-paper town of Kagoshima itself, and set it on fire. When reports of this reached London, it was not fully appreciated that Kuper had only opened fire on the town initially in self-defence and then in retaliation. The reports, too, exaggerated the Japanese casualties and property damage, bad though they were. Many people thought that Kuper's intention in sailing to Kagoshima had been to fire the town. As we have seen, this was not the case, in contradistinction to the later punitive expedition to Shimonoseki. However, attacks on the conduct of the expedition to Kagoshima were widespread.

A debate in the House of Commons on 9th February 1864, on a resolution[116] proposed by Charles Buxton[117], the Liberal Member

---

[116] "That this House, while only imputing to Admiral Kuper a misconception of the duty imposed on him, regrets the burning of the town of Kagoshima, as being contrary to those usages of war which prevail among civilized nations and to which it is the duty and policy of this country to adhere."

[117] Buxton was a wealthy brewer (Truman, Hanbury, Buxton & Co). He followed his father into Parliament, and was proud of his father's advocacy of the abolition of slavery in the British Empire. He commissioned the Buxton Memorial Fountain, now in Victoria Tower Gardens, Westminster: its

RESPECT AND CONSIDERATION

for Maidstone, led to accusations of improper conduct against Kuper by some anti-government members. It was reported that he

> was as warmly defended by a brother flag-officer, who, in the heat of argument, used the word 'damn', and, upon being called to order, created much amusement by apologising for having uttered language which, he said, 'so seldom fell from the lips of sailors'.

Buxton's opening speech, though, was to the point.

> ... my objects in view in bringing this motion before the house are two.
>
> ... There can be no doubt that in the eyes of foreign nations the character of England for humanity had suffered by the act in question. It created a great sensation abroad, and especially in Holland, on account of the connexion of that country with Japan, and, as an American gentleman observed to a friend of his, "when an outcry is made by England about the inhumanity of other nations we must stop her mouth by the one word 'Kagosima'."
>
> ... My hope is that the House of Commons will take the opportunity now offered it of declaring that, whatever rash things might be done by our officers in any part of the world, it was the deliberate resolve of England to treat other nations, whether weak or strong, barbarous or civilized, with unfailing forbearance and humanity. (Hear, hear.)
>
> ... My other object was of still greater importance. This burning of Kagosima, assuming it to be purposefully done, might become a precedent too

---

inscription reads *Erected in 1865 by Charles Buxton MP in commemoration of the emancipation of slaves 1834 and in memory of his father, Sir T Fowell Buxton, and those associated with him: Wilberforce, Clarkson, Macaulay, Brougham, Dr Lushington and others.*

CONTROVERSY IN BRITAIN

easily followed, if not by ourselves, still by others, in future wars.

Mr Layard[118], the Under-Secretary of State for Foreign Affairs, replied.

"..... The hon. Member for Maidstone began by saying he was going to call a number of independent witnesses. Every one must have expected that those witnesses would be persons of a certain standing, whose evidence the House would listen to; but what were they? One was a picture in the *Illustrated London News*. (A laugh.)

..... I do not wish to say anything against that admirable and useful publication, but those who are in the secret know how drawings are made of places at the other end of the world, and I doubt whether any person connected with the *News* was at Kagosima when the engagement took place.[119]"

Austen Henry Layard
GCB

---

[118] Sir Austen Henry Layard GCB, DCL, (1817 - 1894), famed archaeologist, politician, diplomat and statesman.

[119] An editorial in the Illustrated London News of 13th February 1864 protested vigorously that ... "the evidence brought forward by Mr Buxton from our pages was of the highest order, and we had the satisfaction of showing Mr Layard, not only the original sketch, transmitted by Mr Charles Wirgman, our Artist in Japan, but some evidence in unintended but complete corroboration of the accuracy of Mr Wirgman's drawing." However, Sir Rutherford Alcock, refuted this contention in a letter dated 27th April 1864 to Layard, ... "As regards to the *Illustrated London News*, your random shot very nearly hit the mark. And all the flourish of injured innocence, & evidence of the existence of a 'Special Artist' in Japan - but he never saw Kagosima & was not therefore present at the action. The sketches sent to the *Illustrated* & by them engraved, was made by Wirgman here from some sort of sketch made after the action by a mate or midshipman on board the *Euryalus*. So far as the *Illustrated* & its special artist are concerned therefore, your "doubt" whether any person connected with the *News* was at Kagosima when the action took place was perfectly justified by the fact that he was not there at all, before, during or since the action."

RESPECT AND CONSIDERATION

The sentiment of the House was much in Kuper's favour. Among other supportive statements, a government spokesman said,

> Admiral Kuper would have acted improperly if he had aimed his guns at the civilian population deliberately. But that had not been the case, since he had been aiming at the city's fortifications.

There was correspondence in The Times, then a much more prestigious and authoritative journal than it is today. What appeared in its pages *mattered*. These brief extracts from a long letter from Charles Baxton of Cobham are typical:

> I am concerned
> ….. about the second day's fire upon Kagoshima. Most damage was inflicted that day, when its batteries were out of action.
> ….. Firing on the unarmed is a new precedent.
> ….. The Japanese did not even ask Europeans to come to Japan in the first place…

Richard Cobden

Richard Cobden (1804-1865) was a politician and agitator in favour of Free Trade who had spearheaded the successful campaign to abolish the Corn Laws. Palmerston offered him a Cabinet post after his re-election to Parliament as Member for Rochdale in 1859, but he declined, as it would fetter his ability to agitate. He became bitterly opposed to Palmerston's gunboat diplomacy. Here is a lengthy extract from his annual speech to his constituents, delivered on 24th November 1863.

> When I see that Russia is burning Polish villages, I am restrained from even reproaching

them, because I am afraid they will point Japanwards, and scream in our ears the word 'Kagosima!' Now, that word Kagosima brings me to a subject upon which I wish to say one or two words. I see that my noble Friend, the Secretary of the Admiralty[120], who always enters upon the defence of any naval abomination with so much cheerfulness, that he really seems to me to like the task; he has been speaking at a meeting of his constituents, and he alluded to the horrible massacre which took place in Japan, to which, amongst others, I called your attention; and he says it is quite wrong to suppose that our gallant officers ever contemplated to destroy that town of Kagosima, with its 150,000 of rich, prosperous, commercial people—they never intended it—it was quite an accident. Well, unfortunately, he cannot have read the despatch which appeared in the *Gazette*, addressed to his own department, the Admiralty, for it is stated in that despatch that the admiral had himself threatened the Japanese envoys who came on board his vessel the day before the bombardment of that city, that if they did not accede to the demands made upon them, he would next day burn their city. The threat was actually made, and the conflagration was only the carrying out of the threat. But there was another fact in connection with that affair for which I feel greatly ashamed and indignant. It is for the way in which it was managed—the stealthy, shabby, mean way in which it was managed—to make it appear that the Japanese were the aggressors in that affair. Lord Russell's instructions to Admiral Kuper were, that he might go and take this Japanese prince's ships of war, or he might shell his palace, or he might shell his forts. He does not tell him to do all these things; he

---

[120] Lord Clarence Paget

was to go to demand satisfaction, and, in case satisfaction were not given, he suggested to do certain things by way of reprisals, and one of the things he was ordered to do was to take these ships belonging to this prince. Well, the ships were moored—hid, as it were, concealed away—at some distance from the city, and steamers were sent by our admiral to seize these vessels, and they were not within miles of the fort which was firing on our ships. If the admiral had contented himself with trying to seize these ships, which were three steamers of great value, which had been bought from Europeans—had he contented himself, according to his instructions, with trying to seize these steamers, and waited to see if this brought the prince to his senses, there would have been no conflagration. But how did he act? He lashes these steamers alongside his own steamers, and then with his whole fleet goes under the batteries of the Japanese, and waits for several hours; and when the Japanese fire on him, he says that the honour of the British flag required that he should at once commence to bombard the palace, because he had been attacked first.

Now I remember—I remember quite well, in the case of a very analogous proceeding—in the case of our last war with the Burmese, I wrote a digest of the Blue Book giving an account of that terrible war, and to which I gave the title of 'How wars are got up in India'—I remember precisely the same manœuvres were resorted to. Some of the ships of war belonging to the Burmese Government were seized by our naval officers from under their forts, and because they fired on these vessels in the act of carrying off their whole navy, it was said that they commenced the war, and the honour of the British flag required immediately the bombardment of the place. Let us suppose that a French fleet came off

CONTROVERSY IN BRITAIN

Portsmouth, and took three of our ships of war at Spithead, and lashed them alongside their steamers, and then came within range of our forts at Portsmouth; if the commander of these forts had not fired on these ships with all the available resources he had, he would assuredly have been hung up to his own flag-staff on the first occasion. Well, now, is it not deplorable that we English, directly we get east the Cape of Good Hope, lose our morality and our Christianity?—that we resort to all the meanness, and chicanery, and treachery with which we accuse those Oriental people of practising upon us? But we forget what De Tocqueville says in speaking of similar proceedings of ours in India. He says: 'You ought not, as Englishmen and Christians, to lower yourselves to the level of that people. Remember, your sole title to be there at all is because you are supposed to be superior to them.' Do you suppose these things can be done by us Englishmen with impunity—do you think there is no retributive justice that will mete out vengeance to us as a people if we continue to do this; and if there is no compunction on the part of this community?

There is a writer at Oxford University, one who writes bold truths in the most effective manner, who is doing it for the instruction of the next generation of statesmen—that is the Professor of History at Oxford. Mr. Goldwin Smith[121], treating of this very subject, says: 'There is no example, I believe, in history, from that of Imperial Rome down to that of Imperial France, of a nation which has trampled out the rights of others, but that ultimately forfeited its own.' Do you think those maxims, which we tolerate in the treatment of three, four, or five millions of

---

[121] Regius Professor of Modern History, Oxford University, 1858-1868. Renowned as "The Controversialist" on political issues.

people in the East—do you think that they will not turn back to curse us in our own daily lives, and in our own political organization? You have India; you have acquired India by conquest, and by means which no Englishman can look back upon with satisfaction. You hold India; your white faces are predominating and ruling in that country; and has it ever occurred to you at what cost you rule? We have lately had a report of the sanitary state of the army in India; why, if you take into account the losses we sustain in that country by fever, by debauchery, by ennui, and by climate; if you take into account the extra number of deaths and invalids in the army and civil service, in consequence of the climate, you are holding India at a cost—if I may be permitted to use the term—of a couple of battles of Waterloo every year. Is there not a tremendous responsibility accompanied with this, that you are to tolerate your lawless adventurers to penetrate not only into China, but in Japan, in your name?

There were various petitions from a large number of concerned groups around the country. There was, for instance, a public meeting in Margate on 11th January 1864 chaired by the Vicar, which passed on to the Foreign Secretary its resolution:

> In the opinion of this meeting, the bombardment and entire destruction of the great City of Kagosima, in Japan, was an act of barbarous cruelty, and of most questionable policy and that the conduct of the British Agents in employing Armed Force to destroy a large number of innocent lives, and to reduce the homes of 180,000 people to a heap of ashes, was unworthy of the representatives of a Civilized and Christian Nation, and is deserving the several censures of this British Government and People.

CONTROVERSY IN BRITAIN

Not to be outdone, the inhabitants of nearby Ramsgate held a meeting on 13th January and communicated to the Foreign Secretary:

> It was resolved that this meeting has heard with deep regret and dissatisfaction of the employment of a British Naval Squadron to bombard the City of Kagosima & the consequent destruction of the homes of 150,000 people - an act calculated greatly to prejudice the interests of Christianity and civilization in Japan.

The Spectator[122] was appalled by events at Kagoshima:

> And now we are told, not by special correspondents fond of sensation, or ill-informed "eye-witnesses", but by the officials concerned, that Earl Russell, who denounces Mouravieff[123], himself ordered a palace to be destroyed at the risk of everybody in it - for that is what "shelling" amounts to - because its owner then fifty miles away, had committed an assassination, that a British Chargé d'Affaires had commanded the destruction of an immense Oriental city, against which no charge was so

---

[122] A weekly political magazine, founded in 1828 to provide a voice for "educated radicalism". Its new editor and part-owner, Richard Holt Hutton, led the journal towards a more conservative position, and became an opponent of Gladstone and his Irish Home rule policies.

[123] Count Mikhail Nikolayevich Muravyov (1796-1866) was a reactionary Russian imperial statesman, opposed, among other things, to emancipation of the serfs. He was Governor of Northwestern Krai (now Lithuania and part of Belarus) when the January Uprising, a Polish-Lithuanian protest against Russian rule, took place in 1863. Muravyov savagely put down the rebellion, deporting some 9000 people to remote Siberia, hanging 127 rebel leaders, and burning countless villages, rendering their inhabitants homeless. Consequently, he became known as the "hangman of Vilnius". Despite liberal condemnation from the rest of Europe, he was ennobled by the Tsar and held in high esteem by the Russian aristocracy.

much as alleged, and which had not received a moment's warning, and that a British admiral considers the deed one to be described in a tone of triumphant exultation.

... no doubt that the destruction of the town was either intentional, and carried out as the easiest and most complete method of punishing Japanese insolence in firing upon a British squadron, or was one of those "untoward accidents" which those who produce them do not even affect to regret. As yet the balance of evidence inclines to the former view ...

... Colonel Neale repeats and exults in the [destruction of the town of Kagoshima], and throughout the despatches there is not a word of regret over the "hard necessity" which had involved the vast peaceful city in the fate of its batteries, and the prince's palace. The "town" - i.e., the homes of a population nowhere estimated at less than 150,000 - is coolly reckoned up among the property destroyed, and admiral and chargé d'affaires alike demand the approval of her majesty's Government.

... Whether Admiral Kuper be innocent or guilty, innocent of all but the heartlessness of his despatches, or guilty of firing upon an unarmed town, the broad fact will still remain. Great Britain in order to punish an individual assassin, - for the Tycoon had apologized and paid for the official wrong, - has fired a vast and peaceful city, destroyed the commercial sources of wealth of a whole province, slaughtered human beings by the thousand - for thousands must have perished in that conflagration which, says the admiral who produced it, "burnt with unabated ardour for forty-eight hours" - and reduced a population equal to that of a first-class European city to the certainty of beggary and the imminent risk of starvation.

There may be excuses to be made for all those upon the spot. Colonel Neale may have had private instructions which he has misinterpreted. Seamen with shell whistling through their rigging and their comrades falling fast are not expected to reason with philosophic coolness, or even much humanity. But if Englishmen sitting in comfort at home, chuckling over the vast expenditure they have incurred in order to avoid the very suffering they have inflicted on the Japanese, sanction the burning of Kagosima, their remonstrances against cruelty, hitherto so operative, must cease for very shame. Opinion will cease to be executive on the one subject on which it is unquestionably righteous and beneficial. Who listens to gospels preached by men whose hands are stained with blood? Even Berg[124] did not bombard Warsaw because his spy was assassinated, even Mouravieff does not erase cities to punish a single murderer.

And abroad, the *New York Times* ran a leader on 24th November 1863 under the headline "British Barbarity":

The crime, which is to stand forever as almost first on the black list of fearful cruelties committed by the strong against the weak, is the recent burning and shelling of an unprepared Japanese city, containing 180,000

---

[124] Count Fredrik Wilhelm Rembert Berg was a Russian Field Marshal who repressed the Polish element of the 1863 January Uprising,

> inhabitants, against whom there was no war, by
> the British admiral.

Clearly, the reports of the extent of destruction at Kagoshima were inconsistent. In fact, we now know that just five civilian inhabitants of Kagoshima had been killed, in addition to an undeclared number of combatants, so the Spectator, at least, was wildly wrong in its surmises. There is no reliable estimate of civilian or *samurai* wounded. The highest estimate of damage was that a third of the town had been destroyed by shot, shell and incendiary. There were approximately 180,000 inhabitants, so we might guess that up to 60,000 had been rendered homeless. It would be small comfort to the people who lost their homes to reflect that the very reason the buildings were so inflammable was that wood-and-paper is relatively easily replaced, which it was, frequently, in the wake of the earthquakes and volcanic eruptions with which they were familiar.

Having vented a righteous anger, the opponents of gunboat diplomacy and military conquest subsided rather. Nothing could be undone, anyway. Better to recognise the facts and start from where we actually are than from where we would prefer to be.

CHAPTER 25

THE BRITISH SQUADRON IN JAPAN

From the late eighteenth century until the beginning of the First World War in 1914, Britain ruled the waves. The Royal Navy was the largest, best-equipped, best trained, most powerful navy in the world. Since Admiral Nelson's victories over Napoleon's fleets - the battle of Cape St Vincent[125], the stunning victory at Aboukir Bay (known as the battle of the Nile), Copenhagen[126], and finally Trafalgar, not only was Britain's naval supremacy secured and acknowledged, but the British nation itself had an almost mythical belief in the righteousness and invincibility of Britannia's rule. It was the Royal Navy that serviced and protected the vast British Empire. It was the Royal Navy that backed up Britain's trading and diplomatic interests.

The Royal Navy was, after all, Her Britannic Majesty's Navy.

The growing importance of trade with China in the early parts of Queen Victoria's reign convinced the Royal Navy to

---

[125] Nelson was only a Commodore in this action, but his brilliant tactical appreciation and seamanship, together with his inspirational personal heroism brought about the British victory over the French and Spanish fleets. He was promoted Rear Admiral, and appointed Knight Commander of the Most Honourable Military Order of the Bath for his exemplary actions.

[126] Nelson was promoted Vice Admiral of the White three months before Copenhagen, and created a Viscount after the action.

RESPECT AND CONSIDERATION

send a permanent fleet to China and the East Indies. The fleet had various ports that they used as bases: Hong Kong, Malacca, Shanghai, among others. The China station also looked after British interests in Japan, following the treaties of the 1850s.

In September 1862, Rear Admiral[127] Augustus Leopold Kuper CB sailed into Yokohama aboard his flagship, HMS *Euryalus*. To ensure parity with the French, whose senior naval officer in the Far East was a Vice Admiral, Kuper was given acting Vice Admiral's rank. So his ensign, a white one with a red cross, for Kuper was Rear Admiral of the White[128] (rather than of the Red or of the Blue - the three arbitrary divisions of the Royal Navy up to 1864), bore a single red ball marker in the upper left quadrant, and flew proudly from the foremast of Euryalus.

---

[127] When in command of the fleet and using standard sailing-fleet formations, the Admiral was in the middle of the three rows of ships. His deputy, the Vice Admiral, was in the front row of ships, nearest to the enemy, and the third-ranking Admiral - the Rear Admiral - commanded the back row of ships.
[128] During the seventeenth century, the Royal Navy grew large, and administratively had to be broken down into "squadrons". The Admiral's squadron flew a red ensign, the Vice Admiral's a white ensign, and the Rear Admiral's a blue one. The Navy continued to grow until the red, the white and the blue were each commanded by an Admiral, supported by Vice Admirals and Rear Admirals. Their titles became Admiral of the Red, and so on. Promotion was by filling dead men's shoes, as there were only nine Admirals in the whole of the Navy. The ranking structure developed thus (in descending order of rank): Admiral of the Fleet, Admiral of the White, Admiral of the Blue, Vice Admiral of the Red, Vice Admiral of the White, Vice Admiral of the Blue, Rear Admiral of the Red, Rear Admiral of the White, Rear Admiral of the Blue. While C-in-C of the China Station, then, Kuper ranked fifth in the Navy (as had Nelson before him). It was a very senior and responsible position. The colour system was abolished in the 1864 naval reforms. Kuper finished his days as a full Admiral, larded with honours and decorations.

THE BRITISH SQUADRON IN JAPAN

With him on board were *Euryalus'* Captain, James Josling; her Commander, George S. Parkin; her Master, William Parker and some 510 other officers and men. All of these officers had been appointed to *Euryalus* in January and February 1862. Immediately after her arrival in Yokohama, George Parkin was replaced by Edward Wilmot as Commander. Also on board was the ship's surgeon, David L. Morgan F.R.C.S., whose surgeon's log provides interesting, if grim, reading. Extracts will be found elsewhere in this work.

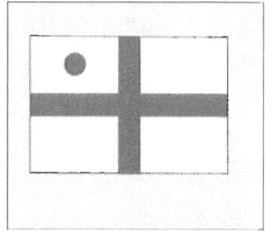

Ensign of the Vice-Admiral of the White

Accompanying Euryalus in August 1863 were a number of other Royal Naval warships. It is interesting that two of the officers went on to attain high naval rank. The Kagoshima action was a good career move. Commander Fox Boxer retired as a Rear Admiral in 1884, and Captain John Borlase retired as a Vice Admiral in 1878.

The Captain was responsible for the ship and made the ultimate decisions on board: the supplies carried, discipline, shore leave, where she should go, how and when to engage in battle, and so on. Only larger ships merited a Captain; lesser ones had Commanders, and the smallest had Lieutenants. The Commander was responsible for sailing the ship. He responded to the captain's orders (if there was one), set the sail, gave orders to the engineers, and re-coaled and re-watered the ship as far as the engines were concerned. The Master was at this time a non-commissioned officer responsible for navigation. He planned the course to the destination required by the Captain, and liaised with the Commander as to the speed of the vessel. In the Navy reforms of 1864, Masters were given the commissioned rank of Commander, in recognition of their special skills. Master Parker was commended for his skill in sailing *Euryalus* so close

RESPECT AND CONSIDERATION

to the shore during the action at Kagoshima, in difficult sea conditions.

I show the squadron in tabular form:

| Royal Naval Vessels at Yokohama August 1863, used in the Kagoshima Expedition ||||||||
	Euryalus	Pearl	Coquette	Argus	Perseus	Havoc	Racehorse
Launch year	1853	1854	1855	1849	1861	1860	c. 1856
Ship Type	Frigate	Corvette	Gun Vessel	Sloop	Corvette	Gun Boat	Gun Vessel
Class			Vigilant		Albacore	Dapper	Cormorant
Size (tons)	2371	1469	677		955	232	695
Horsepower	400 HP	300 HP	200 HP	300 HP	200HP	200 HP	200 HP
Number of major guns (excluding carronades)	35	21	4	6	17	4	3
Propulsion	Screw	Screw	Screw	Paddle	Screw	Screw	Screw
Rear Admiral	Augustus L Kuper 8/2/62	Kuper was Acting Vice Admiral during his command of the Far East Fleet					
Captains	John James Stephens Josling 10/2/62	John Borlase CB 23/8/59					
Commanders	Edward Wilmot 1/8/63		John Hobhouse Inglis Alexander 4/4/62	Lewis James Moore 7/8/62	Augustus John Kingston		Charles Richard Fox Boxer 16/5/62
Lieutenant in command						George Poole	
Masters	William Hennessey Parker 24/1/62	John TC Webb 28/3/59	William Long 4/4/62	Frederick Piper 16/8/62	Robert Gilpin 18/1/62		Bernard B Dowling 17/5/62
Surgeons	David L Morgan 23/1/62	Frederick F Morgan 23/8/59	William G Hill 21/4/67	Thomas B Purchas MD 6/8/62			James E Fawcett 20/5/62

CHAPTER 26

HMS *Euryalus*

HMS *Euryalus* had been built in 1853 at Chatham dockyard. She was a fourth rate[129] steam-powered screw-propelled frigate, with three masts for her longer sailing voyages[130]. She cost the Admiralty £77423 by the time she was ready for commissioning in March 1854. In 1857, she was refitted at a cost of £19130.

Euryalus was 212 ft long (64·62 metres), with an extreme breadth of 50' 2" (15·29 metres). Her Penn engines were two-

---

[129] The rating system, in the days of sail, had six "rates" of ships, depending on their displacement, number of guns and complement of men. Euryalus was exceptionally large for a frigate, at 2371 tons "builder's measure", and her complement was 510-515 men (the standard complements varied from time to time). Her armament was relatively light, however. The only surviving first-rate ship of the nineteenth century Royal Navy is HMS *Victory*, still in commission.

[130] The first steam-engined Royal Naval vessel, HMS *Comet*, had been launched in 1821. Gradually, the new technology ships came into use, all with paddlewheels for propulsion. In the 1830s, screw-propelled vessels were designed. A famous tug-of-war in the mid 1840s between the screw-propelled *Rattlesnake* and the paddlewheeled *Alecto* validated the Admiralty's earlier decision to go for screw propulsion. The engines were useful in getting into and out of harbour, and for manoeuvring during battle, but they were not efficient enough in the middle of the nineteenth century to sustain the ship on long voyages. Thus ships continued to have masts and sail until the first mastless Royal Naval vessel was launched: HMS *Devastation*, unveiled in 1871.

cylinder, nominally rated at 400HP, and achieving 56-60 rpm. In her annual trials in July 1861 at Stokes Bay[131], she achieved 10·036 knots, with her standard 17'2" (5·23 metres) diameter screw.

H.M.S. Euryalus, drawn during her sea trials in 1853

On her main deck she carried 18 muzzle-loading 8-inch guns, each nine feet long (2·74 metres) and weighing 3.25 tons (3302 Kg). There were 4 breech-loading 100-pounder Armstrong guns, ten feet (3·04 metres) long and each weighing 4.05 tons (4115 Kg). On her upper deck, she carried 8 40-pounder Armstrong breech-loaders, 10 feet and 1.6 tons (1626 Kg). And on her forecastle, there were 4 8-inch breech loaders and one Armstrong 100-pounder breech loader[132]. The muzzle-loaded guns could achieve a rate of fire of three rounds in 5 minutes. The Armstrong guns took 50 seconds between rounds. There was, however, a major problem with the breech-loaders and their higher rate of fire. They tended to overheat, causing premature explosions before the breech mechanism had been closed, with devastating consequences for the gun crew.

---

[131] Between Lee on Solent and Gosport, Hampshire.
[132] The shells actually weighed 110 pounds and were 6" in diameter. The gun was officially designated "special gun of large calibre", weighed 65 cwt., and was charged with 12 lbs of gunpowder. It had not fared well in tests, being unable to penetrate 4" armour plate at even a very short range of 50 yards.

HMS *EURYALUS*

Armstrongs were removed from Royal Naval vessels in or around 1864 and not reintroduced until 1879, when improvements had been made to the design of the breech mechanism to deal with the problem.

There were carronades, too, but they were never counted in the firepower reckoning of any ship. A carronade was a low-velocity naval gun, used in ship-to-ship engagements at short range. The relatively low muzzle velocity of its iron shot caused much lethal splintering of the wooden structures of the target ships, and many sailors were killed or severely wounded by splinters. The Royal Navy nicknamed the carronade "the Smasher". It was shorter than other naval guns, but came in a variety of sizes of projectile, from 12 to 68 pounds. Because a carronade typically weighed less than a third of a long gun of the same calibre, it could be mounted on the upper decks without causing the instability that heavier guns would cause. It was never counted in the rating system for ships. *Euryalus* had carronades weighing a total of 24.9 tons, but this cannot accurately be translated into the number of guns. As a guess, it may be in the vicinity of 16 guns.

The calibre of a gun was the ratio between its bore (internal diameter of the barrel) and barrel length. Guns were generally referred to in terms of their poundage. This was a rounded calculation of the weight of a sphere of lead of the same diameter as the bore of the gun. The formula for poundage is

$$P \approx \left(\frac{B}{2}\right)^3 \times \pi \times \left(\frac{4}{3}\right) \times 0 \cdot 4097222$$

where B is the bore of the gun and .4097222 is the density of lead in pounds per cubic inch. We can therefore construct the following table:

RESPECT AND CONSIDERATION

Barrel Diameter in inches	Poundage	Length of Barrel in inches	Calibre
5	25		
6	40	120	20
7	68		
7¾	100	108	13.9
8	110		

The muzzle-loaded guns were smoothbore weapons, with a range of about one and a half miles. The 100-pounder Armstrong guns had a rifled barrel, so making them much more accurate; their range was about two and a half miles. The 40-pounder Armstrongs, again with a rifled barrel, had a range of a little over one and a half miles. The projectiles fired were both shot (balls of iron or stone) and shell (containing explosive, with shrapnel, or with molten iron[133] as an incendiary device). Thus *Euryalus* carried 35 guns, with a combined rate of fire of about 40 projectiles per minute. A total weight of 2600 pounds of shot and shell could be delivered every minute, and the crews could sustain this rate of fire for some time, giving a theoretical total of 70 tons per hour, although this was, of course, never achieved. *Euryalus* carried 76 tons of shot and shell.

In her annual appraisal at the end of 1863, *Euryalus* was said to ride easy at her anchor, and to carry her lee ports well. However, she rolled "uneasy and deep" in the troughs of the sea. She "stayed slowly and well", and she "wore slowly". All of this added up to a ship that sailed well but wallowed about, provoking sea-sickness in those who were prone to it. Her condition was summed up as "a well built strong ship", but with

---

[133] There was a special furnace in the engine-room for melting metal to be loaded into projectiles. These were very effective in setting fire to wooden vessels.

HMS *EURYALUS*

some sign of weakness in her after stern post. Close hauled with smooth water under whole or single reefed topsails and topgallant sails, she sailed at 6½ knots, and before the wind, in a gale, she managed 12½ knots.

She carried supplies and provisions for around three months at sea. Some of the provisions included:

- 3247 8-lb pieces of beef
- 6502 4-lb pieces of pork
- 11 weeks' supply of bread in 468 1-cwt bags
- 13216 gallons of sweet drinking-water
- 800 gallons of wine and spirits
- 400 gallons of vinegar and lemon juice
- 10974 lbs of sugar, tea and cocoa.

Altogether, *Euryalus* normally carried provisions for 98 days, bread for 77 days, spirit for 98 days, and water for just 20 days.

The daily food allowance for sailors in the 1824 Regulations for Her Majesty's Service at Sea provided around 4200 Calories a day. The ration was

- Bread[134], 1 lb.
- Beer[135], 1 gallon
- Cocoa, 1 oz., Tea, ¼ oz.
- Sugar, 1½ oz.
- Fresh Meat, 1 lb.
- Fresh vegetables, ½ lb.

The Captain carried five tons of his own stores. In addition to furniture and clothing, he had his own bath and brought finer

---

[134] Bread in the sailing navy was in the form of a ship's biscuit or hard tack, and needed to be softened with water before eating.

[135] Beer did not keep well and once the supply was exhausted, a daily ration of one pint of wine was issued. If there was neither beer nor wine, half a pint of spirits was issued. This was 95.5º proof (very strong) rum diluted with three parts of water. It was a serious disciplinary offence for a sailor to accumulate several days' spirit ration: he had to drink it on the day of issue, to prevent dangerous drunken binges.

RESPECT AND CONSIDERATION

foodstuffs and alcoholic drinks than were supplied to the rest of the crew. The wardroom, too, brought six tons of furniture, bedding and special foodstuffs.

The Purser ran a shop on board. The Purser was a civilian, and was not paid a salary by the Navy. He made his money from the monopoly sale of commodities to crew members. He was responsible for victualling the ship and issuing provisions to the cooks and crew. He was permitted by custom and practice to account for stores at the rate of 14 ounces to the pound, to allow for 12½% wastage. If he looked after the stores well, the extra two ounces in the pound went, with a nod and a wink from the Admiralty, into his pocket. He could make a big profit and so had to lodge a surety with the Admiralty (£1400 for a First-Rate ship down to £400 for a sixth-rate) to ensure that he conducted himself honestly. On the other hand, any losses were down to him. It was not uncommon for Pursers to become bankrupt. Pursers were regarded with suspicion, even hatred, by the sailors on board, who believed that "14 ounces in the pound" cheated them of proper value for money. In *Euryalus'* inventory, they carried 3½ tons of "Purser's slops" (ready-made clothing for seamen), soap, candles, tobacco and necessaries. An Ordinary Seaman earned £22/16/3d a year, and an Able Seaman £28/17/11d, and could spend some of this at the Purser's store. A sailor might be fortunate enough, if his ship won Prize Money, to be awarded a small fortune, perhaps a year's pay or even more.

Prize Money was awarded by the Admiralty Court. If it were a merchantman that had been legitimately captured, then the sale price of the ship and its cargo was awarded to the Ship's Company; if it was a warship, the Admiralty would purchase it and its contents at a fair price; and there was "head money" of £5 for every enemy sailor captured alive. The Prize Money was distributed by a system of "eighths". The Captain received two

HMS *EURYALUS*

eighths, but had to give one third of that to his Flag Officers (Admirals). The wardroom officers (the Commander, Captains of Marines (if any), Lieutenants, Master and Surgeon) received one eighth between them. The junior officers (Lieutenants of Marines (if any), Admiral's Secretary, Principal Warrant Officers, Masters Mates, and Chaplain) shared one eighth. And the remaining four eighths were shared between midshipmen, inferior Warrant Officers, principal Warrant Officers Mates, Marine Sergeants and the rest of the crew in proportion to their regular pay. Huge fortunes were sometimes amassed by (literally) fortunate senior officers. Nelson's commanding officer at the battle of the Nile, Sir Hyde Parker (1739-1807), was reported to have accumulated £200,000 through Prize Money when he was in command in the West Indies[136] (although the pickings were much leaner in the post-Nelsonian Navy).

Seawater was used for cleaning the decks, and *Euryalus* carried two tons of "Holy stones and sand" for this purpose. *Euralyus* carried 230 tons of coal for her boilers, together with a little under 1½ tons of wood to ignite them.

When Euryalus sailed fully laden on foreign service - "with as much provisions stores and coals as she can conveniently stow" - her draught of water forward was 20 ft. 5 ins., and her draught aft was 23 feet.

---

[136] Equivalent to some £6·4 million in 2011 terms.

CHAPTER 27
WHO WON AT KAGOSHIMA?

Satsuma claimed a victory because the British squadron departed the scene without sending any landing party ashore. Britain claimed a victory because they inflicted enormous visible damage on the town, and put several batteries out of action.

The casualty lists at Kagoshima do not help us very much to decide on the victor. There were thirteen British dead and possibly five Japanese civilians killed. The low figure for Japanese casualties may be explained by the fact that Shimazu Hisamitsu, exercising his powers as regent *daimyō*, ordered that old men, women and children should be evacuated from the town on 14th August, as a precaution. The true figure for *samurai* casualties was never disclosed. As several batteries were hit by naval shot and shell, we would expect some casualties among those manning them. But no reliable figures are available.

The real victory at Kagoshima, and the later Shimonoseki bombardment reinforced the fact, was in defeating the old Japanese way of thinking, and the advancement of the new. The bombardments changed the character of Japanese relations with the West. Demonstrations of western naval and military might had proved enough to convince the majority of *samurai*, even the "men of spirit" opposed to the west, that something more than

WHO WON AT KAGOSHIMA?

personal self-sacrifice would be required if Japan were to challenge the unequal treaties with any expectation of success. Calls for the immediate use of force began to recede.

Instead, plans were made to acquire the most up-to-date western weapons and the skills to manufacture them. Satsuma had been impressed by the firepower and accuracy of the Armstrong guns, notwithstanding their unfortunate tendency to fire prematurely, to the great detriment of the gun crew. They tried, unsuccessfully, to buy some.

Within a very short time, the *bakufu*, the Chōshū *han* and the Satsuma *han* (with a sprinkling of Tosa) all sent students abroad to acquire technological, naval, military and governmental skills. In addition, Satsuma turned to Britain for diplomatic support - with equivocal results - and signed contracts with a Belgian entrepreneur to develop the commercial trade in Japanese produce that would pay for ships and guns from Thomas Glover and others. The *bakufu* strengthened its links with France for similar purposes.

It was a win-win-win situation, although, as so often, the trade in arms ends up in their use for political ends. So it was, here, with the post-restoration "Boshin" civil war, fought ultimately between old-school *samurai* under Saigō Takamori and the modern Imperial forces, equipped with the latest military technology. Saigō's forces were, unsurprisingly, comprehensively defeated. *That* was no contest.

Ironically, he was comprehensively defeated by the new conscript Imperial army, which his brother Saigō Tsugumichi had been instrumental in forming, based on his findings from his mission to France and Germany in 1869. Modern warfare triumphed over the old methods - and weaponry - of the *samurai*. Saigō Takamori's death in battle, though, was seen as heroic in the historic Japanese scale of values. He remains a national hero to this day.

CHAPTER 28
DISTRIBUTION OF THE SATSUMA COMPENSATION

Satsuma, as we have seen, eventually paid £25000 to Britain to compensate the three surviving victims of the Namamugi outrage, and the family of Charles Lenox Richardson. There was correspondence on behalf of the four victims with Lord Russell.

On 15th December 1862, Charles Clarke's uncle, Mr R Few of Covent Garden, London, wrote to the Foreign Secretary. He says that his nephew had gone to Shanghai in the summer of 1860 to act for "an influential House" at Shanghai. There, he had taken charge of a Battery of Volunteer Artillery against the Taipings[137].

---

[137] The Taiping rebellion (1850 - 1864) was a curious and extraordinarily bloody one. At least 20 million people died, and maybe as many as 30 million. The "God Worshippers" were led by Hung Hsiu-ch'üan (revised Pinyin: Hóng Xiùquán), whose mission, he said, came from God. It was to establish a new "heavenly kingdom" (with Hóng - need you ask? - as King) by sweeping aside the demon-worshipping Manchu (Qing) dynasty. Hóng had had a revelation that he was the brother of Jesus. Initially, he had remarkable military success. In August 1860, he made an assault - unsuccessfully - on the western settlement of the city of Shanghai. In February 1861 Admiral Hope and the British forces, supported by French troops and an irregular force under Frederick Townshend Ward put the Taipings to flight, for the first time in the rebellion. It seems, according to a letter from Admiral Hope, that a militia had also been raised among the western settlement in Shanghai. Hóng died from food poisoning from contaminated vegetables (or possibly eating poisonous

DISTRIBUTION OF THE COMPENSATION

While in England, he had been a Lieutenant in a Volunteer Rifle Corps. In July 1861, he had gone to Japan to represent the American House of Messrs Augustine Heard & Co.

Mr Few went on to describe the events of 14th September, and to list the several reasons why it was a particularly heinous crime:

- It was on a highway that foreigners had treaty rights to use
- The four victims were unarmed, innocuous and included a lady among their party
- No warning of the attack was given
- The wounds inflicted were severe: in particular, Clarke was most seriously wounded by a sword cut, "which had nearly severed his arm at the Shoulder, which will thus be disabled for life".

But more serious was his understanding that

> the Representative of Her Majesty in the Colony (Col. Neale) refused, in the first instance, to take any steps whatever for the protection or relief of the party, even when the fate of the three Gentlemen was unknown and further refused when the survivors reached Yokohama to take any action for the apprehension of the offenders or for the redress of the sufferers, tho' urged to do so by the British Consul, and it would seem, by every other Military and Naval Officer on the Station, English and French, as well as by every Foreign Resident in the Colony, including the Representative of the United States.

---

leaves picked from waste land) in the besieged city of Nanjing as his rebellion collapsed. The Qing dynasty was much weakened by the rebellion and finally collapsed in 1912, superseded by the Republic of China. The Taipings purchased their arms and ammunition from the western trading houses in Shanghai throughout the 14 years of the rebellion. Never let the opportunity for profit pass by!

RESPECT AND CONSIDERATION

However, Few was pleased to report that according to a letter received from Japan (from one of the Yokohama committee of residents who initially castigated Neale for inaction) to say that

> every care is being taken of (Clarke), as the estimation in which he is held by all who know him so fully demands; his courage and bearing throughout the whole affair it is hard to speak too highly of.

But, says Few,

> The burden of the letter, thus quoted, is an earnest entreaty that every effort be made to secure the <u>immediate</u> attention of Her Majesty's Government to the transaction, and to the necessity of <u>prompt</u> and decisive measures being taken for demanding redress for this outrage, with a view to prevent a repetition of the same with, too probably, greatly increased enormities.

Few now comes to the point of his letter:

> On the part of my Nephew therefore, I have very respectfully, but earnestly, to enquire, "Whether your Lordship has taken, or is about to take, decisive measures for, in the first place obtaining from the Japanese Government full redress to the sufferers for the severe injuries they have sustained; and, in the second place, securing the English Residents at Japan from all liability to a recurrence of like treatment. Unless, my Lord, both redress for the past, so far as is practicable, and a guarantee against like treatment hereafter, be secured to the English Residents in Japan, and that without delay, the Japanese will doubtless impute inaction to either indifference or timidity on the part of the British Government, and it will be hopeless to make further efforts to establish trade relations between the two Countries to any larger extent. Neither will it be any guarantee to the English Merchants at large if the course of action,

DISTRIBUTION OF THE COMPENSATION

reported in the papers to have been adopted by Her Majesty's Chargé d'Affaires, Col. Neale, (assuming such report to be correct) is not to receive the marked reprehension of Her Majesty's Government: unless very satisfactorily explained and justified.

I should add that, in the private letter received from Japan, the writer says - alluding to Col. Neale - "as one of the Committee I can say that, in our representation of the whole affair going by this Vessel to Earl Russell, much has been omitted for fear it might be considered at the Foreign Office as of a personal nature. There is no doubt that, had the authorities aided the Community as they wished, we should have secured the assassins. When I say 'the authorities' I mean simply 'the English'; both the French Minister and Count d'Harcourt deserve our thanks for their action throughout."

It is some satisfaction to find that this lamentable transaction, and particularly the reported refusal of the British Chargé d'Affaires to aid the sufferers, has called forth in England the same strong expression of indignation, which were on all sides uttered at Japan, and the question among Commercial Men at home in reference to this event is, whether when an Englishman becomes a Resident in another Country, with whose Government friendly relations have been established by the British Government, he is to give up all claim to protection by England of his life and property, however studiously he may comply with the Laws and Customs of the Country where he is residing.

That your Lordship will not fail to protect the English residents in Japan and elsewhere, as Her Majesty's Secretary of State for Foreign Affairs, I cannot doubt; and, in thus addressing your Lordship, I venture to hope, that you will be pleased to give me such a reply as shall assure Mr Clarke and his family, that this outrage will be inquired into, and the rights of Her Majesty's subjects upheld, <u>without delay or hesitation;</u> a communication will be of the greatest comfort to the British Community at Japan, who at present are under the painful misgiving, that for some unknown reason the Japanese are not to be interfered with, until even much greater excesses have been committed, than those I now complain of.

In summary, then, Few was asking for compensation for his nephew, and particularly a strong military response against the Japanese.

On the same date that Few had written, a letter was sent from Wigan by Thomas Marshall on behalf of his brother. His letter is more succinct, though less clearly written[138] than Few's:

> My object in writing, is to ask, that such [steps] may be taken by Her Majesty's Government, as may [seem right] to your Lordship, for the purpose of 1st bringing the offenders to condign punishment, 2nd obtaining pecuniary compensation for [the victims]. 3rd Making such further general arrangements as may be necessary to prevent the recurrence of such acts in future.

An equally succinct and very polite letter was sent on 16th December from JO Borradaile of 10 George Yard, Lombard Street, London:

> As the Brother-in-Law of Mrs. Borradaile, who was one of the party upon whom a murderous attack was made by the Japanese, in the neighbourhood of Yokohama, on the fourteenth of September last, (of which your Lordship has, doubtless received official notification,) permit me, in the absence of my Brother in China, to enquire whether Her Majesty's Government has taken any steps to obtain redress for the injuries received, and to express the hope, that an

---

[138] Doubtful words and phrases are in [square brackets]

DISTRIBUTION OF THE COMPENSATION

investigation has been instituted into the alleged neglect of Col. Neale, Her Majesty's Chargé d'Affaires, to take any proceedings in aid of the party attacked, and the circumstances upon which he may rely in justification of his conduct.

These three letters echoed the poignant letter sent by Charles Richardson senior on 5th December, quoted earlier. On 3rd February 1864, he wrote again to Lord Russell. By now, Richardson senior had prospered in business and moved to "Belle Vue" at Tunbridge Wells. He refers to a note from the Permanent Secretary in November, which stated that £10,000 compensation was to be awarded. Richardson Senior had run up against a bureaucratic wall. He had furnished all the voluminous proofs required by the Treasury Solicitors but no compensation had so far been paid. He asked that settlement should be permitted to proceed, adding:

> that @ my age, that of 69, makes me all the more anxious to have my affairs completed, and, but in a great measure for this circumstance, I should not have ventured to address your Lordship on the present occasion.

Russell replied by return that he was enquiring into the matter. On that same day, Hammond, the Permanent Secretary, wrote to the Treasury:

> His Lordship is of the opinion that the fair arrangement would be that the sum of £10,000 so awarded should be invested in such resources that the interest of the whole amount should be received by the Father & Mother of the late Mr Richardson during their joint & separate lives; & that after the death of both, the money should be divided equally between his sisters who may then be living, provision being made that the children of any sister who may die in the meantime should receive their

> mother's share, which in that case should be equally apportioned between them.

No note of the distribution of the remaining £15,000 to Messrs Marshall and Clarke, and Mrs Borradaile has been discovered. We may presume that Marshall and Clarke would receive more than Mrs Borradaile, since she suffered only psychological injury, which was little understood and sympathised with in those days. But £15,000 is worth nearly £1,000,000 in early twenty-first century terms, and, however shared out, was handsome compensation for the mid-nineteenth century.

Chapter 29
The Allied Chastisement of Chōshū: Shimonoseki

In early 1864, *shōgun* Iemochi visited the Emperor at Kyōto, where he conceded further power to the Emperor. A significant change was that henceforth, on the death of a *daimyō*, his successor would be invested by the Emperor, not the *shōgun*. Thus, over time, the loyalties of the *daimyō* would be towards the Emperor, the fount of power, not the *shōgun*. He also was forced to take on a panel of "advisers" nominated by the Emperor: the *daimyō* of Satsuma, Tosa, Echizen, and Aizu. This effectively ended the *shōgun's* autocracy, and enabled the Emperor to have his way.

Chōshū believed the *bakufu* was shilly-shallying over the expulsion of foreigners. Mori Takachika, the *daimyō* of Chōshū, decided to kick-start what he expected would be a national upwelling of anti-western action that would result in the expulsion of the foreigners and the abolition of the Unequal Treaties. He attempted to close the Strait of Shimonoseki and the Bungo Strait. This had been more than an annoyance to the western nations for over a year. Attacks on USS *Pembroke*, the French packet boat *Kienchang*, the Dutch vessel *Medusa* and a more recent attack on USS *Monitor* had all been calculated to wear down the foreigners' resolve to stay. The Straits of Shimonoseki and Bungo were the only practical route between

RESPECT AND CONSIDERATION

Yokohama and Nagasaki, the two major trading centres operated by the West.

Chōshū, despite having been severely chastised by foreign vessels and realising the superior forces wielded by the foreigners, continued to act in what can only be described, from a western point of view, as a bone-headed manner. They continued to menace shipping passing through the Shimonoseki Strait. Satow commented:

> The batteries had been destroyed but as soon as the foreign men-of-war quitted the scene, the Chōshū men set to work to rebuild forts, to construct others, and to mount all the guns they could bring together. So the hornet's nest was after no long interval in good repair again, and more formidable for attack and defence than before.

The motives of Mori Takachika, though, were not to impress the west, but to embarrass the other *daimyō* in the eyes of the people, so that they would act against the *bakufu* for its failure to expel the barbarians.

Pressure was mounting for action by the western forces against Chōshū. Joseph Heco[139] reported that a local newspaper, in a long editorial, had said,

Kuper's Fleet assembled in Yokohama, preparing to sail to Shimonoseki.
Detail from photograph by Felice Beato

---

[139]Hikozo Hamada (1837-1897) became a naturalised American in 1858 and changed his name. He was the only Japanese person ever to be introduced to President Buchanan, and also met President Lincoln. He worked as an interpreter for the American Legation, was a prosperous agent for other businesses, served as adviser to Itō Hirobumi and Kido Koin and was a civil servant in the Meiji administration.

THE ALLIED CHASTISEMENT OF CHŌSHŪ: SHIMONOSEKI

> We have it from an authentic source that all the Western Powers have come to a full understanding, and will henceforward insist upon the most complete execution of the Treaties. For too long have their most important provisions been evaded, infringed, set at naught by the native authorities of this country, to the serious inconvenience and loss of the foreign as well as of the native traders. We rejoice heartily to think that the time for equivocation or double-dealing has passed; and we can see looming in the distance the dawn of better days, when the patience of our merchants will have its reward.

The western nations decided to put an end to the Chōshū aggression once and for all. Under Vice-Admiral Kuper, a powerful squadron assembled in Yokohama on 17th August 1864. There were 9 British vessels, 5 Dutch, 3 French and 1 American non-combatant ship. In addition to the full complement of sailors, two thousand soldiers and marines were embarked on *Conqueror* and other ships. Kuper had over 5,000 men at his command. In addition to these massive forces, Kuper had another weapon: intelligence. The *bakufu* had had enough of Mori Takachika and his extreme opposition to their policies. They were glad to learn that the west was going to teach Chōshū a lesson. They secretly supplied maps of Shimonoseki and charts of the Straits to the French, who shared the information with their western comrades in arms.

Yokohama was not left unprotected. Fifteen hundred troops, consisting of Her Majesty's 20th and 80 men from the 67th and 300 Indian troops from the 2nd Belochee Regiments, and half a battery of artillery remained there. The 21-gun corvette HMS *Pelorus* under Commander (later Admiral) Boys, and one or two small vessels, as well as the United States' sloop of war

RESPECT AND CONSIDERATION

Jamestown, remained in harbour, to protect the settlement. The gun-vessel HMS *Osprey* was on its way from Shanghai to reinforce *Pelorus*.

On 5th and 6th September, the fleet arrived at Shimonoseki and immediately commenced pounding the batteries of guns that Chōshū had built up. This was not a defensive or accidental bombardment; this was deliberate punishment of Chōshū. After solid bombardment for some hours as the fleet sailed back and forth along the coast, soldiers and sailors from the ships landed and set about destroying the guns and stores not yet destroyed.

The Chōshū forces numbered some 600, according to initial intelligence, but Satow records that he had heard "from a Chōshū man who was present that their force was only half of that". The defenders fought valiantly, but were driven back by better tactics, better leadership, better weaponry, and the high morale and bravery of the western men-at-arms. The *samurai* used bows and arrows to considerable effect. The wounds inflicted by the arrows were troublesome, for the heads remained in the wounds after the shafts had been removed, and sepsis not infrequently set in.

Satow, who had gone ashore with the troops, reported:
> The Japanese could not stand our advance, the sharp musketry fire threw them into disorder, and they had to run for it. ... In only one case was an attempt made to come to close quarters. One fellow had concealed himself behind a door with uplifted sword in both hands ready to cut down a man just about to enter. But contrary to his expectation, his intended victim gave him a prod in the belly which laid him on his back and spoilt his little game.

Three Victoria Crosses, the highest British decoration for gallantry, were awarded for valour at Shimonoseki. The London Gazette citation in respect of seventeen-year-old Midshipman Duncan Gordon Boyes from *Euryalus* read:

THE ALLIED CHASTISEMENT OF CHŌSHŪ: SHIMONOSEKI

> For the conspicuous gallantry, which, according to the testimony of Capt. Alexander CB, at that time Flag Captain to Vice-Admiral Sir Augustus Kuper KCB, Mr. Boyes displayed in the capture of the enemy's stockade. He carried a Colour with the leading company, kept it in advance of all, in the face of the thickest fire, his colour-sergeants having fallen, one mortally, the other dangerously wounded, and he was only detained from proceeding yet further by the orders of his superior officer. The Colour he carried was six times pierced by musket balls

The citation for Thomas Pride, Captain of the After-Guard of *Euryalus*, read:

> Thomas Pride, Captain of the After-guard, the survivor of the two Colour-Serjeants who supported Mr. Boyes in the gallant rush which he made in advance of the attack, is also recommended for the Victoria Cross for his conduct on this occasion.

And the American William Seeley, serving as an Ordinary Seaman on *Euryalus*, was awarded the first V.C. presented to an American:

> For the intelligence and daring which, according, to the testimony of Lieutenant Edwards, Commanding the Third Company, he exhibited in ascertaining the enemy's position, and for continuing to retain his position in front, during the advance, after he had been wounded in the arm.

The Victoria Cross is awarded irrespective of rank
> for most conspicuous bravery, or some daring or pre-eminent act of valour or self-sacrifice, or extreme devotion to duty in the presence of the enemy.

It was created by Queen Victoria and first awarded for valour during the Crimean War. In the 150 or so years since then, a total of only 1,356 VCs have been awarded. Until 1918, the ribbon for the VC was crimson for soldiers and blue for sailors, but after the creation of the Royal Air Force, this was not

RESPECT AND CONSIDERATION

thought appropriate, and all blue-ribbon VCs had to exchange it for a crimson ribbon.

Holders of the VC are unique in terms of military etiquette: however lowly their own rank, they are saluted by all ranks.

THE ALLIED CHASTISEMENT OF CHŌSHŪ: SHIMONOSEKI

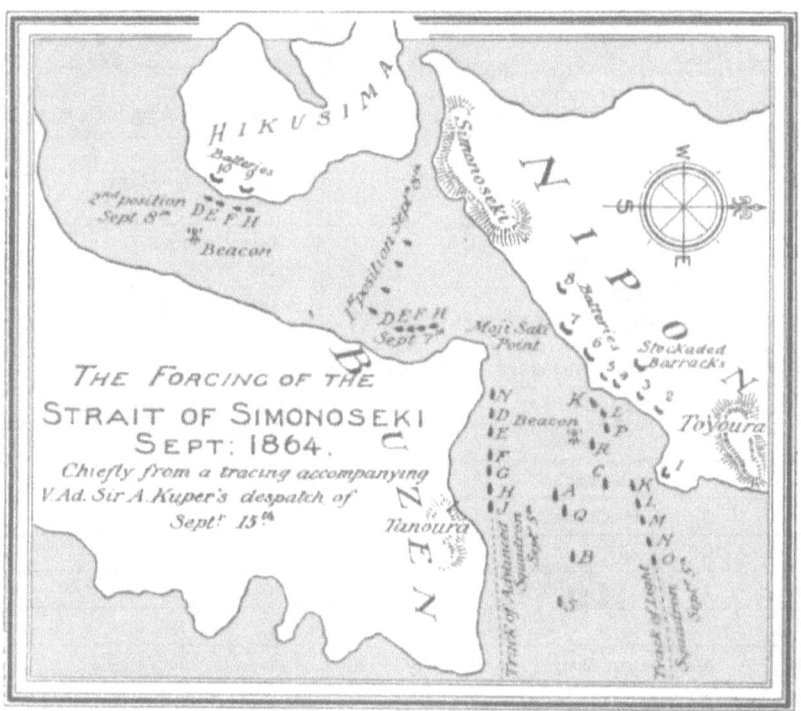

The letters on the sketch correspond to the reference letters for each vessel shown on the table overleaf.

RESPECT AND CONSIDERATION

ALLIED SQUADRONS AT THE FORCING OF THE STRAIT OF SIMONOSEKI, SEPTEMBER 1864.					
NATION	PLAN REF	SHIPS (SCREW UNLESS STATED)	TONS B.M.	GUNS	COMMANDERS
British	A	Euryalus, frigate	2,371	33	Vice Admiral AL Kuper Capt. John Hobhouse Inglis Alexander.
French	B	Sémiramis, frigate		35	Vice-Amiral B. Jaurès Capitaine Du Quilis.
British	C	Conqueror, battleship	2,845	78	Capt. William Garnham Luard[140], Cdr. ET Nott
Advanced squadron under Capt. Hayes					
British	D	Tartar, corvette	1,296	20	Capt. John Montagu Hayes[141]..
French	E	Dupleix, corvette		10	Capitaine Franclieu.
Dutch	F	Metalen Kruis,		16	Kapitein JF De Man.
British	G	Barrosa, corvette	1,700	21	Capt. William Montagu Dowell[142].
Dutch	H	Djambi,		16	Kapitein van Rees
British	J	Leopard, paddle frigate.	1,406	18	Capt. Charles Tayler Leckie.
Light squadron under Cdr Kingston					
British	K	Perseus, sloop	955	17	Cdr. Augustus John Kingston.
Dutch	L	Medusa,		18	Kapitein de Casembroot.
French	M	Tancrède, dispatch vessel		4	Lieutenant Pallu.
British	N	Coquette, gun vessel	677	4	Cdr. Arthur George Robertson Roe[143].
British	O	Bouncer, gun boat.			Lieut. Henry Lowe Holder[144].
British	P	Argus, paddle sloop	281	6	Cdr. John Moresby.
Dutch	Q	Amsterdam, paddle		8	Luitenant Müller.
American	R	Takiang, chartered steamer.		1	Lieut. Pearson, U.S.N. (Chartered for $10000 a month.)
British	S	Pembrokeshire, collier			

[140] Luard (1820-1910) ended his career as an Admiral, a KCB and deputy Lieutenant of Essex. He died in a road accident in his home town of Witham, Essex.
[141] Hayes (b. 1816) ended his career as a Vice Admiral.
[142] Dowell (1825-1912) ended his career as an Admiral and a GCB.
[143] Arthur George Robertson Roe had been Flag-Lieutenant (assistant to the Admiral) on board *Euryalus* at Kagoshima.
[144] Holder ended his career as a Rear Admiral.

THE ALLIED CHASTISEMENT OF CHŌSHŪ: SHIMONOSEKI

The action on land was brief and full of incident. In Kuper's report, he recorded that the landing party had consisted of

Force	Commanded by
Small-arms company from *Euryalus*	Captain JHI Alexander of *Euryalus*, taken over by Lieut. Harington on Alexander being wounded
Small-arms company from *Conqueror*	
Battalion of Marines from *Euryalus*	Lieutenant-Colonel William Grigor Suther, R.M.
Marines from the rest of the British ships	
350 French seamen and Marines	*Capitaine* Du Quilis and *Lieutenant* Layrle, *chef d'état major*
200 Dutch seamen and Marines	*Luitenant* Binkis

The force proceeded, under Kuper's personal direction, to assault and seize the principal batteries on the 6th. The allied force met with little opposition. They dismounted and spiked the guns, burned the carriages and platforms, and blew up the magazines. Kuper decided it would be unnecessarily dangerous to remain on shore overnight, so ordered the entire force to re-embark around 4.00 pm.

RESPECT AND CONSIDERATION

The French and Dutch detachments were the first to set off for their ships. At this point, a strong body of Japanese assembled behind the small-arms companies, who were making their way back to the shore. With no more ado, they attacked the British

The War in Japan: the Naval Brigade and Marines storming the stockade at Simonoseki, September 4th
"from a sketch by our special Artist" (Charles Wirgman). *Illustrated London News*, 24 December 1864

sailors. Colonel Suther's battalion of Marines were close by, on their way back to the shore, and Suther instantly organised an attack on the enemy. The Japanese were driven back to the well-fortified and stockaded barracks, where they mounted a staunch defence. But the Marine and Naval force pressed onwards and the Japanese were eventually dislodged, leaving seven small guns in British possession.

While leading his men towards the stockade, Captain Alexander received a severe and "dangerous" wound in his

THE ALLIED CHASTISEMENT OF CHŌSHŪ: SHIMONOSEKI

ankle[145], and a significant number of British servicemen suffered wounds. Lieutenant Harington took over command from Alexander, and his distinguished leadership earned him swift promotion to Commander. But the Japanese rapidly disappeared, and the force made its way back to their home ships without further incident.

HMS *Perseus* had been driven on shore by an unexpected current during the landing operation earlier that day. She remained fast until midnight on the 7th, when, having been lightened, she was towed off undamaged. Kuper had made contingency plans to burn her rather than leave her in Japanese hands.

On the 8th, an extraordinary incident occurred. A delegation of Chōshū officials arrived under a flag of truce and requested the international force to cease hostilities for forty-eight hours, because the Japanese troops were tired and hungry after the fighting. They needed sleep and food, declared the envoys, and would be in a fit state to resume hostilities two days hence. Kuper and Jaurès, magnanimous in their clear and total victory over Chōshū, permitted the armistice. In the event, hostilities were not resumed.

This break in the action was not unprecedented. During the Belgian revolution, (largely a conflict concerning Dutch versus Belgian/French hegemony over the Low Countries), there was bloody fighting in the streets of Brussels from 23rd-26th September 1830. However, the Belgian and Dutch troops disengaged, by common consent, each day for dinner, and even allowed each other time for a brief snooze afterwards. A chap has to keep his strength up, what?

---

[145] An early report said that it was expected his foot would have to be amputated. It is not known whether this was done or not. Whether amputated or not, his ankle entitled him to a pension for wounds, awarded on 5 October 1865. He remained a Captain in the service, retiring in 1869.

RESPECT AND CONSIDERATION

Ordnance Captured at Shimonoseki, 5-6 September 1864							
Battery	Guns		Howitzers		Mortars		Field Pieces	
	No.	Size	No.	Size	No.	Size	No.	Size
No. 1	1	9-pr.	1	32-pr			2	12-prs.
No. 2	1	9-pr.						
No. 3								
Stockaded barracks			1	12-pd.	1	coehorn	2 3	6-prs. swivels
No. 4	4	30-pr.						
No. 5	1 6	8-ton 24-prs.						
No. 6	2 3	11-in. 78-prs.					3	12-prs.
No. 7					1 1	8-in. 13-in.		
No. 8	1 3 7	8-in. 24-prs. 30-prs.	2	5-in.				
Nos. 9 and 10	6 1 2	30-prs. 24-pr. 9-prs.	1	5-in.			4 2	6-prs 3-prs.
Totals	38		5		2		16	

Coehorn Mortar of c. 1800 (modern mount)

The Coehorn mortar from the stockaded barracks was a standard mortar with a fixed 45º angle and a short, c. 13-inch barrel. It fired a shell or bomb, which usually had to be lit by a fuze before the propellant charge was lit. The standard version has a barrel diameter of 4.4 inches. It was widely used in military and naval versions (naval versions were much larger) from its invention by Baron von Coehorn in 1674 until as late as 1924.

THE ALLIED CHASTISEMENT OF CHŌSHŪ: SHIMONOSEKI

Capture of one of the Shimonoseki batteries.
Photographed by Felice Beato. Probably a staged photograph after the event.

Working parties were landed on the morning of the 7th to begin dismantling the guns captured from the now-silent batteries 1 to 8 (see plan on page 258.). In the afternoon, *Tartar, Metalen Kruis, Djambi,* and *Dupleix* moved round to the westward of Mojisaki Point, preparatory to an attack on batteries 9 and 10. On September 8th, accompanied by *Amiral* Jaurès, Kuper shifted his flag to *Coquette*. *Coquette* and the four ships that had moved to Mojisaki Point on the Buzen coast to the south-west, opened fire on batteries 9 and 10 on Hikushima to the north. There was no response from those batteries, and it was concluded that the Japanese had abandoned them. Parties were landed from the squadron to destroy the structures and carry away the guns. This took until late on 10th September to be completed.

Although the expedition had achieved all it had set out to do, it was not without cost. The casualties are set out on the following pages:

RESPECT AND CONSIDERATION

| Table of casualties at Shimonoseki ||||
Name	Age	Rank	How wounded or killed
HMS *Euryalus*			
Alexander, JHJ	32	Captain RN	wound of right ankle-joint by musket-ball, dangerous
Atkinson, CW	19	Midshipman	wound of finger by musket-ball, slightly
Edwards, Frederick E	22	Lieutenant RN	wound of left foot by musket-ball, slightly
Conner, Bartholomew	28	AB	wound of abdomen by musket-ball, killed.
Baily, Stephen	28	Captain of foretop	wound of groin by musket-ball, killed.
Kidd, Joseph	29	Ordinary	wound of heart by musket-ball, killed.
Wells, George	24	AB	wound of both lungs by musket-ball, mortally, since dead.
Sney, John	27	Private, RM	wound of stomach by musket-ball, mortally, since dead.
Kiley, Thomas	28	AB	wound of throat, ball lodged, dangerously.
Pride, Thomas	28	AB	wound of left side of chest by musket-ball, dangerously.
Lover, Charles	26	AB	wound of right leg by musket-ball, severely.
Dumfoy, George	20	Ordinary	wound of left leg by musket ball, severely.
Atteridge, George	35	AB	wound of left side of chest by musket-ball, severely
Seeley, William	26	Ordinary	wound of right arm by grape shot, severely
Marcham, Joseph	28	AB	wound of right shoulder by musket-ball, severely
Harman, Thomas	20	Ordinary	wound of left leg by musket-ball, severely
Winsby, John	23	Ordinary	wound of right hand by arrow, severely
Butler, Patrick	19	Ordinary	wound of chest by spent ball, slightly
Williams, Thomas	29	AB	wound of right wrist by arrow, slightly
Shylock, James	28	AB	wound of right side of chest by arrow, slightly
Chicks, George	23	Private RM	wound of scalp by a rock splinter caused by shell, slightly
Robinson, James	31	Private RM	wound of neck by a rock splinter caused by shell, slightly
Jones, William	26	AB	wound of forearm by arrow, slightly
Battalion of Royal Marines			
de Courcey NW		captain	gunshot wound of left wrist, severely
Inglis JW		1st lieutenant	gunshot wound of left groin, severely
Adair CW		lieutenant-colonel	temporary concussion from fall of a tree produced by a shot, slightly
Moore, Daniel	22	Private	bullet wound of head, killed

THE ALLIED CHASTISEMENT OF CHŌSHŪ: SHIMONOSEKI

Shaw, Edwin	28	Private	bullet wound of left lung, dangerously
Howard, Samuel	23	Private	shell wound of right knee, dangerously
Cooper, Thomas	28	Private	bullet wound of right thigh, severely
Lethbridge, William	28	Corporal	wound of knees, slightly
Blakemore, Thomas	27	Private	shell wound of left leg, compound fracture, dangerously
Gill, William	22	Private	wound of left wrist by explosion of magazine, slightly
Burrows, John	29	Private	contusion of thigh from explosion of magazine, slightly
Haydon, James	16	Drummer	contusion of left hip, slightly
Allen, William	22	Private	burn of face and hands by explosion of magazine, severely
HMS *Leopard*			
Rowley, Edward	26	Private, RM	wound of left elbow, slightly
Yates, Thomas	24	Private, RM	wound of left leg, dangerously
HMS *Conqueror*			
Greene, George	22	Ordinary	bullet wound of right lung, killed
Lufer, Frederick	22	Private, RM	bullet wound of left lung, killed
Riddles, David	19	Ordinary	bullet wound of back, severely
Kitchener, Henry	21	AB	bullet wound of left wrist, severely
Martin, Henry	22	AB	bullet wound of right leg, severely
Barnes, Ralph	22	Private, RM	bullet wound of abdomen, severely
HMS *Tartar*			
Brownlow, A de V		Lieutenant RN	wound of left hip, dangerously
Wingfield, EJ		Midshipman	wound of left leg, severely
Camplin, Alfred		Private, RM	wound of right shoulder, dangerously
Ford, John		AB	wound of back, severely
Smith, William		Ordinary	wound of arm and face, slightly
Sercombe, Henry		AB	wound of face, slightly
Murphy, John		boatswain's mate	wound of face, slightly
Breeze, Robert		Private, RM	wound of face and head, slightly
HMS *Perseus*			
M'Carlan, John	31	Private, RM	bullet wound of left thigh, severely
Suitors, Charles	27	Leading Seaman	contused wound of left foot, severely
HMS *Barrosa*			
Fountain, George		Private, RM	musketball wound of arm, slightly
HM Gunboat *Bouncer*			
M'Donald, Michael		Corporal, RM	bullet wound of right thigh, severely

RESPECT AND CONSIDERATION

In total, there were eight men killed, and 48 wounded.

But as ever, there was also glory to be had. Following from this action came promotions for some officers:

    Commanders to be Captains:
        John Moresby
        Augustus John Kingston
    Lieutenants to be Commanders:
        Henry Lowe Holder
        William Henry Cuming
        William Arthur de Vesci Brownlow
        Richard Hastings Harington
        Richard Edward Tracey
    Second Master to be Master:
        James Greenwood Liddell
    Assistant-Surgeon to be Surgeon:
        Richard Lovell Bluett Head.

And the following were mentioned in dispatches:

- Lieutenants
    - Robert Peel Dennistoun (flag), (Captain,1873)
    - Cottrell Burnaby Powell
    - Alfred Jephson (Commander, 1873)
- Masters
    - George Williams
    - John Charles Solfleet
    - John Emanuel Chappie
- Paymaster
    - Hemsley Hardy Shanks (Secretary)
- Surgeons
    - David Lloyd Morgan FRCS
    - Christopher Knox Ord, M.D.
- Assistant-Surgeons
    - Samuel M'Bean
    - Edward Alfred Birch

THE ALLIED CHASTISEMENT OF CHŌSHŪ: SHIMONOSEKI

- o John Thomson Comerford
- Midshipmen
  - o Henry Hart Dyke
  - o Edward Plantagenet Hume
- Clerk
  - o Robert N. Haly
- Royal Marines
  - o Lieutenant-Colonel Penrose Charles Penrose
  - o Captain Ambrose Wolrige
  - o Lieutenant John Christopher Hore
  - o Lieutenant William Henry Townsend Morris Dodgin, R.M.A.
- Special
  - o Prussian officer, Herr von Blanc, attached to *Tartar*

All this is ample testimony to the gallantry and skill of the men of Kuper's international force.

There were other losses. Alone, apparently, among the vessels who took part at Shimonoseki, it seems *Conqueror* had a Scrooge on board. For interspersed among the watch-keepers' laconic factual records of being fired on by, and shelling of, the batteries; of death and wounds inflicted and incurred; of shot and shell expended; of courses run and destruction sustained; lie daily notes in another, educated, hand. They concern calamities such as a broken finger glass (Captain's), a cracked pie dish (Captain's), and a lost fork (Captain's).

All the guns from the forts were placed on board the various ships of the squadron. This was with the aid of Japanese civilians from the town, who seemed glad to be rid of them. No *samurai* were to be seen while this operation was carried out.

Lieutenant JMW Silver, RM, commented in 1867

> At the bombardment of the Simonoseki forts, at the entrance of the Suwo-Nada, or 'Inland Sea,' in September 1864, Prince

RESPECT AND CONSIDERATION

> Choisiu's loss, according to one of his own officers, amounted to upwards of 500 killed and wounded; but all had been removed when the brigade of English, French, and Dutch, under the command of Colonel Suther, CB, Royal Marines, took possession of the forts early next day. At the storming of a stockade (which was pluckily defended) by two battalions of Royal Marines and the light-armed companies of the British squadron, the Japanese were noticed carrying away their dead and wounded, and several were unfortunately shot while thus employed.
>
> A few nights afterwards large fires were noticed in the interior, which were said to be the funeral pyres of those who had fallen in the defence of the forts and stockade.

Alarmed at what had occurred, the *bakufu* had sent an envoy to order Mori Takachika to cease hostilities against the west. In an echo of actions by the *bakufu* itself over the last two and a half centuries, the *shōgun's* envoy was captured by Mori's *samurai* and summarily killed. This infuriated the *bakufu*, who thereafter harboured a desire for revenge. But nothing could disguise the fact that Chōshū had been decisively defeated by the west. The Straits were open for the free passage of commercial shipping. And Chōshū had got the message. Like Satsuma before them, they realised that they needed to adopt western methods if Japan were to hold up her head among the nations. And, of course (they hoped) ultimately to drive the detested foreigners away.

On the 10th, a high-ranking Chōshū emissary had brought "humble submissions" to the Admirals. An agreement was

THE ALLIED CHASTISEMENT OF CHŌSHŪ: SHIMONOSEKI

negotiated between the four nations represented at Shimonoseki and Mori Takachika:

> 1. Henceforward all ships of all countries passing through the Straits of Simonosaki shall be treated in a friendly manner. Ships shall be allowed to purchase coal, provisions, wood, and water, and every other necessary. As the harbour of Simonosaki is subject to violent winds and currents, people suffering from stress of weather shall be allowed to land without opposition.
> 2. Not only shall new forts not be built, but no repairs shall be made to the old ones, nor shall guns be mounted thereon.
> 3. Although the town of Simonosaki might have been partly burnt for having fired on foreign ships, it was left standing. A ransom shall be paid for this, and, in addition, the whole expenses of the expedition shall be defrayed by the Prince - the sum to be settled by the Foreign Minister at Yeddo.
> 4. This agreement being merely for the cessation of hostilities upon this occasion, it has nothing to do with questions affecting Chosiu, which have to be settled between the Japanese Government and the Ministers .of foreign Powers.

The allied Ministers decided that Chōshū should pay an indemnity of $3,000,000 to cover the costs of the expedition and the "ransom" agreed upon. Chōshū had no option but to agree, being militarily defeated, stripped of their major weapons, and under pressure from an exasperated *bakufu*. The British and French governments suggested that in lieu of the money, they would prefer that another port be opened to the West. The Dutch and Americans preferred the money. Capitalist principles prevailed, and the *bakufu* agreed to pay it in sixty instalments of $50,000 every month and collect it from Chōshū. In the event, the *bakufu* was unable to pay the first instalment until the following August, nearly a year after the bombardment and agreed settlement, and later instalments too were often delayed. The last payment was not made until the middle of 1874, a full ten years after the bombardment of Shimonoseki.

Japanese xenophobia was, if not dead, heavily muted. Chōshū was now able to concentrate on its over-riding goal: to rid the nation of the Tokugawa shōgunate.

The *bakufu* had agreed to pay a war indemnity of an astonishing three million dollars to cover the western governments' costs in enforcing the Treaties through their actions at Shimonoseki. However, this was later cancelled and replaced by a new commercial deal signed in June 1866, the effect of which was to remove almost all restrictions on foreign trade, and, to the great advantage of the west, to reduce import duties to a lowly 5%.

CHAPTER 30
RESIDUAL OUTRAGES

The defeats at Kagoshima and Shimonoseki did not entirely put an end to outrages committed against westerners. On 21st November 1864, two British officers of the 2nd Battalion of the 20th Regiment of Light Marines, Major George Walter Baldwin and Lieutenant Robert Nicholas Bird were murdered after visiting the island of Enoshima, just a short distance from the tourist attraction of the *daibutsu* at Kamakura, itself just a short excursion southwards from Yokohama. The two men had set out from Yokohama on horseback. Near the statue and between a tea-house and a hut for horses, the bodies of the two men were found, laid out on straw mats, and under a makeshift canopy of mats propped up on sticks. Their bodies were horribly mutilated. A pistol, with one barrel recently discharged, was found by the side of one of them, but the other was still tucked into its owner's belt. They had clearly been taken by surprise.

View near Kamakura where Major Baldwin and Lieutenant Bird were murdered.
Photograph by Felice Beato

RESPECT AND CONSIDERATION

The ringleader of the assassins, *rōnin* Shimazi Seiji, was arrested, tried and sent for public execution. Charles Wirgman, the correspondent and artist of the *Illustrated London News*, reported

> The criminal was mounted on a pack-horse and promenaded through the town. His sentence was written on a large flag carried before him, and also on a board. A guard of twelve Japanese soldiers, with fixed bayonets, marched in front; and the rear was brought up by two mounted officers and a crowd of Europeans on horseback.
> The streets were crowded with Japanese and Europeans. The murderer, who was an athletic man, with a fine head and a determined expression, sang all the time and looked about him with an air of indifference. At the end of the street he smoked a pipe and had something to eat; then he was taken to the execution-ground, where bonfires and torches lighted up the scene; but the execution was put off till next day, because it was too late for the garrison to attend.
> The man was then conducted back to prison; and next morning, at nine o'clock, the whole garrison - Royal marines and light infantry of the 20th Regiment, under the command of Colonel Penrose; and half a battery of artillery, under the command of Lieutenant Wood - marched out to the execution-ground, where they formed a square. The Japanese troops were drawn up on the road. After waiting some time, the prisoner, escorted as before, but carried in a *norimon* or litter, made his appearance. He had some wine and food and then walked to the straw, on which he knelt, with the hole for

The severed head of Shimazi Seiji

RESIDUAL OUTRAGES

his head to fall into in front of him. He had made a request that he should not be blindfolded, which was granted, and also that his body might be buried and sent to the place he named, and that a tablet should be placed over his tomb. After speaking to the executioner, he sang or yelled out a long recitation, which no one seems to have understood, and turned to the executioner, who had his sword ready to strike. Saying 'Wait a little', he settled himself with his head over the hole, and said, 'Now'. The sword came down, but only severed a part of his neck; so that the executioner had to make three cuts before the head was off. A gun was then fired, and the head was taken, in a mat bag, to be exposed at the entrance of the town.

Lieutenant Silver RM reported of the same event:

> After execution, the heads of malefactors are generally exposed[146]: that of Simono Sedgi[147] (the lonin who was decapitated in the presence of the British garrison of Yokohama, for being the organizer of the assassination of Major Baldwin and Lieutenant Bird of Her Majesty's 20th Regiment) was exhibited on the public stand at the guard-house at the entrance of the town.
>
> This man was a fair specimen of the lonin type, and was a most determined ruffian, whose whole life had been a career of crime.

---

[146] The bodies were usually paraded round the town as a warning against wrongdoing, the corpse being propped up at the door of shopkeepers and tradesmen who had failed to pay protection-money to the executioner's assistants.

[147] Silver was no linguist, Simono Sedji was Shimazi Seiji, and "lonin" are *rōnin*.

RESPECT AND CONSIDERATION

When exposed in the streets of Yokohama the day preceding his execution, he conducted himself with great bravado, remarking on the improvements in the town since he last visited it, and expressing his regret that he had not killed a consul.

At the place of execution he made an impassioned speech, in which he declared that he was a gentleman by birth, and had studied the arts and sciences, and never believed the government would sacrifice a Japanese for the death of a foreigner. He said that the days would come when they would repent the encouragement they were now giving to strangers; and ended by complimenting the executioner on his well-known skill.

But such murders and assaults did not achieve their intended object. The Big Picture was not affected by the outrages, and enthusiasm for them among *sonnō jōi* supporters gradually waned. The realisation of the need to westernise eventually filtered through the *shōgun* and his advisory council to reach the Emperor himself. In October 1865, the Emperor ratified all the trading and amity treaties concluded with foreign powers, and promulgated the opening of the country to foreign trading, in particular through the ports of Kōbe and Ōsaka. However, while making these public pronouncements, Emperor Kōmei was privately telling the *bakufu*

Chōshū students in London

not to actually open the ports close to Kyōto.

It was not long before Chōshū sent students to England to learn western ways, and strong and friendly commercial links were forged between Chōshū and Britain.

The *sonnō jōi* movement finally died, to be supplanted by *fukoku kyōhei!* (Enrich the Country and Strengthen the Military!)

On 17th August 1866, Tokugawa Iemochi died in Ōsaka. Hitotsubashi Keiki, Iemochi's guardian (*kōken* 後見) was approached by the *bakufu* and urged to accept the vacant *shōgunate*. Hitotsubashi refused what he saw as a poisoned chalice, but consented to changing his name to Tokugawa Yoshinobu and becoming head of the house of Tokugawa. The *bakufu*, though, saw no other realistic candidates with the requisite experience and skills, and continued to press him to become *shōgun*. Eventually, Tokugawa Yoshinobu bowed to the pressure in January 1867 and became the 15th - and, as it turned out, last - shōgun. He accepted the post with a noticeable lack of enthusiasm, but once in office he attempted to reform the *bakufu* under French guidance. At this time, Britain was supporting Chōshū and Satsuma, and it is clear that both Britain and France were concerned to further their own national causes. Chōshū and Satsuma were in the van in the Emperor's cause, favoured by Britain. They were proponents of the destruction of the power of the Tokugawa clan, who had oppressed both their houses, ever since they had supported the losing side in the Battle of Sekigahara. Even after

Official photograph of Emperor Meiji on his 21st birthday in 1873
Photo by Kusakabe Kinbei

years, wrongs must be righted.

Less than five months after the new *shōgun* took office, on 3rd February 1867, the chronically xenophobic Emperor Kōmei died. His second son was fourteen-year-old *shinnō* (Imperial Prince) Mutsuhito. His older brother died, so Mutsuhito became *kōtaishi* (Crown Prince).

So it was that Mutsuhito ascended the Chrysanthemum Throne. His era name was Meiji ("Enlightened Rule"), which I use to refer to him henceforth. Meiji's father, Kōmei, had had muddled objectives. He wanted to remove power from the *bakufu*, but on the other hand realised that if the foreigners were to be removed from the country, only the *bakufu* could achieve this. The forces at his own disposal were insufficient. Meiji's *sesshō* (Nariyuki Nijo) and his maternal grandfather Nakayama Tadayasu (his close advisers during his youthful imperatorium), though, were completely wedded to the aim of dissolving the *bakufu* and taking all power back into Imperial hands, and Meiji was compliant with their stance.

In early September 1867, a special envoy from the *shōgunate* arrived in Nagasaki to investigate the murder of two drunken British seamen from the screw sloop HMS *Icarus*. Robert Foad and John Hutchings (both aged 23) were murdered on the night of August 5th, 1867. The incident had a tremendous impact on the political situation, particularly in Nagasaki, but also in the relationships between Japan and the international community.

Foreign sailors on shore leave, then as now, are drawn to the entertainment districts of the ports at which they find themselves. Foad and Hutchings were no exception, and found their way into the entertainment district of Nagasaki. As countless sailors have done before and since, they imbibed rather too freely of the local brew, in this case unfamiliar and deceptive *sake*. Their comrades left them sleeping in the gutter in front of a tea house. To a passing xenophobic *samurai*, this was an opportunity not to be missed, and he hacked the two unconscious men to death with his *katana*.

An investigation took place, but there were no witnesses who came forward, and there was no other evidence leading to the identification of a culprit. However, based on his long-held suspicion of the anti-western Tosa clan, the British Consul in Nagasaki, Marcus Flowers, became convinced that the murders had been perpetrated by Tosa *samurai*. These supposed guerrillas belonged to the *kaientai*, or Naval Auxiliary Force, a naval and paramilitary organization created and led by a prominent Tosa *samurai*, Sakamoto Ryoma.

Sakamoto Ryoma

Sakamoto Ryōma (坂本龍馬) (1836-1867) was prominent in the anti-*bakufu* movement. He used the alias Saitani Umetarō (才谷梅太郎) while engaged on operations against the *bakufu*. He came from a family of merchant *samurai* (the lowest rank of *samurai*) that had made its wealth by brewing and selling *sake*. The young Sakamoto Ryōma became a *daimokuroku* (master swordsman) in the *hokushin itto-ryu kenjutsu* (school), which emphasizes techniques useful in one-to-one fighting and duelling. He became active in *sonnō jōi* circles, and entered into a conspiracy to take control of Tosa and then take the clan into war against the *bakufu*. The plot was thwarted, and Sakamoto was forced to flee with some companions, and thus they became *rōnin*.

Sakamoto plotted to assassinate Katsu Kaishū (勝海舟), a leading modernizer within the *bakufu*. However, Katsu talked him round into understanding that modernization of the

RESPECT AND CONSIDERATION

Katsu Kaishū

military-industrial processes of Japan was vital if the westerners were ever to be removed. Sakamoto became Katsu's disciple and assistant. In 1864, as things grew hot for anti-westerners in the wake of *Namamugi jiken* and the placatory actions taken by the *bakufu* against the *sonnō jōi* proponents, and their rueful acceptance of the punitive naval actions at Kagoshima and Shimonoseki, Sakamoto fled south to Kagoshima, which was now a hot-bed and sanctuary for anti-*bakufu* agitators. Sakamoto, as an outside, disinterested, honest broker, was able to negotiate a secret alliance between Chōshū and Satsuma (to be known as *SatChō*), who had previously been dedicated antagonists.

The defeat of the *bakufu* army by Chōshū and Satsuma forces in 1866 caused Tosa to recall its now honoured and victorious son. Sakamoto went on to play a central rôle in negotiating the resignation of *shōgun* Tokugawa Yoshinobu in 1867. Later that year, on his 33rd birthday, Sakamoto was assassinated in Kyōto. Some suspected his own men who had become jealous of his ever-increasing power and influence had killed him. But there is compelling evidence that it was the *shinsengumi* (the band of licensed killers who roamed the streets suppressing dissent against the Tokugawa *bakufu*) who had assassinated Sakamoto Ryōma where he hid, with his comrade Nakaoka Shintarō, in a 2nd-storey room in the house of a Kyōto soya bean dealer. Sakamoto and Nakaoka were at the top of the Tokugawa "most wanted" list. There were several reasons for their hatred of Sakamoto:

- The forging of the *SatChō* alliance, which posed a massive political threat to the *bakufu*, with the propensity

RESIDUAL OUTRAGES

to use the overwhelming military means at their disposal to crush the Tokugawa clan and the *shōgunate* Tokugawa held as their right;
- Sakamoto's call for Yoshinobu to abdicate and power to go to the Emperor;
- Sakamoto's shooting of one, or possibly two, Tokugawa men at the Tereda'ya inn in Fushimi when he had been attacked by *bakufu* forces;
- A civil dispute between Ryōma and the Kii clan (Kii was a cadet branch of the Tokugawa) concerning compensation for a ship and its contraband cargo of smuggled guns that Kii had sunk. It caused humiliation for Kii throughout Japan. For Ryōma had written an insulting ditty that had taken the entertainment quarters throughout Japan by storm. The song was rather jolly[148]:

> It won't be only money we take
> for sinking our ships at sea;
> We won't give up until we've taken
> the entire domain of Kii.

> It won't be only money we take
> for sinking our ships at sea;
> We won't give up until we've taken
> the heads of all the men of Kii.

Kii, and Tokugawa, were incandescent with rage at being made a laughing-stock.

Ōkubo Toshimichi, Satsuma's political mastermind, wrote four days after the assassinations to Iwakura Tomomi (with

Kondo Isami

---

[148] Konishi, Takeshi, Fumio, Saichiro, Kijura, eds., *Sakamoto Ryōma Jiten*, Shinjinbutsu Ōraisha, 1988; and Miyaji Saichirō, ed., *Sakamoto Ryōma Zenshū*, Kōfūsha Shuppan, 1982

Saigō Takamori, the three of them went on to plan the seizure of the Imperial Palace, the event that served to end the *shōgunate*):
> I have heard that that without a doubt it was the *shinsengumi* who killed Sakamoto ... and ... Kondō Isami is the likely suspect.

There was forensic evidence too - a distinctive scabbard that was identified as belonging to *shinsengumi* member Harada Sanosuke, and some *geta* (clogs) that were marked with the name of an inn used by the *shinsengumi* as their regular canteen and accommodation. However, a little thought suggests that these items were planted to frame Harada, possibly by friends of Kondō Isami. Leaving items behind was an offence under the *shinsengumi* code, punishable by *seppuku*, and Harada was known for his fierce adherence to the code. It was unthinkable that he would have left such clumsy clues behind. Furthermore, a *shinsengumi* member later made a statement to the effect that he had been with Kondō and Harada, and that a messenger told them the circumstances of Sakamoto's death. They realised that the assassin had to be an immensely skilled swordsman to dispatch two armed and skilful swordsmen - remember, Sakamoto was a *daimokuroku* - in the confined space of a 2nd-storey room. Later, when someone said that one Imai had done it, they thought that it made sense. Imai was famous for his unmatched prowess with the *wakizashi*, or short sword, which must have been used in the cramped conditions of the little room.

Whether or not it was the *kaientai* who had murdered the British sailors, the British Legation felt that the *bakufu* was dragging its feet on the investigation and prosecution of the perpetrators. Relations between Britain and Japan - or at least the *bakufu* - rapidly soured. There was a clamour from the British community for the British to inflict military retribution on the whole Tosa clan, but the experienced British Minister Sir Harry Parkes skilfully deflected the demands, while still

RESIDUAL OUTRAGES

managing to hold them as unspoken threats in his talks with the Japanese government. Parkes' principal argument was the same one that Lt. Col. Neale had deployed after Richardson's murder: the British were in Japan to trade, not to wage war. There was another good reason not to attack Tosa: the British foresaw that it was very likely that a civil war would break out between the Imperial and the *bakufu* factions, and it would not do to side against what they judged would be the winning side. For Tosa supported the Emperor.

The case, with all its bickering between the governments, dragged on for a year, until a surprising development occurred. Tosa officials, who had denied involvement from the beginning, discovered that the murders had been committed by a Chikuzen[149] *samurai*. It is not at all clear how they obtained this knowledge (probably the information came from a paid spy), but the facts they adduced were undisputed.

It seemed that students from Chikuzen had been drinking at the tea house outside which Foad and Hutchings were sleeping off the alcohol they had overindulged in. The oldest of the students, seeing the drunken sailors, drew his *katana* and amused himself by coolly slashing the unfortunate men to pieces. The matter had been reported to Chikuzen officials and the culprit had been arrested. After a secret enquiry, the offender was ordered to commit *seppuku*, but all details of the offence and the *seppuku* order were kept secret, for fear of blackening the name of the Chikuzen *han*. When Tosa officials learned of these events a year later, the other students in the party were also arrested in early 1869 and were sentenced to be imprisoned. Furthermore, the *daimyō* of Chikuzen was sentenced to internal exile (house arrest) and ordered to pay an indemnity to the families of the murdered seamen.

---

[149] Chikuzen province was at the north-western tip of Kyūshū. It was where Kublai Khan had attempted his invasions of Japan.

RESPECT AND CONSIDERATION

Notorious as the "Icarus Incident", the murders and their unsatisfactory investigation convinced Britain (if further proof were needed) that the *bakufu* was impotent to maintain the security of the foreign settlements against the bands of wandering *samurai* and *rōnin* in the various international ports of Japan. But, by the time the true facts had come to light, the *bakufu* had fallen and Meiji was wielding power. His government imposed the penalties on Chikuzen. That was a good start, from the British point of view.

In October 1867, Tosa representatives presented a petition to the *bakufu*. They proposed a political compromise, whereby the *shōgun's* political authority would be returned, notionally, to the Emperor, while the head of the Tokugawa house retained Tokugawa lands and continued to serve as First Minister. This did not receive a warm reception in any quarter. Because of the adverse response to these proposals, *shōgun* Yoshinobu decided that the Tokugawa family could no longer retain the hereditary *shōgunate*, and that, indeed, the days of the *shōgunate* as such were over. He returned the powers vested in him to the Imperial Court. Yoshinobu convened a meeting of all the *daimyō* in the presence of the Emperor. His intention was that the assembly would, by acclamation, require the Tokugawa family to remain in control of the government. They were, after all, by far the largest landholders in the country.

But Yoshinobu was outmanoeuvred by the brilliant minds behind the Satsuma-Chōshū alliance. The members of the alliance successfully petitioned the Emperor for a decree pardoning Chōshū for its previous misdeeds at Shimonoseki and elsewhere, and, crucially, calling for the *bakufu* and *shōgun* to abdicate. They had asked the Emperor to have Tokugawan landholdings redistributed, and the Emperor had indicated that he would favour the request once the *shōgunate* had ended. *That would avenge 267 years of mistreatment at Tokugawan hands of* the Satsuma and Chōshū *han*! So Yoshinobu's scheme came to nothing, and he acknowledged defeat. On 8th November 1867, Yoshinobu resigned as *shōgun*. The next month, the Court issued a proclamation announcing the restoration of Imperial rule. Japan would return to the system that had prevailed in ancient times, and a new government would be established with the Emperor at its head.

This was not enough for Satsuma and Chōshū. Yoshinobu, though no longer shōgun, still occupied Nijō palace. So on 3rd January 1868, forces from Satsuma, Echizen, Owari, Tosa, & Aki seized Nijō. The Emperor decreed his own restoration to full power, that henceforth the office of *shōgun* was ended, and reduced Tokugawa Yoshinobu to the level of *daimyō*. The Emperor assumed control of the country, and announced the establishment of a provisional government, with representatives of, naturally, Satsuma, Echizen, Owari, Tosa, & Aki – but no Tokugawa. There was to be a Supreme Controller (a sort of Prime Minister), and Junior and Senior Councils of State.

Unsurprisingly, Yoshinobu objected to the Emperor's declaration of 3rd January, and issued a counter-declaration claiming that the Emperor's statement was "illegal". Starting what was to become known as the Boshin War (戊辰戦争 *boshin sensō* "War of the Year of the Dragon"), he massed his forces and attempted to retake Kyōto in a *putsch*. Yoshinobu had 15,000 troops, three times the 5,000 soldiers loyal to the Emperor. Furthermore, Yoshinobu's army had been trained by French military advisers, who were highly regarded[150]. Yet Yoshinobu's

---

[150] Why they were so regarded is something of a mystery, for the French Army had hardly been engaged in any major actions that resulted in victory. Its principal use had been to expand the French Colonial Empire in Africa and Asia, where it met little organised military opposition. Their most recent true military success was in the second Italian War of Independence in 1859, when the French, under Napoléon III, defeated the Austrians who were under the strategic misdirection of an inept Emperor Franz-Joseph. Napoléon III quickly

army was thoroughly routed at the battle of Toba/Fushimi. The attempted *coup d'état* stuttered to a halt.

Enomoto Takeaki
Taken in 1869

Even so, some Tokugawa elements forlornly continued to resist the new règime in the north of the country for some time. So Saigō Takamori[151] led the victorious Imperial forces north and east on a military quest through Japan. Edo fell to Saigō's forces in May, and a month later was renamed Tōkyō, "Eastern Capital". The final, month-long battle took place in Hokkaidō. The Aizu han finally admitted defeat on September 23rd, 1868, leading to the suicide of nineteen *byakkotai* (White Tiger Corps) warriors, most of them between fifteen and eighteen years old. The Tokugawan navy under Enomoto Takeaki and a few French naval advisers (led by Jules Brunet,[152]) had fled to Hokkaidō, where they vainly attempted to establish the independent Republic of Ezo. They were fighting in a cause

---

signed an armistice with Franz-Joseph, because he anticipated that were the Germans to be drawn into the conflict, they would easily defeat the French. The French military reputation, then, was more propaganda than reality; but the Japanese were clearly taken in by it.

[151] Also variously known at different times by other names, including Saigō Kichinosuke, Kokichi, Takanaga, Udo and Nanshu.

[152] Brunet, an artillery officer, was part of the French Military mission sent to train the *shōgunate* forces. When France realised they had backed the wrong side in the struggle between Imperial and *shōgunate* interests that culminated in the *shōgunate* defeat in the Boshin War, the Mission was urgently recalled. Brunet, alone among the French mission, resigned his commission to join the ex-*shogun's* forces and attempted unsuccessfully to see the "Ezo Republic" established in Hokkaidō. Brunet was later rehabilitated into the French Army, and became a General and its Chief of Staff. The Meiji Government subsequently awarded him medals, which does seem strange, as he had fought on the "other" side in the Boshin War.

RESIDUAL OUTRAGES

that was already lost, and eventually they capitulated to Meiji forces in May 1869. The Boshin War was over, and Meiji could get on with establishing the new forms of government.

In the light of what we now know about the circumstances of the death of Charles Richardson, it is interesting to see how the British viewpoint had moved on in six years. Ernest Satow records a semi-formal discussion between himself, Dr Willis and Katsuro Kogyo in 1868 concerning relations between the foreign community and the Japanese once the *shōgun* had ceased to hold power. Satow and Katsuro were firm friends.

On this occasion, among other matters, they agreed that it would be desirable that

Katsuro Kogyo
(1833–1877)

- Foreigners should be informed that to break through a procession is an offence in Japanese eyes;
- Japanese on the other hand should be taught that they must not use weapons, but simply arrest offenders and hand them over to their own authorities;
- When a *daimyō's* train was to pass along a thoroughfare, constables from a mixed force of westerners and Japanese should be stationed to keep the road clear.

Willis, who was present as an observer, dissented from this latter opinion, and maintained that the only way to preserve the peace between foreign rowdies and Japanese bullies was to keep them apart, and to carry the *tōkaidō* round at the back outside Kōbe. Satow and Katsura both demurred from Willis's view, on the grounds that a change of road would give rise to a great deal more ill-will between the two nationalities than even the murder of a few westerners had done. As this was a semi-formal discussion, the matter was not settled; but Satow passed on the matters broadly agreed between himself and Katsuro to Sir Harry Parkes, the British Minister. They were noted, but not specifically acted upon. Neither did Katsuro have any direct success in promulgating the ideas to the Meiji administration.

As late as 1871, there was still a divide between the forces of progress and those of reaction, at least so far as fundamental principles are concerned. Satow wrote an undated note[153] to the British Government in his own hand as follows:

> Information from Kagoshima (very secret)
>
> The Tosa men say that the reason why our country cannot place itself on a level with the other states of the world is the division into four castes[154], in consequence of which, talented men do not arise nor are men skilled in various arts produced, the end being that no measure is successfully carried out. The difference between the four castes ought to be at once abolished and all be converted into 'common people', and the men of capacity ought to be selected and advanced from among the latter.
>
> In the first place a decree ought to be issued doing away with the practice of wearing swords, which would be the first step. We wished this to be proclaimed first, as an experiment, in our province, and then to see it carried out throughout the Empire, if successful here.
>
> We have already carried it out in our *han*, and this is a pattern for the Empire to work by.
>
> The Chōshū men say pretty much the same thing. However, the *han* is not united, and it would be utterly impossible to carry it out at present. More than half the province is averse to leaving off swords, and those who are in favour of it, are simply the men who happen to be in office, who are mere sycophants.

---

[153] This is from Satow's private papers at the National Archives, where its position in the file implies that it was written around May 1871.

[154] *shi-no-ko-sho*, warrior-peasant-artisan-merchant

RESIDUAL OUTRAGES

> Satsuma men say the real weapon of the Empire has always been considered to be the sword, ever since the ages of the gods, which is chief among all the rest. It is considered the most to be venerated among the Three Sacred Treasures. For this reason the sword ought not to be done away with, nor ought the question of abolishing the difference between the four castes to be entertained. Every European Officer wears a sword, different from our swords in form alone. The whole clan firmly holds these opinions. Especially Saigō[155], when he receives, has a small sword at his knee, and thus preserves the form befitting the Empire. Whatever Chōshū and Tosa may say, they will never be able to get the aid of Satsuma to promulgate an order to leave off wearing swords.

In 1869, the *shi-no-ko-sho* caste system was simplified. There were now *kwazoku* (*daimyō* and courtiers), *shizoku* (*samurai* and soldiers), and *heimin* or commoners (everyone else). The visible distinction between the military and commoners soon disappeared: commoners were allowed to adopt surnames and now were permitted to change their occupations and residences. By 1871, the marriages of commoners with *samurai* had been sanctioned. In 1872, (ex-)*samurai* were permitted to marry *kwazoku*, though the price was the banning of the wearing of swords. The distinctive top-knot hairstyle of the *samurai* was no longer permitted.

The old days were gone.

---

[155] Saigō Takamori, a prominent *samurai* of Satsuma, who eventually led rebellious anti-reform forces into annihilation at the battle of Shiroyama (on *tahara-zaka* hill in the outskirts of Kagoshima) in 1877, where he died. He was rapidly rehabilitated as a national hero, was posthumously pardoned by Emperor Meiji on 22 February 1889, and is today venerated as embodying the great Japanese virtues.

RESPECT AND CONSIDERATION

The British Legation Building, Yokohama 1865

CHAPTER 31
EARLY JAPANESE STUDENTS IN BRITAIN

As the policy of *sakoku* fell by the wayside, the forward-looking, ambitious, pro-western *han* of Chōshū and Satsuma sent young men to the west to absorb the latest European knowledge. Later many studied at Cambridge University and a smaller number at Oxford University until the end of the Meiji era.

In 1862, the *bakufu* sent fifteen students including Nishi Amane[156] and Tsuda Mamichi[157] to the Netherlands, to study western medicine among other subjects.

The "Chōshū five" (長州五傑 *Chōshū Goketsu*) were chosen from the Chōshū *han* of western Japan and studied in England from 1863 at

Nishi Amane
1829–1897,
Philosopher

---

[156] He was sent to the University of Leyden to study political science, constitutional law and economics. On his return, Nishi advocated the rejection of Confucian ethics as the basis for Japanese government, preferring a more pragmatic, western model. John Stuart Mill was a big influence on his thinking. His ideas influenced much of the early Meiji structures, particularly the Imperial Army.

[157] In parallel with Nishi, Tsuda returned to Japan with western ideas. He codified Japanese laws and was engaged in diplomatic negotiations with China

RESPECT AND CONSIDERATION

William Alexander Williamson
1824–1904

University College London[158] under the guidance of Professor Alexander William Williamson[159]. It was still illegal to leave Japan when they left, as *sakoku* was still in force.

A Mr. Weigal, Thomas Glover's[160] manager in Yokohama, put the Chōshū youths, disguised as English sailors, aboard a reluctant Captain J. S. Gower's vessel (owned by Jardine Matheson) at 1000 ryō[161] each, bound for Shanghai where they were sheltered on an opium storage ship before dividing into two groups for the long voyage to London. When they reached London, the Chōshū students were introduced by William Matheson to Professor Williamson.

---

[158] Sir Ernest Satow had studied here as an undergraduate.

[159] Alexander William Williamson studied medicine at Heidelberg University under Graham and Liebig, and soon turned to chemistry. Appointed Professor of Practical Chemistry in 1849 and also Professor of Chemistry 1855-1887 at University College, London. He discovered the structure of alcohols and ethers and devised a method of classifying organic compounds into types according to structure. He formulated the concept of dynamic equilibrium of a reaction and demonstrated the catalytic action of sulphuric acid in the synthesis of ether from alcohol.

[160] Thomas Blake Glover (6.6.1838 - 13.12.1911), had been a buyer of green tea for Jardine, Matheson in Nagasaki but left in 1861 to form his own trading house, *Guraba-Shokai*. He was highly respected in Japan for his many contributions to its modernization. He imported and sold ships, guns and gunpowder to Satsuma and other anti-*bakufu han*, and later railway locomotives and engineering equipment and much else to Japan in general. He was probably the most successful (despite a bankruptcy *en route*) foreign trader with Japan. He helped found a shipbuilding company that grew into the mighty Mitsubishi *keiretsu*, and a brewery that became the Kirin brewery, whose original brewery at Tsurumi-ku is at Namamugi-cho 1, close by the scene of Richardson's murder. Glover's Japanese wife Yamamura Tsuru was said to have been the inspiration for Puccini's opera *Madama Butterfly*.

[161] Gold coin = 60 *monme* = 4 *kan*

EARLY JAPANESE STUDENTS IN BRITAIN

Inoue Kaoru (1835-1915) and Itō Hirobumi (1841-1909), destined to be two of the greatest Japanese statesmen of the age, worked as deckhands aboard the 1500 ton steamer *Pegasus* on the voyage to Europe. They also returned earlier than the other three when they realised that the Chōshū clan was in danger of attack by the allied powers for trying to oust the foreigners by firing on their ships in the Straits of Shimonoseki.

Itō Hirobumi

The five students from Chōshū in 1863 were Itō Shunsuke (later Itō Hirobumi), Inoue Monta (later Inoue Kaoru), Yamao Yozo, Endo Kinsuke, and Nomura Yakichi (later Inoue Masaru).

Prince Itō Hirobumi 伊藤 博文 (1841-1909) was also called Hirofumi/Hakubun and Shunsuke in his youth. He was born in Hagi, Yamaguchi. He became the first Prime Minister of Japan (and the 5th, 7th and 10th).

Inoue Kaoru 井上 馨 (1836-1915) Originally named Inoue Monta until his visit to England. After returning from England with Itō Hirobumi to prevent warfare between Chōshū and Satsuma, Endo served as joint interpreter (with Endo Kinsuke) between Chōshū and Sir Harry Parkes on his visit in 1865. Inoue was a Japanese statesman, serving as Finance Minister and as Foreign Minister in the Meiji administration.

Inoue Kaoru

Yamao Yozo (1837-1917) later studied engineering at the Andersonian Institute,

Yamao Yozo

RESPECT AND CONSIDERATION

Glasgow from 1866 to 1868 while working at the River Clyde shipyards by day. He lodged with a Colin Brown. Yamao became Vice Minister of Public Works and as such was responsible for setting up the Japanese Imperial College of Engineering as well as the Imperial College of Art. He was made an Earl (*hakushaku*) and claimed to have introduced the Scottish song (presumably learnt from Colin Brown) "Auld Lang Syne" to Japan. Japanese words have been set to that melody: *hotaru no hikari* ("The light of the firefly"), and the tune is commonly played in large stores in Japan to inform their customers that they are about to close; many Japanese are adamant that it is in origin a Japanese song.

Endo Kinsuke: a faded photograph

Endo Kinsuke 遠藤謹助 (1836-1893). On returning from England, Endo served as joint interpreter (with Inoue Kaoru) between Chōshū and Sir Harry Parkes on his visit in 1865. From 1881 to 1883, Endo was head of the Mint (*Zōheikyoku*) at Ōsaka. His lasting legacy is that he opened the grounds of the Mint each spring so that the people could enjoy the spectacle of the magnificent *sakura* - cherry blossom - from its many trees.

Inoue Masaru as a student

Inoue Masaru 井上勝 (1843-1910) was known as the "Father of the Japanese Railways". He was born at Hagi, Yamaguchi. He briefly was adopted into the Nomura family and became known as Nomura Yakichi, though later he was restored to the Inoue family.

In 1865, fifteen Satsuma students, one from Tosa and one from Nagasaki were sent to Britain with two *ometsuke* (supervisors).

EARLY JAPANESE STUDENTS IN BRITAIN

This group also studied at University College London, which was open to students of all religions[162]. Notable students included Mori Arinori, Godai Tomoatsu (joint leader of the group and instigator of the plan to send the 15), Terashima Munenori (joint leader), Sameshima Naonobu and Nagasawa Kanae.

Here are brief biographies of these five particularly notable students, which illustrates the high calibre of person who seized the opportunity to study abroad, to the great benefit of Japan:

Mori Arinori

Mori Arinori 森有礼 (23.8.1847 - 12.2.1889) was sent to England to study mathematics, physics and naval surveying. During his studies of navigation, he once sailed from Newcastle to deliver coal to Russia. In 1871, he was appointed the first Japanese Ambassador to the United States of America. He embraced the American liberal education ethos. Such was his assimilation into American culture, that on his return to Japan, he advocated the universal abandonment of the Japanese language in favour of English. He was successively ambassador to China, senior vice-Minister for Foreign

---

[162] Until well into the nineteenth century, admission to Oxford and Cambridge universities was restricted to members of the Church of England, later expanded to non-conformist Christians, and at the end of the century, to Roman Catholics. The Japanese students, from a Buddhist/*shintō* culture, found difficulty coping with aspects of Christianity that had been absorbed into British culture, such as the Easter and Christmas holiday arrangements, and the historical-clerical origins of the universities. They also struggled with the British "gentleman-amateur" approach to university education still then prevalent, where many students did the minimum necessary to obtain a low-grade degree, whereas the Japanese ideal, then as now, was to strive unswervingly for excellence.

RESPECT AND CONSIDERATION

Affairs, ambassador to Great Britain, a member of the *Sanjiin* (legislative advisory council) and Minister of Education. On the day the Meiji Constitution came into force, he was assaulted by a reactionary, Nishino Fumitaro, and died the following day.

Godai Tomoatsu

Godai Tomoatsu 五代友厚 had studied naval science and technology and fought for Satsuma at Kagoshima in the Anglo-Satsuma war. After studying in England, he established relations with French business interests, who went on to invest in Satsuma. A shipyard and a silk-spinning works were established by them, to go with the extensive cotton-spinning industry Godai had established by buying machinery from Platt Brothers of Oldham when he was studying in England. Godai was so successful in his negotiations with the French that Satsuma was treated as an independent country in the Paris Exhibition of 1867. Satsuma ware was one of the most popular exhibits. Godai went on to become a junior councillor in the Meiji administration, but from 1869 turned his attention to business. He founded several large international trading companies, and became a major banker and shipping magnate. He later founded Ōsaka Chamber of Commerce and the Ōsaka Stock Exchange.

Terashima Munenori 寺島宗則 studied at University College, London, and travelled widely in Europe during his time in the West. He returned to Satsuma in time to take part in the defence of Kagoshima during the Anglo-Satsuma War detailed earlier. In 1873, he was appointed Foreign Minister of Japan, and negotiated the Treaty of St Petersburg that fixed the national boundaries between Russia and Japan. He failed, however, to renegotiate the Unequal Treaties; he had come to terms with America, but Britain refused to budge, so all the negotiations fell through, and the Unequal Treaties remained.

Terashima Munenori

Sameshima Naonobu 鮫島尚信 (1844-1881) was sent from the small town of Kaseda in Satsuma. Later he became Envoy Extraordinary and Minister Plenipotentiary from Japan to France. Under Laurence Oliphant's patronage, Sameshima became a member of Thomas Lake Harris's utopian quasi-Christian community, the Brotherhood of the New Life[163].

---

[163]This was founded in 1861 on Swedenborgian-utopian principles and soon moved to Brocton on Lake Erie, with about sixty converts, including five clergymen, Sameshima and Nagasawe, a number of American women enamoured of Harris, and Laurence Oliphant and his mother. A winemaking industry was established. In reply to teetotallist objections, Harris declared that the wine he vinted was "filled with the divine breath" so that "all noxious influences" were neutralized. He also strongly advocated the use of tobacco. Like many a cult leader since, he demanded absolute obedience from his disciples, and found many women disciples eager to obey his sexual commands. The Brotherhood, though, required marital celibacy of its rank-and-file members until they had attained a "sense of marital chastity". Harris developed his ideas: there were interplanetary empires; the early humans had been taught agriculture, technology and spiritual secrets by astronauts (paralleling Amaterasu, perhaps?), and those within the Brotherhood would be caught up into the "Celestial Sphere" come the millennium. Helen Blavatsky picked up many of these ideas and used them as a basis for her "Theosophical" movement. The Oliphants broke away from Harris in 1881 and successfully sued him for thousands of pounds they claimed he had robbed from them. The Oliphants remained faithful to the principles of the brotherhood, though. Harris's followers believed that he had attained the secret of immortal life on

RESPECT AND CONSIDERATION

Nagasawa Kanae

Nagasawa Kanae 長澤鼎 Nagasawa (originally Hikosuke Isonaga) too became a member of the Brotherhood of the New Life. He arrived in America via Scotland, where his English picked up a Scottish accent, a source of great amusement to the people he met. He was the only one of the Satsuma students who failed to return to Japan and take up influential positions in the Meiji governmental infrastructure. He left "Father Faithful" - Thomas Lake Harris - eventually, and went on to found the first Californian winery, Fountaingrove Round Barn & Winery, in 1875 in Santa Rosa, Sonoma. Nagasawa became known as the "Grape King of California". His product was the first Californian wine exported to England. For many years, Fountaingrove regularly produced 84,000 cases annually (756,000 litres).

Hayashi Tadasu

In 1865, the *bakufu* itself decided to send six students to Russia. A year later, as the *bakumatsu* gathered pace, the *shōgun* sent 12 students and two supervisors to England in the wake of the Chōshū and Satsuma delegations. The supervisors were Kawaji Taro and Nakamura Keisuke. The students were Naruse Jogoro, Toyama Sutehachi, Fukuzawa Einosuke, Hayashi Tozaburo (later Hayashi Tadasu), Itō Shonosuke, Okukawa Ichirō, Yasui Shinpachirō, Mitsukuri Keigo and his younger brother Mitsukuri Dairoku (later Kikuchi Dairoku), Ichikawa

---

earth, and after he ceased moving on 23 March 1906 declared that he was only sleeping. Holding their noses, they ruefully announced three months later that he was, in fact, dead.

EARLY JAPANESE STUDENTS IN BRITAIN

Morisaburo, Sugi Tokujiro and Iwasa Genji. Mitsukuri Dairoku was only eleven years old when he was sent to Britain.

Once again, these were high-calibre individuals. For example:
- **Count Hayashi Tadasu** 林董 (1850-1913), was born in Chiba prefecture, the son of Sato Taizen, a physician practicing Dutch medicine for the Sakura clan. He became Industry Minister and Vice Foreign Minister. He was appointed ambassador to China, Russia and then Britain and later Foreign Minister.

Kikuchi Dairoku 菊池大麓 17.3.1855 - 19.8.1917, was born in Edo. From a family of astonishing academics (many of his ancestors, contemporaries and descendants to this day have had glittering careers), as a graduate from London (B.A.) and Cambridge (M.A.) universities, he was a Wrangler (senior mathematician) at Cambridge University;  he was showered with honorary Doctorates from Britain and America, and had a Japanese D.Sc.; he became a professor and Dean of the faculty of Science and eventually president of Tōkyō Imperial University; Minister of Education; and president of Kyōto Imperial University. He was made a baron in 1902, and was the eighth president of *Gakushuin* (School for the children of the Aristocracy) and briefly the first President of the Science Research Institute of Japan.

By 1867, other parties of students were sent by the *bakufu* to France and elsewhere. In 1871, to the great interest of the Japanese public, a group of five young girls including Tsuda Umeko (aged 6) travelled to the United States to study. Some students went for military training: soldiers to France, and sailors to England. Among them was Heihachirō Tōgō who trained as a naval cadet aboard the Thames Marine Officer Training School HMS *Worcester* in 1873-4. Before long, it was a

RESPECT AND CONSIDERATION

regular practice to send young men and women abroad for study[164].

High-calibre students again:

Tsuda Omeko

Tsuda Umeko 津田 梅子 (31.12.1864 - 16.8.1929) went, aged six, to stay with the childless Charles Lanman (former Secretary to Mori Arinori q.v.) and his wife. She returned to Japan aged 18 and worked as a tutor to the children of Itō Hirobumi. In 1889, she returned to America and took a degree in biology and education; she also studied for a short time at St. Hilda's College Oxford. Returning to Japan, she agitated for equal educational opportunities for girls, against much conservative opposition. She went on to found (for women of all backgrounds) *Joshi Eigaku-juku* (女子英学塾 the Women's Institute for English Studies) - now Tsudajuku College in Kojimachi, Tōkyō. She was also a novelist and (having become a Christian at the age of nine) was President of the Japanese Y.W.C.A.

Tōgō Heihachirō as a student in Britain 1871–78

Tōgō Heihachirō 東郷 平八郎 (1848 – 1934) rose to become a Count and *gensui* (元帥 Fleet Admiral) and was a motivating force in the structure and organisation of the Imperial Japanese Navy (IJN). He served as a gunner in the battle between Satsuma and the British fleet

---

[164] The Oath in Five Articles (*Gokajō no Seimon*) on March 14, 1868 was signed by the Emperor as one of his first ruling acts. Its last article says, "Knowledge shall be sought throughout the world so as to strengthen the foundation of Imperial Rule" (*Chishiki wo sekai ni motome, dai ni kōki wo shinki subeshi.*) On February 11, 1871, the Order concerning Study Abroad (*Kaigai Ryugaku Kisoku*) was promulgated. Only students recommended by a Japanese university were eligible to study abroad. The Order required the Japanese university to regulate the foreign programme of study that the student would follow.

at Kagoshima in 1863. He volunteered as a junior officer in Satsuma's new Navy and fought against the *bakufu* in the battles of Miako and Hakodate. Tōgō joined the Emperor's new Navy and applied to go for training to Britain. In 1874, he finagled his way into HMS *Worcester*, a Royal Naval training school, claiming that he was 16 years old, not 26. He later graduated with honour from the Royal Naval College at Greenwich. On behalf of the IJN, he supervised the building of their frigate *Fusō* 扶桑 at the Samuda boatyard on the Isle of Dogs in 1877.

Imperial Japanese Battleship *Fusō*

He rose to glory when, as Admiral, he defeated the Russian fleet - twice - in 1904 and 1905. Tōgō's life in many ways paralleled that of Admiral Lord Nelson, whom Tōgō admired and modelled much of his actions on.

As the brief biographies show, these eager students from Japan went on to have illustrious careers, mainly in the service of Japan. Some were chosen from aristocratic stock, but most were selected for their aptitude for learning. The men among them went on to provide a strong backbone for the Meiji government, and had a lasting effect on Japanese culture and government.

For example, the Meiji education system was modelled on the British system. Term times are very much as British terms are today. The importation of British engineering and other machinery led to the adoption of Imperial measures for these purposes, and the Whitworth screw thread standards became Japanese standards too. The standard width (two pages) of

RESPECT AND CONSIDERATION

Japanese broadsheet newsprint is 32 inches, the same as the imported British printing presses. Like the British Empire, the rule of the road became - and still is - to drive on the left.

Emperor Meiji and his government and advisers were aware of Western progress, and "learning missions" were sent abroad to absorb as much of it as possible. One of the most important was the "Iwakura Mission", led by Iwakura Tomomi in the role of Ambassador Extraordinary and Plenipotentiary, assisted by four vice-ambassadors, three of whom - Ōkubo Toshimichi, Kido Takayoshi, and Ito Hirobumi - were also ministers in the Japanese government. Such was the importance of the Mission that the Government even commissioned a renowned historian, Kume Kunitake, as the official diarist.

Ōkubo Toshimichi

On 23rd December 1871, they sailed from Yokohama for San Francisco. From there they travelled overland to Washington, DC, then by sea again to Britain, France, Belgium, the Netherlands, Russia, Prussia, Germany, Denmark, Sweden, Austria, Italy and Switzerland. It was a comprehensive tour. But they were not finished even then. During their return to Japan, they made brief calls on Egypt, Aden, Ceylon, Singapore, Saigon, Hong Kong and Shanghai, finally returning to Yokohama on 13th September 1873.

Kido Takayoshi

The purposes of the mission were:
1. to secure high level international recognition for Japan's newly restored Imperial règime

EARLY JAPANESE STUDENTS IN BRITAIN

2. To open discussions on the renegotiation of the unequal treaties with the USA, Britain and the other European countries that had been entered into in the 1850s and 1860s.
3. To gather information on education, technology, culture, and military, social and economic structures from the countries visited that would be of value in the modernization of Japan.

Of these goals:
1. the first succeeded, as the west accorded them a friendly, not to say enthusiastic, reception.
2. The second failed. Western governments saw no advantage in ceding the valuable concessions their earlier diplomats had wrung so painfully from Japan. In their vain attempts to renegotiate the treaties with better conditions, the Mission went beyond their mandates, and stayed abroad much longer than planned, which did not please the Emperor or the government.
3. The third succeeded admirably.

As this book is concerned with British-Japanese relations, I will confine myself to just one part of the Mission. After arriving in London in August 1872, they split into independent groups to visit Britain's northern centres of industrial and commercial power: Liverpool, Manchester, Glasgow, Edinburgh and Newcastle-upon-Tyne. They arrived in Newcastle on 21st October and were accommodated in the Royal Station Hotel. Their arrival excited much interest in the local

Heads of Iwakura Mission, photographed in London in 1872
Iwakura is in the centre

populace. The Newcastle Daily Chronicle of 23rd October commented:

> The gentlemen were attired in ordinary morning costume and except for their complexion and the oriental cast of their features, they could scarcely be distinguished from their English companions.

The statement was intended as a compliment.

During their visit, they met the industrialist Sir William Armstrong at his Elswick Engine and Ordnance Works outside Newcastle-upon-Tyne and looked closely at the manufacture of the Armstrong guns they had seen in action at Kagoshima and Shimonoseki. Armstrong had by now nearly cracked the premature firing problem, but not quite. (When he did eventually solve it, the Japanese bought many from him, and the Armstrong guns played a decisive part, on 27th - 28th May 1905, in the Japanese naval success at the Battle of Tsushima in the Russo-Japanese War.) They also examined the organization of the Works, and were impressed with the hydraulic equipment and the boring and turning departments.

During their visit to the north-east of England, they also visited a colliery, an Iron Works, an iron-ore mine and a couple of Chemical factories. Everywhere they made comprehensive notes and drawings, which in time would lay the foundations for the nascent Japanese industrial flowering of the early twentieth century.

Sir William Armstrong

EARLY JAPANESE STUDENTS IN BRITAIN

Newly opened Port of Yokohama, 1860 by Sadahide Utagawa
This is a view of *honchō–dōri*, a favoured shopping street for foreign visitors keen to buy curios. Note the trading logo of the long-established House of Mitsui on the building on the left. Mitsui was the largest Trading House during the latter days of the Edo period. They were involved in "dry goods" (textile fabrics: cottons, woollens, linens, silks, laces, etc.), and latterly in banking, especially money lending and foreign exchange. They also served as tax collectors for the *bakufu* in various places. Later they became heavily involved in international trade and shipping, and remain as one of Japan's largest businesses today. Its gross revenues for the year to 31 March 2007 were 4,880,741,000,000 Yen. If Mitsui were a country, it would currently rank around 60th out of 183 countries in the world in terms of GDP.

The Mitsui logo
Still in use today. It is composed of the stylised *kanji* for
"three" - *mitsu* 三 - within the stylised kanji (tilted through 45°) for "well" - *i* 井
mitsu - *i* becomes Mitsui "three wells".

Chapter 32
Why did the Tokugawa *shōgunate* Fall?

There were two strands of pressure that combined to bring down the Tokugawa règime in 1868. The first was the internal discontent and decay that gradually manifested itself during the first part of the nineteenth century.

The great strength of the Tokugawa *shōgunate* had been to create relative economic stability over two and a half centuries. Its wealth gave it absolute control over the great cities and the economically advanced areas of the country, and it was able to manipulate the economy to its own advantage. Inflation was virtually zero throughout their reign.

The great weakness of the Tokugawa *shōgunate* was its favouritism of certain of the *daimyō* over others. In particular, the Satsuma, Chōshū, Tosa and Hizen *han* were subjugated as *tozama*, and they represented a powerful economic and military force that resented their treatment at the hands of Tokugawa. Satsuma had 27,000 *samurai* and Chōshū 11,000. These were highly trained, well-led, and totally loyal to their domain chief, eager to give their lives if required.

A further weakness along similar lines was the rigid distinction that had grown up between *shōgunate* and Imperial Courts. The Emperor was accorded divine status in theory, but in practice, all political direction was in the hands of Tokugawa. The *shōgunate* had, in effect, subjugated the Imperial Court. It

WHY DID TOKUGAWA FALL?

was the unspoken but deep-seated feeling that the *shōgunate* had gone too far in excluding the *kuge* and the Emperor from power that gave moral support to the movement to restore the Emperor to his rightful place as supreme ruler.

Because of the relative peace over 250 years of the Tokugawa *shōgunate*, the *samurai* had become largely redundant as fighting men, and many had become the civil service of the national and domain governments. The retainers who served as bodyguards and in other military capacities became restless at their lack of real purpose. It was unthinkable that any member of the *samurai* might turn to farming or craftsmanship or, worst of all, trade. But idle hands readily turn to mischief.

The peasants had become discontent with their lot. They were conscripted as soldiers, kept in economic poverty, forced to ask permission to marry, and generally treated below their rightful place in the *shi-no-ko-sho* system.

Finally, the *shi-no-ko-sho* system placed merchants firmly at the foot of the status ladder. Yet many of them had become rich and economically powerful. So these *chōnin* too were resentful of their low-caste status.

Thus a strange anti-Tokugawa alliance gradually coalesced: resentful *daimyō*, resentful *kuge*, resentful *chōnin*, resentful peasants, the whole loose alliance led by resentful lower-ranking *samurai* and *rōnin*. And a key component in this was the financing of the alliance by the *chōnin*. The Osaka branch of the trading house of Mitsui has a minute in its records that says

> The loans required for the military operations of the
> Imperial forces were largely furnished by the
> House of Mitsui

It needs to be emphasised that this anti-*bakufu* alliance was not a parallel to the class-based conflict that had characterised the bloody French revolution. The united Japanese revolutionaries came from all classes, from the highest to the lowest. Perhaps it had something in common with the American revolution, in that it represented a struggle against bad government. And the protagonists for change were not agreed on any one single policy other than the need to restore power where it rightfully belonged - to the hands of the emperor. In that regard, there were some parallels with the Unification of Italy.

The second strand was the external pressure applied by the western powers. Once Perry had made his initial Friendship Treaty in 1854, there was an inevitable cracking of the nutshell exposing the kernel inside. The British chastisement of Kagoshima and the British-led punishment of Shimonoseki had exposed the Tokugawa règime as unable to protect its peoples. Defence of the realm is usually cited as the primary duty of any state, and Tokugawa had failed in its primary duty. The naval engagements had also convinced Satsuma and Chōshū that the west had much to offer by way of technology - particularly military and naval technology - and expertise. They had no qualms about concluding amicable trading agreements with their erstwhile antagonists in Europe, and equipped themselves well for the forthcoming battles with the *shōgunate* - and later for the Boshin War.

The *shōgunate*, too, realised that the genie was out of the bottle and they had to make an accommodation with the west. Their fault was being too slow to grasp the point, unlike Satsuma and Chōshū.

It is not true to say that Tokugawa fell because of the incursion of western merchants, but it is clear that their advent accelerated the process greatly. The first strand of internal Japanese discontent would have caused the change, but doubtless many years - maybe decades, given the Japanese talent for prevarication - later. It is ironic that the lowest form of life in the *shi-no-ko-sho* system - the merchants - were the catalyst for the destruction of the centuries-old Japanese system of government.

After the dust had settled and Emperor Meiji had assumed the reins of government, it might have been the opportunity for the *sonnō jōi* movement to seize the moment and throw the foreigners out of Japan. This, however, did not happen, because the new Meiji government was composed of men who took a strategic view of Japan's opportunities. They realised that Japan, in world terms, was in a backwater. To come out of a feudal past into a technological future, to move from an ineffectual nation to a powerful state, they needed the help of the west. The new government and the dynamic *han* started hiring western experts like technicians, railway and marine engineers, architects, agriculturalists, university teachers, doctors and military and naval advisers on a large scale. At the same time, they sent out some of their brightest young talents in the nation to the west to be educated in western science and law and government and military and naval matters.

Although the élite were seizing the opportunity for enlightenment, the embracing of the West was not as readily undertaken in the backwaters of Japan. Between 1917 and 1922, JW Robertson Scott had collected this *bon*[165] song from a dancer in rural Akita in northern Honshū. Even then, more than 60 years after the arrival of the West, there was veiled regret at the arrival of the foreigners and the changes they had brought about:

---

[165] *O-bon* お盆 is an annual Buddhist summer festival to honour the departed spirits of one's ancestors. It has developed into a family reunion akin to America's Thanksgiving, but still contains many of the ancient elements of dance and music performed collectively by the inhabitants of the village or district. Each community has its own traditions of distinctive song and dance.

RESPECT AND CONSIDERATION

>Mr. Potato of the Countryside
>Got his new European suit.
>But a potato is still a potato.
>He took one and a half rin[166] out of his bag
>And bought amé[167] and licked at it.

A potato is still a potato, and a Japanese is still a Japanese.

---

[166] A *rin* 厘 is one-tenth of a *sen*, which in turn was one hundredth of a *yen* 円 (*yen* is pronounced "en"). The *yen* replaced the *mon* as part of a major economic reform by the Meiji administration in 1870. The *sen* had but a negligible value and a *rin* far less. The *rin* and *sen* were withdrawn from circulation in 1953.
[167] A kind of barley sugar.

Epilogue

It is a perennial pastime of historians to speculate on the consequences if events had not occurred, or if some factor(s) had been different. In the events recounted here, what if...

- ... Kublai Khan had successfully conquered Japan in the late thirteenth century?
- ... Fernão Mendes Pinto and his companions had not washed up on the shores of Tanegashima in 1543?
- ... Francis Xavier had been entirely successful and Japan had become a Catholic country?
- ... the Tokugawans were expansionist world traders?
- ... Japan had followed a parallel course with the West in their evolution from feudalism to a recognisable form of democracy?

More germane to the subject matter of this book, though, is: What if Perry had not been sent to open Japanese ports up to international trade? Let me conject.

The obvious first conclusion is that *sakoku* would have continued for some time. Japan would have continued to slumber while the world around her became more industrialised and prosperous. Because there would have been no treaties, there would have been no visiting naval and military forces sent to protect the diplomats and traders. Japan would not have been on any regular shipping route, and Charles Lenox Richardson would have found an alternative passage home, bypassing Japan, and keeping his life. There would have been no naval engagements at Kagoshima and Shimonoseki. There would have been no purchases of warships and other *materiel*, and western military principles would have remained with the west.

Admiral Togo at the time of the Russo–Japanese War 1904–5

Following on from that, Japan would not have become the formidable naval force she became, vanquishing Russia in 1905. She would not have been a valued military ally with Britain and the west against Austria-Hungary, Germany and the Ottoman Empire in the 1914-1918 war. Japan would not have invaded mainland China in the 1930s, nor would she have waged war against America and the western allies in the 1939-1945 war. Or at least, she would have been several decades behind the west in terms of military and industrial technology and military training. Had Japan not been in a position to wage war in World War II, no atomic bombs would have been dropped on Hiroshima and Nagasaki. And perhaps America would not have engaged in what would have been the European war against fascism.

There would have been no *Japonisme* in Europe and America in the last quarter of the nineteenth century. So the impressionist and post-impressionist output of Manet, Henri de Toulouse-Lautrec, Degas, Renoir, Whistler, Monet, van Gogh, Pissarro, Gaugin and Klimt, among others, would have been very different. The Art Nouveau movement with its flowing lines and flat contrasty colours clearly owes its inspiration to *ukiyo-e*. And the later abstract art movement in the west owes its origins to the Japanese woodcut style with its blocks of colour.

EPILOGUE

In music, there would be no *Madama Butterfly* by Puccini, nor *The Mikado*[168] by Gilbert & Sullivan. In poetry, the unique forms of Japanese verse would be unknown to the West. The western world would have been much the poorer artistically.

The reader may think I have made too much of poetry in this book. However, poetry has a special place in Japanese culture. *Kojiki* says the very first *waka* was composed by no less than the *kami* Susa-no-o himself (see Appendix 1-1). It reads:

八雲立つ	yakumo tatsu
出雲八重垣	izumo yaegaki
妻籠みに	tsuma-gomi ni
八重垣作る	yaegaki tsukuru
その八重垣を	sono yaegaki wo

Translation is always a difficult art, particularly when it is poetry that is to be translated. And compound this with the archaic Japanese in this case! So I am grateful to Mr Stephen Denney for his meaning-for-meaning translation, which I take responsibility for doctoring to fit my English style:

>THE EIGHT CLOUDS STAND
>The eight-layer fence of Izumo[169].
>Those actively billowing clouds form an eight-layered[170] fence to surround the palace[171] in order to keep my[172] wife safe[173];
>That magnificent 'eight-layered' fence of cloud[174].

---

[168] The Japanese ambassador made a formal protest to the Foreign Office when *The Mikado* was first staged in 1885, complaining that it painted a very different picture of Japan (and particularly the Emperor) than was the truth.

[169] City in Shimane prefecture, Northern Japan, where Susa-no-o slew the dragon.

[170] i.e. impenetrable.

[171] Or Castle, or Fortress

[172] "My" is not in the Japanese, but is needed to make English sense.

[173] The form of the Japanese carries a suggestion that the wife is cloistered against her will.

RESPECT AND CONSIDERATION

With a pedigree reaching back before the birth of the first emperor, poetry can claim to be the primary art-form of Japan. And the west readily took to the forms of Japanese poetry. The *haiku* and its near-identical predecessor the *hokku* has been a particularly popular international form (a 2011 internet search for "haiku" produced some 10·8 million results). Most schoolchildren in Britain will have tried to write English *haiku*, as part of their creative writing attempts.

---

[174] This line presents particular difficulties. A direct translation says something along the lines of "The clouds make the eight-layered fence of that beautiful/splendid cloud"; but the interjection is nearer the meaning of the Japanese.

EPILOGUE

JAPONISME'S INFLUENCE IN WESTERN FINE ART

Ukiyo–e
Katsukawa Shunsho

La Courtisane
Vincent van Gogh

La princesse du pays de porcelain
James McNeill Whistler

RESPECT AND CONSIDERATION

The influence on western painters of Japanese art forms is plain to see. The (reversed) S-shaped human figure was not known in western art before the Japanese forms became known. Japanese colours had an influence, too. The woodblock printing process led to the use of blocks of intense colour, and this intensity of colour was taken up by western artists too. The monochrome printing of this book does not do justice to the three portraits shown here. Dozens of other western painters could have been chosen than the two shown, but these two demonstrate the *Japonisme* effect very well.

Namamugijiken–sankohkan

At the little museum[175] in Namamugi, Asaumi Takeo, its enthusiastic founder and voluntary curator, says that in a strange way, he is glad Richardson died. At least his death was not ultimately pointless. Without his death, Japan perhaps would never have engaged the west, or dragged herself out of sterile feudal *shōgunate* rule, until much later. Asaumi-san is the one who tends the graves of Richardson, Marshall and Clarke. He even contributed out of his own pocket, alongside the Shimazu family and the British Embassy, to have Richardson's grave restored and his and Marshall and Clarke's graves moved to their present location. And each year he organises, conducts and personally pays for a ceremony at the graveside attended by Satsuma and British representatives. It is a ceremony of homage and respect for a

---

[175] Namamugijiken-sankohkan, 1-11-20 Namamugi, Tsurumi-ku, Yokohama. Phone 045-503-3710. Opening hours 10:00-17:00, but may open upon request since facility is privately owned. Admission Free.
http://www.city.yokohama.jp/me/tsurumi/shokei/99-05/19tenbyo.html (Japanese)

EPILOGUE

man whose death was a pivot for so much to happen to the long-term benefit of Japan.

It is fitting that these graves should be tended and cherished, for they speak of the moment when Japan, willingly or not, took its first tentative steps to joining the modern community of nations. This should be recognised as a site of national importance by the Japanese Government, who owe their form, function, prerogative and history to the events of the *bakumatsu*. Is it too much to ask that they should shoulder the major part of the costs involved in keeping fresh the memory of the three Englishmen?

**2006 Ceremony.
Chairman of Shimazu Corporation, Representative from British Embassy and Asaumi–san.**
Photo: Stephen Denney

APPENDIX 1-1
ANCIENT AND MODERN

In order to understand the various strands that led to the death of Charles Richardson and the ensuing events, it is useful to make a broad sweep through the Japanese past. Bear with me, for there are many threads in the complex matrix of Japanese history that echo throughout the centuries, and continue to resonate today. The Japanese do not share our historical European background, and so Japanese culture is unfamiliar - indeed, one is tempted to say, inscrutable - to our western eyes. We need to put aside our western preconceptions and venture into the Japanese mind-set, the unspoken yet all-encompassing beliefs that the Japanese have about themselves. We need to look - and look with admiration - at the complex political and cultural systems that set the scene for the events that we have seen unfolded. It is a fascinating culture we are looking at, with European parallels here and there, and completely alien dissimilarities too. We need to begin at the beginning, with …

THE JAPANESE CREATION MYTH AND THE IMPERIAL LINE

There are various Japanese creation myths. I have chosen to recount parts of the earliest on record. In 712 AD, the first compilation (in Japanese) of Japanese legends and myths - *kojiki*

ANCIENT AND MODERN

("record of ancient things") – was assembled by Oono Yasumaro, who was ordered to note down the sayings of an Imperial storyteller, Hiedano Are. In 720, another collection of myths - *nihongi* or *nihon shoki* - ("chronicles of Japan") were written down in Chinese. The two collections have considerable similarities but also differ in some respects. Both of them serve to legitimise the divine origins of the Imperial line. After all, Emperor Temmu (r. 673-686) commissioned them both.

According to *kojiki*, (and this is a very much condensed version of it) first there was nothing. Then something light arose and became the plain of heaven. Three Creating Deities formed. Over a great period of time, a primordial soup of matter started to separate into heavier and lighter parts. The heavier part sank and formed the earth, and muddy waters covered it. A green shoot grew until it reached the clouds and was transformed into a god. The god felt lonely and started to create other gods and goddesses. Among them were Izanagi (伊邪那岐命 "He who invites") and Izanami (伊邪那美命 "She who invites"). The gods commissioned these two to turn the earth into something useful.

Izanagi wondered what lay beneath the muddy waters, and thrust his jewelled spear Ama-no-Nuboko deep into them. As he wrenched it free from the cloying mud, some clumps fell back into the sea and began to harden. These became the many islands of Japan.

Izanagi and Izanami, who had a tempestuous - not to say murderous – relationship, start separately to explore the islands. Each, seeing the potential of the land, creates plants to cover the land. When they meet up again, they decide that plants are not enough, so they resolve to populate the land. Izanami dies of burns while giving birth to the fire god Hinokagutsuchi. Izanagi, grief-stricken, kills Hinokagatsuchi and chops him into eight pieces that form eight active volcanoes. He then follows Izanami to Yomi, the netherworld, to bring her back to the land of the living. She is embarrassed when he sees her putrefying body, and chases him away, splashing him inadvertently with her suppurations. While washing the contamination of the putrefaction away, Izanagi bears (from his left eye) a child of dazzling, radiant beauty named Amaterasu-ō-mi-kami (天照大御神 "lustrous goddess who lights up the heavens"). Amaterasu, the Sun Goddess, is usually regarded as female, though this is not clear from the ancient Japanese texts.

Izanagi then gives birth to a second child, Tsuki-yomi-no-mikoto (月夜見の尊 "the blessed - behold the moonlit night") from his right eye; Tsuki-yomi becomes the moon (in Japanese *tsuki* means "moon"); and then a third and unruly son, Susa-no-o-mikoto 須佐之男命, is born from Izanagi's nose, and is sentenced to the sea, where he creates storms. Other children include Owatatsumi, the sea god. Izanami decides Amaterasu is far, far too beautiful for muddy earth, even for beautiful Japan, so he sends her up the celestial ladder to the High Celestial Plain. Her radiance is visible to us today, for she became the sun.

A malachite magatama
Jōmon period
(1000BC–538AD)

Susa-no-o was a troublesome boy who exasperated the gods, and fought bitterly with his sister Amaterasu. She took umbrage and withdrew to the Yasugawara cave in Takachiho, in the middle of Kyūshū. Amaterasu was only enticed out again by the entreaties of eighty myriads of gods. One of them, Ama-no-Uzumeno-Mikoto (the "Terrible Heavenly Female") performed a lewd comic dance[176] that drew Amaterasu's

---

[176] *Iwato kagura* dances imitating Uzumeno's are still performed every evening at the *Takachiho-jinja* (Takachiho shrine), and in the darkest months of the year, these may last all night.

ANCIENT AND MODERN

attention to some gifts with which they wished to entice her. These were a bronze mirror, in which she could see herself, and a necklace of comma-shaped jewels called *magatama* (*tama* means "gem"). These neolithic adornments are often found in Japan in the *kofun* (古墳 keyhole-shaped tumuli) where early Emperors were buried, possibly as offerings to the gods. They are also found in Korea, just 130 miles (210 km) over the sea.

Susa-no-o was banished to the netherworld, but took his time going there and had to be chased. While being pursued around Japan, he fought and slew a fearsome dragon at Izumo. It has been speculated that the pursuit of Susa-no-o was an allegory of a real series of battles fought between two Japanese tribes in the Bronze Age, the winning one being the predecessors of the Imperial line. However, in one of the eight tails of the monster, Susa-no-o found a sword, which he called *kusanagi* "the grass-cutter". He presented *kusanagi* to Amaterasu as a peace-offering. In 1984, a cache of 358 2000-year-old bronze swords was unearthed at Izumo. Izumo was clearly an important Bronze Age sword factory.

The *yasakani no magatama* (八尺瓊曲玉, necklace), the *yata no kagami* (八咫鏡, bronze mirror) and *kusanagi* (草薙劍, the sword) comprise the Japanese Imperial regalia to this day. The Imperial regalia, known as *Sanshu no Jingi* (三種の神器, the Three Sacred Treasures) carries moral and mythical significance. The sword *kusanagi* represents valour, the mirror *yata no kagami* represents wisdom, and the stone or necklace *yasakani no magatama* represents benevolence. Valour, wisdom and benevolence are the three primary Imperial virtues in the Japanese reckoning. The regalia are used in the ceremony of Imperial Accession. No one other than the Emperor is permitted

Three Sacred Treasures

to see *yata no kagami*, which is kept in the inner recesses of the Imperial Palace in Tōkyō, so whether it is a stone, an orb, a necklace or something else has become a matter of speculation.

Sake Barrels at Itsukushima *jinja* (shrine). Author's photograph.

Amaterasu went on to create rice fields or paddies (*inada*), to invent the art of weaving with the loom, and she taught the people how to cultivate wheat and silkworms. Rice (*gohan*) and silk remain supremely important to the Japanese people right up to the modern era, not merely as economic products, but as icons deep within the Japanese psyche. Rice wine, or *sake* (酒) plays an important part in *shintō* ritual. Rice is also more than a staple of the diet: it is a sign of the commonality of all Japanese people. The cultivation of rice was, after all, a secret imparted by Amaterasu herself for the perpetual benefit of Japan. Even in 2006, the question of Japanese prevention of importation of rice from other countries was a matter of major dispute within the World Trade Organization. Some Japanese politicians, with the interest of their rice-farmer constituents in mind, seriously suggest that foreign rice would weaken the Japanese national spirit; and thus they seek to justify the ban on imports.

Amaterasu's main sanctuary is Ise-Jingu situated at Ise, on the island of Honshu. The main temple in this temple complex is dismantled every twenty years and then rebuilt exactly to its original plan. The chief priestess at Jingu must be a member of the Imperial family. Even the building that houses *yata no kagami* is forbidden to the public, and its possession makes this the most sacred of all *shintō* shrines.

ANCIENT AND MODERN

Amaterasu had a son named Ame-no-Oshihomimi-no-Mikoto and through him her grandson Ama-tsu-hiko-hiko-ho-no-Ninigi-no-Mikoto. Ninigi-no-Mikoto married Princess Konohana-Sakuya near Mount Takachiho, where Amaterasu had sent him to cultivate rice. He brought with him as evidence of his authority the jewels, the mirror and the sword.

Among their three sons was Hikohohodemi-no-Mikoto (a.k.a. Yamasachi-hiko), who married Princess Toyatama. She was the daughter of Amaterasu's brother Owatatsumi. They had a single son called Hikonagisa-Takaugaya-Fukiaezu-no-Mikoto. The boy was abandoned by his parents at birth and consequently raised by Princess Tamayori, his mother's younger sister.

Hikonagisa and his aunt Princess Tamayori eventually married and had four sons. The last of them became Emperor Jimmu ("Divine Might"), the first Emperor of Japan, born on the first day of January 711 BC. He fought for, and gained, his Imperial dignity in 660 BC. Although the many present-day followers of the Imperial cult, *arahitogami* ("God who is a human being") claim that the Emperors can trace a direct line back to Jimmu, the occupants of the Chrysanthemum Throne[177] can only be traced back with any certainty to Ōjin, who reigned from 270 to 310 AD. It is still the longest traceable lineage of any hereditary ruler.

Kikukamonshō, the Chrysanthemum Crest

It was the decree of Amaterasu that the unbroken line of emperors would rule the nation "until the end of time". Thus absolute fealty was required of every Japanese, and the

---

[177] The 16-petal Chrysanthemum (菊 *kiku*) is the crest (紋章 *monshō*) of the Emperor of Japan. The Chrysanthemum Crest (菊花紋章 *kikukamonshō*) is the common name of the Imperial Throne.

RESPECT AND CONSIDERATION

Emperor's will had to be obeyed without thought or demur: it was Amaterasu's declaration.

So much for the legend. But the power of legend should not be underestimated. Thanks to the powerful mythology of the creation story, the Emperor (天皇 *tennō* = "heavenly sovereign") is regarded as the embodiment of the nation. Loyalty to the Emperor, or loyalty to the *shōgun*[178]'s government? Could the two be reconciled? These questions permeated Japanese political life in the *bakumatsu* period. *Bakumatsu* is the word used to denote the period between Commodore Perry's arrival in 1853 and the Meiji Restoration in 1868. They were, to say the least, turbulent years.

In the late eighteenth century, Motoori Norinaga (1730-1801), a paediatrician who was enamoured with ancient Japanese language and culture, wrote an epic commentary on the *kojiki* that set the tone for the subsequent *shintō* mind-set. *Shintō*, according to Motoori, demonstrated and validated the essence of Japanese nationhood. Its scholarship became known as *kokugaku*, or "National Learning".

Self-portrait of Motoori Norinaga

The key doctrine was the direct line of descent of the Emperor from Amaterasu, the sun-goddess. She had declared that her descendants would rule the nation "until the end of time"; and, good or bad, right or wrong, the Emperor was entitled to absolute and immediate obedience from every Japanese person, whatever their rank or position in life. The Japanese people needed no ethical basis for their nationhood, because, in the same manner as their Emperor, and in the same manner as the very country of their birth, each Japanese was of divine origin, though of lesser

---

[178] See Appendix 1-2 "The *shōguns* and the sweep of history"

degree, and thus intrinsically good. As proof, the Japanese could look at the centuries-long unbroken line of Imperial succession: only divine approval could have caused that world-beating record.

When Motoori wrote his commentary, the ideas he put forward were disregarded by the Tokugawa dynastic government as being risible. The last ghostly laugh, though, was from Motoori: within one hundred years, the Tokugawa would be swept away and Motoori's ideas would be embodied in a new written constitution and learned by heart by Japanese schoolchildren.

That these notions of Japanese-ness were widely accepted is attested by the death poems[179] written by some of the two officers and eighteen rank-and-file Tosa *samurai* who had ambushed and dishonourably killed Midshipman Guillou and ten sailors from the French corvette *Dupleix* on 8th March 1868 at Sakai, an old sea-port near Ōsaka. The incident became known as *Sakai jiken* (堺事件). The warriors had been ordered to commit *seppuku*[180] in the presence of M. Léon Roches, the French *Ministre*

---

[179] *jisei no ku* (辞世の句). A death poem within the *seppuku* ritual was almost always a *tanka* with its 5-7-5-7-7 syllable format. A poem of this nature must not have even accidental rhyme, so solemn is its content. Poetry was regarded as one of the essential accomplishments of the *samurai* and *daimyō* classes. See Appendix 5 for a note on another form of Japanese poetry, with an example relevant to the *bakumatsu*.

[180] *Seppuku* was a form of ritual suicide. Under the *bushidō* code, transgressors might be ordered, by the feudal superior in the name of the Emperor, to commit suicide. Formal execution entailed the loss of the family's land and wealth and a blackening of the family name in perpetuity, but *seppuku* was regarded as a sufficient and honourable death, so ordering *seppuku* was a merciful act. The suicide took the form of slicing open the abdomen (*hara kiri* "belly slitting") and then being beheaded by a trusted second or friend to prevent undue suffering. Apart from transgressors, a man might choose to commit *seppuku* if he felt he had disgraced himself or failed to live up to the *bushidō* code in some way. It was a noble death. It was said (and believed by the Japanese) that in 1860, the Prince of Satsuma had ordered five boys aged

RESPECT AND CONSIDERATION

and *Capitaine* (later *Vice-Amiral*) Abel-Nicolas Georges Henri Bergasse Dupetit Thouars of the *Dupleix*.

In the event, after witnessing the dignified, though bloody, ritual deaths of eleven men, Roches begged for an end to their punishment. The nine men thus spared were mortified that their noble end had been averted, and left in disgrace. It was said that several of them shortly committed *seppuku* on their own behalf to expiate the dishonour of having been considered unworthy of a noble death. There was a widespread feeling in the foreign community that Roches' action had been motivated, not by humanity, but shameful revenge: he should not have intervened to save the remaining nine, because an eye-for-an-eye, eleven-for eleven, was vengeance, not justice. Roche later vainly claimed that he had intervened because it was getting late and he needed to return to his quarters, which is perhaps even more disgraceful. Death, even that of a criminal, is worthy of more than usual consideration and respect.

The death poems written by some of the dead Tosa *samurai* give an insight into the depth of their feelings for Japan, and of the political mindset they had adopted. Written in contemplation of imminent death, they are unrestrained expressions of their deepest feelings:

---

between 8 and 13 to commit *seppuku* for the crime of drawing their swords and setting about each other in the precincts of his palace in Kagoshima.

ANCIENT AND MODERN

Though I regret not my body which becomes as dew scattered by the wind, my country's fate weighs down my heart with anxiety

As I also am of the seed of the country of the gods, I create for myself today a glorious subject for reflection in the next world. The sacrifice of my life for the sake of my country gives me a pure heart in my hour of death.

Unworthy as I am I have not wandered from the straight path of the duty which a Japanese owes to his Prince

Though reproaches may be cast upon me, those who can fathom the depths of a warrior's heart will appreciate my motives

In this age, when the minds of men are darkened, I would show the way to purity of heart

In throwing away this life, so insignificant a possession, I would desire to leave behind me an unsullied name

The cherry flowers[181] too have their seasons of blossoming and fading. What is there for a Japanese soul to regret in death?

Here I leave my soul and exhibit to the world the intrepidity of a Japanese heart

---

[181] The cherry blossom (桜 sakura) that spreads on millions of trees South to North through Japan from February to May each year is a potent symbol for the Japanese even today. It wistfully symbolises life: birth, blossoming, death and decay, as its flowers appear, flourish, and fall away within a week. The leaves of the tree appear after the blossom has gone, so the brief moment of blossoming shows a sea of palest-pink-flowered trees that are extremely beautiful. *Kamikaze* aircraft in World War II would usually have cherry blossom painted on them to symbolize the fragility of life, and there was a popular belief that the souls of dead pilots were reincarnated in the cherry blossom of the next year.

RESPECT AND CONSIDERATION

As late as March 1937, the Ministry of Education published *Kokutai no Hongi* (国体の本義 "Cardinal Principles of the Nation"), which was to be instilled into Japanese schoolchildren and university students. It described the Japanese Nation in these terms:

> The unbroken line of Emperors, receiving the Oracle of the Founder of the Nation, reign eternally over the Japanese Empire. This is our eternal and immutable national entity. Thus, founded on this great principle, all the people, united as one great family nation in heart and obeying the Imperial Will, enhance the beautiful virtues of loyalty and filial piety. This is the glory of our national entity.

This lengthy, illiberal, and to modern eyes, totalitarian, document goes on to describe the Emperor as a "deity incarnate" and "a direct descendant of Amaterasu". Serving him is not a question of duty or acceptance of authority but "a natural manifestation of the heart"; the Emperor and his subjects "arise from the same fountainhead". The highest manifestation of Japanese-ness is "the climax of harmony in the sacrifice of the life of a subject for the Emperor". This high-blown rhetoric was widely accepted, not just by its youthful target audience, but also by all the "children of the gods[182]", including people in the highest reaches of Government and the military. *Kokutai* was directly behind the aggression of the military-dominated government in its plans for the "liberation" of South-East Asia and the Pacific War. The infamous attack by the Imperial Japanese Navy on Pearl Harbor on 7th December 1941 was a product of *kokutai no hongi*.

---

[182] A phrase from a *noh* play *"hagoramo"* by the playwright Zeami Motokiyo (世阿弥 元清 c.1363-c.1443 AD) and taken by Japanese nationalists to apply to the Japanese nation.

ANCIENT AND MODERN

In 1945, Emperor Hirohito[183] startled the nation by speaking to them by radio after the surrender to the Allied forces. Only the Emperor's inner circle had ever heard his voice before[184]. In what sources describe as a curious high-pitched thin monotone, using arcane Court language, he disclaimed any form of divine ancestry[185]. One of his key statements was

> The ties between Us and Our people have always stood upon mutual trust and affection and do not depend upon mere legends and myths. They are not predicated on the false conception that the Emperor is divine, and that the Japanese people are superior to other races and fated to rule the world.

However, to this day, some, mainly older, Japanese believe that the Emperor's disclaimer was only for political convenience, and they still believe that the Emperor is a direct descendant of Amaterasu. *Arahitogami* supporters argue that, although the descent from Amaterasu cannot be proved, it has so far not been disproved either, so why change the beliefs of 2700 years?

Initially the supreme and active ruler of the nation, the Emperor tended, from the twelfth century onwards, to withdraw from political life, concentrating on his rôle as Chief *shintō* Priest for the nation. Until the latter days of the *bakumatsu* that are the subject of this book, the occupant of the Chrysanthemum Throne mostly remained aloof, distant from the politics and daily life of the nation, a puppet for successive dynasties of *shōgun*. At the time of the Meiji restoration around 1868 AD, however, the Emperor took an active part in wresting

---

[183] After his death in 1989, he was named *Shōwa* (昭和 "Enlightened Peace"): the *nengo* (era name) of his record 63-year reign is the *shōwa* Era.

[184] A little searching on the internet will unearth an audio file of this broadcast. Try *gyokuon-housou* as a search term.

[185] On 1 January 1946, the Emperor issued two documents that would reshape Japanese government and society. They are known as the *ningen-sengen* ("Humanity Declaration").

power from a discredited *shōgunate*. To Emperor Meiji's credit, he oversaw the creation of a new constitution for Japan that came into effect in 1889, sharing power with an elected diet. The constitution remained in effect until 1947.

There was a limited franchise under the 1889 constitution with voting rights for about 2% of the (male and wealthier) population. The cabinet was not accountable to the people by the ballot box, but to the Emperor, who had the right to appoint and dismiss ministers. Prime Minister Kuroda Kiyotaka explained it thus:

> The government must always steadfastly transcend and stand apart from political parties, and thus follow the path of righteousness.

The Emperor today is the ceremonial head of state, but has no powers, not even reserve powers. Nonetheless, whether or not they subscribe to the Emperor's divinity, the Emperor is still much revered by the Japanese, and his divine status remains deep within the subconscious bones of the nation.

ANCIENT AND MODERN

THE MARCHING SONG OF THE *KAMIKAZE* PILOTS

You, sir, and I, sir,
   Are cherry blossoms of a kind, sir,
      Blooming in the garden of the naval academy.

And if we bloom, sir,
   We are ready, too, to fall, sir.
      Let us fall in splendour for the sake of the country.

APPENDIX 1-2
THE *SHŌGUNS* AND THE SWEEP OF HISTORY

Japanese society until 1868 was feudal. In the beginning there were wealthy clan chiefs who ruled their fiefs with more or less unfettered power. Above these was the Emperor, who ruled over the entire nation, assisted by a few high aristocrats, often related to the Emperor, or who had been in Imperial service for generations. In 668 AD, Emperor Tenji bestowed the honourable Fujiwara name on the Nakatomi family in gratitude for loyal and effective service to the court.

The Fujiwara clan gradually became ascendant in the practical government of the nation and held the highest civil office in the land, *kanpaku*, chief adviser. From time to time, they provided the *sesshō*, regent for the Emperor in the time of his minority (or if the heir to the throne was female). However, in 1156, a power struggle erupted within the Fujiwara clan; other families, especially the Taira and Minamoto families, were enlisted by one branch or another[186]. The Taira family were victorious in the military clash that ensued, and Taira no Kiyomori assumed almost total power, and remained *kanpaku*

---

[186] This was Japan's "War of the Roses", presaging England's wars between the House of Lancaster (red rose) and the House of York (white rose) some three centuries later (1455-85). On this occasion, though, the white roses won: Taira wore the white, and Minamoto the red.

THE SHŌGUNS AND THE SWEEP OF HISTORY

until his death in 1181. Thereafter Minamoto no Yoritomo conquered the Taira in a series of battles and naval engagements.

By 1195, Minamoto no Yoritomo was supremely powerful. In 1192, he had sought, and had been granted by the Imperial Court, the title of *seii-tai-shōgun* ("barbarian-subduing generalissimo"), a term usually shortened to *shōgun*. His government was known as the *bakufu* ("tent headquarters"), a term used of military headquarters during a mobile campaign, reflecting the fiction that the *shōgun* was merely the military arm of the Imperial government.

Yoritomo based his government by the sea at Kamakura, while the Emperor remained in the official capital, Kyotō. The separation by distance of the Imperial and *shōgunate* courts was a recurring feature throughout the era of the *shōguns*. It was a strong component of the governmental system in the late Edo period, and had a direct effect in the events of 14th September 1862.

Yoritomo ruthlessly eliminated potential rivals, and even assassinated his own half-brother, as well as several other relatives and rivals. This left a problem when Yoritomo mysteriously died in a riding "accident": he left no clear successor. Yoritomo's widow Hōjō Masako arranged to murder two of her own sons to prevent their appointment, and plotted to appoint the *sesshō*, whom she controlled. She was known as *ama shōgun*, the nun-*shōgun*, for she had taken Buddhist nun's vows on becoming widowed. She saw off one serious challenge to her *de facto* power, exiling the retired Emperor Go-Toba to Oki, a remote island, where he died, a tragic figure.

During the Hōjō period, on two occasions, serious threats to Japan's security occurred, which were to have an important and lasting effect on the Japanese view of themselves. Kublai Khan had inherited the enormous Great Mongol Empire. The name of

RESPECT AND CONSIDERATION

his grandfather, Genghis Khan, was a byword for ruthless military might and conquest. Some estimates say that 30 million people were slain by Mongol troops as Genghis Khan put together his empire. The Mongol domain covered Northern China, and Korea, and they exacted tribute from as far west as Vienna. Kublai sought to extend the empire into southern China, where the Song dynasty held sway. But he had an overriding ambition to annex Japan, where his grandfather had never ventured. This was Kublai's personal project. Perhaps he had a psychological need to get out of his grandfather's shadow.

In 1268, Kublai sent a letter to "the King of Japan" demanding that he should acknowledge Mongol overlordship and should pay tribute to him. Failing this, he would invade Japan and take by force what was not given voluntarily. The Japanese ignored this and further missives from Kublai Khan. The *bakufu*, though, prudently sent soldiers to northwest Kyūshū, where any invasion force would be likely to arrive, and prepared for invasion.

In November 1274, Kublai Khan fulfilled the *bakufu's* worst fears. Nine hundred ships with 40,000 men sailed from Korea and landed at Hakata in northwest Kyūshū. The Japanese defenders retreated inland. The Mongols made a puzzling decision never satisfactorily explained: not to push inland immediately while they held the initiative with vastly superior forces, but to return to their ships, there to sleep overnight. No sooner had they re-embarked than a huge storm blew up, many ships were sunk, and the survivors straggled back to Korea. Around 14,000 men had been lost, and several hundred vessels. Kublai Khan sent further envoys in 1275 and 1279, each time repeating his demands. The Japanese unceremoniously beheaded them as their reply. Kublai Khan was enraged.

The Mongol leader then concentrated his efforts at overcoming the Song dynasty, and achieved their downfall in

THE SHŌGUNS AND THE SWEEP OF HISTORY

1279. His reign marked the beginning of the Yuan dynasty throughout China. He immediately set about planning the conquest of Japan. He commandeered all the considerable shipbuilding capacity in south China, and ordered them to make as many boats as possible. The military resources of China and Korea were directed towards Kublai Khan's plan. As soon as he had amassed sufficient naval and military strength, Kublai Khan tried yet again to invade in June 1281. Considerable numbers of the Mongol forces were conscripted Chinese and Korean auxiliaries, who had no interest or desire to help their subjugator or further his ends.

The initial part of the force that set out from Korea - some 900 ships with 42,000 men - arrived on 21st June and was surprised to be met by fierce and determined resistance from the Japanese warriors. The Japanese forces had been strengthened and trained to meet such an invasion. The Japanese defensive plan included the building of a low wall along the coast, together with stakes in the mud flats and beaches, to impede the large-scale manoeuvring of their horses, on which much of the Mongol force's tactics depended. The *samurai* made silent night assaults on the men in the boats, killing significant numbers of them. Having made little progress, and suffering attrition, the Mongol fleet withdrew to Tsushima to await the arrival of their reinforcements from China - a further 3500 ships and 100,000 men. Together they planned a fresh all-out assault on Japan on 15th August, but just as they set sail, another enormous typhoon destroyed most of the fleet. Only 200 ships and 28000 men made it back to base.

Ocean-going vessels even in those days were designed to withstand fierce storms at sea. A deep keel helps the boats to stay upright, and the deep holds that come with deep keels could hold stabilising ballast. However, boats designed for the rivers of China and shallow coastal waters of Korea have no

RESPECT AND CONSIDERATION

such keel or ballast hold, and so a sea storm renders them unstable and liable to capsize. In his haste to build an invasion fleet, Kublai Khan conscripted the river- and coastal-boat builders of China and Korea. As the Chinese and Korean shipbuilders detested the Mongol forces that had occupied their country and usurped their Emperors, none of them explained the folly of using a river boat to ply the seas.

In the summer, the prevailing winds in Japan are westward, blowing from Japan towards the continent. In August and September, five or six typhoons can be expected to arrive over Japan, bringing considerable destruction in their wake. So the enormous two-day storm starting on 15th August might have been expected, although it is apparent that the Mongol fleet was taken by surprise. One account described it as bigger than any typhoon ever encountered, and so it caused the unprepared, keel-less, unballasted boats to ship water and founder and capsize, drowning their complements of men.

There is an alternative theory that would explain why even ocean-ready boats with keels also sank. The Mongols had brought the new weapon of war: heavy cannon, with gunpowder. Poor stowage of the guns might have caused loose cannon to career around the lower decks, breaching the hull; and mishandling of the gunpowder during the storm might have caused explosions below the waterline. If this is true, it may explain why the Japanese, who so readily adopted and copied small arms when they arrived from Portugal in 1543, showed no desire to copy cannon from the Mongols.

The reputation of Mongol invincibility was thus demolished, and this marked the beginning of the decline of the great empire that the Mongols had built up. The obsessed Kublai Khan continued to nurse his ambition to annex Japan, and only his death in 1294 stopped him launching another invasion, despite his advisers' unanimous objections.

THE SHŌGUNS AND THE SWEEP OF HISTORY

The Japanese saw that the storms had saved them. Japan - the land created by the gods - had been protected by those gods. They had sent a divine (神 *kami*) wind (風 *kaze*) to defend them. From that day onwards (and this was consciously exploited in the latter days of the second world war[187]), the *kamikaze* have been seen as the saviours of Japan. The partiality of the gods in saving the nation from foreign invasion confirmed the Japanese belief that they are specially favoured among the nations. This formed the basis of the xenophobia seen later under the Tokugawa *shōguns*.

---

[187] The Japanese naval "divine wind special attack units" (神風特別攻撃隊 *shinpū tokubetsu kōgeki tai*) of 1944-45 were "suicide" pilots seeking to crash aircraft filled with explosives on targets such as aircraft carriers. (*Shinpu* is the "Chinese" reading of the characters normally read as *kamikaze,* and was used at the time in Japan for such units: *kamikaze* was an American usage that has subsequently become universal). The four sub-units of this force were given names (underlined) taken from a patriotic *tanka* by our old chum Motoori Norinaga:
    Shikishima no Yamato-gokoro wo hito towaba, asahi ni niou yamazakura bana
        If someone asks about the <u>yamato</u> spirit of <u>shikishima,</u>
        It is the flowers of <u>yamazakura</u> that are fragrant in the <u>asahi</u>."
Yamato, denoting a historic period that saw Japan emerge as a nation, represents the "Spirit of the Empire"; *shikishima* is a poetic name for Japan; *yamazakura* are cherry blossoms on the mountains, representing wistful passing beauty; *asahi* is the Rising Sun, symbol of Japanese glory.

RESPECT AND CONSIDERATION

Go-Daigo *tennō* 後醍醐天皇

But back to the Hōjō *bakufu*. The cost of the defence of Japan had been heavy. The *bakufu* coffers were very nearly empty, and it reneged on its promises to reward the warrior clans who had mounted Japan's defences. There was a ferment of resentment among the dissatisfied *daimyō* and *samurai*. A new assertive emperor, Go-Daigo confronted the *bakufu* and there was much political manoeuvring which for a time saw two rival Emperors - Go-Daigo and Kōmyō.

Over time, the power of the *shōguns* declined as the wealth of the aristocratic families expanded. Their edicts were progressively ignored, and the powerful families refused to pay taxes to the *shōgunate*. The families fought between themselves, and there was in effect a state of sporadic civil war from the middle of the fifteenth century. The weakened *shōgunate* was unable to quell this fighting. The next 100 or so years became known as the *sengoku* (warring states) era.

THE SHŌGUNS AND THE SWEEP OF HISTORY

A *daimyō's* procession at Namamugi, 1860s
Japanese woodcut

APPENDIX 1-3
FIRST CHRISTIAN ARRIVALS FROM THE WEST

In the middle of the *sengoku*, the first recorded westerners arrived in Japan. Passengers aboard a Chinese vessel blown off-course, Fernão Mendes Pinto and two other Portuguese traders set foot on Japanese soil at Tanegashima in southern Kyūshū on 25th August 1543. Pinto sold two arquebuses[188] - an early firearm - to Tanegashima Tokitaka, 14th *daimyō* of the island of Tanegashima, who had them copied by the local swordsmith. The 15-year-old *daimyō* paid 2,000 *ryō* for them - some £500,000 in early twenty-first century value. Pinto later presented one to Shimazu Takahisa, the 15th *daimyō* of the Shimazu clan of Kyūshū, who befriended him. The firearm caused great excitement and was soon copied in numbers and marketed by the enterprising Takahisa and had a marked effect on inter-family warfare in succeeding decades. By the end of the sixteenth century, it was said that guns were almost certainly more common in Japan than in any other country in the world[189].

Pinto is also credited with the introduction of the Christian faith to Japan. But there had probably been an earlier Christian presence, though the evidence is slim:

---

[188] It was a relatively short-barrelled smoothbore muzzle-loaded predecessor to the much longer (and more accurate) musket. For reasons that need no explanation, the Japanese for "arquebus" became *tanegashima*.

[189] Perrin, Noel, *Giving Up the Gun*, David R. Godine Publisher, Boston.

FIRST CHRISTIAN ARRIVALS FROM THE WEST

Kūkai 空海 (774 - 835 AD)

known posthumously as **Kōbō Daishi** 弘法大師 , "the great Master who spread the Buddhist teachings". He studied under the Chinese Buddhist Master Hui Kuo and returned in 806 AD, bringing Shingon Buddhism to Japan. He also brought a commentary on Christ's *Sermon on the Mount* and Matthew's gospel to Japan

He founded the *Nishi-Hongan-ji* (temple) in Kyotō. The Kawasaki Daishi temple was founded in his honour by a former *samurai*, Kanenori Hirama, and the Buddhist priest Sonken. Kanenori had a dream; Kōbō Daishi appeared to him and told him that he had carved an image of himself and had cast it into the sea. Kanenori was to retrieve it, and his hopes and aspirations would be fulfilled.

Kanenori cast his nets at the spot indicated in the dream, and dredged up a wooden statue of Kōbō Daishi. Kanenori and Sonken set about building a temple to house the image. The temple - the destination for the ill-fated Richardson party - is now Kawasaki Daishi Heikenji Temple, Grand Head Temple of the Chisan Sect of Shingon Buddhism. Shingon was later eclipsed in Japan by Pure Land Buddhism and to a lesser extent, by Zen Buddhism.

Kōbō Daishi died on Mount Kōya on April 23, 835, but many devotees believe that he remains in eternal *samadhi* (deeply concentrated meditation) in his bodily form within the inner shrine on the mountain. To that end, monks bring food and fresh clothing to the place of his interment on a daily basis.

Apart from his spiritual significance and many philosophical works, Kōbō Daishi is revered as a great poet and calligrapher, and is credited with the invention of *hiragana*, the Japanese syllabic writing system. He was also an energetic civil engineer, restoring a reservoir and constructing grand buildings.

RESPECT AND CONSIDERATION

- Two beams of an ancient temple, dating from the late seventh century, with crosses on them and Syriac (the Eastern Aramaic language spoken by Christian communities in the Middle East from 100-800 AD) inscriptions, are in the Tōkyō National Museum.
- The *Shoku Nihongi*[190] refers to the return from China in 736 of an envoy who brought with him "a Persian by the name of Limitsi and another dignitary of the church of the Luminous Religion (i.e. Christianity - because Christ is 'The Light of the World') called Kohfu". The Christianity referred to is Nestorian Christianity of the Assyrian Church, which was very active in missionary work eastwards from its Bagdad headquarters. Limitsi is also known as Rimitsu, a physician. The Empress Kōmyōshi, from the Fujiwara *han* (consort of Emperor Shōmu), was very much influenced by Rimitsu's teaching and built a leprosarium, a hospital, and an orphanage, common enough charitable works for wealthy Christians, but not of the Buddhists of that era.
- At the Nishi-Hongan-ji Temple in Kyotō, founded by Kobo Daishi on his return in 806 AD from China's capital and contact with the Christian monastery there, is a manuscript he brought back: *The Lord of the Universe's Discourse on Almsgiving*, which is a commentary on the Sermon on the Mount and other passages from Matthew's gospel.

There are unattested stories that Shimazu Takahisa and his wife became Christian converts, along with their sons and many servants. The Shimazu family crest is a circle divided into four

---

[190] The *Shoku Nihongi* （続日本紀） is the second of the *Rikkokushi* (六国史) or "six histories of the nation", following directly after *Nihon Shoki*. It is a key primary historical source concerning the Nara period (710 - 794 AD) as it covers the years from 697 to 791 AD. It was published in 797 AD.

FIRST CHRISTIAN ARRIVALS FROM THE WEST

orthogonal segments and it was wrongly suggested by an early American missionary that this is the Christian symbol of the Cross. In fact, it was a representation of a horse's bit-ring. But Christianity (*kirishitando*) was of considerable interest among the Shimazu family, particularly the womenfolk. The Christian faith was initially welcomed - or at least, tolerated - in the Shimazu domain.

In fact, Christianity received a greater acceptance in Kyūshū than in any other part of the country. Two prominent Kyūshū *daimyō*, Konishi Yukinaga 小西 行長 and Takayama Ukon 高山右近 became convinced Christians. Takayama died in Manila, after the Tokugawa expulsions of Christians from Japan in 1614 AD. Konishi, who fought against the Tokugawa at Sekigahara, refused (because of his Christianity) to commit *seppuku* after the battle and was therefore executed by the victors.

Pinto's reception paved the way for the first Jesuit missionary, Francis Xavier, to start work at Kagoshima in 1549. Pinto funded the first Christian church in Japan, for Francis Xavier's use. Christianity flourished in Japan until the vicious Tokugawa clamp-down on "foreign practices" in the seventeenth century. Throughout the period from 1543 to the *bakumatsu*, "Christianity" meant Roman Catholicism in the main, and attracted disquiet in the *bakufu* because of the Catholic Church's chequered political history in Europe. It reminded them only too well of the former power in Japan of the Buddhist monastic establishments, who like the Pope, claimed superiority and jurisdiction over the temporal rulers.

Curiously, these fears were mirrored by ex-President Fillmore when he headed the "Know Nothing Party", responding to suspicions about Papal influence over the large numbers of Irish and German Catholic immigrants to the United States in the 1850s. Pope Pius IX was regarded with great suspicion. He was widely thought of as being illiberal and opposed to the values of America's Founding Fathers by the protestant majority in the United States[191].

---

[191] Giovanni Maria Mastai-Ferretti died, aged 85 in 1878, having been Pope for 32 years. This is still the longest papal reign since the Papacy was defined as such. It was he who proclaimed the Roman Catholic doctrine of Papal Infallibility, (when speaking *ex cathedra* on a matter of faith or morals). The Pope also defined the dogma of the Immaculate Conception of the Blessed Virgin Mary, stating that Mary, the mother of Jesus Christ, was conceived without original sin and that she lived a life completely free of sin. These doctrines are viewed with great disdain - not to say repugnance - by Protestants. He was known as a political reactionary, and published his still controversial *Syllabus of Errors*, which condemned "modernism", particularly as evidenced in liberal democratic forms of government. His papal name - Pius IX - is pronounced in Italian as "Piu nono", and he became lampooned for his regressive views as Piu No-No.

APPENDIX 1-4
THREE LEADERS

It took the efforts of three successive leaders to reunite Japan into the cohesive nation she had once been. They were sharp and ruthless operators, each with his own way of achieving his ends.

The first was 織田信長 - Oda Nobunaga. Oda had risen to prominence among the aristocracy by a series of battles in the 1550s and 1560s. His brilliant generalship gave him victories over superior forces, particularly at the battle of Okehazama (near Nagoya) in 1560. He was completely ruthless, and had several members of his own close family murdered. He was accustomed to massacre his defeated enemies. At the Enryaku-ji Temple on Mount Hiei in Kyotō, 10,000 people were surrounded and systematically killed in 1571; the victims included Buddhist priests, women and children. Oda had a particular distrust of Buddhist priests, seeing in them a source of opposition, and put hundreds of them to death. And at

Oda Nobunaga

RESPECT AND CONSIDERATION

ホトトギス 子規

The different approaches of the three men who unified Japan in the late 16th and early 17th centuries are illustrated by a famous set of three *senryū*, poems similar in form to *haiku*, but concerning human nature. They do not require a *kigo* or season word, as *haiku* do.

Oda was notorious for his mercilessness; Tomotomo for his inventiveness, and Tokugawa for his doggedness.

The *senryū* concerns a *hototogisu* - a Mountain Cuckoo - that would not sing its melancholy, plaintive song. Asked what to do to make it sing, each of the three leaders replies as follows:

ODA NOBUNAGA: *nakanunara,*
koroshiteshima,
hototogisu

TOMOTOMO HIDEYOSHI: *nakanunara,*
nakashitemiseyō,
hototogisu.

TOKUGAWA IEYASU: *nakanunara,*
nakumademató,
hototogisu.

Which translates as

ODA NOBUNAGA: If the cuckoo does not sing, kill it
TOMOTOMO HIDEYOSHI: If the cuckoo does not sing, coax it.
TOKUGAWA IEYASU: If the cuckoo does not sing, wait for it.

THREE LEADERS

Nagashima in 1574, 20,000 people were burned alive, including thousands of innocent civilian bystanders.

Oda Nobunaga, with 1000 (later accounts say 3000) untrained *arquebusiers*, won the seminal Battle of Nagashino in 1575 against the renowned cavalry of Takeda Katsuyori, who opposed Nobunaga's intention to unify Japan. Nobunaga's men routed the cavalry by cyclical firing of their guns[192], a brilliant and inventive tactic not developed in Europe for another 30 years.

Oda pursued a cult of personality greatly super-ego-ising that of twentieth century dictators. His birthday was an official holiday. He built a temple dedicated to himself so that the aristocrats of Japan could worship him. He even refused the exalted title of *shōgun* because that would mean that whoever conferred it would by definition be superior to him. And Oda recognised no such person, not even the Emperor.

In 1568, Oda seized Kyotō on behalf of the weak *shōgun* Ashikaga Yoshiaki. Oda was the real power behind the *shōgun*, and was even bold enough to issue public rebukes to Yoshiaki himself. The motto on Oda's official seal explains his single-minded aim:

tenka fubu (天下布武) "cover those things that are under the sky with the sword", coded language for "a unified realm under military rule".

Oda died violently, possibly forced to commit *seppuku*, but certainly burned while locked in a blazing temple (Honno-ji) by a rebel *samurai* general, Akeche Mitsuhide. Oda had murdered

---

[192] The *arquebusiers* formed in three ranks. The front rank fired their weapons from a standing position then dropped to their knees to reload. The second rank then did exactly the same, followed by the third rank at the back, who did not need to kneel to reload. By this time the front rank had reloaded, so they stood up and fired then dropped to their knees. And so on. It meant that a steady and devastating rate of fire in salvos could be maintained against the enemy for long periods.

RESPECT AND CONSIDERATION

Mitsuhide's mother, and Akeche Mitsuhide was embarked on a course of personal vengeance.

Toyotomi Hideyoshi (豐臣秀吉) was the second of the three reunifiers of the country. Toyotomi was a senior retainer in Oda's service, having commenced service as an *ashigaru* - a lowly foot soldier. Oda treated him with affection, giving him the jokey nickname *saru* - monkey - because of his prominent ears, and Toyotomi bore the nickname stoically. It appears that Toyotomi was born with two thumbs on his right hand, which further marked him out physically. Toyotomi was an accomplished general in his own right, and deeply loyal to Oda. On Oda's demise in 1582, Toyotomi pursued and defeated Akeche Mitsuhide, who had seen to the death of Oda.

There was an ensuing succession struggle between Oda's sons. Nobutada had died with Oda at Honno-ji. Nobutaka (the father of Hidenobu) was murdered by Toyotomi and Nobukatsu, the third son. Nobukatsu sought to succeed his father, but was outmanoeuvred by Toyotomi. Toyotomi thereupon successfully schemed to have Oda's infant *grand*son Hidenobu appointed *shōgun*, with himself as *kanpaku* (関白 regent). Toyotomi could not be appointed *shōgun* in his own right because of his lowly birth.

Toyotomi Hideyoshi

One of Toyotomi's early acts as regent was to commission a survey of the landholdings of Japan, rather in the manner of William the Conqueror's Domesday Book survey of

THREE LEADERS

England of 1086. It was he who decided to measure the *daimyōs'* wealth in terms of the rice that their land could produce each year. Armed with these statistics, the *shōguns* would be able to control the wealth and therefore the power of the *daimyō* by confiscating and granting land, and ensuring the wealthier *daimyō* lived as far away from Edo as possible.

Toyotomi extended his regency powers by military force. A notable victory was in 1587 over the Shimazu clan of Satsuma in southern Kyūshū, who were themselves trying to extend their own fiefdom northwards. Toyotomi redistributed lands forfeited by the Shimazu family among his own followers, so strengthening his network of supporters. He instigated the policy of keeping the families of the aristocracy hostage at his seat of power in Momoyama, near Kyotō. He also made a decree forcing the peasant class to hand in their swords. This was known as the *katanagari*, or "sword-hunt" of 1588. Actually, all forms of weaponry were confiscated, including considerable quantities of firearms. Toyotomi's avowed object was to melt the swords and other weaponry to make the biggest statue of the Buddha ever known. His true object was to prevent rival lords from raising peasant armies. Henceforth, only the *samurai* were licensed to bear weapons.

Toyotomi issued further laws to stratify society more distinctly. The so-called "class-freezing" regulations of 1591 made it illegal for peasants to leave their fields to pursue any other work; forced *samurai* to live in the castle towns belonging to the *daimyō*; and made collective responsibility the standard control over personal behaviour. Entire neighbourhoods or even towns would be punished - including the death penalty – for the wrongdoing of individuals. This inculcated something in the Japanese psyche that is reflected today in the general reluctance of the Japanese to become involved with people outside the "group" (be it work colleagues, family, school or otherwise). It

RESPECT AND CONSIDERATION

instigated the formal stratification of society into four main classes: *shi-no-ko-sho* (士農工商), meaning warrior-peasant-artisan-merchant in descending order. The classification excluded priests, nuns and court nobles. There were also the outcast subclasses *eta* ("great filth" – their descendants, the *burakumin,* even today commonly regarded as untouchable) and the *hinin,* or "non-persons". The *eta* were engaged in "unclean" activity such as butchery, tanning, and burial of the dead, and the *hinin* in suspicious activities such as acting and peddling. The warriors - *samurai* - made up about 6% of the population and provided, besides military capability, the civil service.

Toyotomi finally brought the far northern provinces of Japan under his control in 1591. The central government now held control over almost the whole of Japan.

Toyotomi went on to become paranoid about people he assumed were a threat to him. He forced his nephew, adopted son and designated successor Hidetsugu to commit *seppuku,* had his head exhibited on a pole, and put his wife and infant children to death, as a warning that he would tolerate no dissent from anyone. He would put messengers bringing bad news to a cruel death, and required many friends and officials to commit *seppuku,* purely in case they might pose a threat. He sought a greater Japanese kingdom, and tried to invade Korea in 1592 and 1597, but failed militarily, partly because his troops had no faith in a general who remained safely in his palace instead of leading them into battle.

Toyotomi had sought to prevent succession problems arising after his death. He had created a council of "Five Great Elders" (五大老 *go-tairō*) to govern temporarily pending the appointment of a successor by them[193]. In 1598, the dying

---

[193] These were Ukita Hideie (宇喜多秀家) of Bizen and Mimasaka, Maeda Toshiie (前田 利家)of Arako Castle, Uesugi Kagekatsu (上杉 景勝)of Echigo and Aizu, Mori Terumoto (毛利 輝元)of Hiroshima, and Tokugawa Ieyasu (

THREE LEADERS

Toyotomi asked the Great Elders to look after his five-year old son Hideyori and appoint him to the *shōgunate* in due course. The five Elders acted as joint regents for Hideyori but Tokugawa Ieyasu entered secret alliances with other *daimyō* opposed to Hideyori's succession. After regent Toshiie died, Ieyasu captured Osaka castle, with Hideyori its resident and hostage. The three remaining *tairō* were angered by this peremptory action, and soon a war of words erupted into real warfare. The war ended within a few months in October 1600 with Ieyasu's victory at the battle of Sekigahara. Toyotomi's son Hideyori would never become *shōgun*.

Three years later, in 1603, Tokugawa Ieyasu was finally prevailed upon to accept the office of *shōgun* himself. The Tokugawa dynasty went on to rule Japan for 264 years up to 1867, when power was wrested back by, or on behalf of, the Emperor. The period of Tokugawa rule (1603-1867) is known as the "Edo period", Edo[194] being the city whence the Tokugawa *shōguns* ruled. Edo is subsumed in present-day Tōkyō. The Emperor resided in Kyotō, once again keeping the Imperial and *shōgunate* courts at a distance.

In the Edo period, the definition of a *daimyō* was related to the amount of rice his land could produce annually. He had to own land producing in excess of 10,000 *koku* of rice annually. A *koku* was approximately the amount of rice needed to sustain a man for a year, and was about 180 litres. There were some 260 to 275 *daimyō* (the number varying according to rice production capacity), the wealthiest, other than Tokugawa Ieyasu himself, being the *daimyō* of the Kaga domain, which produced 1.2

徳川家康)of Mikawa and later Edo. Ieyasu was the wealthiest and therefore most powerful, with an astonishing personal 2.5 million *koku*.

[194] Edo was commonly referred to as "Yedo", "Yeddo", or even "Jeddo" by the foreign community during the *bakumatsu*. "Edo" means "rivergate".

million *koku*. Few domains produced more than 40,000 *koku*, however.

Ieyasu formalised his style of government by adopting Confucian ideas[195], with weight given to loyalty. However, the father/son relationship, the central tenet of Confucianism, was soon tacitly replaced by an emphasis on ruler/ruled. Some inimical Confucian tenets were quietly dropped - the notion that bad rulers could legitimately be deposed, for example, and the desirability of having no warriors.

Ieyasu put the ruler/ruled relationship into practice in a determined way. The *daimyō* who had supported him in his power struggle, and in particular at the battle of Sekigahara, became known as the "Inside Lords" or *fudai*, and those who had fought against him were the "Outside Lords" or *tozama*. The *fudai*, together with the *shinpan* (members of the Tokugawa clan) got all the best jobs and wielded more national power than the *tozama*. There were approximately 25 *shinpan*, 150 *fudai* and 100 *tozama*, though this fluctuated according to the political climate.

Much land was redistributed in favour of the *fudai* and *shinpan* and the *shōgunate* itself, at the expense of the *tozama*. Between 1603 and 1653, 213 *daimyō* lost all or part of their lands through having offended the *shōgun*, while 172 newly-favoured *daimyō* were created by giving them sufficient land. 206 *daimyō* were given extra land, and 281 *daimyō* were relocated entirely. The shōgun's domination of the *daimyō* was absolute. However, some of the *tozama* remained among the wealthiest in Japan, and quite able to support armies of tens of thousands of men. Prominent among this wealthy *tozama* aristocracy were the Shimazu family of Satsuma and the Mori family of Chōshū.

Chōshū was based at Hagi. The Mori family had been banished there and their land reduced from 1.2 million *koku* to

---

[195] Confucianism - more precisely, Japanese neo-Confucianism - was a central subject of the Japanese education system right up to 1945.

THREE LEADERS

369,000 by Ieyasu, despite having agreed to withhold their forces from opposing him at Sekigahara. They regarded this as a great betrayal and harboured an unquenchable grudge against Tokugawa as a result. They even had a tradition at their annual New Year clan gathering of ritually asking, "Is it time to overthrow the Tokugawa?", to which the leaders of the subsidiary families would reply, "Not yet, the shogunate is still too powerful".

In August 1615, Ieyasu formalised the powers of the *shōgunate* over the *daimyō* by issuing thirteen regulations, the *buke shohatto*. The regulations stated that:

1. *daimyō* were forbidden to give sanctuary to lawbreakers;
2. The plans and conspiracies of neighbouring domains were to be reported immediately;
3. *daimyō* could not build new castles;
4. *daimyō* could not repair existing castles without the consent of the *shōgun*;
5. *daimyō* could not marry without the consent of the *shōgun*;
6. advisers to the *daimyō* must be men of ability as approved by the *shōgun*;
7. *daimyō* must dress in accordance with a specific dress code;
8. *samurai* must not dress extravagantly or inappropriately;
9. *daimyō* must travel with exactly the prescribed number of retainers, according to his rank;
10. unranked persons were forbidden from being carried by palanquin;
11. *samurai* must lead a simple and frugal life, and study the military and civil arts;
12. no person should take up residence in a new domain;
13. there must be no wanton revelry, drunkenness or licentiousness.

RESPECT AND CONSIDERATION

Ieyasu also issued rules of conduct, the *kinchū narabini kuge shohatto*, for the Imperial court and the nobility, thus declaring the *shōgunate's* ascendancy over the Imperial Court. They included:
1. The Emperor and the courtiers should devote themselves to scholarship and the liberal arts
2. The Emperor and the courtiers should not study government
3. Appointments to high office in the court were to be made on *shōgunate* advice and would be based on rank and ability
4. Ranks and titles were not to be conferred on *daimyō* without the *shōgun's* assent
5. Refusal to bend to the *shōgun's* wishes in matters of substance would result in the banishment of the offending courtier

There were other rules that served to limit potential troublemaking. They included:
1. Travel between domains required an official permit;
2. There was a universal curfew, preventing movements at night without permit, especially outside the traveller's home town boundaries;
3. Many bridges were demolished, thus channelling travel through a few controllable points, and enabling checks to be made on the identity of travellers and their purposes for travel;
4. Carts and other wheeled transport were banned for the general public;
5. A secret police force was established to monitor suspicious activity of any kind

APPENDIX 1-5
BACK AND FORTH TO EDO

From the outset of the Tokugawa *shōgunate*, as an exercise in authority and control, the *shōgun* required each *daimyō* to spend equal amounts of time cooling his heels in Edo, and in his own domain. For those whose lands were distant from Edo, they had to spend alternate years there; for a few of those who lived closer, the rotation was every six months. This was known as *sankin kōtai*, or "alternate attendance" which was formalised by *shōgun* Iemitsu's revision of *buke shohatto* in 1635. It was dressed up as the *daimyō* being needed by the *shōgun* for their wisdom and advice, but its primary by-product had the desirable effect of keeping them from making mischief and fomenting rebellion. It also theoretically provided on hand the assessed number of *samurai* for *bakufu* war-service from each *han*, for they had to accompany their Chief to and from Edo.

Whenever the *daimyō* returned to his fiefdom to see to his estate, he left behind, effectively as hostages, his wife and heir, together with appropriate servants. He was also financially crippled by the need to maintain at least two households in the prescribed style and to live and travel in accordance with the rules, maintaining large retinues. This prevented the *daimyō* from becoming too rich for the *shōgun* to dominate. One estimate is that *sankin kōtai* cost each *daimyō* 50% of his income.

Between Edo and their domains, the *daimyō* had to travel along prescribed routes that were guarded by the *shōgun's* men.

RESPECT AND CONSIDERATION

There was little scope for them to conspire against the *bakufu*. Sankin kōtai was finally rescinded as late as the end of 1862.

Part of the reason for the eventual withdrawal of *sankin kōtai* was the forceful reaction of Sir Rutherford Alcock to a note received in mid-January 1862 from the *bakufu*. It required westerners to stay off the *tōkaidō* for a week to permit various *daimyō* and their retinues to pass unhindered. The French Minister (to Alcock's disgust) cravenly acceded to this request, and issued an *order* to the French residents of Yokohama to keep away. Alcock, though, refused to prevent British subjects from travelling on the road, but agreed to issue a circular *requesting* them to avoid the road on two specific days. At the beginning of the week specified by the *bakufu*, the Japanese shut the gates of the foreign settlement, thus positively infringing the Treaty.

Directly Alcock heard this, he sent an indignant letter remonstrating with the Governor of Kanagawa, reminding him that the gates were there, not for the imprisonment but the protection of foreigners, and telling him that unless they were immediately reopened, a force, with explosives, would be landed from one of the Royal Naval warships currently in the Bay of Yokohama, and they would destroy the gates entirely. The Governor was taken aback and made a stammering excuse that the *yakunin* at the gate were alone responsible. Notwithstanding his attempt to save face, it was clear that the order had emanated from higher quarters.

The speed and vehemence of Alcock's response took the Japanese officials by surprise, and they never again put out such a demand. They did, however, always announce when any particularly great man was about to pass with a large cortège. It was the practice of the Legation to inform the foreign community that a procession was about to pass by and suggesting it might be better to keep out of the way for the few

BACK AND FORTH TO EDO

hours that it might take to pass. The British Legation received no notification concerning Sunday 14 September.

Stitched panorama of Edo, 1865/6, showing the multi-roomed Satsuma *daimyō* house for him and his many retainers, as required by the *sankin kōtai* rules
Five albumen prints by Felice Beato make up the panorama

Appendix 1-6
The *Samurai*

The Richardson murder involved members of the *samurai* class. In order to understand something of their motives and mindset we should first understand what it was to be a *samurai*, and what impact this had on the events on that fateful Sunday afternoon.

The warrior class were initially mercenaries for hire, but in time started to develop a sense of the nobility of their status. In the tenth century, one of these mercenary warriors was Taira Masakado, a descendant of the Emperor Kammu who reigned from 781 to 806 AD. Taira Masakado sought political independence for the Kantō region. He proclaimed himself Emperor. Emperor Suzaku took exception to this, and warfare erupted. Masakado was killed in combat by his cousin Sadamori in 940AD. Sadamori hacked off his head and displayed it on a gatepost in Kyotō, to prove that Masakado was dead. It was then believed miraculously to have been spirited away by non-human hands and arrived in the little fishing port of Shibasaki, which later grew into Edo. There, it was preserved in a wooden casket. As his legend grew, the warrior class started to venerate Masakado, and he was eventually

Casket in which Masakado's head was kept

THE *SAMURAI*

proclaimed *gunshin* - the divine spirit of the *samurai*. The casket containing Masakado's head became an object of veneration.

The *tsuku-do* shrine near the Imperial Palace was built to house the grisly relic, which remained there until the shrine and its contents were destroyed by an American air raid in 1945, 1005 years after Masakado's death. The shrine was rebuilt twice after that, and the latest building won a prestigious architectural award in 1994 for its audacious postmodern design. There is a monument close by at Ōtemachi 大手町 in Tōkyō, where, it is said, Masakado's *kami* resides. After the Great Tōkyō Earthquake of 1923, rioting mobs murdered some 6000 Korean workers, whose presence, so the rumour was, had upset Masakado's *kami*. To this day, local financial institutions take care not to seat their employees with their backs to the monument, which would be insulting to Masakado. It seems the Long-Term Credit Bank of Japan ignored this when they reorganised their offices in 1998, and very soon had to be rescued from a sea of bad debts. The Marubeni Corporation put their shame at being involved in the 1976 Lockheed bribery scandal down to annoying Masakado's *kami*. The Matsui Insurance Company requires its employees to make a monthly pilgrimage to the monument and offer prayer and votive offerings of beer and *sake*. Ancient beliefs resonate in modern Japan.

In time, the *samurai* became bound by a strict but initially unwritten ethical code - *bushidō* - during the Edo period. *Bushidō* 武士道 - "the way of the warrior" - was in some ways parallel to the code of chivalry of the knights of Europe of an earlier time. It combined the ascetic frugality and self-effacement of Zen Buddhism with Confucian conservatism, with its emphasis on loyalty and hierarchy and filial piety. A warrior espoused several virtues in *bushidō*. These were 義 *gi* (rectitude), 勇 *yu* (courage), 仁 *jin* (benevolence), 礼 *rei* (respect), 誠 *makoto* or 信

RESPECT AND CONSIDERATION

shin (honesty), 名誉 *meiyo* (glory and honour), 忠義 *chugi* (loyalty); and some subsidiary virtues *chu* (maintaining an ethical stance), 孝 *kō* (filial piety), 智 *chi* (wisdom) and 悌 *tei* (care for the aged). The well-known true story of the 47 *rōnin* that ends this chapter gives a flavour of the code of *bushidō*.

Samurai were expected to set a strong example in proper behaviour to the inferior classes. They were totally loyal to their *daimyō*, and were sworn to give their lives for him or at his command. From as early as the eleventh century, *samurai* subscribed to the noble concept of *bun-bu ryō-do* meaning "literary arts, military arts, both ways". One scribe recorded it as "The pen and the sword in accord." *Samurai* were supposed, then, to be as accomplished in the most refined aspects of Japanese culture and learning as they were with the sword. Through military conquest, assassinations, political machinations and recognized intellectual ability, some *samurai* rose to become *daimyō* in their own right, and these in turn furnished the families who became *shōgun*. Zen was influential on *samurai* thinking in the 13th century: its austerity chimed with the hard life of the soldier.

Bushidō made its impression on the peasant classes too, and they held strongly to its virtues until well into the Meiji era. Townspeople, though, were far less enamoured of the sobriety of the code and far more ready to espouse the fleshly delights their townships offered.

Disdaining Zen, the general populace preferred the heavily ritualised "Pure Land" (or "Amida") Buddhism, with its promise of physical delights to come when the pure land was established.

THE *SAMURAI*

THE 47 *RŌNIN* AND THE CODE OF *BUSHIDŌ*

The "47 *rōnin*" is a defining national legend for Japan. Unlike most such legends, the story is true.

Asano Takumi no kami Naganori, the 50,000-*koku daimyō* of Akō (now in Hyōgo prefecture), was appointed by *shōgun* Tokugawa Tsunayoshi to the élite group of *daimyō* who represented the *bakufu* in dealings with the Imperial Court. To train him in the elaborate Court ritual, the *bakufu* appointed the *kōzukenosuke* (senior protocol master) Kira Yoshinaka as his mentor. The men detested one another. Kira took to insulting Asano in public by calling him a country bumpkin, after Asano had declined to pay Kira for the tuition, which the rigidly Confucianist Asano held to be part of a *kōzukenosuke's* normal duties.

The situation eventually exploded within the *shōgun's* palace. Kira insulted Asano once again, and Asano drew his sword and aimed a blow at him. Kira was marginally wounded on his face by the sword strike. Asano was immediately arrested and confined. It was clear that Asano had acted illegally by attacking an official with a weapon. Worse still, though, was the fact that this had been done, unthinkably, within the *shōgun's* palace. Asano had no defence and said little to the three *ometsuke* who investigated on the spot. Asano's only statement was that he regretted the insult to the *shōgun* and that he was ashamed that he had failed to kill Kira. The *shōgunate* had no option but to order Asano to commit immediate *seppuku*. Such was the gravity of Asano's offence, though, that even *seppuku* would not save his family from ruin: his fief at Akō was forfeit, and his brother was to be imprisoned. Many took this to be unnecessarily harsh.

Asano took his life in the prescribed manner. When the news of this reached his *samurai* retainers, they were thrown into turmoil. Some advocated an acceptance of the situation, with a quiet retirement from their duties. Others demanded armed resistance to the *bakufu*, if not outright rebellion, for what they saw as an injustice. Others, led by Ōishi Kuranosuke, urged that the retainers should appear to accept the situation but at the same time, prepare to exact revenge against Kira. Ōishi's view prevailed, the men vowing to sacrifice their lives for their dead master.

Kira clearly expected some attempt on his life, and strengthened his bodyguard. Asano's men, by now *rōnin* or leaderless *samurai*, set aside a cache of weapons and then sought to lull Kira into a sense of false security by apparently dispersing and leading dissipated lives. Ōishi even left his wife and began consorting with prostitutes and brawling drunkenly in public. On one occasion, it is said, a Satsuma *samurai* found Ōishi drunk in the street and spat upon him, cursing him as never having been a true follower of *bushidō*.

In time, Kira relaxed. But on 14 December 1702, almost a year after their master's death, the 47 *rōnin* struck. Armed and armoured, they set out for Kira's mansion in Edo. They split into two groups, one entering through the rear of the compound and the other through the front, smashing down the gate to do so. Kira's men were taken by surprise but put up a valiant defence. They killed one of the 47 rōnin, but suffered 16 deaths and 22 woundings in return, such was the ferocity of the *rōnin*. Kira was discovered hiding in an outbuilding, and brought before Ōishi. Ōishi offered Kira the opportunity to commit *seppuku* with the same *tantō* that Asano had used, but Kira, though trembling with fear, refused to answer a mere *rōnin*. Thereupon, Ōishi hacked off Kira's head with the dagger.

Kira's head was then put in a bucket and carried to the *sengaku-ji*, Asano's burial place. Ōishi and the other remaining 45 *rōnin* offered the head to the *kami* of Asano, and then gave themselves up to the *bakufu*. This presented the *shōgun's* Court with a pretty dilemma: the men had lived up to the standards expected under the code of *bushidō*, and there had been earlier dissent among some *daimyō*, many Court officials, and indeed the people generally, against the harsh treatment of Asano and the contrasting leniency shown to Kira. However, they believed that the stability of the nation was at stake, and there was no alternative but to order the surviving *rōnin* to commit *seppuku*. The *rōnin* respectfully obeyed, and were interred near their master in the *sengaku-ji*.

An unverified topper to the legend has it that the Satsuma *samurai* who had spat upon Ōishi in the street came to that same temple and committed *seppuku* to atone for his unjustified insult.

The 47 *rōnin* are revered in Japan even today as examples of men driven by duty, persistence, honour and loyalty, putting righteousness ahead of their very lives. Such are the qualities the Japanese expect of themselves.

RESPECT AND CONSIDERATION

Graves of the 47 *rōnin* at Senkakuji, Takanawa, Minato, Tōkyō

Appendix 1-7
Other Ranks

Hatamoto (旗本) - literally "at the base of the flag", hence "bannermen" - were the direct feudal retainers of the *shōgun*. Under the Tokugawa *shōgunate*, their primary historical function was to act as bodyguards for the *shōgun*, clustering round his banner to protect him. Before the Tokugawa assumed power, most *daimyō* had their own *hatamoto*, but this was discouraged by the Tokugawa, and the term after the early years of the seventeenth century applies exclusively to the *shōgun's* men. There were *hatamoto* present in Shimazu Saburō's *gyoretsu*, protecting the *shōgun's* envoy, on *the tōkaidō* on 14th September 1862.

Despite the proverbial saying, "eighty thousand *hatamoto*", there were only about 5000 of them. It just *seemed* that there were eighty thousand, for they controlled almost every aspect of life for the working man. *Hatamoto* fell into two major classes: the *kuramaitori*, who took their incomes straight from Tokugawa granaries, and the *jikatatori*, who held land scattered throughout Japan. All of them ranked below *fudai daimyō* in having less than 10,000 *koku*. The highest-ranked among them had the right of face-to-face meeting with the *shōgun*. Unlike the *daimyō*, most *hatamoto* did not have to travel back and forth to Edo (see appendix 1-5). They were thus saved a great deal of expense. On rare occasions, a *hatamoto* might be promoted to the rank of *daimyō*.

Hatamoto served in many administrative and civic positions, including the police force as *yoriki* (superintendents), Edo magistrates, and magistrates and tax collectors in districts owned by the Tokugawa. They could even be appointed as one of the 4-6 "junior elders" of the *wakadoshiyori*, the council that supervised the rest of the *hatamoto*, as well as all the Edo artisans, physicians and civil engineers. They were in effect the officer class in the Tokugawa civil service.

Officers need men to command, and so they were provided with *gokenin* (御家人). The 17,000 or so *gokenin* ("housemen") ranked below *hatamoto*, as non-commissioned officers, to continue the analogy. None had any right of audience with the *shōgun*. Most of them had modest landholdings of their own, measured in hundreds, rather than thousands, of *koku*.

APPENDIX 1-8
JAPANESE RELIGION AND PHILOSOPHY: A BRIEF INTRODUCTION
SHINTŌ, BUDDHISM (*BUKKYU*) AND NEO-CONFUCIANISM

Shintō (神道), meaning "the way of the gods", and formerly the State religion of Japan, is a form of animism. It involves the worship of *kami*, which are sacred spirits within such things as wind, rain, mountains, trees and rivers; there are also *kami* relating to issues such as fertility. Some *kami* are local and can be regarded as the spirit of a particular place, but others have greater importance and significance - such as Amaterasu. The *kami* display human-like characteristics: they can, for instance, make mistakes, and can be happy or angry; and the earthly ones live in the same world and breathe the same air that we do.

Shintō, unlike every other major religion, has neither sacred scriptures, nor any extensive codified rules for its adherents. There are four main forms[196] of *shintō*, but their beliefs and

---

[196] These are : Shrine or *jinja shintō* (神社神道), the oldest and central core of *shintō* belief and practice; Folk or *minzoku shintō* (民俗神道) which incorporates shamanism and primitive local elements; Sect or *shūha shintō* (宗派神道), a 19th century movement that eschews shrines and conducts worship in halls and on mountains and has numerous spin-off sects (some only distantly related to *shintō*); and State or *kokka shintō* (国家神道), which

practices have much in common. *Shintō* venerates some mythological texts, such as the *kojiki* and *nihon shoki*, but these are historical documents, not devotional ones. They are vague about the afterlife; there is reference to the "Dark Land" - an unclean place of the dead - but there is no discussion of life after death. Ancestors, however, are revered, even worshipped, and in August, there are local *bon* festivals when Japanese travel to their "home" location and take part in dances and ceremonies in honour of their ancestors.

There are four "affirmations" within *shintō*:
1. tradition and the family. The family is seen as the main mechanism by which traditions are preserved. The main *shintō* celebrations relate to birth and marriage;
2. love of nature. Nature is sacred; to be in contact with nature is to be close to the Gods. Natural objects are worshipped as having or housing sacred spirits;
3. physical cleanliness. Followers of *shintō* take baths, wash their hands, and rinse out their mouths often;
4. *matsuri* - festivals dedicated to particular *kami*.

There is also a less-defined desire for peace and harmony.

Purification rituals are an important feature of *shintō* practice. Throughout Japan there are countless *shintō* shrines (*jinja*); they each have at least one (and sometimes thousands of) distinctive  (often vermilion-painted) *torii* or gate, with two tall uprights and two crossbars or lintels. The *torii* marks the border between the earthly world and the world of the *kami*. A *torii* is never closed. *Torii* literally means "bird-place" - where birds, the messengers of the gods, can rest on the lintels. Believers respect animals as messengers of the Gods. A pair of statues of *koma-inu* ("Korean-"

A *torii*

---

followed on from the Meiji restoration and emphasises the Imperial and national aspects of *shintō*.

JAPANESE RELIGION AND PHILOSOPHY

= "guard-" dogs) usually face each other near the entrance to the temple grounds. Here and there, the guardians differ: at shrines dedicated to Inari, the *kami* of rice and prosperity, the guardians are usually foxes, the messengers of Inari and therefore a sacred animal. Occasionally, the guardians are a pair of demon-kings; this is a Buddhist motif, and shows how syncretistic the Japanese are in their complaisant mingling of *shintō* and *bukkyu*.

Shintō is a religion of the here and now, so most Japanese funerals are carried out under Buddhist auspices: because Buddhist belief is centred on a cycle of birth, death and re-birth. Rarely does a Japanese celebrate marriage under Buddhist auspices: *shintō*, and increasingly nowadays, Christian, marriage ceremonies are preferred.

Japanese parents will seek protection for their children from the *kami*. The *hatsumiyamairi*, (first shrine visit) puts the newborn child under the protection of the *kami*. It takes place on the 32nd day after birth for a boy and the 33rd day for a girl. On November 15th each year, Japanese girls aged three and seven and boys aged three and five should be presented at an appropriate shrine for a blessing by the priest in the *shichigosan* (*shichi* = seven, *go* = five, *san* = three) ritual.

Shintō beliefs and practices underlie a great deal of modern Japanese etiquette and culture. For example:
- The concept of harmony with nature is expressed in *ikebana*, or Japanese flower-arranging.
- *Sumō* wrestling has *shintō* ceremonial garb for wrestlers in the opening ceremonies; there is a purification-by-salt ritual before each bout; and the referee (*gyoji*) wears old-style *shintō* robes.
- Even such everyday matters such as the etiquette of using wooden chopsticks (*hashi* or *otemoto*) and the removal of shoes before entering a building have *shintō* origins.

RESPECT AND CONSIDERATION

Japanese Buddhism, *bukkyo*
Buddhism, in origin, is more a philosophy than a religion. From India around 550 BC, it spread through Asia, (notably along the Silk Road) and arrived in Japan nearly 1000 years later. During its long journey, many changes took place.

The Buddha had been concerned with just one thing - how to end suffering. He believed in a cycle of birth, life and death, followed by birth, life and death, and so on. He reasoned that if we can break free from this cycle, the suffering that inevitably accompanies life would be negated. He postulated four "noble truths":
1. All existence is suffering.
2. Suffering is caused by desire.
3. If you end desire then you end suffering.
4. Following the Eight Fold Path will enable you to end desire.

The Eight Fold Path is a complex set of methods of living to achieve "enlightenment". Many disciplined lifetimes must be lived to attain perfection and so transcend the cycle of birth and death.

The eight elements can be organised into three groups (these are not a series of linear steps, but all eight are to be undertaken simultaneously, in parallel). Each has two stages, preliminary and higher. The eight elements are, in outline:

1. Wisdom
    a. Right understanding, view, perspective (understanding of the four noble truths and the impermanence of being)
    b. Right thought, intention, resolve, aspiration (having proper reasons for following the path of the Buddha)
2. Ethical conduct
    a. Right speech

(not lying, not being contentious, not being abusive, abstaining from gossip)
    b. Right action, conduct
(abstention from taking life, stealing, sexual misconduct, intoxication)
    c. Right livelihood
(not making a living by harming any living creature or that might lead to such harm, such as arms dealing, animal slaughter, dishonest acts, slave trading, prostitution)
3. Mental discipline
    a. Right effort, endeavour
(keeping the mind free of distractions from the Truths and the other Paths; replacing ill wishes towards someone with good wishes; banishing laziness in meditation)
    b. Right mindfulness, memory
(remaining in the present, being aware, but not disturbed by, what is happening around the follower)
    c. Right concentration
(sinking into a detached state during meditation, leading to transcendent experience)

Once the eightfold path has been well trodden, the follower finds himself led on to two further, advanced elements:

4. Right knowledge
(a full understanding of the meaning of life, and the wisdom to see his own place in the scheme of things)
5. Right liberation, release
(a state leading ultimately to release from the birth-life-death-rebirth cycle)

RESPECT AND CONSIDERATION

According to *nihon shoki*, Buddhism arrived in Japan in 552 AD from Korea. The original Buddhism of 552 AD developed over time into different schools, each emphasizing different aspects of the Buddha's teaching, and each appealing to different sorts and classes of people. The Imperial court, for instance, was drawn to ritual and intellectualism, while commoners generally went for the simpler sects that promised them salvation in return for little beyond financial support and attending major knees-up festivals. The soil in which Buddhism was planted was of course one in which *shintō* had flourished for a very long time.

Buddhist monk Nichiren Daishōnin

The first flourishing of Buddhism in Japan was in the Nara period (c. 710-794 AD). Six major schools of Buddhism lived side by side, sometimes within the same temples: *ritsu*, *joyitsu*, *kusha*, *sanron*, *hosso* and *kegon*. They were largely distinguished by which sacred texts they admitted were canonical.

In the Heian period (c. 794-1185 AD), the Chinese-influenced *shingon* ("true word") and *tendai* (a Chinese mountain) sects developed, and towards the end of the period, the native Japanese *nichiren* school was founded by Nichiren Daishōnin, the "great sage". These were all forms of "esoteric" Buddhism, with great emphasis on its transcendent aspects.

Starting in the Kamakura period (1185-1333 AD) to the present day, Japanese Buddhism developed into two broad schools, although elements of earlier schools still exist. The two "modern" schools are Amida, or "Pure Land" Buddhism, and Zen Buddhism, though *shingon* Buddhism straddles all schools.

There are many quasi-Christian elements to Pure Land Buddhism, which developed in China around the second century AD under the influence of a monk from Parthia, where Nestorian Christianity had already made its mark. It was

JAPANESE RELIGION AND PHILOSOPHY

brought to Japan in the fourth century. Pure Land Buddhists seek the help of Amida Buddha to lead them to Nirvana. The great *daibutsu* statue of Buddha at Kamakura is of Amida Buddha. Pure Land Buddhism is by far the largest school of modern Buddhism in Japan, and indeed, in the world. It offers a path to enlightenment through devotion to Amitabha Buddha (Japanese 阿弥陀如来 *amida nyorai*), a celestial buddha of great merit. *Jodo* (浄土) - "Pure Land" - was in fact founded in China around 180 AD but did not flourish for another 400 years.

Zen (禅) Buddhism ("meditative" Buddhism) had been founded in China around 500 AD (the exact dates are disputed) by Bodhidharma, an Indian monk. Everything in Zen Buddhism leads to meditation, and no activity does not have a meditative aspect, nor is any task too menial to be performed. Your feelings and your sufferings are inconsiderable. Even the abbot of a Zen monastery performs such tasks as sweeping the floor. Zen claims an unbroken line of teaching right back to the Buddha himself. Zen is notable for its use of *kōan* (公案) for meditation. These are riddles or paradoxical sayings whose contemplation is supposed to lead to enlightenment. You decide. Some notable examples are:

- A monk asked Dongshan Shouchou, "What is Buddha?" Dongshan said, "Three pounds of flax".
- Huìnéng asked Hui Ming, "Without thinking of good or evil, show me your original face before your mother and father were born".
- Two hands clap and there is a sound. What is the sound of one hand?

Zen teaches the false nature of material things, the need for obedience to one's master, the impermanence of life, and enlightenment through a life lived well.

According to a 1997 survey by Japanese Government Agency of Cultural Affairs, ("ACA"), the number of Japanese people who say they are "close to" various religions is (excluding "No Religion" responses):

Religion	ACA
	%
shintō	49
bukkyo	44
kirishitando[197]	2
Other/not stated	5

Many Japanese regard themselves as followers of both *shintō* and *bukkyu*. The percentage of self-proclaimed non-believers in any religion is high: various surveys show from 52% to 63%, with a median around 55%. However, over 70% of Japanese admit to visiting a shrine, temple or church at least once a year, which rather contradicts the 55% finding. Neither *shintō* nor *bukkyo* expects its devotees to turn up at the shrine or the temple on a weekly basis.

In their day, the *samurai* found Zen Buddhism perfectly suited to their needs, especially, perhaps, the need to die at anytime without any hesitation at the behest of their master.

Confucianism
The third religious/philosophical strand to influence Japan was Confucianism, or, more properly, neo-Confucianism.

Confucius was a Chinese thinker who lived from 551 to 479 BC. He developed a systematic theory of personal and governmental morality embodying concepts of social relationship, sincerity, and justice. To study was man's highest attainment. Confucius' philosophy was primarily pragmatic. He was renowned for formulating the "Golden Rule".

---

[197] Christianity

JAPANESE RELIGION AND PHILOSOPHY

> Adept Kung asked, "Is there any one word that could guide a person throughout life?" The Master replied, "How about 'shu': never impose on others what you would not choose for yourself?"

As always happens with great teachers, his immediate students elaborated Confucius' straightforward thoughts, and successive generations of followers built on their predecessors' elaborations until there was a complex, rule-laden structure that would probably have been unintelligible to Confucius himself. He championed strong familial loyalty, the worship of ancestors, respect of elders by their children and of husbands by their wives, and the family as a basis for an ideal government. His moral system was based upon empathy and understanding others, rather than laws imposed by a deity. There are no deities in Confucianism.

Some of Confucius' aphorisms are self-evidently wise:
- Before you embark on a journey of revenge, dig two graves.
- Forget injuries, never forget kindnesses.
- It does not matter how slow you go so long as you do not stop.
- Life is really simple, but men insist on making it complicated.
- Respect yourself and others will respect you.
- The only constant is change.
- To see what is right and not to do it is want of courage.
- When anger arises, think of the consequences
- If the people be led by laws, and uniformity sought to be given them by punishments, they will try to avoid the punishment, but have no sense of shame.
- If the people be led by virtue, and uniformity sought to be given them by the rules of propriety, they will have the sense of shame, and moreover will become good.

RESPECT AND CONSIDERATION

These last two sayings spell out his political theory. You can't rule by threats; virtuous leadership will rule by the people's own volition. And finally, Confucius had a strong streak of asceticism in his make-up:

> With coarse rice to eat, with water to drink, and my bended arm for a pillow, I still have joy in the midst of these. Riches and honours acquired by unrighteousness are to me as a floating cloud.

The neo-Confucianism that influenced Japanese political thought was a Confucianism formulated by Zhu Xi (1130-1200 AD) that had absorbed some Buddhist and some Taoist ideas. This resulted in an almost Gnostic view of a dualism between outward appearance and inward reality. Human nature is essentially good, says Zhu Xi, but each human needs to be purified to reveal the goodness within.

Zhu Xi

The three belief systems influenced much of the Japanese way of life over the centuries. Perhaps the easiest for us to understand is the *samurai bushido* code of conduct. The asceticism and conservatism of neo-Confucianism, the rigour and clarity of purpose of *Zen*, and the loyalty elements of *shintō* appealed to the soldiery:

- they lived a hard and austere life with no fripperies
- their valour and respect for the enemy were right actions that resulted in being respected
- they were ready to cast off "self" completely by giving their lives for their master
- their souls would either
  - be promoted in the next life, or
  - they would be revered by their descendants.

And the tenets of the belief systems, particularly the neo-Confucian ones, were the bedrock for the *bakufu* under the Tokugawa *shōgunate*. Consistent justice, sincere and honest governance, respect for the hierarchy, and applying the methods of the past to present situations were the ideals they sought after.

APPENDIX 1-9
SAMURAI WEAPONS

In the early days of the rise of the *samurai*, they were primarily archers and horsemen. They used a variety of weapons, including the longbow (*yumi* or *daikyu*), knives, spears (*yari*), darts and axes. Gradually, they began to become expert in the use of swords. In the fourteenth century, Okazaki Masamune (岡崎正宗), a swordsmith, developed new techniques of sword-making. His technique was to make the core of the body of the sword of relatively soft steel ("pearlite"), giving the sword slight flexibility and the ability to withstand the shocks that might otherwise snap the metal when used as intended. To this, he added a cutting edge of hard steel ("martensite"). It could be honed to phenomenal sharpness. The blade of the sword had a curve that enabled the user to slice his opponent instead of hacking at him; this was much more efficient.

The *samurai* Suenaga facing Mongols, during the Mongol invasions of Japan.
(Moko Shurai Ekotoba, c. 1293.) The bows and arrows of the *samurai* are clearly visible. The Mongol horseman has just thrown an explosive bomb at the *samurai*

SAMURAI WEAPONS

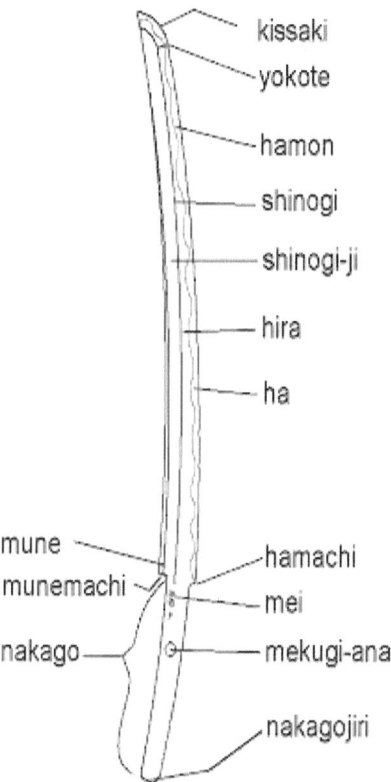

Parts of a *katana* blade

Samurai would have their *katana* tested on the corpses of executed criminals. There were prescribed cuts to be made on a corpse to test various aspects of the blade. A really good blade could cut through three corpses at one stroke, and on one noted occasion, a single stroke bisected seven corpses. It was not uncommon for a *samurai* to pay the executioner to use a new sword for an actual execution as a test to see whether the sword was worth its high price. Sometimes, if the criminal were executed for a particularly heinous crime, he would not be beheaded, but would be tied to a frame and cut in two through his right shoulder diagonally through to his left waist with a single blow. The best executioners might despatch 350 criminals in a good year. They were despised socially, and were sometimes not paid the standard 7 *bu* fee, but they did have the right to the condemned criminal's liver, which they sold to manufacturers of medicines, the warmer and fresher the better.

The techniques for sword-making were taken up and improved further by other swordsmiths. The Japanese sword mightily impressed Europeans on first acquaintance:

> Their swords and daggers are made in the fashion of a scimitar with a slight curve, of medium length and are so sharp that draping a sheet of soft paper on the edge and blowing on it cuts it ...

according to a French memoir of October 1615.[198]

There were a number of renowned swordsmiths. A Japanese account of the murder of Charles Richardson says that the *katana* that first cut him was wielded by Narahara Kizaemon[199]. His sword, it is said, had been made by the celebrated swordsmith Fujiwara Tadahiro[200], in or around 1624. If true, it would have

---

[198] *Le ses epees et dagues sont faictes en fasson de simmetterre tres peu courbe, et de moyenne longueur et sont sy fort tranchantz que y mettant un feuillet de papier et soufflant ilz couppent le papier* ... Relations of Mme de St Troppez, October 1615, Bibliothèque Inguimbertine, Carpentras. (Author's loose translation from mediæval French). Hasekura Rokuemon Tsunenaga travelled with a large retinue to Mexico ("New Spain"), then to Spain and on to Italy from 1613 to 1620, even meeting the Pope. Bad weather caused them to put into St. Tropez for a few days, when Hasekura became a sensational celebrity. The French were amazed at the "two small sticks" with which he ate, and the disposable tissues on which he blew his nose. The used tissues became highly-prized trophies of his visit, which says as much for the French as for the Japanese.

[199] The second, and more efficient *samurai* to attack Richardson was, according to a Japanese source, Hisashi Kukimura.

[200] Born Hashimoto Heisakuro in 1614, he took over the duties as the master smith of the Hizen school when his father Tadayoshi died in 1632. Tadahiro had been forging swords for the previous nine years.

SAMURAI WEAPONS

been handed down through several generations of the Narahara family as a treasured heirloom.

As previously noted, the arquebus, an early firearm, had been brought accidentally to Japan by Fernão Mendes Pinto, the Portuguese victim of shipwreck. He had bought his way into favour by presenting one to the Shimazu *daimyō* who gave him shelter. Not long after Pinto's arrival in 1543, the enterprising Shimazu clan had set up a plant to manufacture these matchlock weapons and the gunpowder and ammunition required. The arquebus was taken up by the *samurai* and played an important part in the near-civil war that culminated in Tokugawa Ieyasu's victory at Sekigahara in 1600. Despite furnishing the decisive weapon of the campaign, the Shimazu clan were on the losing side, and so became *tozama*. Purists among the *samurai* disdained the arquebus: not quite in the *bushidō* spirit.

Apart from minor skirmishes, warfare died out in Japan from the beginning of the seventeenth century. *Samurai* increasingly became token warriors, but active courtiers and civil servants. By the time of the *bakumatsu*, each *daimyō* had a retinue of *samurai* bureaucrats and administrators. Some of these were immensely able and went on to become senior ministers in the early Meiji governments.

The *samurai* continued to wear the *daishō*, but this was more and more symbolic. The *daishō* are the two *samurai* swords, the badge of their rank. The *katana* (long sword) and *wakizashi* (short sword) normally make up the pair. To counter the decline in the arts of swordmanship, a number of *samurai* formed schools to teach the techniques. Each school emphasized different techniques - single-handed, two swords simultaneously, the short sword, and so on. There was rivalry between the schools, and much discussion as to which taught the best techniques.

There was a complex etiquette in the wearing of the sword, relating to the speed with which they might be drawn and their

RESPECT AND CONSIDERATION

readiness for use. "Two-sworded men", as *samurai* were known, still had the legal right to cut down any person of lower degree who did not show proper respect. That right was claimed by the *samurai* of Shimazu Saburō on the *tōkaidō* on 14th September 1862.

Appendix 2
Text of President Fillmore's letter to the Emperor of Japan

GREAT AND GOOD FRIEND: I send you this public letter by Commodore Matthew C. Perry, an officer of the highest rank in the navy of the United States, and commander of the squadron now visiting Your Imperial Majesty's dominions.

I have directed Commodore Perry to assure your Imperial majesty that I entertain the kindest feelings toward your majesty's person and government, and that I have no other object in sending him to Japan but to propose to your Imperial majesty that the United States and Japan should live in friendship and have commercial intercourse with each other.

The Constitution and laws of the United States forbid all interference with the religious or political concerns of other nations. I have particularly charged Commodore Perry to abstain from every act which could possibly disturb the tranquillity of your Imperial majesty's dominions.

The United States of America reach from ocean to ocean, and our Territory of Oregon and State of California lie directly opposite to the dominions of your Imperial majesty. Our steamships can go from California to Japan in eighteen days.

Our great State of California produces about sixty millions of dollars in gold every year, besides silver, quicksilver, precious stones, and many other valuable articles. Japan is also a rich and fertile country, and produces many very valuable articles. Your Imperial majesty's subjects are skilled in many of the arts. I am

RESPECT AND CONSIDERATION

Commodore Perry bringing gifts for the Emperor and Commissioners on his return in 1854

The presents included Audubon's *Birds of America* and *Quadrupeds*; sundry other Books; Charts; Clocks; a Telegraph; a Telescope and Standard U.S. Measures; Farm implements; Potatoes; Seeds; a Miniature locomotive, tender, coach and track (on which the Japanese officials rode with great and joyous abandon: the locomotive is visible in the engraving); Patent lifeboats; Perfume for the ladies of the Court; Small arms and ammunition; Stoves; Tea; Whiskey and Wine (which latter two were particularly gratefully received). Many of these were, of course, effectively samples of items that the Americans hoped to trade.

In return, they received gifts from the Japanese of:
Lacquer work; Silk; Crêpe; Pongee (a soft thin cloth woven from raw silk); Dolls; Foodstuffs; Porcelain; Umbrellas and Handicrafts - and a collection of obscene paintings. The Japanese clearly recognised that the gifts from the Americans were largely tradable items, and so were shrewd enough to respond in kind. Perry and the American officers were somewhat unimpressed with the gifts from the Japanese. "The meager display and the lack of rich brocades and magnificent things always associated with our ideas of Japan.... I think these presents will prove a great disappointment to our people, whose ideas of Japan have been so exaggerated."

TEXT OF PRESIDENT FILLMORE'S LETTER TO THE EMPEROR OF JAPAN

desirous that our two countries should trade with each other, for the benefit both of Japan and the United States.

We know that the ancient laws of your Imperial majesty's government do not allow of foreign trade, except with the Chinese and the Dutch; but as the state of the world changes and new governments are formed, it seems to be wise, from time to time, to make new laws. There was a time when the ancient laws of your Imperial majesty's government were first made.

About the same time America, which is sometimes called the New World, was first discovered and settled by the Europeans. For a long time there were but a few people, and they were poor. They have now become quite numerous; their commerce is very extensive; and they think that if your Imperial majesty were so far to change the ancient laws as to allow a free trade between the two countries it would be extremely beneficial to both.

If your Imperial majesty is not satisfied that it would be safe altogether to abrogate the ancient laws which forbid foreign trade, they might be suspended for five or ten years, so as to try the experiment. If it does not prove as beneficial as was hoped, the ancient laws can be restored. The United States often limit their treaties with foreign States to a few years, and then renew them or not, as they please.

I have directed Commodore Perry to mention another thing to your Imperial majesty. Many of our ships pass every year from California to China; and great numbers of our people pursue the whale fishery near the shores of Japan. It sometimes happens, in stormy weather, that one of our ships is wrecked on your Imperial majesty's shores. In all such cases we ask, and expect, that our unfortunate people should be treated with kindness, and that their property should be protected, till we can send a vessel and bring them away. We are very much in earnest in this.

Commodore Perry is also directed by me to represent to your Imperial majesty that we understand there is a great abundance of coal and provisions in the Empire of Japan. Our steamships, in crossing the great ocean, burn a great deal of coal, and it is not convenient to bring it all the way from America. We wish that our steamships and other vessels should be allowed to stop in Japan and supply themselves with coal, provisions, and water. They will pay for them in money, or anything else your Imperial majesty's subjects may prefer; and we request your Imperial majesty to appoint a convenient port, in the southern part of the Empire, where our vessels may stop for this purpose. We are very desirous of this.

These are the only objects for which I have sent Commodore Perry, with a powerful squadron, to pay a visit to your Imperial majesty's renowned city of Yedo: friendship, commerce, a supply of coal and provisions, and protection for our shipwrecked people.

We have directed Commodore Perry to beg your Imperial majesty's acceptance of a few presents. They are of no great value in themselves; but some of them may serve as specimens of the articles manufactured in the United States, and they are intended as tokens of our sincere and respectful friendship.

May the Almighty have your Imperial majesty in His great and holy keeping!

In witness whereof, I have caused the great seal of the United States to be hereunto affixed, and have subscribed the same with my name, at the city of Washington, in America, the seat of my government, on the thirteenth day of the month of November, in the year one thousand eight hundred and fifty-two.

TEXT OF PRESIDENT FILLMORE'S LETTER TO THE EMPEROR OF JAPAN

Your good friend,
MILLARD FILLMORE

EDWARD EVERETT,
Secretary of State

A report of the mode of submission of the letter includes this paragraph:

> The United States flag and the broad pennant were borne by two athletic seamen, who had been selected from the crews of the squadron on account of their stalwart proportions. Two boys, dressed for the ceremony, preceded the Commodore, bearing in an envelope of scarlet cloth the boxes which contained his credentials and the President's letter. These documents, of folio size, were beautifully written on vellum, and not folded, but bound in blue silk velvet. Each seal, attached by cords of interwoven gold and silk with pendent gold tassels, was encased in a circular box six inches in diameter and three in depth, wrought of pure gold. Each of the documents, together with its seal, was placed in a box of rosewood about a foot long, with lock, hinges, and mountings all of gold. On either side of the Commodore marched a tall, well-formed Negro, who, armed to the teeth, acted as his personal guard. These blacks, selected for the occasion, were two of the best-looking fellows of their color that the squadron could furnish.

Clearly, the magnificence of the American ceremonial and accoutrements was intended to impress the Emperor. That it was the *shōgunate* he was dealing with was a fact of which the commodore was blissfully unaware. Perry insisted the letter be taken at once to the Emperor, who would not have known what to do with it had it reached him, so far outside the real world did he reside. The *shōgun* replied evasively:

> ...It is quite impossible to give satisfactory answers at once to all the proposals of your government. ... a change is most positively forbidden by the laws of our imperial ancestors ... (because of the recent installation of a new Emperor) there is no time to settle other business thoroughly. Moreover his majesty the new Emperor at his succession to the throne promised to the princes and high officers of the empire to observe the laws; it is therefore evident that he cannot now bring about any alterations in the ancient laws ...

It was classic *bakufu* temporising - but to no avail. The treaties would inevitably come.

APPENDIX 3
DRAMATIS PERSONAE
BIOGRAPHICAL AND OTHER NOTES ON VARIOUS PEOPLE MENTIONED IN THE TEXT.

ALCOCK, SIR (JOHN) RUTHERFORD (1809-97)
British Head of Legation to Japan: he was in England (to be married on 8th July 1862) at the time of Richardson's murder. He trained as a doctor at Edinburgh University. After service as Minister Plenipotentiary in Japan from 1858 to 1864, he fell out with Lord Russell and did not return to Japan. He was known for his vague and over-long despatches. Instead of Japan, he was appointed Ambassador to China. On retirement in 1871, he became President of the Royal Geographical Society. He wrote extensively about Japanese culture and language and was the first non-Japanese to ascend Mount Fuji. CB 1860, KCB 1862, hon. DCL Oxon 1863.

ALEXANDER, COMMANDER JOHN HOBHOUSE INGLIS, RN
Commanded HMS *Coquette* at Kagoshima. Promoted Captain of *Euryalus* 1864. Severely wounded by a bullet in the ankle at Shimonoseki.

Sir Rutherford Alcock

DRAMATIS PERSONÆ

APPLIN, LIEUTENANT

Commanded the mounted guard at Yokohama. Satow wrote of him:

> a good, harmless sort of fellow, whose only weakness was for fine uniforms and showy horses. It was whispered about that he had assumed the insignia of a field-officer which is undoubtedly a serious offence against discipline ... the blaze of gold which decorated his person was wonderful to behold, and on at least one occasion, when we were going in solemn procession to an audience of the Tycoon, caused him to be mistaken for the Envoy by the Japanese officials, who gave him the salutes that rightly belonged to his less conspicuously adorned diplomatic chief.

Applin led the troop improperly ordered by Captain Vyse to pursue the killers of Richardson. Willis, writing of his departure from Japan, refers to him as Captain Applin.

ASPINALL, WILLIAM GREGSON

Liverpool-born Tea inspector and general merchant in Yokohama; formed partnership with Frederick Cornes as Aspinall, Cornes & Co. Retired 1873. The inquest into Richardson's death was held in Aspinall's house, which must therefore have been capacious. He was a pallbearer at Richardson's funeral.

BORLASE, CAPTAIN JOHN, CB, RN

Captain of HMS Sloop *Pearl*. Ordered by Adm. Kuper to seize three ships at Kagoshima. Retired to Penzance as Vice-Admiral, 1878. d. 1895

BORRADAILE, MRS MARGARET

Sister in law of William Marshall; accompanied CL Richardson on the fateful excursion. Died in England in 1869.

RESPECT AND CONSIDERATION

BOXER, COMMANDER CHARLES RICHARD FOX, RN
Son of Rear-Admiral Edward Boxer (1784-1855) who died of cholera while port-Admiral of Balaclava during the Crimean War. Charles commanded HMS *Racehorse* at Kagoshima. Retired as a Rear-Admiral in 1884.

CLARKE, WOODTHORPE CHARLES
Silk inspector of Yokohama, accompanied CL Richardson on the fateful excursion. Richardson and Clarke were old friends, going back to Clarke's days working in Shanghai.

CORNES, FREDERICK (1837-1927)

Partner of William Aspinall. He had been out riding with Elias Ellis when the news of the Namamugi Incident first spread through the community. He sought Richardson's body with Ellis. His partnership with Aspinall ended in 1873, and today the firm of Cornes & Co trades as Ferrari, Maserati, Rolls-Royce and Bentley dealers, are agents for P&O and Lloyds, supply agricultural machinery and high-technology equipment in Japan and the Pacific Rim countries, and has other maritime and insurance interests.

DE BELLECOURT, GUSTAVE DUCHESNE
Envoy Extraordinary of His Majesty the Emperor of the French - the French Minister in Japan from 1859 to April 1864.

ELGIN, EARL OF
James Bruce, the 8th Earl of Elgin and 12th Earl of Kincardine (20.7.1811 - 20.11.1863), was a career diplomat, and at

The Earl of Elgin

DRAMATIS PERSONÆ

various times Governor General of the Province of Canada and Viceroy of India. In 1857, he became High Commissioner to China, and he stayed there in 1858-9, where he oversaw the end of the 2nd Opium War. On his visit to Japan, Elgin brought with him a steam yacht, the *Emperor*, as a gift from Queen Victoria to the Emperor of Japan, as from a mighty Empress with a colossal empire to a local Emperor confined to his own territory.

ELIAS, ELLIS

With Cornes, he discovered Richardson's body and gave evidence at the inquest.

HAMMOND, SIR EDMUND, PC (1802-1890) (1874, ennobled as Baron Hammond of Kirkella, in the town and county of the town of Kingston-upon-Hull)

Permanent Secretary at the Foreign Office, 1854-71 under successive Foreign Secretaries the Earls of Clarendon, Malmesbury, Russell, Clarendon (again) and Granville. His father, George Hammond, was Under-Secretary of State for Foreign Affairs from 1795-1806 and 1807-1809.

HITOTSUBASHI, KEIKI

Regent for the young *shōgun* Iemitsu 1862. As Tokugawa Yoshinobu (q.v.) he became 15th and last of the Tokugawa *shōguns*.

HOPE, ADMIRAL OF THE FLEET SIR JAMES, GCB (1808-81)

Sir James Hope was Commander-in-Chief in the East Indian and China seas from 25th January 1859 to 8th February 1862, in the rank of Rear Admiral; he flew

Tokugawa Yoshinobu in French military uniform

his flag in the frigate HMS *Chesapeake*. A Scotsman, he ordered the design of a special uniform, including a Balmoral bonnet, for Scottish sailors in the Royal Navy, but the experiment failed due to opposition (some said jealousy, and others, derision) from the other nationalities serving alongside their Caledonian brothers-in-arms. (He followed in a noble naval tradition. In 1853, Commander, later Admiral, Eardley-Wilmot of HMS *Harlequin* paid for his crew to dress as harlequins, an event that was widely regarded as bringing the Royal Navy into disrepute.) Hope took a close interest in the welfare of his men, and regarded all who had sailed with him as lifelong comrades. He was in turn very popular with the men.

HOWARD-VYSE, CAPTAIN FRANCIS

An Officer in the Royal Regiment of Horse Guards (The Blues), 1865

Captain Francis Howard-Vyse (bapt. 15 Sep 1828, d. 1891) was the tenth and youngest of eight sons and two daughters of Frances (*née* Hesketh) and Richard William Howard-Vyse JP, MP of Stoke Place, Buckinghamshire. Francis' father Richard was said to have been a "trial to his family, who were anxious to get rid of him". He was a "trial" because he had no heart for the family business of soldiering, and yearned to be an archaeologist[201].

---

[201] He excavated extensively in Egypt, and discovered, among other things, an anomalous hieroglyphic cartouche inside the Great Pyramid (there are no other such inscriptions inside the Great Pyramid), which discovery he made without witnesses. It has divided scholars ever since. Many allege that it was a

DRAMATIS PERSONÆ

There was a distinguished military ancestry: Ann Howard, daughter of Field Marshal Sir George Howard, married General Richard Vyse in 1780, thus conjoining the surnames. Eight generations back through the Howard line, the family sprang from the Dukes of Norfolk.

One of Francis' brothers had a distinguished military career, retiring as a Colonel: he also held the Royal appointment of Silver Stick in Waiting. Another brother was also an officer in the family regiment, the Royal Regiment of Horse Guards (The Blues). Another was a Northamptonshire vicar in the Church of England. Yet another was a Member of Parliament.

Vyse's family continued to serve with some distinction in the regiment through two world wars, and Sir Richard Granville Hylton Howard-Vyse was its Colonel from 1951 to 1962.

Francis was appointed a Cornet[202] in the regiment, on 29th November, 1844. He was sixteen years old. His family was wealthy and powerful, and the Army or the Church were fitting professions for younger sons of influential families, for they would not, of course inherit the family estate. His commission as Cornet was, naturally, purchased for him. His older brother Richard also purchased his own commissions. As Richard promoted himself rank by rank (eventually to Major in the Regiment but a Lieutenant Colonel as far as the rest of the Army was concerned), on each of the same days young Francis purchased *his* promotions. Francis purchased his Lieutenancy

---

forgery by Richard Vyse, but all we can say is that the jury is still out. He also discovered, indisputably, an iron plate wedged in a joint of the Pyramid: it had previously been thought that iron was not made in Egypt before 650BC, but the pyramids are undeniably 2600 BC: thus the Egyptian Iron Age is much earlier than had been thought.

[202] Cornet was the lowest commissioned officer rank in the cavalry. A cornet in a cavalry regiment carried the troop standard, known itself as a "cornet". Vyse's regiment even today refers to second Lieutenants as "Cornets".

RESPECT AND CONSIDERATION

on 5th February 1847 and his Captaincy on 21st April 1854. In May 1857, he was "sold out"[203] after 13 years service.

During Francis' service, the regiment won no battle honours, and remained largely a ceremonial and social regiment. They were deployed domestically on occasion, in the absence of a police force, to prevent riots, particularly of Chartist meetings. Their blue uniform coats with red facings, together with their highly-polished armour, made for magnificent ceremonial. Unlike the modern army, where the successors to the Royal Horse Guards (Blue) are a fine light tank regiment, the Blues of Vyse's time rested on the laurels they had won in the Napoleonic wars. It was not until 1875 that the regiment, now renamed the Royal Horse Guards, was sent abroad again on service, when they served in Egypt.

---

[203] At this time, Army commissions in ranks up to Colonel could be purchased from a retired or deceased officer, making use of the Regimental Agent for this purpose. Vyse would have sold his Captain's commission to the highest bidder. A Royal Horse Guards Captain's commission in 1858 was going for a regulation £3,500, a Lieutenant's £1785, a Cornet's £1,260. Majors' commissions cost £5350, and Lieutenant Colonels' £7250. The "regulation" was the highest amount a commission could be sold for. "Over-regulation" payments were prohibited, though sometimes a retiring officer's military equipment might be sold to his successor for extraordinarily high prices. From 1850 onwards, a cornet had additionally to pass an examination to be commissioned as a Lieutenant, and a Lieutenant a Captain. General Officer ranks (above Colonel) were not purchasable: they had to be earned by merit (though friends in high places helped). It was possible for a Cornet to be promoted free of charge through the ranks if he showed outstanding bravery and soldierly skills. £3500 was a very large sum of money in those days: over three times the annual pay of a Rear-Admiral, for instance. On that basis, Vyse's £3500 would equate to around £300,000 at the beginning of the twenty-first century. The purchase and sale of commissions was abolished by Royal Warrant in the Cardwell army reforms of 1871. By the Army Reform Act 1871, the rank of Cornet was abolished and replaced by that of Second Lieutenant. However, the Blues and Royals Regiment to this day unofficially styles its Second Lieutenants as "Cornets".

DRAMATIS PERSONÆ

Twenty-two months after resigning his commission, Vyse joined the consular service and was appointed Vice Consul in Edo on 7th February 1859. His letter of appointment informed him that his salary would be £750 per annum, and granted him £250 for "outfit" - the necessary purchases of uniform, clothing and essentials for personal use in this remote and subtropical country. The letter of appointment from Lord Malmesbury[204] contained an unusual paragraph, which sheds light on the depth of antagonism expressed by his superior in Japan (Lt. Col. Neale) when the Namamugi Incident occurred, for Vyse clearly disobeyed Malmesbury's instruction. It read:

> I have especially to point out to you that it is indispensable that you should avoid giving any just cause of offence to the Japanese Authorities or people. You will demean yourself courteously on all occasions towards those authorities, and if any case should appear to you to be inconsistent with the rights and privileges secured by Treaty to British Trade, you will abstain from entering into any lengthened discussion on the subject and you will at once state your intention to refer the matter to your official superior, by whom the question at issue must be settled.

The letter concludes with travel instructions. Passage had been booked on a ship from Marseilles to Alexandria and thence to Hong Kong by Packet. As was customary, Vyse would have to make his way to Marseilles at his own expense. In a Foreign Office estimate of the annual costs of operating the Consulate in

---

[204] James Howard Harris, 3rd Earl of Malmesbury (1807 - 1889) was Foreign Secretary in Lord Derby's Conservative administration from 26 February 1858 to 18 June 1859. He was known as a Tory of the "Old School". Malmesbury's "old school" was Eton, followed by a "gentleman's degree" at Oriel College, Oxford. Such a degree entailed only dining regularly at the college and not materially offending the authorities. No studies or examinations were required. He was succeeded as Foreign Secretary by Lord John Russell.

RESPECT AND CONSIDERATION

Japan, passages to Japan for student interpreters and assistants were shown as costing £125. These were, of course, costs for second-class passages. Vyse travelled in greater pomp, as befitting a Vice-Consul in Her Britannic Majesty's service. The Admiralty conveyed the consular party for the final legs of their voyage from Hong Kong to Japan in HMS *Sampson*, a paddle frigate. Their report requesting that the costs of the voyage be charged to the public purse shows:

NAMES	CAPA-CITY	FROM	TO	EM-BARK	DISEMBARK	NOTE
R Alcock	Consul General	Hong Kong	Jeddo	17 May	July 5	At Captain's Table
Capt. FH Vyse	Vice Consul	-do-	-do-	-do-	-do-	-do-
CP Hodgson[205] with wife and daughter	Consul	-do-	Nagasaki	-do-	June 13	-do-
Capt. FH Vyse	Acting Consul	Jeddo	Kanagawa	17 July	July 21	-do-

Abel Gower was also on board, but as a lower ranking official, did not merit a seat at the Captain's table. Pierre Rossier, the Negretti & Zambra photographer, was on board as well.

Vyse replied to Malmesbury on 22nd February from 15 Dover Street, Piccadilly, expressing his "most grateful thanks" to Lord Malmesbury, and requesting that the £250 outfit money be given to him immediately in England to defray his costs.

There was some controversy over Vyse's appointment, which was not by the normal promotion from a junior rank within the

---

[205] C. Pemberton Hodgson was the first, temporary, Consul at Nagasaki, serving from 13th June 1859, handing over to the delayed GS Morrison on 6th August 1859.

DRAMATIS PERSONÆ

Foreign Office Consular Service. A question was asked in the House of Commons on 18th February 1859 by John Ayshford Wise, the Liberal Member of Parliament for Stafford. William Robert Seymour Vesey-FitzGerald, the Under-Secretary for Foreign Affairs, denied that Vyse had been improperly appointed. Certainly, the other twelve Japanese appointments made the same day had been under regular Consular Committee rules, but Vyse had "only" been appointed as vice-Consul, and would serve "under the supervision of a chief of great eminence". The Under-Secretary was

> at a loss to understand what recommendations were referred to which rendered objectionable the appointment of an excellent and intelligent gentleman to a very subordinate office.

We must draw our own conclusions. If he was so "excellent", why was he being appointed to a "very subordinate office"? Maybe there were no better candidates for the post. Certainly at that time, whom you knew was more advantageous than what you knew[206].

Exactly six months later Vyse was given more independence as acting Consul in Kanagawa, and on 12th December 1860, he was confirmed as substantive British Consul there. The following year the post was renamed as Consul in Yokohama. Yokohama was the pinnacle of the consular service in Japan, for a great proportion of the commerce passed through it, with many ships and people passing through as well. So much for Vyse "only" being appointed a "vice-Consul under supervision".

Might we speculate that Vyse was eager to make up for his unblooded years of service in the Blues by seeking some kind of

---

[206] The 1854 Northcote-Trevelyan reforms of the Civil Service were finally implemented, as far as open competitive examination entry into the Foreign Office was concerned, as early as 1914. Such was the fervour with which the reforms were pursued.

RESPECT AND CONSIDERATION

glory in leading a punitive expedition to bring retribution on Shimazu Saburō? At the head of the cavalry? Lest I be accused of painting a biased picture, here is a tribute paid to Vyse by his friend Edward Barrington De Fonblanque[207], who was Vyse's guest for ten months, in an account published in 1862:

> Howard Vyse, ever kind, considerate and unselfish, and, in spite of his military administration of consular law, no unworthy representative of English manliness and honour; as is sufficiently testified by the respect in which he is universally held by his countrymen, and the unusual regard entertained, by the Japanese of all classes, for the "Consul with the big heart".

What De Fonblanque meant by "military administration" we can only guess. Perhaps it meant meticulous administration. Perhaps it meant unthinking, *befehl ist befehl*[208] (orders are orders) administration.

Precisely three months after his hot-headed actions in Yokohama, big-hearted Vyse was "removed" to the remoter port of Hakodate, in Hokkaidō, as Consul on 14th December 1862. The Hakodate Consul (Dr C.A. Winchester), was appointed Consul in Yokohama, with Marcus O. Flowers appointed as his Vice-Consul. This was a humiliation for Vyse that lasted 2½ years. In time, though, Vyse was rehabilitated when appointed Consul at busy Nagasaki on 25th May 1865.

Vyse continued to seek for glory, even then. Sir Harry Parkes, the then Minister Plenipotentiary, sent him a note on 19th July 1865. Parkes tartly informed him that Vyse's design for a new flagstaff for the Nagasaki Consulate was too expensive and could not therefore be approved.

---

[207] De Fonblanque was a member of the British Legation under Sir Rutherford Alcock.
[208] The defence put up at, but refuted by, the Nuremberg Military Tribunals after World War II.

DRAMATIS PERSONÆ

Vyse was required to resign from the Consular service because of a scandal relating to his apparent part in the illicit acquisition and sale of *Aino* skulls and skeletons. See Appendix 10 for details.

II NAOSUKE (1815-1860) 井伊 直弼

Ii was *daimyō* of Hikone and *tairō*, the "great elder", who presided over the *gorogio* and was effectively deputy to the *shōgun*. It was Ii who signed the first Treaty with Townsend Harris.

He was a noted exponent of the tea ceremony in the *sekishūryū* style, and wrote two books on the subject. He was the fourteenth son of his father, and had no expectations of becoming *daimyō*. However, all his brothers died or were adopted into other families, and in 1850, Ii was extracted from the Buddhist temple he inhabited to inherit the domain.

Ii Naosuke

Ii was enthusiastic about opening up relations with the west. He instigated the "Ansei Purge" of 1858 and 1859 to remove the violent proponents of *sonnō jōi*, and those who aggressively resented his appointment of Tokugawa Iemochi over the Mitō candidate, Hitotsubashi Keiki. Some 100 people were deposed from their positions in the bakufu and the Imperial court; several of the *han* were downgraded, and eight people were executed. This earned him everlasting hatred from his opponents, and several attempts were made on his life. One finally succeeded, by the Sakurada Gate of Edo castle.

It was an unusually cold and snowy morning. On 3rd March 1860, the procession of *tairō* Ii was approaching the Sakurada Gate of Edo Castle. An eighteen-strong band of *samurai* (all from

RESPECT AND CONSIDERATION

Sakurada Gate in 2006

Mitō, save one from Satsuma) lay in wait to attack Ii. The band of conspirators had spent the previous night at the *dozōsagami* inn, and had plotted their action in the *inaba-ya* teahouse. Ii was not excessively guarded by the standards of the day. His *norimon* was surrounded by 26 two-sworded men, and 40 foot-soldiers armed with spears. All of Ii's entourage were wearing heavy coats to protect themselves against the icy weather, and this made it difficult for them to draw their *katana* to defend the *tairō*.

Mori Goronosuke, a *samurai* from Mitō, had been elected to initiate the assassination attempt. He approached the procession as if he wished to hand a complaint to the *tairō*, a common (though illegal) practice at the time. As he reached the *gyoretsu*, Mori drew his sword, slew one of the guard and ran off, as planned. Ii's bodyguard unthinkingly charged after Mori, leaving Ii unprotected. By this time, Kurosawa Chūsaburō had fired a pistol as a signal for the rest of the assassins to attack in force. Within two minutes, most of Ii's men lay dead. Then, Arimura Jizaemon, the only member of the group from Satsuma, proceeded to attack Ii's *norimon*, stabbing at it repeatedly. His thrusts went through the norimon and into Ii, who was trapped helplessly within, unable to draw his own sword to protect himself. Jizaemon opened the norimon, pulled the wounded Ii out, sliced off his head and impaled it on the tip of his *katana*. Mission accomplished.

IWAKURA TOMOMI (1825-1883) 岩倉具視

Iwakura was recognised as an intellectual in the Imperial court. He rose to become a chamberlain to Emperor Kōmei in 1854. Like almost everyone else in the Kyōto court, Iwakura was opposed to the *bakufu's* intention to open Japan to the foreigners.

DRAMATIS PERSONÆ

From 1860, he supported *kobu-gattai*. This caused the more extreme *sonnō jōi* faction to brand Iwakura as a supporter of the *shōgunate*, which was far from the truth.

Nonetheless, Iwakura was forced to leave the court and move to his fief north of Kyōto. From there, he embarked on a vigorous correspondence with his friends in the Imperial court, especially the Satsuma faction. After the death of Emperor Kōmei, Iwakura took his opportunity. On 3rd January 1868, with Ōkubo Tochimichi and Saigō Takamori, he seized the Imperial Palace, precipitating the Meiji Restoration.

Iwakura Tomomi

Iwakura's close and trusted relationship with Emperor Meiji gave him access to real power. He suggested and helped draft the "Oath in Five Articles", read out and assented to by some 400 nobles at the coronation of Emperor Meiji on 7th April 1868. This was effectively the first post-*shōgunate* Constitution. The Oath was:

> By this oath, we set up as our aim the establishment of the national weal on a broad basis and the framing of a constitution and laws.
> - Deliberative assemblies shall be widely established and all matters decided by open discussion.
> - All classes, high and low, shall be united in vigorously carrying out the administration of affairs of state.
> - The common people, no less than the civil and military officials, shall all be allowed to

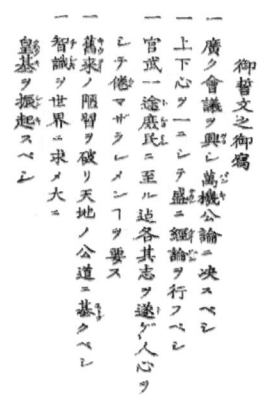

The Oath in Five Articles

pursue their own calling so that there may be no discontent.
- Evil customs of the past shall be broken off and everything based upon the just laws of Nature.
- Knowledge shall be sought throughout the world so as to strengthen the foundation of Imperial rule

As *udaijin* - Minister of the Right - Iwakura was the second most important man in the government. He drafted the order putting an end to the venerable *han* system, and headed the Mission to western nations that bears his name.

VICE-AMIRAL CONSTANT LOUIS JEAN BENJAMIN JAURÈS (1823-1889)

Amiral **Benjamin Jaurès**
Photographed in 1870

Jaurès was a nineteenth century French Admiral and later Senator. He was second-in-command at the Bombardment of Shimonoseki. He was also present during the Boshin War of 1868-9, when France unwisely backed the pro-*bakufu daimyō*. Ambassador to Madrid 1878-92 and then to St. Petersburg until 1883. He became Minister of Marine and the Colonies from 22nd February 1889 but died in office just 21 days later, on 13th March, in Pierre Tirard's second administration under the Presidency of Marie François Sadi Carnot. *Grand-croix de la Légion d'honneur*

JOSLING, CAPTAIN JOHN JAMES STEPHENS RN (1818[?]-1863)

Captain of HMS *Euryalus*, killed in action at Kagoshima. His London home was in Mornington Crescent. He had served as a Lieutenant under the then Captain Kuper in HMS *Thetis* from 1850.

DRAMATIS PERSONÆ

At St. James's Church, Emsworth, Hampshire, England, is a black-and-white marble memorial tablet. Its inscription reads:

> SACRED TO THE MEMORY OF
> JOHN JAMES STEPHENS JOSLING
> CAPT RN,
> WHO WAS KILLED WHILST
> COMMANDING H.M.S. EURYALUS,
> AT THE SIEGE OF KAGOSIMA;
> ON THE 15TH OF AUGUST 1863
> AGED 38 YEARS,
> AS A TRIBUTE TO HIS MANY ESTIMABLE
> AND ENDEARING QUALITIES, THIS
> TABLET IS
> ERECTED AS AN AFFECTIONATE
> REMEMBRANCE,
> BY HIS FONDLY ATTACHED SISTER.
> BLESSED ARE THOSE SERVANTS, WHOM
> THE LORD WHEN HE COMETH SHALL
> FIND WATCHING. LUKE 12.37

Captain John James Stephens Josling RN, *Illustrated London News* 14 November 1863

RESPECT AND CONSIDERATION

KATSU KAISHŪ (勝海舟) (1823-1899)

Kaishū was a nickname that he took from a piece of calligraphy, *Kaishū Shōku* (海舟書屋) by one Sakuma Shōzan. His actual name was Rintarō. He was fluent in Dutch, and at the age of 15 became head of his minor *samurai* family in the Tokugawa service and an interpreter during the newly-opened relationships with the West. He developed a particular knowledge of western military and naval matters. In 1860, Katsu was assigned as commanding officer of Dutch-built IJN *kanrin-maru*, Japan's first sail/screw warship. He took the 1860

Imperial Japanese Navy ship *kanrin maru*

diplomatic mission across the Pacific Ocean to San Francisco, where he remained, taking in all he could learn about American technology (especially military technology) and culture. In the Tokugawa navy, he rose to become *gunkan-bugyō* (commissioner). He was tasked with negotiating between the *bakufu* and Chōshū in 1866; his success in that led to him becoming the chief negotiator for the *bakufu* in the transition to the new Meiji règime. Although his personal and intellectual sympathy was with the reforming pro-Imperial cause, Katsu remained loyal to his Tokugawa roots during the Boshin War. When the *shōgun's* forces were finally defeated, Katsu was charged with negotiating the terms of surrender of Edo castle to the "*SatChō*" (Satsuma-Chōshū) alliance under Saigō Takamori on 3rd May 1868. Katsu served as Vice-Minister for the Navy in the Meiji administration in 1872, and then as First Minister for the Navy from 1873 to 1878.

DRAMATIS PERSONÆ

KIDO TAKAYOSHI (1833-1877)

Kido was a Chōshū *samurai*. Initially a radical loyalist, but later he helped to negotiate the Satsuma-Chōshū alliance. He invaded Hagi castle in Chōshū; and became joint clan chief with Takasugi Shinsaku. He was the major representative of Chōshū in the early Meiji government. He had used the name of Niibori Matsusuke when he had been working against the *shōgunate*. Another alias - used when negotiating with foreigners - was Katsura Kogoro, or Kogyo. A member of the Iwakura mission, he supported Ōkubo in the 1873 crisis, but left the government in 1874 in opposition to the (disastrous) Taiwan Expedition, a punitive expedition by the Meiji military forces in response to the murder of 54 crew of a wrecked Ryūkyūan merchant vessel by native tribesmen in Taiwan in December 1871. It was the first deployment of the new Imperial army and navy. Katsura died of natural causes at the height of the anti-Meiji revolt later led by Saigō Takamori. He was married to Ikumatsu, a Japanese Mata Hari - a *geigi* and lover-spy. Ernest Satow regarded him highly.

KINGSTON, COMMANDER AUGUSTUS JOHN, RN

Commander of HMS Perseus at Kagoshima and Shimonoseki. Promoted Captain 1864.

KŌMEI, EMPEROR (1831-67) 孝明天皇

121st Emperor, son of Emperor Konin, reigned 1846-67. In contrast to previous Emperors of the Edo period, he refused to be a puppet of the *shōgunate* and strongly criticized *shōgun* Tokugawa Iesada for abandoning *sakoku* in 1853. He became the hero of the xenophobes, but many *samurai* and *daimyō* felt betrayed when he accepted

Emperor Kōmei
The photograph appears to have been retouched

RESPECT AND CONSIDERATION

kobu-gattai by agreeing to marry his sister to *shōgun* Tokugawa Iemochi. Kōmei died in 1866, allegedly of smallpox, but he was widely suspected to have been poisoned. Kōmei was the last Emperor to have multiple *nengo* or era names during his lifetime.

They were:

Kōka	弘化	"Becoming vast"	Dec 1844 - Feb 1848
Kaei	嘉永	"Eternal esteem"	Feb 1848 - Nov 1854
Ansei	安政	"Quiet Government"	Nov 1854 - Mar 1860
Man'en	万延	"Immortal name"	Mar 1860 - Feb 1861
Bunkyū	文久	"Literate story"	Feb 1861 - Mar 1864
Genji	元治	"Original rule"	Mar 1864 - Apr 1865
Keiō	慶応	"Jubilant answer"	May 1865 - Oct 1868

KUKIMURA RIKYŪ （久木村利久）

Kukimura's real given name was Jikyū (治久), but at some time it was mistakenly written as Rikyū and this stuck ever since. Kukimura was nineteen at the time of the incident. He was from one of the important, rich, *samurai* families within the Shimazu clan. Young Kukimura was earmarked for greatness, and on that fateful afternoon of 14th September 1862, he was given the honour, as a Shimazu messenger, of being stationed in the gun troop close by Shimazu Saburō's *norimon*.

Kukimura was the first to draw his sword and attempt to attack the British intruders. He was inexperienced, nervous, but eager to impress. This was the first time he had drawn his sword in anger. *Samurai* swords were bound tight to the *samurai's* side. In the heat of the moment, the binding of Kukimura's *katana* proved too tight for him to release. Kukimura gave up trying to unsheathe the big sword but managed to release his smaller *wakizashi* and lunged at Richardson with it. This sword hit Richardson's stirrups. Such was the strength of Kukimura's youthful blow that the sword was bent. There is a photograph of

DRAMATIS PERSONÆ

the damaged sword in the Namamugi museum. Shimazu Saburō commanded his men to maintain a wall of silence over the events at Namamugi. He could ill afford to give up any of his *samurai* to justice, as was demanded by Britain. The men involved, including Kukimura, were too valuable to the clan for the present and future administration of Shimazu affairs.

Kukimura went on to have a long and successful military life. He rose to the rank of *chūjyū* - three star general (Lieutenant General in the British equivalent rank) - and died on 10th September 1937 aged 95, four days short of the 75th anniversary of the Namamugi incident.

KUPER, ADMIRAL

Augustus Leopold Kuper, b. 16th August 1809, was a career naval officer. He joined the Royal Navy as a midshipman[209] in 1823. On 23rd June 1829, he had been appointed Mate[210], Lieutenant on 26th February 1830, Commander on 27th July 1839, Captain on 8th June 1841, and Rear Admiral (of the White) on 29th July 1861. He went on to be appointed Vice Admiral on 6th April 1866, and Admiral on 20th

Admiral Augustus Leopold Kuper

---

[209] Midshipmen were almost always from wealthy or aristocratic families intending a senior naval career for their son. There was no certainty that a midshipman would gain promotion, for this depended on the patronage of their commanding officers. There were no competitive examinations for naval officers at this time. Kuper was apparently a good officer, for he was appointed post captain at the age of 31, a little earlier than average. Nelson, an exceptional officer (whose uncle Maurice Suckling, helpfully, was Comptroller of the Navy) gained *his* post captaincy at the incredibly early age of 20.

[210] The modern equivalent is Sub-Lieutenant.

RESPECT AND CONSIDERATION

October 1872. He was put on the inactive list[211] on 10th September 1875. He died on 28th October 1885, aged 76. In his naval service, Kuper spent a total of 18 years and 47 days at sea.

With rank came decorations. He was appointed Companion of the Most Honourable Order of the Bath[212] in 1842 for his conduct during the first China war. He was promoted to Knight Commander on 25th February 1864 in recognition of his service in the aftermath of the Richardson affair and the bombardment of Kagoshima and its consequences. On 2nd 1869, Kuper was promoted to Knight Grand Cross. Along the way, he picked up a couple of foreign decorations. In early 1865, in respect of Kuper's leadership at the bombardment of Shimonoseki, he was made a Grand Officier du Légion d'Honneur[213] and for the same event was made a Commander of the Order of William of the Netherlands[214].

Kuper picked up another, unusual, distinction during his service: an island was named after him. In 1851, he had been in charge of a naval survey of the Straits of Georgia off British Columbia. The survey officers named two of five tiny islands

---

[211] Admirals never retired. The fiction was that they could be called on to give the benefit of their naval experience should a crisis arise. Kuper had been awarded a Good Service Pension on becoming inactive, equating to his full pay.

[212] At the time, the Order of the Bath was Britain's fourth most senior order of chivalry, after the Orders of the Garter, the Thistle and St Patrick.

[213] The *Ordre national de la Légion d'honneur* is a French Order that can be awarded to any person who has distinguished himself in any field of endeavour. There were five classes: Grand-Croix, Grand Officier, Commandant (now Commandeur), Officier and Légionnaire (now Chevalier). A Grand Officier wore the badge of the order on a rosetted ribbon on the left chest, plus the star of the order on the right chest

[214] The Netherlands' Military Order of William (*Militaire Willemsorde*) equates to the Legion d'Honneur but is awarded much less frequently, and always for bravery in battle. The Commander equates to the French Grand Officier; the holder wears the badge of the order on a necklet, plus an identical breast cross on the left chest.

DRAMATIS PERSONÆ

respectively Kuper Island and Thetis Island, after Captain Kuper and his ship, HMS *Thetis*.

Sir Ernest Satow claimed that, prior to his service in Japan, Kuper had not seen a shot fired in action. This was untrue, for Kuper had distinguished himself during the first China War (1840-42) and had been involved in the fighting and operations that led to the capture of Canton (now Guangzhao). These are detailed below. Kuper had been appointed Commander-in-Chief, East Indies and China, on 8th February 1862, in succession to Admiral Sir James Hope. From his journal and correspondence, it is clear that Kuper was a level-headed officer with considerable diplomatic talent.

Diplomatic talent was a requisite for the high commanders of Royal Naval stations abroad. Communications at that time were slow and unreliable, for frequently ships would be lost on the high and stormy seas. In his letter to Earl Russell, Thomas Marshall, dated 15th December 1862, says:

> The Mail due a day or two since, by which I was expecting to receive further communications having been lost in the Colombo[215], I have thought it best to write, without delay, to your Lordship.

Thus the commanders had to operate under their own initiative, and this required not only a thorough grasp of British foreign policy, but a rapid appreciation of the nuances and balance of power at any given instant and circumstance. Wisdom went hand-in-hand-with courage, discretion with valour. The Naval forces under an Admiral's command were mighty forces, and needed to be used judiciously.

---

[215] Mail recovered from the Colombo arrived in London between 26 Dec 1862 and 24 Jan 1863. Some 530 boxes of mail were eventually recovered, but much was damaged by immersion. The Colombo was *en route* from Calcutta via Galle (Ceylon) to Suez on 19 Nov 1862 when she foundered on Minicoy Island in the Maldives.

RESPECT AND CONSIDERATION

On 19th June 1837, Lieutenant Kuper married Emma Margaret, eldest daughter of Rear Admiral Sir James John Gordon Bremer, who was Commander-in-chief, East Indies and China from 17th January 1840 to 7th October 1841. Bremer, too, had the distinction of having a geographical feature - Bremer Bay in Western Australia - named after him. Governor James Stirling named it after Bremer, then captain of HMS *Tamar*, engaged on a survey of Western Australia in 1835. In turn, the river Bremer is named after the bay. Kuper certainly followed in father-in-law's footsteps with *his* island.

Commodore Bremer temporarily commanded the fleet in early actions during the 1st Opium War in 1840. He blockaded the river Canton, silenced the defences of Chusan, and occupied the town. This was regarded as a fine action in the absence of an Admiral (Rear-Admiral Sir Frederick Lewis Maitland, KCB had died suddenly just before this, and his replacement, Rear Admiral the Hon. George Elliot CB, had not yet arrived). Bremer sent commendations in his dispatches for a number of officers for their skill and valour during this episode, including a Commander (Acting Captain) Augustus Leopold Kuper, in command of 28-gun sailing ship HMS *Alligator* (which Bremer had commanded himself from 1837 to 1840, with Kuper as his Lieutenant.) Kuper had been ordered to maintain a blockade at Amoy, and had to fight off and destroy a number of Chinese gun boats that attacked *Alligator*. He failed, however, to force open the passage between Kolangso and Amoy harbour, so the action resulted in a stalemate. Nonetheless, Kuper had distinguished himself several times in action before he sailed to Japan.

DRAMATIS PERSONÆ

MARSHALL, WILLIAM

William Marshall, wounded at Namamugi, was a prominent silk merchant in Tōkyō. He regularly played billiards with his good friend Woodthorpe Clarke. His wife was the older sister of Mrs. Borradaile, who was visiting her sister on vacation from Hong Kong. When an Anglican church building was constructed in Yokohama in 1863, Marshall was appointed one of the trustees. John Black, the journalist, said of Marshall, "the peculiarly single-minded, truthful and conscientious character of Mr. Marshall, gave him in early days a leading position among foreign residents, which he maintained unchallenged during the remainder of his career, and until his sudden decease in September 1873."

MEIJI, EMPEROR (1852-1912)

The 122nd Emperor, he was the son of Emperor Kōmei and reigned from 1866 to 1912. Born in 1852, Mutsuhito was only 14 when he ascended the throne and adopted his regnal name. He was the central figure of the movement to abolish the *shōgunate* and deal with the west on an equal footing. He recognised that it was vital to transform feudal Japan into a country governed in the modern way. Under the 1889 constitution, he had untrammelled power and authority. The Japanese victories over China (1895) and Russia (1905) gave him the reputation of great wisdom and cleverness. Keeping up the aristocratic poetic tradition, he wrote an astonishing 100,000 *waka* in his lifetime. Died 1912.

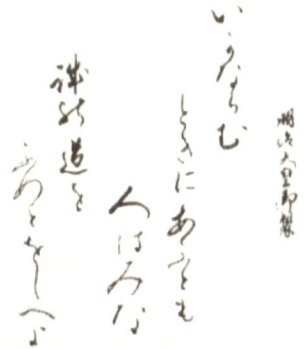

Waka by Emperor Meiji, in his own hand
For the times to come
And of meeting what must be met
All of our people
Must be taught to walk along
The path of sincerity

RESPECT AND CONSIDERATION

MOORE, COMMANDER LEWIS JAMES, RN

Moore commanded HMS *Argus* at Kagoshima and carried Satow and Willis on board. Satow admired Moore's audacity and courage as commander. Moore was promoted Captain in 1868 and given command of the brand-new HMS *Eclipse*. He was dismissed that year from her command for "suffering the ship to ground off Heligoland on the 22d of July, to the hazard of the same ship". He was subsequently forgiven, it appears, for he was given the Captaincy of HMS *Barrosa* at the end of 1869. *Barrosa* was one of the ships designated as "flying squadron" vessels: ships whose duties were to train sailors and to "wave the flag" - or intimidate other countries - without firing a shot. *Barrosa* was part of Rear-Admiral Hornby's flying squadron of ten ships that toured the world from mid-1869 to the end of 1870.

MORI TAKACHIKA

Mori Takachika 毛利敬親 (1819-1871) was *daimyō* of Chōshū. He closed the Shimonoseki Straits in 1863 to foreign shipping and his batteries fired on foreign shipping. This precipitated the Shimonoseki bombardment. Mori was consequently barred from Kyōto and stripped of court rank for the embarrassment his extreme anti-foreigner views had caused the *bakufu*.

MORRISON, GEORGE S (1830-1893)

Morrison was the son by his second wife of Rev. Robert Morrison D.D., an early Presbyterian missionary to China, who was the first to translate the New Testament into Mandarin (and later jointly translated the Old Testament), and compiled an Anglo-Chinese dictionary. George Morrison was British Consul at Nagasaki from August 1859. He was wounded by Mitō samurai in their attack on the British Legation on 5th July 1861. He returned to Britain to recuperate, came back to Japan 2 years

DRAMATIS PERSONÆ

later, but soon thereafter finally retired to Britain, broken in health.

NEALE, LIEUTENANT-COLONEL EDWARD ST. JOHN

The official records concerning Neale the man are scanty. No record has been traced of his birth[216]. His father was Daniel Neale, a judge in Madras, and his grandfather a clergyman from Hertfordshire, according to his brief obituary in the *Illustrated London News* of February 1867 following his death in Quito on 11th December 1866. The Foreign Office Lists of 1862 and 1865 tell us of the salient parts of his career. We are fortunate that Sir Ernest Satow gives his own comments about the Colonel, else we should know little about the man.

What we do know is this. Edward St. John Neale joined the Liberating Army of Portugal on 20th September 1832, and was appointed to the Regiment of Scottish Fusiliers. He served throughout the protracted Siege of Oporto and the Campaigns of 1833 and 1834, and was sent in Command of a Company in every action in which the British Troops in the service of Portugal were engaged to the end of the war[217]. He left the service of Portugal, and took up an appointment to the Staff of the British Ancillary Legion of Spain, under the command of

---

[216] As he is unlikely to have been under the age of 20 when enlisting in the Liberating Army, we may guess that he was born in the decade before 1812.
[217] This was the so-called Liberal War, something of a re-run of the Peninsular war.

RESPECT AND CONSIDERATION

Lieut.-General Sir George de Lacy Evans[218], effective from 5th July 1835.

Neale was later Aide-de-Camp to Brigadier-General Sir Charles Shaw[219], who commanded the volunteer British Auxiliary Legion in Spain[220]. Subsequently Neale became Brigade-Major[221] of the Light Brigade. He took an active part in the several engagements and sorties before Bilboa, St. Sebastian, Fuenterabia, and Victoria. As recognition of his bravery and military leadership, Neale was promoted to the rank of Major on

---

[218] Evans, (1787-1870) served in the Peninsular War, fought at Quatre-Bras and Waterloo, commanded the British Legion sent to assist Queen Isabella in Spain. He commanded the second division of the army in the Crimea and the East; and distinguished himself at the Battle of the Alma. Knighted 1837; promoted Lieut.-General and GCB in 1861. Served as a Member of Parliament 1830-1865 while continuing his military career.

[219] Shaw served in the army in Spain and Belgium, including the Battle of Waterloo. In 1831 he joined the liberating army of Portugal in the Azores, and commanded a regiment during the whole of the civil war in Portugal. In 1835, he was appointed Brigadier-General of the British Auxiliary Legion in Spain. He was knighted in 1838. From 1839 to 1842, he was Chief Commissioner of Police in Manchester and Bolton. Shaw was also a Knight Commander of the Portuguese Order of the Tower and Sword, and Knight Commander of San Fernando of Spain.

[220] This was during the first Carlist War in Spain (1835-37), which concerned issues of succession to the Spanish Throne - whether King Ferdinand VII's successor would be his brother Carlos or his nominated daughter Isabella. King Philip V of Spain (1683-1746) had affirmed the Salic Laws that prevented any woman ascending to the Throne. Ferdinand countermanded the Law by promulgating the *Pragmática Sanción* to give effect to his wish that his daughter Isabella would become monarch after him, rather than his brother Carlos. There was a Basque dimension to the conflict that echoes even in modern Spanish politics.
Sir Rutherford Alcock (later British Minister in Japan), while a doctor, had served as Deputy Inspector General of Hospitals in the first Carlist War. He made a collection of bones that had suffered musket and sabre injuries, which are still on display at the Anatomical Museum of the University of Edinburgh, and advanced the cause of battlefield surgery at the time.

[221] Brigade-Major was the Chief of Staff of a brigade.

DRAMATIS PERSONÆ

6th May 1836, and to Lieutenant-Colonel on 19 January 1837. He also received the Spanish Royal Military Order of St. Ferdinand of the 1st Class, and a medal, conferred upon him by Queen Isabella of Spain herself, for "gallantry in the attack on the enemy's lines in front of St. Sebastian, on the 4th May, 1836."

Neale retired from the Spanish Service, to accompany Colonel (later Sir George Lloyd) Hodges[222] CB, British Consul-General to Serbia, in May 1837. While in Serbia, Neale was attached to the Consulate-General at Belgrade for nearly two years, and was in charge of it for eight months. He was then appointed Vice-Consul at Alexandretta in Turkey on 22nd February 1841; and thence Consul at Varna in Bulgaria on 31st May 1847. Neale remained in Bulgaria during the whole period of the Allied occupation and Russian War from 1853 to 1856. While between Alexandretta and Varna, on 22nd March 1847

Neale took time to marry Adelaide Sewell, daughter of Henry Sewell, a civil servant of Madras. She drops from the narrative accounts immediately, so whether she lived, died or retired in seclusion somewhere we do not know. According to his will, they had a daughter, Adelaide Harriet Eliza, and two sons, Henry St. John Dudley and William Buchanan. The will also refers to Neale's brother, William Trevor. His executor was his cousin Major Henry Clarinbold Powell. Neale's estate was declared as "under £9,000" and his children were to be disinherited if they became Roman Catholics or entered a convent or monastery.

Neale was next detached on duty to Omer Pasha's[223] Headquarters at Shumla for two months in 1853; in May 1855,

---

[222] Hodges (1792-1862) was knighted KCB, and served in the diplomatic corps after his military exploits.

[223] Omer Pasha was an outstandingly successful Ottoman general who inflicted several defeats on the Russian forces during the Crimean War. Neale might well have been involved in helping Omer to plan his victory over the Russians at Oltenitza.

he accompanied General Charles Frederick Havelock to Shumla and Roustchouk for the purpose of recruiting and raising the 3rd regiment of Osmanli Irregular Cavalry. He was transferred as Consul to Patras, in February 1858; and was appointed Consul for the Morea of Greece[224] in July 1858. He then was transferred to Bosnia (including Herzegovina and Montenegro) in September 1858, but the Foreign Office List is silent about his appointment or his duties.

Neale was appointed Secretary of the British Legation in China on 3rd January 1860. Two years later, on 25th January 1862, he was appointed Secretary of the British Legation in Japan. Neale was unusually appointed CB in 1863, an honour beyond his rank, in recognition of 'the patience, good temper, and firmness' which he displayed following the Namamugi Incident and the Bombardment of Kagoshima. It was the final validation of the propriety of his stance in the immediate aftermath of the murder of Richardson. Willis said that Neale's CB "pleased him awfully".

When he left Japan in 1864, Neale was not in good health, and the Foreign Office decided he was not fit to serve again in Japan. Instead, he was made Secretary of the Legation in Athens in April 1865, and then in August was appointed Consul-General in Guayaquil, Ecuador. When he died there in December 1866, his son Henry was with him.

Satow (q.v.) says that Neale was

> an old warrior who had seen service with the Spanish Legion commanded by Sir de Lacy Evans, and who, gossip said, regarded Sir R. Alcock, formerly attached to the Marine Brigade of Portugal in the quality of surgeon, with no friendly feelings. … He had great command of his pen, and composed most dramatic Notes to the Japanese Government. …

---

[224] The Peloponnese Peninsula.

DRAMATIS PERSONÆ

> Neale was in stature considerably less than the average Englishman, he wore a heavy grey moustache, and thin wisps of grizzled hair wandered about his forehead. His temper was sour and suspicious. ... In his jovial moments he easily unbent, and would entertain his companions with snatches of operas of which he carried a large assortment in his memory. At this period he was about fifty-five, and probably already affected with the beginnings of the disease which carried him off a few years later at Quito.

Little else is known of his character, but he had a reputation as a martinet and was even said to have "a short fuse". Satow complains that Neale was a hard taskmaster who diverted him from his proper trade of learning the Japanese language in order to act as a Legation clerk. Dr Willis thought Neale "an old woman" for his refusal to attack Shimazu's retinue, though Satow was much more complimentary, stating that Neale had been decisive and right in his decision to hold back. Neale had remarked to Satow that the western community (of whom the British were the leading component) was in Japan to trade, not to engage in senseless tit-for-tat hostilities. Moreover, Satow says, Neale had no doubt seen many dead bodies at close quarters in his military career, and was not willing to see many more.

RESPECT AND CONSIDERATION

PALMERSTON, LORD

Henry John Temple, 3rd Viscount Palmerston, KG[225], GCB, PC (1784-1865). Initially Tory[226] Member of Parliament 1807 for the pocket borough of Newport, Isle of Wight (a "pocket borough" was one in which there was no electorate, just a patron). He was immediately appointed junior Lord of the Admiralty. Invited to become Chancellor of the Exchequer in 1809, he demurred but accepted appointment as Secretary of State for War, which office he happily kept for 20 years. On the collapse of the traditional-Tory government following Lord Liverpool's death, a liberal-Tory and Whig[227] administration took over: Palmerston was invited to become Chancellor of the Exchequer, and he accepted.

---

[225] Knight Companion of the Most Noble Order of the Garter: England's (not Britain's) premier order of Knighthood. The order is restricted to the Sovereign, the Prince of Wales and no more than 25 Knights, whose are appointed by the Sovereign alone. Additionally, there are supernumerary Knights, usually foreign monarchs or statesmen, or members of the British royal family. Four Japanese Emperors have been made supernumerary Knights: Meiji (1905), Taishō (1912), Shōwa (1929, degraded 1941, restored 1971) and Akihito (*nengo:* Heisei) (1998).

[226] "Tories" were originally Irish guerrilla fighters against Cromwell's army sent in 1649 AD to subdue the rebellious Irish. The term was subsequently applied to those who supported the Church of England against attacks made on it by King James II. Alternatively, their name derives from a hard-drinking, debauched, style of life of the land-owning classes: "Rory-tory-ranter-boys". The Tories were succeeded by the formally-constituted Conservative (and occasionally) Unionist Party.

[227] The Whigs were a loose political grouping in late 17th Scotland and England to mid-nineteenth century Great Britain. They were succeeded by the formally-constituted Liberal Party. The term was originally an insult: "whiggamores" were cattle-drivers.

DRAMATIS PERSONÆ

However, there was Royal interference in the composition of the government, and Palmerston remained Secretary of State for War, though this time with a seat in the Cabinet.

A succession of weak governments followed and in 1828, Palmerston, for the first time, found himself in opposition. In 1830 the Duke of Wellington tried to induce Palmerston to join his Cabinet. Palmerston declined, but when the Whig administration under Lord Grey came into power later that year, Grey prevailed on his friend Palmerston to accept the office of Foreign Secretary. He was more of a Whig than a Tory by now. He held the Foreign Office from 1830 to 1834, from 1835 to 1841 (under Viscount Melbourne), and from 1846 to 1851 (under Lord John Russell), all Whig administrations. Even out of office, though, he wielded great influence on foreign affairs. He was punningly nicknamed "Lord Pumice-stone" on account of his abrasive nature, and it was he who used the Royal Navy ruthlessly to maintain British interests abroad: he was the father of "gunboat diplomacy"[228].

---

[228] An example of Palmerston's gunboat diplomacy was the "Don Pacifico Incident" of 1850. David Pacifico, a Portuguese Jewish merchant born in Gibraltar, traded in Athens. In 1847 his business premises had been attacked by an anti-Semitic mob. King Otto's government declined him compensation. Pacifico was British by virtue of his place of birth, and appealed in 1850 to the British Government for help. Palmerston sent a Royal Naval squadron to seize Greek ships and property to the value of Pacifico's claims; in the event, they blockaded the port of Piraeus. Greece was under tripartite protection: British, French and Russian. The French took umbrage at Britain's actions and temporarily ceased diplomatic relations. Otto's government climbed down and paid compensation to Pacifico. The British House of Lords condemned Palmerston's actions, but their censure motion was decisively reversed by the House of Commons, though with some dissenting voices, notably Cobden's (q.v.). Doubtless the Commons were inspired by Palmerston's rhetoric. He set out the basis for gunboat diplomacy when he said in his speech on 29 June 1850:

> As the Roman, in days of old, held himself free from indignity, when he could say, Civis Romanus sum [I am a Roman

RESPECT AND CONSIDERATION

In 1852, Palmerston was appointed Home Secretary in Lord Aberdeen's Peelite government. Through Palmerston's hawkish anti-Russian sentiment, the government was induced to embark on a war with Russia, to keep them from encroaching on Ottoman territories. The Crimean War was to a considerable extent instigated by Palmerston. Aberdeen's government fell in 1854 because, due to the findings of an enquiry into the conduct of the war; there had been widespread public anger at the inept conduct of the Crimean campaign. (The noble and heroic Charge of the Light Brigade was widely seen as a demonstration of government incompetence.) Although Palmerston was at least as much to blame for the Crimean War as the rest of the Cabinet, he was the natural choice to succeed the hapless Aberdeen as Prime minister.

In December 1855, Palmerston formed his first - Liberal - Cabinet. In 1858, his government fell and Palmerston was out of office for seventeen months. On the fall of the Earl of Derby's Conservative government, Palmerston was invited to form his second Cabinet. He remained in office from June 1859 to October 1865, when he died in office.

Palmerston had a considerable personal charm and a ready wit. He is once said to have claimed of the "Schleswig-Holstein problem"[229]: "Only three people have ever understood it. One was Prince Albert, who is dead; the second is a German professor, who has gone insane; and the third is myself (Palmerston), and I have forgotten it." He was regarded as something of a womaniser (*The Times* nicknamed him Lord Cupid), and was said to be secretly proud of being cited as co-respondent in a divorce case in 1863, when he was aged 79.

---

citizen], *so also a British subject, in whatever land he may be, shall feel confident that the watchful eye and the strong arm of England will protect him from injustice and wrong.*

[229] A complex territorial dispute between Denmark and Germany.

DRAMATIS PERSONÆ

PARKES, SIR HARRY SMITH (1828-1885)

Parkes was orphaned and raised first by an uncle and then, aged 13, by a cousin who lived in Macau. Parkes diligently set about learning Chinese. In 1842, aged just 14, he received a British consular appointment due to his proficiency in Mandarin. In 1843, he worked under Sir Rutherford Alcock in the British Consulate in Fuchow. In 1849, he was called to the Foreign Office in London to work on Chinese affairs, and returned to China as Interpreter in 1851. After a spell as Secretary to the British Mission in Bangkok, he was appointed Acting Consul in Canton. Parkes took a firm hand in having the Royal Navy chastise Commissioner Yeh, a Chinese warlord who held some British sailors from the *Arrow* hostage in Canton during the 2nd Opium War. After the city fell to the British, Parkes was the virtual sole governor of this large city for three years, and was appointed Companion of the Most Noble Order of the Bath for his work.

Sir Harry Smith Parkes

Parkes then served as Interpreter and Adviser to Lord Elgin, and was captured and imprisoned with others, against the usages of diplomacy, while discussing the commencement of peace negotiations with the Chinese. He was eventually released, but Elgin ordered the burning of the Old Summer Palace as retribution for the Chinese misdeeds. In 1861, Parkes returned to England, and was promoted Knight Commander of the Most Noble Order of the Bath.

Sir Harry Parkes returned as Consul to Shanghai, and then in 1865 was appointed Minister (the highest diplomatic rank there at the time) in Japan, which post he held until 1882. He astutely supported the Emperor against the *bakufu*, and thus retained

RESPECT AND CONSIDERATION

British influence in the subsequent Meiji government. This influence waned as time progressed, due in part to Parkes' refusal to countenance alterations to the Unequal Treaties. This, of course, made him very popular with the British merchants in Japan. But it made him even more unpopular among *bakufu* supporters, who three times attempted to assassinate him. Parkes always exhibited coolness and courage in such moments.

He encouraged Ernest Satow and William George Aston, interpreters on his staff, to make deep and comprehensive studies of all matters Japanese. Aston published the first translation of *"Nihongi: Chronicles of Japan from the Earliest Times to A.D. 697"*. They both appreciated the freedom he gave them, but found him difficult and sometimes cantankerous. Parkes was transferred to China as British Minister in 1882, and died of malaria, still working, in Peking in 1885.

PERRY, COMMODORE MATTHEW CALBRAITH, USN (1794 - 1858).

Commodore Matthew Calbraith Perry, USN

"Old Matt" Perry was born in South Kingstown, Rhode Island, the younger brother of Oliver Hazard Perry. Matthew Perry obtained a midshipman's commission in the Navy in 1809, and was initially assigned to USS *Revenge*, which was under the command of his elder brother. Like Nelson, a little bit of patronage allowed the first foothold in a glittering naval career.

Perry's early career saw him assigned to several different ships, including the frigate *President*, where he was aide to Commodore John Rodgers. On 16th May 1811, 1576-ton *President* scored a victory against the 460-ton British sloop HMS *Little Belt*, as a prelude to America declaring war on Britain and Canada in 1812. During that war, Perry was transferred to USS *United*

DRAMATIS PERSONÆ

States, and consequently saw little fighting in the war afterwards, since the Royal Navy trapped *United States* in harbour at New London, Connecticut.

After the war, Perry served on various vessels. At one point, while in port in Russia, Perry was offered a commission in the Imperial Russian Navy, which he declined.

Perry commanded USS *Shark* from 1821-1825, and from 1826-1827 acted as fleet captain for Commodore Rodgers. Perry returned for shore duty to Charleston, South Carolina in 1828, and in 1830 took command of USS *Concord*. From 1833 to 1843, he was assigned as second officer of the New York (later Brooklyn) navy yard, where he pioneered the application of steam power to warships. He was promoted to Captain in 1837 and commanded the *Fulton*, the first steam vessel in the U.S. navy.

Perry acquired the courtesy title[230] of commodore in 1841, and was made first officer of the New York Navy Yard in the same year. He saw action in 1843-44 while commanding the African Squadron, whose duty was to suppress the slave trade. He then commanded the Gulf Fleet and saw action in the Mexican war, taking part in the taking of Veracruz.

In 1852, Perry embarked from Norfolk, Virginia for Japan, and his success there is recounted elsewhere in this book. Perry died in 1858 in New York City. His remains were removed to the Island Cemetery in Newport, Rhode Island in 1866, where they remain to this day.

---

[230] At that time, the United States Congress refused to countenance any higher rank than Captain. "Commodore" was a temporary office, denoting a Captain with more than one ship under his command. Once having held the office of Commodore, the courtesy title was retained. In 1862, Congress changed its policy and appointed Commodores and Admirals as ranks in the Navy.

RESPECT AND CONSIDERATION

POOLE, LIEUTENANT GEORGE, RN
Temporarily commanded HMS *Havoc* at Kagoshima. Immediately thereafter transferred to the China station, and two years later transferred to H.M. Coastguard.

RICHARDSON, CHARLES LENOX (1833-62)
Merchant, murdered in Japan, 14th September 1862. Son of Charles Richardson (1796-1865+)

ROCHES, LÉON (1809-1901)
French Minister in Japan from April 1864 to 1868, as successor to Gustave Duchesne De Bellecourt. He and the British Minister, Harry Parkes, were often working against the interests of the other's government, and there was some personal animosity between them. In the struggle between the Imperial and *shōgunate* courts, Roches persuaded the French government to side with the *bakufu*, whose demise led to a long period in the Meiji era during which Franco-Japanese relations were at a low ebb.

RUSSELL, LORD JOHN (LATER EARL)
John Russell, 1st Earl Russell, KG, GCMG, PC (18.08.1792-28.05.1878), known as Lord John Russell before 1861. He was the 6th son of the Duke of Bedford, with no expectation of inheriting the dukedom. Educated at Edinburgh University, he did not take his degree, entering the House of Commons as Whig Member for Tavistock on 18 August 1813, as soon as he was legally permitted to do so, on his 21st birthday. An activist for reform of parliament, he became Paymaster of the Forces in Earl Grey's 1830 administration, and was soon admitted to the Cabinet. There followed periods as leader of the Whigs in the House of Commons, and as Home Secretary. On the fall of Sir Robert Peel's government in 1846, Russell became Whig Prime

DRAMATIS PERSONÆ

Minister, remaining in office until 1852. There was disunity among the Whigs, and Russell had difficulty with Lord Palmerston, his headstrong Foreign Secretary[231]. Out of office until 1859, Russell re-established relationships with Palmerston, and accepted office as Foreign Secretary in the new Liberal administration.

Russell was elevated to the peerage as Viscount Amberley, of Amberley in the County of Gloucester and of Ardsalla in the County of Meath, and Earl Russell, of Kingston Russell in the County of Dorset, in 1861. On Palmerston's sudden death in late 1865, Russell again became Prime Minister. Little was achieved in a disunited Cabinet, and Russell's parliamentary Liberal Party fell apart. Russell and his government resigned in June 1866, and Russell retired from public life.

SAIGŌ TAKAMORI 西郷 隆盛 (1827-1877)

A Satsuma *samurai*, Saigō was promoted by Shimazu Nariakira from very low rank to become his assistant in efforts to reconcile the Imperial and *shōgunate* Courts in Edo. The turmoil of the 1858-59 Ansei Purge was coupled with the death (by natural causes) of Nariakira, and Saigō fled back to Kagoshima. The long arm of the *bakufu* had him arrested and banished to Amami Oshima, one of the Ryūkyū islands. He was pardoned by the *bakufu* in 1861, but had scarcely set foot in Kagoshima when Shimazu Hisamitsu had him arrested and banished again until 1864. Hisamitsu rehabilitated him and appointed Saigō as his representative at the Imperial Court in Kyōto.

While there, Saigō, in alliance with Aizu forces, prevented a *coup d'état* by the Chōshū clan. He unenthusiastically

---

[231] It was Palmerston's recognition, with neither Royal nor Cabinet approval, of Napoleon III's 1851 *coup d'état*, that led to Palmerston's resignation and the fall of Russell's administration.

RESPECT AND CONSIDERATION

commanded the punitive expedition against Chōshū, and declined to join a later similar expedition, for he was secretly conducting negotiations with Chōshū that would result eventually in the *SatChō* alliance.

When *shōgun* Yoshinobu finally ceded power to the Emperor in 1868, Saigō was opposed to the terms of settlement. He demanded that Tokugawa - the *han* that had denied power and status to Satsuma for 260 years - be stripped of lands and all vestiges of power. Saigō's intransigence on the issue was a major cause of the *Boshin* War. Saigō led the Imperial forces during that conflict, and had the satisfaction of receiving the surrender of the Tokugawan forces at Edo castle.

Saigō Takamori
National Diet Library, Japan
Note Shimazu crest on his coat

Saigō was prominent in the first effective Meiji government, and promulgated reform of the *han* system. During the currency of the Iwakura Mission, Saigō was caretaker Prime Minister. Subsequently, Saigō became something of a hawk in the government, seeing military expansion as an opportunity to absorb the large numbers of unemployed *samurai*. He famously opposed the creation of the Japanese railway network, wanting the huge investment to be spent instead on the military and naval forces. After failing to persuade the government to wage war against Korea (who refused to accept the legitimacy of the Meiji government), Saigō resigned from the government. He went into self-imposed exile in Kagoshima, where he founded a school to teach the *bushidō* code and *samurai* skills.

DRAMATIS PERSONÆ

Eventually, in 1877, Saigō was reluctantly prevailed upon to lead the anti-government forces in what became known as the Satsuma rebellion. The rebels were finally crushed at the battle of Shiroyama (the mountain behind Kagoshima), where Saigō died. It is generally said that he committed warrior's *seppuku*, though there is confusion as to whether he died from his wounds, or whether a comrade performed *todome*, or whether he did indeed commit *seppuku*. Whatever the case, the Meiji government was clever enough to rehabilitate him. He was declared a national hero and embodiment of Japanese nobility, in which light he is generally regarded today.

SATOW, THE RIGHT HONOURABLE SIR ERNEST MASON, PC, GCMG (1843-1929)

Satow, aged 19, arrived in Yokohama just after Richardson's murder, to take up a post as student-interpreter at the British Legation. He was thus an eye-witness to many of the events described here. He was born in Clapton to Hans David Christoph Satow, a naturalised former Swedish/German, and his wife Margaret Mason. He was educated at Mill Hill School[232] in London and then University College, London (whose Chair of Japanese Law is named after Satow).

Ernest Satow, c. 1865

Satow lived in Japan as man and wife with Takeda Kane, who bore him two sons in 1880 and 1883. Diplomatic and societal

---

[232] Mill Hill School is a private foundation, created by non-conformist merchants and ministers in 1807, outside the then boundaries of London. It is now in London NW7. It was so located to guard against "dangers both physical and moral, awaiting youth while passing through the streets of a large, crowded and corrupt city". Doubtless this grounding served Satow well in his service in Yokohama and Tōkyō.

pressures of the day prevented Satow from marrying her. Satow remained in Japan until 1883.

Satow became a fluent speaker, reader and writer of Japanese, and contributed much to the understanding of Japan by the West. He was a keen amateur botanist and, it is said, presented several specimen plants to Kew Gardens in London.

He then served in Siam (modern Thailand) from 1884 to 1887, Uruguay from 1889 to 1893 and Morocco from 1893 to 1895, steadily gaining promotion in the Diplomatic Corps.

In 1895, Satow returned to Japan, this time as Envoy Extraordinary and Minister Plenipotentiary and having been invested as KCMG[233] just prior to his departure, for his Morocco service. He remained in the Japanese post for five years, disappointed that he had not been named as the first British Ambassador to Japan, as his successor was. Nonetheless, he headed the British Mission to Japan and oversaw the implementation of the Treaty of Shimonoseki. He observed the build-up of Japanese military and naval forces to prepare for the eventual humiliation of Russia as a result of the "Triple Intervention[234]". He also implemented, much to his personal

Takeda Kane, 1870

---

[233] The Order of St Michael and St George concerns itself with distinguished service on behalf of the country. British Ambassadors are routinely appointed CMG on first taking up their position. Its three ranks are Commander (CMG), Knight Commander (KCMG) and Knight Grand Cross (GCMG). As early as Satow's day, they were wryly nicknamed "Call me God", "Kings call me God" and "God calls me God". This doesn't work for the Dame Commanders (DCMG).

[234] The "Tripartite Intervention" was a diplomatic intervention by Russia, Germany and France to negate some of the terms of the Treaty of Shimonoseki that ended the first Sino-Japanese War in April 1895. Under the Treaty, Japan had been awarded the Liaodong Peninsula, which included the naval harbour

DRAMATIS PERSONÆ

satisfaction, the abolition of the extraterritoriality provisions of earlier treaties, as ended by the Anglo-Japanese Treaty of Commerce and Navigation of 1894. A personal gratification was his summons to return to England for Queen Victoria's Diamond Jubilee in 1897, when he had the privilege of being received by Queen Victoria at Osborne House in 1897. During this second stint in Japan, Satow renewed his relationship with his Japanese "family", with whom he remained in touch - if only ultimately by letter - until his death.

From 1900 to 1906, Satow served as British High Commissioner and then Minister in Peking. Satow was pleased about his promotion. As a more highly-regarded post, Satow earned £5000 a year in Peking instead of the £4000 he had received in Japan. He negotiated the compensation claims of all the powers after the Boxer Rebellion, and signed it on Britain's behalf. He returned to Britain

---

of Post Arthur, seized by Japan from China during the war. The European powers were unhappy about Japanese territorial ambitions on the mainland, and their likely effects on Chinese stability. The Intervention from the three powers was to suggest that Japan should return the territory seized. They hinted at the stick of war if Japan failed to comply, but offered the carrot of larger cash indemnities if they complied. The British and Americans sat on the sidelines, and Japan felt forced to comply: it was not in any position to fight another war immediately after the heavy conflict with China. They complied, and duly received further cash from China. As soon as the Japanese vacated the territory, to their consternation, Russia swept in to replace them, and the other powers, including Britain, seized various ports. Japan felt cheated. The situation resulted in the Japanese policy of *Gashin Shōtan* ("Persevering through Hardship for the sake of Revenge"). There was a heavy build-up of industrial strength and an enlargement and re-equipping of the Japanese armed services, particularly the Navy. It required much sacrifice on the part of the Japanese people to achieve. It culminated in the Russo-Japanese war of 1904-5, which was decisively and surprisingly won by the Japanese.

RESPECT AND CONSIDERATION

in 1906, and was appointed a Privy Counsellor. In 1907, Satow was Britain's second Plenipotentiary at the second Hague Peace Convention, which laid down agreed standards of conduct for nations and people engaged in warfare, which, modified, persist today.

THE SHIMAZU FAMILY

Shimazu Nariakira (1809–1858)
Note the Shimazu crest on his lapels

Although one of the *tozama*, Satsuma was one of the wealthiest and best armed *han*. Because of its size and wealth, the *daimyō* of Satsuma was classed as a *kokushu*, or provincial lord, the highest rank of *daimyō*, and consequently was permitted to build a castle. The Shimazu family had Kagoshima as its castle town and Satsuma province in southern Kyūshū as its domain. Kagoshima was a thriving little port on the shores of beautiful Kinko Bay. The clan's lands were extensive, and the Shimazu were very wealthy. They were *tozama*, though, because Shimazu Yoshihiro (1535-1619) fought against the Tokugawa clan at Sekigahara - and lost.

In the nineteenth century, the key members of the family were
- Shimazu Narioki 島津斉興 (1791-1859), the 27th daimyō
- Shimazu Nariakira 島津斉彬 (1809-58), the 28th daimyō
- Shimazu Tadayoshi (島津忠義) (1840-97), the 29th daimyō
- Shimazu Saburō (島津三郎) (1817-87), formerly Shimazu Hisamitsu (島津久光), the father and regent of Tadayoshi

DRAMATIS PERSONÆ

Saburō's given name was Hisamitsu, but the name Saburō was conferred on him by the Emperor as a token of favour when he was commissioned to carry the Emperor's summons to the *shōgun*. He was returning with the *shōgun's* reply when the incident at Namamugi occurred. Saburō was the de facto ruler or regent of the Satsuma domain in the years immediately preceding the Meiji Restoration of 1868. His father was Narioki and his mother was Yura, Narioki's mistress. Saburō had tried to usurp his older half-brother Nariakira on the death of Narioki. There had been a short but bloody conflict, and Saburō had been defeated. Willis noted that he "enjoyed the consistent reputation that he never forgave anybody that offended him and that he never lost an opportunity of doing a spiteful act".

Nariakira was probably the most progressive *daimyō* of his era. It was Nariakira who was first to envisage the inevitable westernisation of the craft-based Japanese industries and the sword-and-spear military. He embraced western technology and knowledge. He built an iron foundry, an armament factory, and ceramic[235] and glass[236] factories at his castle town, Kagoshima, the first such enterprises in Japan. Looking ahead, he could see problems looming with the crumbling of the *bakufu*, so he placed his own-manufacture muzzle-loading artillery in defensive gun batteries in strategic locations along Kinko Bay, on which Kagoshima sits. Nariakira was one of the prominent backers of Hitotsubashi Keiki as *shōgun* in succession to Tokugawa Iesada, the 13th Tokugawa *shōgun* against the wishes of Ii Naosuke, the *tairō*. (Iesada's 3rd wife was Nariakira's adopted daughter.) The

---

[235] Satsuma ware is exquisitely hand-decorated earthenware produced from the 1850s onwards. Much early twentieth century ware was specifically designed for the Western domestic market and decorative taste (e.g. tea services, vases, bowls, etc)
[236] Satsuma glass is a highly prized copper-ruby coloured cut-glass ware, widely exported during the Japanese craze that engulfed Europe in the 1870s and beyond.

RESPECT AND CONSIDERATION

failure of that political campaign led to the "Ansei purge"[237], where a number of nobles were required to commit *seppuku* or were otherwise severely punished. Nariakira would certainly have been among them had he not conveniently died in 1858.

Saburō was the father of Shimazu Tadayoshi, for whom he acted as regent. Tadayoshi was 22 years old in 1862 and should not have needed a regent. It was put about by Saburō that Tadayoshi was feeble-minded and unfit to govern, but we have only Saburō's word for that. Saburō supported *kobu-gattai* ("Shaking the Emperor's hand" – the union of the court and *shōgunate* by a marriage link).

Matsudaira Yoshinaga

In August and September 1862, he was in Edo, first pressing for the appointment of Hitotsubashi Keiki as *shōgun*, but found himself outmanoeuvred. Tokugawa Iemochi was appointed instead. As a sort of Plan B, he successfully pressed for Tokugawa Yoshinobu and Matsudaira Yoshinaga to be appointed advisers to young *shōgun* Iemochi, but only managed to have Hitotsubashi Keiki appointed Iemochi's regent. He made an unprecedented demand on behalf of the Imperial court, that Iemochi should come to Kyotō to hear the Emperor's wishes first-hand. Saburō left Edo in anger at his failure to have Hitotsubashi appointed *shōgun*, compounded by his failure to have his nominees chosen as advisers, and set off to return to the Imperial court in Kyotō. At least he carried a

---

[237] The Ansei purge (安政の大獄 *Ansei no taigoku*) was instigated in 1858-9 by Ii Naosuke, the *Tairō* ("Great Councillor") of Japan, to put an end to dissent over his signing the treaty of Amity and Commerce with the United States. There was also disquiet over his handling of *shōgunal* succession issues. Over 100 *daimyō* and senior Imperial Court officials were removed from office, and eight of them were put to death.

DRAMATIS PERSONÆ

message from the *shōgun* to the Emperor, accepting the Emperor's offer-you-can't-refuse invitation to visit him in Kyotō. This was a great diplomatic triumph for Saburō, for no such visit had been made for over 250 years.

Saburō's procession had passed through the first three stations of the *tōkaidō*: Nihonbashi ... Shinagawa ... Kawasaki ... and were on the way towards Kanagawa. They reached the sleepy village of Namamugi. The procession was large and impressive. His entourage on his earlier journey from Kyotō to Edo had comprised some 700 men; and he had had to leave 300 of them behind in Edo. As a senior daimyō, Saburō travelled in a palanquin, or *norimon*, carried by eight bearers. This was a large, richly lacquered wooden affair, with silk cushions and hangings inside, large enough for Saburō to lie down. There were windows covered with bamboo screens, so that Saburō could see out without himself being seen.

Saburō's procession included a substantial bodyguard of the best swordsmen surrounding his *norimon*; other *samurai* and spearmen before and behind; servants carrying clothing and armour for the *daimyō*; packhorses carrying other luggage; and carts for the largest and heaviest items. Saburō, it was said, also brought with him a great cannon, mounted on a cart.

THE DUKE OF SOMERSET (1804-1885)

Edward Adolphus Seymour, 12th Duke of Somerset, KG, PC was a British Whig aristocrat and politician, who served in various cabinet positions in the mid-nineteenth century. He served in Lord Melbourne's administration from 1835 to 1841; was a member of Lord John Russell's cabinet in 1851; and First Lord of the

The 12th Duke of Somerset,
1869, by Carlo Pellegrini

435

RESPECT AND CONSIDERATION

Admiralty from 1859 to 1866 (he was appointed KG in 1862). In 1863, for his public service as MP and Cabinet Minister, he was created Earl St Maur of Berry Pomeroy (what *can* you give a duke as a thank-you gift?).

STIRLING, ADMIRAL SIR JAMES (1791 - 1865)

James Stirling was born into a Scottish naval family. His maternal grandfather and uncle were both Admirals. One of James' early appointments was to serve under Uncle Charles in his flagship *Glory* in the West Indies. He continued to serve under Sir Charles in successive flagships *Sampson* and *Diadem*.

Admiral Sir James Stirling

By 1811 he was flag Lieutenant to his uncle in the West Indies Station at Jamaica. He received his first command, HMS *Moselle*, in 1812. Given a larger sloop, HMS *Brazen*, he harassed American shipping at the mouth of the Mississippi during the short war of 1812 with America.

Stirling surveyed the west coast of Australia, and lobbied the British government to establish a colony there. He succeeded and, as Captain Stirling, was appointed Lieutenant-Governor of the Swan River Colony from 1829, for which service he was knighted KCB in 1833. In 1840, with the threat of war with France, he returned to sea, commanding *Indus* and later *Howe* in the Mediterranean fleet. He was knighted by the King of Greece for his services for that country.

In July 1851, Stirling was promoted Rear Admiral, serving in the Admiralty. From January 1854 to February 1856 Stirling was Commander in Chief of the China and East Indies Station, flying his flag in HMS *Winchester*, and commanding the partially

DRAMATIS PERSONÆ

successful naval campaign during the second Anglo-Chinese War of 1856-57.

Stirling signed the Anglo-Japanese Friendship Treaty on his own initiative on 14th October 1854. He came under some disapprobation from the armchair admirals at the Admiralty for concentrating on Japan at the expense of his primary duty, of finding and destroying the Russian Pacific squadron. The treaty only allowed for the repair and revictualling of ships, not for commerce.

This was the time of the Crimean War. The unpopular First Lord of the Admiralty, Sir James Graham, led the criticism of Stirling in this regard. However, Graham himself was later heavily criticized by the inquiry into the conduct of the Crimean war, and he retired from public life in disgrace.

The rest of Her Majesty's government, however, did not share Graham's views and enthusiastically commended Stirling's actions in Japan. The Treaty was readily ratified. In 1862, Stirling was promoted Admiral.

TOKUGAWA

Following the defeat of the Toyotomi clan and its supporters at the battle of Sekigahara on 21 October 1600, Tokugawa Ieyasu became the *de facto* governor of Japan. The Tokugawa family ruled Japan from 1600 AD to 1867. 15 successive *shōguns* were provided from the clan. Only six of them relevant to the matters dealt with by this book are given brief biographies here. There are a large number of *shintō* shrines, called *Tōshō-gū*, that are dedicated to Tokugawa Ieyasu, the founder of the dynasty of *shōguns*. The most well-known *Tōshō-gū* is in Nikkō. There is a buddhist temple - *Kan'ei-ji* - dedicated to the family in

Tokugawa family crest: the Triple Hollyhock

RESPECT AND CONSIDERATION

Tokyo. The dynasty's power through some 267 years was so great that "Tokugawa era" is synonymous with "Edo period". This is a list of all the Tokugawa *shōguns* in order of accession:

Name	Birth	Reign from	Reign to	Death
Tokugawa Ieyasu 徳川家康	1542	1603	1605	1616
Tokugawa Hidetada 徳川秀忠	1579	1605	1623	1632
Tokugawa Iemitsu 徳川家光	1604	1623	1651	1651
Tokugawa Ietsuna 徳川家綱	1641	1651	1680	1680
Tokugawa Tsunayoshi 徳川綱吉	1646	1680	1709	1709
Tokugawa Ienobu 徳川家宣	1662	1709	1712	1712
Tokugawa Ietsugu 徳川家継	1709	1712	1716	1716
Tokugawa Yoshimune 徳川吉宗	1684	1716	1745	1751
Tokugawa Ieshige 徳川家重	1711	1745	1760	1761
Tokugawa Ieharu 徳川家治	1737	1760	1786	1786
Tokugawa Ienari 徳川家斉	1773	1786	1837	1841
Tokugawa Ieyoshi 徳川家慶	1793	1837	1853	1853
Tokugawa Iesada 徳川家定	1824	1853	1858	1858
Tokugawa Iemochi 徳川家茂	1846	1858	1866	1866
Tokugawa Yoshinobu 徳川慶喜	1837	1866	1868	1913

TOKUGAWA, IEMOCHI (1846-66) 徳川家茂

The 14th *shōgun* 1858-66; possibly poisoned in response to his fruitless marriage to the Emperor's sister, Princess Kazu (Kazumiya or Kazunomiya Chikako), to "show to the world that the Imperial family and the house of Tokugawa agreed in their political views". He was *daimyō* of the Kii *han* (now Mie/Wakayama province), one of the three branch houses of the Tokugawa.

TOKUGAWA, IESADA (1824-1858) 徳川家定

The 13th *shōgun* 1853-1858. He was childless and suffered poor health. It was put about that he was feeble-minded, but

DRAMATIS PERSONÆ

this might have been a slander perpetrated by his enemies, for it was Iesada who signed the various treaties with the west that opened the country to foreign influence.

Tokugawa Ieyasu (1543-1616) 徳川 家康

The first *shōgun* of unified Japan (1603-1505). He was born Matsudaira Takechiyo 松平竹千代, changed his name to Matsudaira Jirōsaburō Motonobu 松平次郎三郎元信 (on coming of age in 1556) and then Matsudaira Kurandonosuke Motoyasu 松平蔵人佐元康 (on marriage in 1559). In 1567, he finally changed his name to Tokugawa Ieyasu. For complex historio-linguistic reasons, he was thereby claiming descent from the Minamoto *han*, a claim for which there is no evidence. "Minamoto" 源 was a surname bestowed by the Emperor in the Heian period (794-1185 AD) on any sons and grandsons who were not eligible to succeed to the Chrysanthemum Throne. 源 can be read as "Genji" in the Chinese reading, and it was used to indicate nobility in the family name, much as the Germans used "von".

Tokugawa Ieyasu as *shōgun* by Kano Tan'yū (1602-74)

Ieyasu founded the Tokugawa shōgunate following his victory at the battle of Sekigahara in 1600. He formally abdicated as *shōgun* in 1605, but continued to rule the country as *ogoshō* (大御所) - "cloistered *shōgun*" - from behind the scenes until his death in 1616. He made a start in founding the Tokugawa dynasty by taking nineteen wives and concubines, and siring eleven sons and five daughters. He was not a sentimental man: he ordered his first wife and his eldest son to be executed. He had plenty more to be going on with.

RESPECT AND CONSIDERATION

TOKUGAWA IEYOSHI (1793-1853) 徳川 家慶

The 12th *shōgun*, reigning from 1837 to 1853. He was married to Princess Sachi, sister of Tokugawa Yoshinobu's mother. He failed to name an heir, and thus sparked a succession dispute. Some said his death was occasioned by the shock of having to deal with barbaric foreigner Commodore Perry and the demands of President Fillmore.

TOKUGAWA NARIAKI (1800-1860) 徳川斉昭

The *daimyō* of Mitō and father of **Hitotsubashi Keiki** (who later became **Tokugawa Yoshinobu**). Nariaki was idolised by the loyalists; and championed both Western learning and the pro-Imperial, antiforeigner cause. A man of action, he was famous for declaring, scathingly:

> In these feeble days, men tend to cling to peace; they are not fond of defending their country by war.

TOKUGAWA YOSHINOBU (1837-1913) 徳川慶喜

Formerly **Hitotsubashi Keiki.** The seventh son of **Tokugawa Nariaki,** of an inferior branch of the Tokugawa clan. He had been talent-spotted by Abe Masahiro, head of the *roju* (council of elders) under *shōgun* Tokugawa Ieyoshi.

Abe let it be known that the *shōgun* would look favourably on the Hitotsubashi family (one of the three Tokugawa minor families who could, in extremis, provide an heir for the *shōgun*, should the main Tokugawa line fail) adopting Keiki.

DRAMATIS PERSONÆ

Indeed, Keiki was a candidate for *shōgun* in the 1858 vacancy on account of his success in governing the house of Hitotsubashi at an early age. But he was unwilling to accept the *shōgunate*. So Ii Naosuke seized the opportunity caused by Keiki's refusal, and appointed Tokugawa Iemochi on his own authority. Ii consolidated Iemochi's appointment by placing many opponents and potential opponents, including Keiki, under strict house arrest. He also took on the rôle of Iemochi's chief adviser: perhaps "manipulator" would be a better description.

Wistful photograph of
Tokugawa Yoshinobu
National Diet Library, Japan

Iemochi's *shōgunate* was marked by incompetence and corruption. In 1860, Ii was assassinated and Hitotsubashi became *de facto* regent. In 1866, he was by far the best candidate to succeed the late Iemochi, and he eventually was prevailed upon to become the 15th - and last - *shōgun*. He embarked on an energetic programme of reform, in a forlorn attempt to strengthen the country militarily, economically and diplomatically in order to expel the barbarians. His most enthusiastic proposers and advisers had been *sonnō jōi* supporters; as *shōgun*, Yoshinobu ceded power to the Emperor on 14th October 1867, after being defeated in the Boshin War. This ended 675 years of *shōgunate* rule. After many years of involuntary, then voluntary seclusion, Yoshinobu was ennobled as a *kōshaku* (Prince) in 1902.

RESPECT AND CONSIDERATION

WILLIS, DR. WILLIAM

Dr William Willis

William Willis M.D. (1837-1894) was a young Irish physician and surgeon (MRCS 1859, FRCS 1881) who joined the British mission in Japan in May 1861 (it was the United Kingdom of Great Britain and Ireland at that time, of course). Willis, on arrival in Japan, initially stayed with Thomas Glover in Nagasaki. Willis was the first British doctor in Japan. He had trained at Edinburgh University, and thereafter accepted an appointment at the Middlesex Hospital. He had not been there for very long when he precipitately left the Middlesex to join the British Legation in Japan. His haste might be explained by the fact that he left behind one Maria Fisk, a hospital housemaid, and their illegitimate son Edward Herbert, ultimately adopted by Willis's brother George. It was said that he remitted money for the upkeep of both Maria and his son.

Willis was 6' 3" tall (1.905 metres) and was said to be of "mountainous" proportions; at any rate he weighed 280 pounds (20 stone, or 127 kilograms). His size intimidated even the refractory *rōnin* and *samurai* sometimes encountered. On one occasion, the gatekeeper at Hachiōji (an important road junction and post-town along the Kōshū highway) declined to open the gate for Willis and his companions to ride through. Willis spurred his horse to charge through the gate, whereupon the gatekeeper saw that his gate would be smashed, and so, courage failing him, he flung the gates open just as Willis was about to gallop through.

Within two weeks of his arrival in Japan, Willis was present at the British Legation on the night of the attack by the Mitō *samurai* in which the two British Marines were killed and Oliphant and Morrison were wounded.

He was present in Yokohama on the day of the Incident and treated Messrs Clarke and Marshall, and confirmed Richardson's death. He conducted an autopsy at 11.00 pm that night and gave evidence at the ensuing inquest at the Consular Court.

Willis rapidly became fluent in Japanese and became a friend of many of the key players in the Meiji Restoration. In 1868, he accompanied government troops to Aizu to assist the wounded. He was instrumental in founding the *Ignacio* (later the faculty of medicine of Tōkyō University) and was appointed professor and chief clinical physician there. In 1869, Willis founded and published the first Japanese medical journal *Nikko Kilburn* ("Records of Daily Lectures"). In 1870, his close friend Saigō Takamori invited Willis to open a hospital and medical college in Saigō's home town of Kagoshima, and Willis resigned his posts to do so. It is now the medical department of Kagoshima University.

When the Satsuma rebellion[238] broke out in 1877, Willis remained for a time in Kagoshima, ostensibly because the ship sent to evacuate him refused to allow Willis's Japanese wife Aye Koki (27) and their sons George (12) and Albert (2) on board but in reality to provide medical aid to the huge numbers of combatants (said to be 40,000 rebels against 300,000 Imperial troops). Willis eventually did make his way to Tōkyō on the *Kory Mari* and resumed work in the Tōkyō medical faculty. However, by this time, the Japanese had decided to adopt the

---

[238] Led by Saigō Takamori, this was a movement to restore the position of the *samurai* and return to the old ways. The Meiji democratic modernisations were too difficult for the old guard to swallow. Their traditional fighting methods were no match for the much larger Imperial army. The final defeat of Saigō and his few surviving followers was 24 September 1877, when Saigō committed *seppuku* in a cave at Shiroyama, Kagoshima.

RESPECT AND CONSIDERATION

Willis with Satow, from *Japan Punch*, 1863.
In reference to his Irish roots (he was born at Maguire's Bridge in County Fermanagh), Willis is shown holding a shillelagh. *Japan Punch* was published in Yokohama by their mutual and close friend, the artist Charles Wirgman, from 1862 to 1887, who drew this affectionate cartoon.

DRAMATIS PERSONÆ

German medical system and not the British one. Willis was uncomfortable with what he regarded as an alien approach to medicine, saying that the German method did not regard the patients as people, but as cases. He returned without Aye to England in 1881, and later spent time with his great friend Ernest Satow in Bangkok.

WILMOT, COMMANDER RN

Commander of HMS *Euryalus*; killed in action at Kagoshima. He was entitled to a Captaincy and a ship of his own through seniority. But the Royal Navy did not have infinite numbers of ships available, and there were many demands on their resources. In respect of Wilmot's appointment (and *dis*appointment at having been given no ship), the First Lord of the Admiralty wrote to the Foreign Secretary:

Commander Edward Wilmot RN
Illustrated London News
14 November 1863

> Dear Lord Russell
> I have already sufficient difficulties in sending out ships for Mexican operations. I have had more men during all these months than the number voted by Part. And having already increased the vessels in the African station, I cannot send another vessel without adding to the risk of an excess on the sum voted by Part. for the service of the navy. I should be sorry to have to go to the H of Commons for a supplementary vote on account of Mexico, but this will become inevitable unless I am allowed to retain the other stations without an increase of vessels.

RESPECT AND CONSIDERATION

The position of affairs will not allow of a reduction on the China station or in New Zealand. We have an insufficient force in the Pacific for the demands which the war may bring upon us. Capt. Wilmot must therefore be contented to go without a vessel of war at his disposal. Whenever the Mexican operations are concluded (so far as the fleet is concerned) I will do all in my power to further your views in repressing the slave trade.
   Believe me, Yrs very faithfully, Somerset

WINCHESTER, DR.

Dr. Willis recorded that Winchester was *as fat as a pork butcher. He is a very good man and easy to get along with, with no pride or nonsense about him. He is passably clever, will do whatever he is ordered and nothing more.* Mrs Winchester, says Willis, was prone to interfere in her husband's business. She was *an immensely big woman six feet high and about nineteen stone* (266 pounds, 121 kg.). *She has the lord and master all under her thumb and, indeed, she is the Chargé d'Affaires.* He goes on to say that because of her physique, she was nicknamed "Daiboots" after the *daibutsu* at Kamakura.

DRAMATIS PERSONÆ

A Curio Shop, photograph by Felice Beato.

Beato's caption reads:
NOTHING attracts a stranger so readily as the sight of a Japanese Curio Shop. The ingenuity and cleverness displayed in the manufacture of the exquisite little articles of ivory carving, cabinets, lacquered-ware, bamboo and straw work, paper, crockery, egg-shell china, &c., are admirable.

The lacquered-ware of Japanese inlaid shell, mosaic with gold tracing, or plain, is of very fine quality, —far superior to that made in China,—is peculiar to the country, and is unequalled. Lacquered wooden dishes, cups, &c., often of elegant design and workmanship, are used for refreshments, —tea, saki, and other hot things. After use they are washed with warm water and wiped dry; and thus the luster is preserved for years. The prices asked for really old lacquer are almost fabulous.

Of ivory carvings there are some of superior workmanship, but expensive. The bamboo work, however, such as cigar cases, &c., and the paper imitations of leather, are cheap; and for their peculiarity well worth purchasing.

Appendix 4
Dr Willis' Autopsy Report on Richardson's body

EXAMINATION of the body of Charles Lennox Richardson, on the 14th September 1862, at 11 P.M.[239]

Rigor mortis marked.

No wound of head.

1. Transverse wound of throat extending from the angle of the lower jaw on one side to a corresponding point on the opposite side; severing the structures down to the vertebrae, which are partially divided. The wound extends through upper part of the Thyroid cartilage, passing back above the Arytenoids Cartilages. The deep vessels cut through on the left side. Uninjured on right.
2. About 2 inches below the clavicle of the left side there is a clean transverse wound, about 5 inches in length, extending from the medial line interiorly, downwards, outwards and backwards, severing the 2nd and 3rd ribs and opening into the cavity of the chest.
3. An extensive incised wound commencing at the coracoids process on the left side, and passing obliquely round the arm

---

[239] Note that this was carried out at 11.00pm, by the light, presumably, of oil lamps or candles. This is not to doubt the report; the wounds were gross enough to be obvious. Willis was obviously under pressure to complete the post mortem examination as soon as possible so that the inquest could go ahead.

THE AUTOPSY REPORT

to a point opposite posterior, severing the humours about 2 inches below the joint.

4. About the middle of the left upper arm there is an obliquely transverse wound, extending downwards and outwards, severing the biceps, but not injuring the bone.
5. Near the commencement of the fingers, the left hand is almost entirely divided across.
6. About an inch above the right wrist, there is an obliquely transverse wound extending upwards severing both bones of the forearm; the hand is attached merely by integument.
7. About 3 inches below the uniform cartilage[240] there is a transverse wound about 3 inches in extent opening into the abdominal cavity and through which part of the large intestine is protruded.
8. One inch above the latter there is a punctured wound, an inch in extent opening into the abdominal cavity.
9. Four inches below and to the right of No. 7 there is a punctured wound of the same size as preceding, and also opening into the abdominal cavity.
10. An extremely large incised wound, extending from middle line posterior, nearly opposite the lower angle of the scapula, downwards and outwards round the left side, to a spot 2 inches above the anterior superior spinouts process of the ileum, severing the ribs and through which part of the lungs, stomach, large and small intestines is protruded. Length of wound 16 inches.

Remarks

The transverse wound of the neck from its position and direction appears to have been inflicted whilst the body was on the ground.

The wounds in the front of the abdomen appear to have been inflicted by a weapon of the nature of a Japanese small sword, or lance thrust.

The large wound of the shoulder was inflicted whilst the arm was raised in the posture of defence. The large wound of the chest and abdomen was received whilst sitting in the saddle. The two latter wounds were seen inflicted by those in company with Mr. Richardson.

---

[240] The modern term is "Xiphoid Process" the lowest, bony part of the sternum

APPENDIX 5
A well-known, apparently anonymous, *kyoka*
On the arrival of the Black Ships

JAPANESE SCRIPT	ROMAJI	OPEN TRANSLATION	HIDDEN TRANSLATION
泰平の	*taihei no*	Awoken from sleep	The Pacific has its
眠りを覚ます	*nemuri o samasu*	from a peaceful quiet world	peaceful slumber broken
上喜撰	*jōkisen*	by Jōkisen tea;	by the steamships.
たった四杯で	*tatta shihai de*	with only four cups of it,	A mere four boats are enough
夜も眠れず	*yoru mo nemurezu*	no more sleep possible at night	to make us lose sleep at night

A *kyoka* ("mad song") is a humorous or satirical form of Japanese poetry, often, as here, in the *tanka*[241] 5-7-5-7-7 syllable[242] style. The humour of this particular poem comes from the puns (*kakekotoba* or "pivot words") it contains.

The puns are these:

---

[241] A *tanka* is the modernized form of the *waka*, as the *haiku* is the modernized form of the *hokku*. The modernization was proposed by Masaoka Shiki towards the end of the nineteenth century.

[242] Technically and phonologically, Japanese uses not syllables but morae. A *mora* is akin to a syllable, but need not be a consonant+vowel combination. For example, the Japanese word *nippon* is <u>four</u> morae: ni-p-po-n.

A *KYOKA* ON THE BLACK SHIPS

- *taihei* means "tranquil", but can also mean "Pacific Ocean".
- *jōkisen* was a brand of expensive and caffeine-laden green tea, but also means "steam-powered ships".
- *shihai* means "four cups", but can also mean "four vessels".

The first-glance "open" reading is almost an advertising jingle for *Jōkisen* brand tea. The poem's hidden meaning shows the alarm of the Japanese after such a long period of *sakoku*. It is also interesting that their fear had to be concealed from a first-glance reading; it could not be voiced openly, for the *bakufu* had made the treaties, and the *bakufu* at that time was not to be openly opposed. The Japanese peoples' fears were of two kinds: the fear of the *bakufu* and the fear of the foreigners. Time would tell which of the two had greater power. Their repressed concerns gained expression ultimately in the *sonnō jōi* movement.

Appendix 6-1
Personnel of the British Legation

On 23rd March 1862, Sir Rutherford Alcock, the British Minister Plenipotentiary, left Japan temporarily. He had been granted leave to return to England in order to be knighted KCB, to marry[243] and to receive an honorary DCL from Oxford University. Dr Winchester, the British Consul, became acting Chargé d'Affaires pending the arrival of Lieutenant-Colonel Edward St. John[244] Neale. Neale, appointed officially as Secretary to the British Legation and acting Consul-General in January 1862, was the second most senior diplomat, after Sir Rutherford himself. Alcock did not return until 1864, so Neale represented Britain in Japan from his arrival in May 1862 through very turbulent times. Neale served in Japan until 11 March 1864, when he departed on board HIMS *Sémiramis* for Shanghai where he would pick up a passage in the mail steamer for home.

There were British Consuls in Hakodate, Nagasaki, and Kanagawa/Yokohama. The function of the consul was to administer (extraterritorial) British law in the areas defined by Treaty (acting as magistrate, coroner, notary or judge as

---

[243] On 8 July 1862, he married the widow of Rev. John Lowder. Alcock was himself a widower.

[244] "St. John", when used as a Christian name, is pronounced "Sinjohn".

BRITISH LEGATION PERSONNEL

occasion demanded), and to protect the rights of British subjects when threatened by Japanese actions. Under the eyes (or eye, at this particular moment) of the Head of Legation and Consul-General, extraterritoriality was strongly enforced, and was greatly resented by the Japanese.

In mid- 1862, the Legation had, as senior staff, under Neale:

- The "Japanese Secretary" was next most senior to Col. Neale. Sir Ernest Satow, who arrived as a student interpreter a week after the murder of Charles Richardson, says that this particular Japanese Secretary - Richard Eusden - spoke no Japanese. He did, however, speak Dutch (the only European language at all understood in Japan). Despite his title, he was really "secretary in charge of correspondence with the Japanese Government".
- Then followed the "First Assistant", Abel Anthony James Gower. Satow describes the 1862 model of First Assistant as "a polyglot and musician but no lover of hard work. The accounts fell 18 months in arrear, and the registers of correspondence 2 years." Eventually he was relieved of these administrative duties, which were passed on to Dr. Willis. In 1864, he served as Acting Consul in Nagasaki.
- There were two Legation doctors, who also acted as "Second assistants" in the Chancery. One - Dr Jenkins - shortly retired from the service and set up a lucrative practice in Yokohama. The other - Dr William Willis - was "greatly conscientious; no man was more tender or sympathetic towards a patient". It was he who cleared up the Augean mess left by the First Assistant. After nine years service (i.e. in 1870) Willis was promoted to Vice-consul, but the Japanese offered him four times his Legation salary to lure him away to medical service in

RESPECT AND CONSIDERATION

Japan. His gigantic stature made him conspicuous among the Europeans of Yokohama.
- Besides these, the legation staff included Russell Brooke Robertson and Ernest Satow, as student-interpreters.

Then there was the military contingent, the officers of the mounted escort and infantry guard. The latter, according to Satow,

> was commanded by Lieut. Price of the 67th Regiment[245], and was soon replaced by fifty marines under the command of a man widely known in the service to which he belonged as "Public-spirited" Smith. The cavalry escort consisted of a dozen men from the Military Train, a corps which went by the honorary title of "Pig-drivers", and at their head was a lieutenant (Lieut. Applin), a good, harmless sort of fellow, whose only weakness was for fine uniforms and showy horses. It was whispered about that he had assumed the insignia of a field-officer, which is undoubtedly a serious offence against discipline. ... the blaze of gold which decorated his person was wonderful to behold, and on at least one occasion, when we were going in solemn procession to an audience of the Tycoon, caused him to be mistaken for the Envoy by the

Tozen–ji around 1861

---

[245] In 1862, twenty-eight men of the 67th (South Hampshire) Regiment of Foot went to Japan to reinforce the military train. They remained there until March 1864 when they were relieved by the 2/20th Regiment of Foot. In July 1864, the detachment in Yokohama was increased to five companies by adding three companies of the 67th under Major Miller. There were further units from the Royal Artillery, the Royal Engineers and the Royal Marine Light Infantry.

BRITISH LEGATION PERSONNEL

Japanese officials, who gave him the salutes that rightly belonged to his less conspicuously adorned diplomatic chief.

As soon as his Chief had departed for England, Neale decided to show his "old-soldier" bravado by moving the British Legation from Alcock's sanctuary in Yokohama back to its erstwhile home in the Tozen-ji Temple in Edo. No sooner had the move been completed (to the considerable misgivings of the Legation staff) but the startling incident of 27th June 1862 occurred, when the two British servicemen were killed. Neale immediately reversed his decision and the Legation and their archives and their staff and retainers scuttled back to Yokohama, where, Satow informs us, they installed themselves in a house hastily leased from a Mr. Hoey on the site of what was to become the Grand Hotel. Satow complains that Hoey

> took advantage of my inexperience and the love of books he had discovered to be one of my weaknesses to sell me an imperfect copy of the Penny Cyclopaedia for more than a complete one would have cost at home.

At the time of Col. Neale's arrival in Japan, the Emperor was sending repeated orders to the *shōgun* to close Yokohama and drive the "ugly foreign barbarians" away. He had not approved of the *bakufu's* negotiation of the treaties with the western nations. The *bakufu* replied to the Emperor's demands with promises that his will would be done, but then actually did nothing to implement it.

At the same time, the Governor of Kanagawa was actually offering to allot 25,000 *tsubo*[246] of land on the "Bluff" for foreigners to build residences for themselves. The foreign community, however, considered the area on offer to be grossly

---

[246] A *tsubo* was 3.306 m², approximately the area of two *tatami* mats. In fact, a single *tatami* mat is conventionally 90 cm. × 180 cm. or 1.62 m². 25,000 *tsubo* amounted to about eight and a quarter hectares or twenty and a half acres.

inadequate to meet their needs. They suggested he offer them a much greater area, extending from the face of the "Bluff" all the way from the "Canal" to "Treaty Point", and reaching back from the coast for a considerable distance. It was between four and five times the Governor's initial offer of 25,000 *tsubo*. The foreign community's requirements were eventually met in full in 1867.

Appendix 6-2
British Diplomatic and Naval Emoluments at December 1863

SALARIES PAID TO MEMBERS OF THE BRITISH LEGATION IN JAPAN			
Name	**Situation**	**Annual Salary**	**Notes**
Lt. Col. E. St.John Neale	Chargé d'Affaires	£800-0-0	
-do-	Acting Consul-General	£1095-0-0	£3 per day
Richard Eusden	Japanese Secretary	£700-0-0	
Abel A.J. Gower	1st Assistant	£472-10-0	
Marcus O. Flowers	Acting Japanese Secretary	£700-0-0	
W. Willis	Medical Officer & 2nd Assistant	£500-0-0	
L. Fletcher	2nd Assistant	£300-0-0	
John Macdonald	-do-	£300-0-0	
A. von Siebold	Supervising Interpreter	£300-0-0	
E. Satow	Student interpreter	£200-0-0	
Nakamura Seitaro	Mr Siebold's teacher	$96.00	=£20-00-00
Takaoka Kaname	Mr Satow's teacher	$96.00	=£20-00-00

457

RESPECT AND CONSIDERATION

Bunsko	Messenger	$60.00	=£12-10-00
Rinzo	-do-	$60.00	=£12-10-00
Matzungoro	Head Boatman	$48.00	=£10-00-00
Ginzo	Boatman	$36.00	= £ 7-10-00
Gingiro	-do-	$36.00	= £ 7-10-00
Tokuhitei	-do-	$36.00	= £ 7-10-00
Sebi	Watchman	$36.00	= £ 7-10-00
Seihitei	Office Coolie	$36.00	= £ 7-10-00

The British Legation personnel were able to take advantage of the "scandal" that Satow refers to, increasing their pay by more than 39¼%. See Page 33.

BRITISH LEGATION PERSONNEL

REMUNERATION OF VARIOUS BRITISH NAVAL RANKS			
Name	**Situation**	**Annual Salary**	**Notes**
e.g. Augustus Leopold Kuper	Rear Admiral, RN	£1095-0-0	
do	Rear Admiral, RN, "Table Money"	£1095-0-0	For dining, entertaining, etc
e.g. John Borlase	Captain, RN	£365-0-0 to £547-10-0 Plus >600 men £219-0-0; 350-600 men £155-2-6; <350 men £91-5-0	
e.g. Edward Wilmot	Commander, RN	£310-2-6 plus £45-12-6 if in command	
e.g. Alfred Jephson	Lieutenant	£182-10-0 to £219-0-0	
e.g. William H Parker	Master	£182-10-0 to £365-0-0	
	Rear Admiral's coxswain	£41-1-3	
	Able Seaman	£28-17-11	
	Rear Admiral's cook	£24-6-8	
	Rear Admiral's domestic	£24-6-8	
	Rear Admiral's steward	£24-6-8	
	Ordinary Seaman	£22-16-3	

Appendix 7
The 1860 Japanese Diplomatic Mission to America

The 1860 Japanese Mission to the United States. Photograph by Mathew Brady

New York *Times*, 18th June 1860
Report on the Parade
of 76 Japanese Ambassadors and their Hosts.

The procession was one of the finest displays of the kind ever witnessed in the City, and comprised no less than six thousand men of our First Division of Militia ... beside the long line of carriages. First, came a corps of Police, mounted and on foot. The Washington Grays and Seventh Regiment troop, and the Eighth Regiment Engineer Corps, Drum Corps, and Guard of Honor. This last completely surrounded the Common Council Committee and

THE 1860 DIPLOMATIC MISSION TO AMERICA

Japanese guests, so that even without the aid of the police, four of whom guarded each carriage, the Japanese would have traversed the entire line of march without any of that impertinent scrutiny at the very sides of the carriages which has characterized their visit to other cities.

In the first carriages rode the Common Council Committees and their Secretary and Sergeant at-Arms. Next came the first, second and third Ambassadors, in separate open barouches, accompanied respectively by Capts. Dupont, Lee and Porter, of the Naval Commission. The Japanese Treasurer, Governor and Secretaries followed in couples, occupying open barouches, and immediately after the feature of the procession—the triumphal car, or pagoda, containing the treaty box ... One of Adams' Express wagons, drawn by six of the finest horses in the city, constituted the vehicle, but so completely was this transformed that it seemed to have been entirely built for the occasion. Nothing of the wagon appeared but the bright painting and silver hubs of the wheels. There was a platform covering all else, profusely decorated with flags and banners, and festoons and wreaths of flowers, the whole surmounted by a canopy, the apex of which was a huge red ball—the Japanese insignia. The interior was carpeted and decorated, and provided with velvet-seated chairs for "Tommy" and his attendants, who guarded the treaty, and in order that none should mistake the affair, the words "Japanese Treaty" were painted on the four sides, together with Japanese inscriptions, doubtless appropriate to the occasion ...

To attempt a detailed description of the scenes along the route of the procession would be to multiply the same story for every point from the Battery through Broadway, Grand street, Bowery, around Union-square, down Broadway to the Metropolitan. Everywhere the same eager, jostling, tired, curious crowd, patiently enduring for six hours under a sweltering sun the dangers of *coup-de soleil* for a view of the display. Of all the public demonstrations yet witnessed by the Japanese, this must have been the most impressive. Everywhere as far as the eye could reach a dense mass of human beings greeted their eyes, while the display of gayly dressed females lent a brilliancy to the scene rarely equalled. Every window, house top, tree, box, awning post, brick pile, fence, and in short every stand point along the route had its tenant; and yet, to the credit of the Police be it said, the procession moved along almost unobstructed through the sea of humanity. At the Museum, the various hotels, the corners of the streets, at Union-square, and at the Metropolitan particularly, the crush was terrible to endure, and fearful to witness.

By 1866, some 150 Japanese had been sent on official missions to The United States, England, France, Holland and Germany, to bring back information on western ways. One of their findings was that Dutch was not the language for international use, and started a widespread programme to learn English. The envoys to England were particularly impressed by the Royal Navy, and Japan adopted English naval uniform in 1866. They bought the former Confederate warship *Stonewall Jackson* from the United States and renamed her *Azuma*.

One of the envoys' purposes was to renegotiate the Unequal Treaties, and in particular, to have the extraterritoriality provisions annulled. They were unsuccessful at the time, but laid the foundations for eventual renegotiation.

THE 1860 DIPLOMATIC MISSION TO AMERICA

Cartoon from *Harper's Weekly*, 26 May 1860
ALDERMAN TOOLE, who is to have charge of the Japanese in New York, finds, on reading Lord Elgin's book, that in case anything goes wrong with the reception, Japanese etiquette requires him to perform the Happy Despatch, *i.e.*, rip his bowels open. He acquaints Mrs. Toole and the family generally with the fact, and declares his intention of doing his duty at all hazards.

John McLenan's cartoon refers to *Narrative of the Earl of Elgin's Mission to China and Japan*, written by Laurence Oliphant, which had achieved a wide circulation in America. "Alderman Toole" is a thinly disguised caricature of Alderman Francis Boole, one of the corrupt Democrats who ran Tammany Hall in New York.

Appendix 8
On the Japanese Mission
From the New York *Times*, 27th June 1860

The Errand-Bearers
(later, "A Broadway Pageant")
By Walt Whitman (1819-1892)

1

OVER the Western sea hither from Niphon come,
Courteous, the swart-cheek'd two-sworded envoys,
Leaning back in their open barouches, bare-headed, impassive,
Ride to-day through Manhattan.

Libertad! I do not know whether others behold what I behold,
In the procession along with the nobles of Niphon, the errand-bearers,
Bringing up the rear, hovering above, around, or in the ranks marching,
But I will sing you a song of what I behold Libertad.

When million-footed Manhattan unpent descends to her pavements,
When the thunder-cracking guns arouse me with the proud roar love,
When the round-mouth'd guns out of the smoke and smell I love spit their salutes,

THE ERRAND–BEARERS

When the fire-flashing guns have fully alerted me, and heaven-clouds canopy my city with a delicate thin haze,
When gorgeous the countless straight stems, the forests at the wharves, thicken with colors,
When every ship richly drest carries her flag at the peak,
When pennants trail and street-festoons hang from the windows,
When Broadway is entirely given up to foot-passengers and foot-standers, when the mass is densest,
When the facades of the houses are alive with people, when eyes gaze riveted tens of thousands at a time,
When the guests from the islands advance, when the pageant moves forward visible,
When the summons is made, when the answer that waited thousands of years answers,
I too arising, answering, descend to the pavements, merge with the crowd, and gaze with them.

2
Superb-faced Manhattan!
Comrade Americanos! to us, then at last the Orient comes.
To us, my city,
Where our tall-topt marble and iron beauties range on opposite sides, to walk in the space between,
To-day our Antipodes comes.

The Originatress comes,
The nest of languages, the bequeather of poems, the race of eld,
Florid with blood, pensive, rapt with musings, hot with passion,
Sultry with perfume, with ample and flowing garments,
With sunburnt visage, with intense soul and glittering eyes,
The race of Brahma comes.

RESPECT AND CONSIDERATION

See my cantabile! these and more are flashing to us from the procession,
As it moves changing, a kaleidoscope divine it moves changing before us.

For not the envoys nor the tann'd Japanee from his island only,
Lithe and silent the Hindoo appears, the Asiatic continent itself appears, the past, the dead,
The murky night-morning of wonder and fable inscrutable,
The envelop'd mysteries, the old and unknown hive-bees,
The north, the sweltering south, eastern Assyria, the Hebrews, the ancient of ancients,
Vast desolated cities, the gliding present, all of these and more are in the pageant-procession.

Geography, the world, is in it,
The Great Sea, the brood of islands, Polynesia, the coast beyond,
The coast you henceforth are facing-you Libertad! from your Western golden shores,
The countries there with their populations, the millions en-masse are curiously here,
The swarming market-places, the temples with idols ranged along the sides or at the end, bonze, brahmin, and llama,
Mandarin, farmer, merchant, mechanic, and fisherman,
The singing-girl and the dancing-girl, the ecstatic persons, the secluded Emperors,
Confucius himself, the great poets and heroes, the warriors, the castes, all,
Trooping up, crowding from all directions, from the Altay mountains,
From Thibet, from the four winding and far-flowing rivers of China,
From the southern peninsulas and the demi-continental islands, from Malaysia,
These and whatever belongs to them palpable show forth to me, and are seiz'd by me,

THE ERRAND-BEARERS

And I am seiz'd by them, and friendlily held by them,
Till as here them all I chant, Libertad! for themselves and for you.

For I too raising my voice join the ranks of this pageant,
I am the chanter, I chant aloud over the pageant,
I chant the world on my Western sea,
I chant copious the islands beyond, thick as stars in the sky,
I chant the new empire grander than any before, as in a vision it comes to me,
I chant America the mistress, I chant a greater supremacy,
I chant projected a thousand blooming cities yet in time on those groups of sea-islands,
My sail-ships and steam-ships threading the archipelagoes,
My stars and stripes fluttering in the wind,
Commerce opening, the sleep of ages having done its work, races reborn, refresh'd,
Lives, works resumed-the object I know not-but the old, the Asiatic renew'd as it must be,
Commencing from this day surrounded by the world.

3
And you Libertad of the world!
You shall sit in the middle well-pois'd thousands and thousands of years,
As to-day from one side the nobles of Asia come to you,
As to-morrow from the other side the queen of England sends her eldest son to you.

The sign is reversing, the orb is enclosed,
The ring is circled, the journey is done,
The box-lid is but perceptibly open'd, nevertheless the perfume pours copiously out of the whole box.

Young Libertad! with the venerable Asia, the all-mother,
Be considerate with her now and ever hot Libertad, for you are all,

RESPECT AND CONSIDERATION

Bend your proud neck to the long-off mother now sending messages over the archipelagoes to you,
Bend your proud neck low for once, young Libertad.

Here the children straying westward so long? so wide the tramping?
Were the precedent dim ages debouching westward from Paradise so long?
Were the centuries steadily footing it that way, all the while unknown, for you, for reasons?

They are justified, they are accomplish'd, they shall now be turn'd the other way also, to travel toward you thence, They shall now also march obediently eastward for your sake

Libertad

Appendix 9
Extracts from David L Morgan's surgeon's logbook

Surgeon Morgan's logbook provides a fascinating insight into the sailor's life. The diseases of the day - dysentery, syphilis, tuberculosis and so on - were serious enough to warrant the sufferer a return to England. In 1864, there was an outbreak of smallpox on board, and 42 crew members died. The cramped living quarters on board HMS *Euryalus* doubtless helped the virus to spread. Injury and accident were hazards of everyday life as a sailor. Perhaps being brained by a Chinaman, as Ordinary Seaman Fox was, was an exceptional occurrence, and we have to wonder at the masthead punishment meted out to poor 2nd Class Boy Richards that resulted in his death by drowning. What had he done to deserve being placed in such hazard?

But it is the awful wounds received during the Kagoshima engagement on 15th August 1863 that concerns us particularly. The laconic descriptions of the victims and their treatment cannot convey the horror that those on board must have witnessed. And of course, there were deaths and wounds inflicted among the Satsuma people, too, and perhaps their medical treatment was of a more primitive nature. The "ten-inch shell" wounds are the results of the explosion of the Armstrong breech-loading gun that went off prematurely.

David Morgan appears to have been an honours graduate of the Standard Medical Calligraphy school, so not all of his notes are completely legible. He was also putting pen to paper immediately after stressful experiences on a ship sailing stormy waters, so we might forgive him the quality of his handwriting.

A glossary of medical terms used by Surgeon David L Morgan is given after the log.

Surgeon's Logbook HMS Euryalus 1863, extracts				
Date	Nature of disease or hurt	Name, Rank	Age	Notes
01 Jan	Dysentery	James Laid, OS[247]	24	To hospital & thence to England
03 Jan	Dysentery	John Colt, Lieut	22	To hospital & thence to England
03 Jan	Pleurisy, syphilitic rheumatism & Bronchitis	Charles Gregory, Marine Private	28	To hospital & thence to England
05 Jan	Syphilis, secondary	James Type, OS	22	To hospital & thence to England
07 Jan	Syphilis	James Page, AB[248]	20	To hospital
08 Jan	Rheumatism following Dysentery & Jaundice	Samuel Hibbard, Gunner	39	To hospital & thence to England
11 Jan	Phthysis	Charles Jones, OS	23	Invalided out

[247] Ordinary Seaman
[248] Able Bodied Seaman

SURGEON MORGAN'S LOG BOOK

13 Jan	Syphilis	Richard hill, AB	21	To hospital
20 Jan	Dysentery	Francis Pitt, OS	20	Died 30 Jan
19 Jan	Dysentery	James Page, armourer	24	Sent to England
19 Jan	Dysentery	William Wade, sick berth steward	40	Self-treated for a long time with mercury: invalided out
19 Jan	Syphilis	Cuthbert J Layton, Second Master	22	Discharged to hospital
01 Feb	Wound of scalp	William Fox, OS	24	Hammer blow by Chinaman; bone damage; invalided home
07 Feb	Dysentery	William Blight, Leading Stoker	31	Invalided out
10 Feb	Syphilis	William Hayes, OS	23	Discharged to hospital but later returned to ship
17 Feb	Otorrhoea	Joseph Hutchinson, 2nd Class Boy	17	Not suited to climate; sent home
22 Feb	Bronchitis	Ebenezer Griffiths, AB	29	Sent to hospital and then back to ship
22 Feb	Syphilis	William Hutchinson, AB	24	Discharged to hospital but later returned to ship

RESPECT AND CONSIDERATION

22 Feb	Syphilis	Frederick W King, AB	24	Transferred from "Vulcan"; immediately discharged to hospital
22 Feb	Syphilis	Henry Urquhart, AB	31	Discharged to hospital but later returned to ship
22 Feb	Dysentery	William Collins, Capt. Crew[249]	32	Discharged to hospital but later returned to ship
24 Feb	Secondary syphilis	John Woodham, AB	24	Discharged to hospital and thence invalided out
22 Feb	Anaemia	Robert Thompson, AB	26	Discharged to hospital
05 Mar	Drowned	Edward I. Richards, 2nd class Boy	16	Fell overboard from rigging while undergoing masthead punishment
28 Apr	Small Pox	Paul Mootheir, 1st Marine	20	Died 10 May
05 Jun	Compression of the Brain	William Stewart, Bandsman	38	Drunk; fell down companionway; died 6 June
15 Jun	Phthysis	Alfred Clark, RHA Gunner	29	Discharged to Yokohama hospital 17 June; died there 12 August

---

[249] This was a senior rating, not an officer.

SURGEON MORGAN'S LOG BOOK

15 Aug	Gunshot wound	John JS Josling, Captain	36	Head shattered by a round shot from a field piece. Frontal, parietal and occipital bones smashed, and the Brain scattered about the Deck. Struck by the same shot as Commander Wilmot
15 Aug	Gunshot wound	Edward Wilmot, Commander	32	Struck on the back of the head by a round shot whilst on duty on the bridge during the action with the Fort of Kagosima. Upper half of the occipital and portions of the parietal bones shattered together with the corresponding portion of the Brain and its membranes. Death instantaneous.
15 Aug	Gunshot wound	Michael Haggerty, AB	22	Struck whilst working at one of the Main Deck guns on the starboard side by a piece of ten-inch shell which struck the side of the post and exploded between decks. Bones of the face, skull, brain and its

				membranes shattered
15 Aug	Gunshot wound	Patrick Flemming, Private, RULI	22	Supposed to have been struck by a splinter of wood on the head whilst working at the main deck gun where the ten-inch shell struck the side of the post and tore off the timber. Extravasation of blood into the cavity of the aruchavid and a fracture of the base of the skull extending through the petrous posterior of the temporal bones and the sphearid bone. Death instantaneous.
15 Aug	Gunshot wound	Richard Lindsay, AB	26	Supposed to have been struck on the head by a splinter of wood whilst working the main deck gun where the shell exploded during the action with the Fort of Kagosima on the 15th of August. Fracture of the base

SURGEON MORGAN'S LOG BOOK

					of the skull and extravasation of blood within the aruchuridean cavity as in the former case. The brain in this case was found to be much softer than natural - death inst.
15 Aug	Gunshot wound	John Warren, OS	18		Struck by a piece of the ten inch shell alluded to in the former cases whilst working at the same gun. Frontal, Parietal and occipital bones shattered together with the Brain and its membranes
15 Aug	Gunshot wound	James Smith, AB	22		Killed by the same shell as the above cases whilst working at the gun already mentioned during the action at Kagosima. Compound comminated (sic) fracture of skull and compound comminated fracture of pelvis
15 Aug	Gunshot wound	William Yardley, AB	22		Killed by the same shell as the above cases during the action. Compound comminated fracture

RESPECT AND CONSIDERATION

				of the skull and laceration of the Brain and its membranes.
15-Aug	Gunshot wound	John Hawkins, OS	18	Struck by a piece of the ten inch shell which caused so much destruction among the men working the main deck gun above mentioned. Brought into the cockpit in a state of complete collapse; general surface cold and pulse fluttering and scarcely perceptible. He was perfectly tranquil and apparently free from pain. He did not appear to have bled much judging from the state of his under clothing and trousers. Upon examination, there was found a large ragged and irregularly shaped wound in right groin. There was another wound in the right nates also jagged, and irregularly shaped.

					Although the whole of the large vessels were torn and divided, there was no bleeding and in consequence of the pulpy and disorganized state of the tissues, at the seat of injury no trace of them could be found. There was also a compound fracture of left arm which was evidently a splinter wound. There was found upon a minuter examination a fracture of the horizontal arm of the pubis which was completely shattered, together with the head and neck of the femur. Attempts were made to establish reaction by means of stimulants, but without avail as the poor fellow died from exhaustion at 7.30 pm viz four hours and a half after being wounded.

15-Aug	Gunshot wound	Thomas Harding, 1st class Boy	18	Brought into the cockpit with Hawkins at 3 pm. Compound comminated fracture of right arm at the insertion of deltoid muscle and division of the vessels and nerves. An enormous wound of the corresponding side of the chest; the soft parts were found to be completely torn off from the ribs below the right axilla the 5th 6th and 7th ribs were broken in several places and were found driven in the pleura and lungs which were lacerated in three separate places. Great Dyspnea and hurried respirations; cough; and spitting of florid frothy bloody air passing out of the wound with a loud whiff; pulse 140; complexion livid. As chloroform was quite out of the question it was

deemed imprudent to amputate the arm at the shoulder joint in this case. He clearly had but a short time to live which would in all probability be still shorter if an operation had been attempted. Nothing therefore was done but the administration of opiates and stimulants. On the 16th the dyspnea became greater if anything in consequence of general emphysema, although there had not been any bleeding the humeral artery was searched for and discovered to be contracted at its divided extremity and firmly closed by a plug of coagulation. It was secured by a ligature about half an inch above, where it was seen pulsating. Died at 10pm

15-Aug	Gunshot wound	William Howden, Private Marine	26	Ten-inch shell wound. Face & neck frightfully torn and shattered.. Blood poisoning, alarming haemorrhages. Died 17th of asphyxiation: blood and infection seeping into lungs.
25-Aug	Accident	Henry Bray, Able Seaman	22	Compound comminuted fracture of frontal bone; brought in "insensible". Was coiling a rope in the launch on the upper deck when ord. seaman Grover fell from the Main Top and alighted on him whilst he was in a stooping position with his head inclined downwards and propelled him with great force against a ring bolt. Grover only had a few bruises. Bray died from his injury.

SURGEON MORGAN'S LOG BOOK

GLOSSARY OF MEDICAL AND ANATOMICAL TERMS USED BY SURGEON MORGAN	
Aruchavid	Unclear, but almost certainly he meant "arachnoid", a web-like membrane that lines the inner surface of the brain cavity
Aruchuridean cavity	Unclear, but almost certainly he meant "arachnoid" cavity
Axilla	Armpit
Comminated	"Commin<u>u</u>ted" (of bone) means "shattered"
Deltoid muscle	The muscle that forms the rounded part of the shoulder
Dyspnea	Shortness of breath
Emphysema	Obstruction of the lungs; leads to hyperventilation, air trapped in the chest
Extravasation	Bleeding
Frontal bone	Major cranial bone that forms the forehead and front top of the head
Humeral artery	Artery that supplies blood to muscles in the shoulder and upper arm, including the deltoid muscle
Mercury	Widely used for bowel conditions (though not dysentery at this time), sometimes mixed with chalk as "blue mass". It was, of course, a cumulative poison that led ultimately to death.
Nates	Buttocks
Occipital bone	major cranial bone at the lower back of the head
Otorrhoea	Discharge from the ear
Parietal bone	Major cranial bone that forms part of the top, back, and side of the head
Phthysis	Tuberculosis
Pleura	Membranes that cover the lungs
Sphearid bone	Unclear, but almost certainly he meant "sphenoid" bone, which adjoins the temporal bone
Temporal bone	Cranial bone on the side of the head that extends down behind the ear towards the jaw

APPENDIX 10
CONSUL VYSE AND AINO BONES

Such is the title of file FO 46/88 in the National Archives. The volume of handwritten correspondence and official documents is thick. And the unfolding story is remarkable.

The Japanese governor of Hakodate had complained in 1866 to the British Consul, Captain Francis Howard-Vyse, that graves had been desecrated and bones stolen from them in two Ainu villages in Hokkaido. Three skeletons and four skulls had been stolen from graves at Mori, and 13 skulls from Otoshibe. A Japanese servant of an Englishman had been arrested and told the story to the governor.

The Aino (today "Ainu") people have a distinct physiology and culture. They were neither Japanese, Chinese nor Korean in general appearance. Their language was unlike any other in the region. At the time, their particular skeletal features were a matter of intense interest among Darwinian scientists in Europe, and there was a trade in their bones. Bodysnatching had only died out in Britain some 30 years previously, with the passing of the Anatomy Act in 1832.

Vyse had three Britons - Trone, Kemish[250] and Whitely - arrested. The first two were the keeper of the British Jail and the Constable of the Consulate respectively. Whitely's occupation was not stated. Vyse opened the trial, took no evidence beyond the statements of the Japanese governor, entered a "guilty" verdict, and held the case over for sentence. It was strange behaviour. Instead of following Court rules as to evidence, and

---

[250] K e m i s h or K e r n i s h; the handwritten records are indistinct.

CONSUL VYSE AND AINO BONES

then coming to his own judicial decisions, he sought advice on sentence from Sir Harry Parkes, the Minister Plenipotentiary, who had no authority in the Consular Courts. The Japanese governor then approached Vyse and sought to bring witnesses from the villages who would testify to what had occurred and how serious it was. Vyse refused to hear them, as he had already heard the case and determined the guilt of the three men.

On Parkes' advice, two lay assessors were called in to help conclude the case. When they reviewed the Court papers, they declined to assent to the guilty verdict, since it was clear that the normal British judicial process had not been followed. But to Vyse's relief, the three men confessed to the crime and pleaded guilty. Vyse thereupon sentenced them to twelve months imprisonment with hard labour, and two of them were given a further month for violent conduct upon their arrest.

The stolen bones were returned to their villages, and apologies and 1000 *ichibu* compensation were given. But one skeleton and four skulls remained unaccounted for. The men claimed to have thrown them into the sea "because of the stench they emitted". Vyse arranged for the sea to be dragged at the indicated site, to no avail.

Parkes was unhappy with whole farrago, and feared a great anti-Western backlash if the matter were not laid to rest. He personally questioned Whitely, the most talkative of the three perpetrators, who admitted their story was not true. The bones had not been dumped, but had in fact been shipped to England, though he refused to say where. The file goes on, "after consultation with the other two prisoners, Whitely returned and gave the address in question as *Colonel Vyse, Stoke Park, Windsor*, which is the name and residence of a brother of Captain Vyse". They were shipped from Shanghai on the vessel *Earl of Dalhousie*. Consul Vyse evinced astonishment at this statement.

RESPECT AND CONSIDERATION

He requested instant leave to return to England to get to the bottom of things. Parkes acceded to his request.

On his arrival in England, Vyse had a correspondence with the Foreign Secretary, The Earl of Clarendon, via the Permanent Secretary Sir Edmund Hammond. Vyse reported to Clarendon that he had recovered the bones and sent them back to Japan. "I further have the honor to inform your Lordship, that I did not find the bones at the residence of my brother, as stated by the prisoner Whitely." There is a marginal note in Hammond's hand saying, "A portion of them had been purchased from him for £50. - !"

Capt Vyse was required to furnish better explanations. In a letter of 4 July 1866, he says:

First: The bones were illicitly placed by Trone in three packing cases that Vyse had in his offices for the purpose of sending curios to his brother in England. His own goods were removed by Trone and replaced by the bones without his knowledge. Trone's brother was to take delivery of the cases in Eton, though how the intercept was to be done was not stated. (Eton lies about three quarters of a mile from Windsor.)

Second: He (Capt. Vyse) had no knowledge of the sale of the bones, nor that they were produced at a scientific meeting in London.

Third: The cases never were delivered to Col. Vyse, but went to a naturalist named Davis from Shelton, Staffordshire. (A marginal note by Hammond questions how the cases could have been redirected to Davis, and a later letter asks Capt Vyse to answer the point.)

Fourth: He (Capt. Vyse) had procured the bones from Davis and despatched the three boxes to the Consul in Hakodate in the care of Messrs. Dent & Co of Shanghai. (How he had traced them, and why he paid out of his own pocket, were not stated.)

CONSUL VYSE AND AINO BONES

Hammond summarised the case and commented "Captain Vyse's explanations can hardly be said to be satisfactory. ... The other view would be that Captain Vyse was a party to the transaction, that it was by his connivance if not by his directions that the bones were shipped to England and that his peculiar management of the complaint as first lodged by the Japanese Authorities was prompted by a desire to screen those who had acted as his agents in the business."

Vyse gave half-answers to each of the successive points relayed to him by Hammond. But every explanation furnished by Vyse only raised further doubts as to his veracity. To ensure he had not erred in judgement, Hammond had the Foreign Office Counsel, Mr Egerton, look at the documents. Hammond noted in a Memorandum of 22 Sep 1866, "I cannot depart from the conclusion at which Mr Egerton has arrived, as stated in his minute of the 20th instant, as to the necessity of removing Captain Vyse from the Consular Service".

Despite pleas from Vyse's brother, the trusted and eminent Colonel Vyse, and depositions from the three convicts that Vyse was not involved, he was given the choice of resigning or being dismissed. Either was socially ruinous, but one more than the other, so Her Britannic Majesty's Consul, Captain Francis Howard-Vyse, tendered his resignation from the Consular Service on 7 December 1866, still protesting his innocence. His resignation was readily accepted.

RESPECT AND CONSIDERATION

At the time of the events described in this book, a distinct cultural feature among the Ainu was the extensive tattooing of women. The most obvious was the tattooing of the lips. Young girls would sport a spot in the centre of their lips, which would be extended until the mature woman's tattoo ranged almost from ear to ear. Elaborate tattooing of the hand and forearm in traditional patterns was also commonplace. Some examples are sketched above.

The most striking feature of the Ainu man was the luxurious beard generally worn. The beard was thought to tie the man in with a key religious symbol: the bear. The animist beliefs of the Ainu gave a primary place to the bear, seen as powerful, self-sufficient and feared, characteristics the Ainu thought of as theirs, too.

An Ainu family photographed c.1902.
"Aino" was a spelling used in the mid-19th century by foreigners

RESPECT AND CONSIDERATION

			All Royal Naval vessels mentioned			
HMS	Launched	Hull	Prop-uls'n	Type	BM	Displacement
Alecto	9/7/1839	Wood	Paddle	Sloop	800	878
Alligator	29/3/1821	Wood	Wind	6th rate	500	
Argus	15/12/1849	Wood	Paddle	Sloop	981	1630
Arrow	26/06/1964	Wood	Screw	Gunvessel	477	586
Barrosa	03/10/1960	Wood	Screw	Corvette	1700	2302
Bouncer	23/2/1852	Wood	Screw	Gunboat	232	
Brazen	23/2/1856	Wood	Screw	Gunboat	232	
Centaur	6/10/1845	Wood	Paddle	2nd Class frigate	1270	2100
Chesapeake	27/9/1855	Wood	Screw	Frigate	2377	3334
Conqueror	10/6/1833	Wood	Wind	First rate	2694	
Coquette	25/10/1855	Wood	Screw	Gunboat	677	
Devastation	12/7/1871	Iron	Screw	Turret Ship	4406	9387
Diadem	14/10/1856	Wood	Screw	Frigate	2483	3880
Eclipse	14/11/1867	Wood	Screw	Sloop	1276	1760
Euryalus	5/10/1853	Wood	Screw	Frigate	2371	3125
Havoc	20/3/1856	Wood	Screw	Gunboat	232	
Howe	28/3/1815	Wood	Wind	1st rate	2619	
Icarus	22/10/1858	Wood	Screw	Sloop	580	868
Indus	16/3/1839	Wood	Wind	2nd Rate		2653
Kestrel	20/5/1856	Wood	Screw	Gunboat	233	
Leopard	5/11/1850	Wood	Paddle	1st class Frigate	1406	
Moselle	?/?/1804	Wood	Wind	Sloop		
Osprey	22/3/1856	Wood	Screw	Gunvessel	682	
Pearl	13/9/1855	Wood	Screw	Corvette	1469	2187
Pelorus	5/2/1857	Wood	Screw	Corvette	1462	2330
Perseus	21/8/1861	Wood	Screw	Sloop	955	1365
Racehorse	19/3/1860	Wood	Screw	Gunvessel	695	877
Rattler	18/3/1862	Wood	Screw	Sloop (1862: Corvette)	950	1280
Rattlesnake	9/7/1861	Wood	Screw	Corvette	1705	2431
Renard	23/4/1856	Wood	Screw	Gunvessel	682	850
Ringdove	22/2/1856	Wood	Screw	Gunvessel	674	
Sampson	1/10/1844	Wood	Paddle	2nd class frigate	1299	2100
Tamar	5/1/1863	Iron	Screw	Troopship	2812	4650
Tartar	17/5/1854	Wood	Screw	Corvette	1322	1965
Victory	17/5/1765	Wood	Wind	1st rate	2142	
Winchester	21/6/1822	Wood	Wind	4th rate	1487	

CONVENTIONS USED IN THE TEXT

	All Royal Naval vessels mentioned		
Initial Guns	Fate	ADM 135/	Note
4	1865		
28	1865		1841 d.s. 1842 troopship. 1846 hospital ship
6	1881		
2	1862	25	
21	1877	38	
4	1871	58	
4	1864		
6	1864		
51	1867	89	
120	1918		1859 screw. 1862 = Conqueror. 1876 = Warspite t.s. 1918.01.20 burnt in Thames
4	1868	102	
4	1908		
32	1875	131	
6	1921	147	Laid down as Sappho. 1888-1892 lent War Dept. (1876: Corvette)
51	1867	163	
4	1871	224	
120	1854		
11	1875	246	
80	1898		1860 guardship
2	1866	265	1859.06.25 wrecked in action, Peiho Forts, China; salvaged, reentered service
18	1867	276	
18	1815		
4	1867	343	Vigil 1867.06 wrecked off South Africa
21	1884	349	
21	1869	351	
17	1931		1904=Defiance II
3	1864		1864.11.04 wrecked Chefoo, China
17	1868	387	1868.09.24 wrecked China station
21	1882		
4	1866	394	
4	1866	400	
4	1864		
3	1941	465	1897 base ship. 1941 scuttled at Hong Kong
18	1866	466	ex-Russian *Wojn*, seized on stocks
100			1801 rebuilt 2164 bm.1824 h.s. 1922 drydocked. Still in commission.
52	1921		1861 = Conway, t.s. 1876 = Mount Edgcombe

RESPECT AND CONSIDERATION

Note on Conventions Used in the Text.

Western dates have generally been used. The Japanese dating system depends on Imperial *nengo*. So Charles Richardson was murdered on 14 of 9 of *bunkyū* 2, or 14th September 1862.

Obviously, BC and AD have no intrinsic meaning in Japanese culture, but they have been used for ease of reference for western minds.

Japanese names are given in Japanese style, family name followed by given name. Only the *samurai* classes and above in fact had a family name. It was quite common for higher-class people to change their name whenever a significant life event occurred. Promotion by the Emperor might be such an occasion, or coming of age, or the birth of a child, or being exiled or downgraded. It was common for young people to be given for adoption or as hostages by another family for strategic reasons, and so completely new names would be taken. I have used the name most commonly used by the person at the time of the events described. Once a Japanese person has been introduced within a section of the text, I subsequently refer to him by his family name, unless there are several bearing that name in the section: in that case, I have used the personal name. I have altered the spelling of names in documents to achieve consistency. In particular, the English often spelled Shimazu as Shimadzu, and Saburō as Saboolo.

There are no plurals in Japanese, so, for example, *daimyō* might mean one *daimyō* or several, depending on the context. Similarly, there are no capital letters, so these only appear when a Japanese word starts a sentence.

CONVENTIONS USED IN THE TEXT

A NOTE ON PRONUNCIATION:

In *romaji* script, Japanese is written syllabically, not letter by letter. Every letter is pronounced, except that "u" in the middle of names is hardly voiced at all, and at the end of words is usually similarly unvoiced. A vowel with a macron over it is longer than the vowel without it. Thus the name Ōkano Shinsuke is something like o~o-ka-no shin-s'-kay.

GLOSSARY OF JAPANESE TERMS, WITH EXPLANATORY NOTES

arahitogami	現人神	Cult that reveres the Emperor as a divine being
ashigaru	足軽	"light-foot", meaning "lightly armed" The lowest-ranking members of the feudal class, having status below that of *samurai* proper. They served as the highly disciplined rank and file of a feudal army, or as clerks, guards and messengers in time of peace. A distinctive uniform item was the *jingasa*, a protective conical hat made out of hard lacquered leather, a specimen of which was plundered by Ernest Satow when the Japanese ships were burned at Kagoshima.
bakufu	幕府	"Tent headquarters", the headquarters of a commander in the field. A term used for the *shōgunate* government from 1192 to 1868.
bakumatsu	幕末	The "End of the *shōgunate*" - the process that began after Commodore Perry's arrival in 1853 and culminated in the Meiji Restoration of 1868/9.
betto		Groom, servant who looked after horses, and often ran alongside the horse and rider.
bu		Unit of currency. See *ichibu*.
bugyō	奉行	Governor, commissioner. *Gai-koku-bugyō* were commissioners for foreign affairs, equivalent to British permanent under-secretaries.
Bushidō	武士道	Code of the *samurai*
Chōnin	町人	Townsman. Non-*samurai* inhabitants – artisans, labourers, merchants. Peasants - *nōmin* - by definition, are not town dwellers.

JAPANESE GLOSSARY

Choutei	Emperor, also "Imperial Palace"; refers to the Emperor in the sense of an institution.
daibutsu	大仏 or 大佛 A huge (大 *dai*) statue of the Buddha (仏 or 佛 *butsu*), one of the most famous being the one at Kamakura. There is a larger one in the temple of Tōdai-ji in Nara.
daimyō	大名 "Great name" i.e. Lord: wealthy feudal aristocrat. There were between 260 and 270 *daimyō* at any given time.
daishō	大小 "big and small" denotes the pair of swords worn by a *samurai*. The *katana* 刀 is the long sword and the *wakizashi* 脇差 the short. Colloquially the *katana* is the *daitō* 大刀 ("big sword") and the *wakizashi* is the *shōtō* 小刀 ("small sword"). Combined, **daitō** + **shōtō** = **daishō**. Confusing (or enlightening) Japanese *kanji* lesson: 刀 has the *kun'yomi* - Japanese reading - *katana* and the *on'yomi* - Chinese reading - *tō*.
Edo period	The period of Tokugawa rule, from the battle of Sekigahara in 1600 to the Meiji restoration in 1868. The Tokugawa capital city (originally a fishing village called Shibasaki) was Edo (now 東京 Tōkyō)
fudai	譜代 "Inside" Lords, whose ancestors supported Tokugawa Ieyasu at the battle of Sekigahara.
fukoku kyōhei	富國強兵 "Enrich the Country and Strengthen the Military!" - the successor slogan to *sonnō jōi* when it was realised that the *bakufu* was doomed.
gokenin	御家人 "houseman". The lowest rank of *samurai* proper, ranking immediately below *hatamoto*. Many *gokenin* were direct retainers of the *shōgun*. There were about 12000 of them, and their stipend was restricted to 260 *koku* or less..
gorogio also gorojiu	"August elders" or "noble old men" according to context - the great Council assisting the *shōgun*
gyoretsu	行列 The *daimyō's* procession. It was preceded by a group of men clapping blue-painted bamboo rods together and shouting "*shitanero!, shitanero!*" ("down!, down!") to announce the *gyoretsu's* impending arrival. Anyone in the vicinity was required to kneel with forehead touching the floor (*dogeza*) until the *gyoretsu* passed.

RESPECT AND CONSIDERATION

han	藩 Clan, fief, domain.
hatamoto	旗本 Direct retainers of the *shōgun*, whose annual rice revenue of less than 10,000 *koku* (but more than the *gokenin's* 260 *koku*) did not qualify them as *daimyō*. There were about 5000 *hatamoto*. See also *gokenin*.
ichibu	A (usually silver) coin, increasing in exchange value against British money from 10d in 1862 to 1s 8d in 1882
inada	Rice-fields
kago	Palanquin. "Basket". A version of the norimon (q.v.) made out of bamboo and used by lower classes of people. A *hikido kago* was upmarket, for use by officials, and had sliding doors. A *kiribo kago* was suspended from a pole (of Paulownia wood. q.v.)
kaikoku	"Open country", the policy of the Tokugawa *bakufu* after the arrival of Commodore Perry, replacing *sakoku*.
kakuro	"The old ones" - the common, rather disrespectful, expression for the *gorogio*
kami	神 The objects of worship or respect in the *shintō* religion: spirits of the objects of veneration. Used as a title, it means "Earl" or "Baron" in conjunction with a province, but "Minister" when used in conjunction with a government department. Roughly equivalent in ministerial usage to archaic English "Sire".
kanji	漢字 "*Han* ("Chinese") characters": the signs that along with *hiragana* and *katakana* syllabaries (the characters represent syllables, not letters) make up the Japanese writing system.
karo	家老 Senior hereditary counsellor of a *daimyō*
katana	刀 Long (>61cm) two-handed sword borne by *samurai* tucked into their *obi* or sash. There was spiritual significance embodied in a *samurai's* sword, and he venerated it. The hard and immensely sharp cutting edge is matched by the more pliable backbone of the sword: combined with the curve of the sword, this is widely regarded as the finest cutting weapon ever designed. See *daishō, wakizashi, tantō, samurai*.

JAPANESE GLOSSARY

kinsatsu	"Gold-note". Paper currency, used in the trading of rice, and therefore used widely as general currency.
kobu-gattai undo	The movement for "Shaking the Emperor's hand" – the political scheme hatched in 1861 by Ando Nobumasa to unite the Emperor's Court and the *shōgun's* Court by marrying the Emperor's sister Kazu-no-miya Chikako to Tokugawa Iemochi. Iemochi died shortly after the marriage had taken place, possibly poisoned by opponents of the scheme.
kojiki	古事記 Earliest collection of folk-myths about Japan, commissioned by Emperor Temmu and completed under Emperor Gemmai in 712 AD.
koku	石 An approximation of the amount of rice to sustain one person for a year - about five British bushels or 182 litres. Wealth was measured in the number of *koku* someone's lands could produce annually. A *daimyō* had to have 10,000 *koku* to hold his rank.
kokudaka	Measurement of land in terms of its rice yield in units of *koku*.
kokugaku	国学 "National study", or "Native Studies". Japanese-centred learning promulgated from the late eighteenth century, as opposed to the classical Chinese-centred learning of earlier days. Ancient works were translated into modern Japanese, and there was a conscious perception of a golden age of Japanese culture and society. This weakened the philosophical "Chinese" basis for the Tokugawa system of government and contributed to its later downfall.
kokushi	国司 Honorific title for descendants of *daimyō* whose ancestors used to be of importance and influence in pre-Tokugawa days.
kokushu	"Provincial Lord", the highest rank of *daimyō*, usually granted because of his wealth or armed strength. Permitted to build a castle.
kuge	公家 The nobility. Two levels of nobility existed: the senior were the *dōjō* 堂上 who sat on the floor near the Emperor and to whom all significant government posts

495

	were granted, and the *jige* 地下 who were not permitted to come that close.
meiji	明治 "Enlightened rule" - the *nengo* given to the period from the end of the *bakufu* (1868) to the death of the Emperor (1914)
Namamugi jiken	The Namamugi Incident, known widely in the west as the Richardson Affair; the killing of Charles Lenox Richardson at Namamugi and its consequences
nengo	The name given to the era starting on the accession of a new Emperor (or when a significant event in the life of the nation occurs). In the modern era, it is only on the accession of the Emperor that a *nengo* changes. Nowadays, year one starts on the accession and ends on 31 December, so will normally be shorter than other years.
norimon / norimono	Palanquin for use by a *daimyō* or high court official. Often richly lacquered and furnished, with soft cushions and elaborate drapery. The bearers - up to eight of them for a V.I.P. - carried *norimon* of junior personages on their shoulders, but senior ones low by their sides. People of lower status might be carried in a *kago* (q.v.). Wheeled transport for humans was prohibited before westerners arrived, though carts for the conveyance of heavy cargo were to be seen. Horse-drawn carriages first appeared in 1869, and in 1872, the first railway was built by British engineers. It ran the 18 miles from Tōkyō to Yokohama.
ometsuke	Supervisor or overseer; in the governmental context referred to an official observer (akin to the later commissars of the Soviet Union) who reported back to the *bakufu* that the officials they supervised had carried out their duties properly and nothing had been done outside their remit.
Paulownia	A deciduous tree, a commercially important hardwood, used, among other things, for the poles of *kago* and *norimon*, in the manufacture of the *koto*, a zither-like instrument, and the wooden clogs still worn in Japan. *P. tomentosa* is known in Japan as *kiri*, or the "Princess Tree". It is used symbolically as the badge of the Government of

JAPANESE GLOSSARY

	Japan (the Chrysanthemum being the Imperial badge).
rangaku	"Dutch knowledge" - information gained from Dutch textbooks (mainly confined to botany, economics and medicine). See *yogaku*.
ri	里 Measure of distance: how far a man can walk in an hour - about 4 kilometres.
rōnin	浪人 "wave man" (one who is tossed about like a wave in the sea). *Samurai* with no allegiance to a *daimyō*. Many turned to ruthless banditry to make a living. See also *shishi*.
ryō	両 A coin, equivalent to 60 *monme*, or 4 *kan* (approximately ⅓ Mexican dollar in 1862)
sakoku	鎖国 "Closed nation" - the inward-looking doctrine that excluded foreigners from the country and made it a capital offence to travel abroad. *Sakoku* literally means "chained country"
samurai	侍 or 武士 "those who serve in close attendance to nobility". Hereditary soldiers and administrators for the *daimyō* and the *bakufu*. Only the *samurai*, the *daimyō* and a small number of medical doctors were permitted to own or wear swords. Commonly known as "two-sworded men". The wearing of swords was prohibited in 1876.
sankin kōtai	参勤交代 "Alternate attendance" - the system whereby *daimyō* had to visit 江戸 Edo for six months and then return to their province for six months (or 12 months and 12 months in some cases). Their wives and family had to remain in Edo permanently. The policy was abolished in October 1862; the cohesiveness that the policy had enforced no longer existed, and this contributed inevitably to the break-up of the whole *bakufu* system, and cession of power to the Emperor. A *bakufu* Edict of September 1863 seeking to reimpose *sankin kōtai* was disregarded by every *daimyō*, even the pro-*bakufu* faction.
satsu-ei sensō	薩英戦争 The Satsuma-England war - the Japanese name given to what the British call the Bombardment of Kagoshima
seppuku	切腹 Ritual suicide by painfully but determinedly cutting

	into the abdomen. Also known - though the term is considered vulgar and generally used only by foreigners - as *hara-kiri* 腹切り, "belly slitting" (note the kanji used for *seppuku* and *hara-kiri* are the same but in reverse order). The ritual granted a noble memorial to a defeated or wounded, or disgraced *samurai*: his slate was wiped clean. Forfeiture of property and land, and family disgrace, which followed a regular execution, was avoided by *seppuku*. The ceremony, when undertaken without pressure of time, became more "refined" over the years until it involved the writing of a stylised death poem, prayers, and the taking of *sake* before the rip into the belly, and the use of an assistant (介錯人, *kaishakunin*) who would behead the suicide with his *katana* immediately after he sliced into himself with his *wakizashi*, to save him suffering. The object of the *kaishakunin* was *daki-kubi:* the head should, ideally, remain attached to the body by a sliver of flesh. *Seppuku* on the battlefield by a defeated or wounded *samurai* was far more perfunctory.
sesshō	摂政 Regent of a young Emperor. A *kanpaku* 関白 was a chief adviser and first secretary to an adult Emperor. A *sesshō* often, seamlessly, became a *kanpaku*, and the two offices were indistinguishable, and referred to collectively as *sekkan* (摂関).
shimonoseki sensō	下関戦争 The Shimonoseki War, known to the West as the Bombardment of Shimonoseki
shi-no-ko-sho	士農工商 the four traditional castes of mainstream Japanese Society in the Edo period: warrior-peasant-artisan-merchant in descending order, taken from the Confucian system, but substituting warriors for scholars. Warriors rule; peasants grow things; artisans make things; merchants merely make profits.
shinpan	Relatives of the Tokugawa *shōguns* who were entrusted with major administrative rôles.
shinsengumi	新選組 "Newly selected corps", a ruthless force recruited from *rōnin*, used to suppress anti-*bakufu* factions as the

JAPANESE GLOSSARY

	end of the *shōgunate* loomed. They had a strict code of discipline and honour, but were widely regarded by outsiders as uncontrolled, licensed killers
shishi	*Samurai* of the lowest class. They were xenophobic and politically active and ready to use their weapons in furtherance of their policies. Many of them were *rōnin*.
shōgun	将軍 From 征夷大将軍 *sei-i tai shōgun* - barbarian-quelling generalissimo – the *de facto* hereditary ruler of Japan for most of the period from around 1185 to 1868.
sonnō jōi	尊皇攘夷 or 尊王攘夷 "Revere the Emperor! Expel the barbarians!" - the slogan under which anti-*bakufu* factions rallied from the late 1850s onwards.
tairō	大老 "Great Councillor" - the highest office in the *bakufu* below the *shōgun* himself.
tantō	短刀 "short sword". Dagger, short stabbing weapon. The three weapons - *katana*, *wakizashi* and *tantō* - were proverbially said to be "one weapon in three sizes".
tennō	天皇 "heavenly sovereign" – Emperor. Some other names for the Emperor include *Zenzi*—"Son of Heaven"; 帝 *Mikado,*—"Emperor"; and *Dairi* or *Kinrai*—"Grand Interior" (the latter denoting the perpetual seclusion of his person).
todome	*Coup de grâce*, beheading of a profoundly wounded adversary as an act of mercy. Inflicted on Richardson.
tōkaidō	東海道 The coastal "east sea route" that linked the Imperial capital 京都市 Kyotō with the governmental capital 江戸 Edo (now 東京 Tōkyō). Along the route, there were 55 "stations" where food and lodgings could be had. The famous artist Hiroshige Ando (1797-1858) painted several series of 55 paintings of the stations. The road averaged 5.5 metres in width and mainly comprised sand over crushed gravel, though bare earth was found here and there. Where needed, some sections were paved with stone. The entire road was lined with fir trees, to provide shade for the travellers. It took about two weeks to travel the 520 kilometres or so (325 miles) between Edo and Kyotō even using teams of professional "walkers" to carry the *norimon*. An alternative, inland route from Edo

	to Kyotō was the *nakasen-dō* 中山道 - the "Road through the Central Mountains" - but this was longer, more arduous, and much less popular for travel.
tozama	外様 "Outside" Lords, whose ancestors had opposed Tokugawa Ieyasu at the battle of Sekigahara.
tycoon	大君 Used (mistakenly) by the western powers to refer to the *shōgun*. It was never used so by the Japanese, because *tycoon* means "Great Prince", a title properly belonging to the Emperor
wakizashi	脇差:わきざし "Side arm" Short (30-61cm) sword worn by a *samurai*. Made to the same high standards as the *katana* (q.v.), it was used as a stabbing weapon, a sword for indoor use and close personal combat, and was often used for *seppuku*. See *daishō, tantō*.
yakunin	An official.
yashiki	One of a chain of inns designed to accommodate *daimyō* and their retinues while travelling the *tōkaidō*. Also used of a counting-house, where the *daimyō's* officials received rent and payments in kind.
yogaku	"Western knowledge". *Rangaku* (q.v.) was widened to encompass more than the original fields of knowledge imparted by the Dutch.
yonin	Junior hereditary councillor of a *daimyō*, inferior to *karo*

SELECT BIBLIOGRAPHY

In addition to the sources noted below, I made extensive use of original documents from the National Archives; the Internet has been fruitful too. I have listed many of these sources on the website associated with this book, www.japanhistory.co.uk

Alcock, Sir Rutherford, *The Capital of the Tycoon: a narrative of a Three Years' Residence in Japan*, Longman, Green, Longman, Roberts & Green, 1863 (e-text on Google books)	Head of British Legation's detailed notes on events, including the attack on the British Legation.
Auslin, Michael, *Negotiating with Imperialism: The Unequal Treaties and the Culture of Japanese Diplomacy*, Harvard University Press, 2005	U.S.-Japanese diplomacy in the bakumatsu
Beasley, W.G, *The Japanese Experience*, Weidenfeld & Nicolson, London, 1999 [Professor Bill Beasley, 1919 - 2006]	Excellent illustrated and authoritative history, a commanding overview of Japanese history, political, cultural and social.
Beasley, W.G, *The Meiji Restoration*, Stanford University Press, Stanford, 1972	Scholarly account of events leading up, and subsequent, to the Restoration
Beasley, W.G., *Great Britain and the opening of Japan: 1834 – 1858*, Luzac & Co., London, 1951	Details of the Stirling and Elgin negotiations with Japan
Beasley, W.G., *The Foreign Threat and the Opening of the Ports*, in Marius B Jansen (ed.) *The Cambridge History of Japan (vol. 5) The Nineteenth Century*, Cambridge University Press, 1989	Emphasis on the commercial history of the period

RESPECT AND CONSIDERATION

Beasley, W.G., *The Rise of Modern Japan: Political, Economic, and Social Change Since 1850*, Phoenix Press, Toronto, 2000	Much scholarly detail and discussion of the *bakumatsu* and later events
Bird, Isabella L., *Unbeaten Tracks in Japan*. John Murray, London,1880	An 1878 account of travels in the interior including visits to the aborigines of Yezo and the Shrine of Nikko
Black, John Reddie, *Young Japan, Yokohama and Yedo, a narrative of the settlement and the city from the signing of the treaties in 1858, to the close of the year 1879.*, N. Trübner & Co., London, 1881	A journalist's contemporary accounts of all relevant events.
Booth, Alan, *The Roads to Sata, a 2000-mile walk through Japan*, Kodansha International, 1985	A modern travelogue with much incidental observation and anecdote. Includes the Song of the *kamikaze* Pilots
Bruce, Anthony, *The Purchase System in the British Army 1660-1871*, Royal Historical Society, 1980	Purchase and sale of commissions by officers.
Buruma, Ian, *Inventing Japan, from Empire to Economic Miracle 1853-1964*, Weidenfeld & Nicolson, London, 2003	A concise broad-brush history, mainly concerning post-Restoration events. Has a chapter on the *bakumatsu*.
Carroll, John, *Trails of Two Cities: A Walker's Guide to Yokohama and Kamakura*, Kōdansha International, Tōkyō 1964	Brief account of the incident
Clavell, James, *Gai-jin*, Hodder & Stoughton, London, 1993	Novel set in Japan in 1862, very loosely based on events recounted in this book. Many historic inaccuracies and characterisations, and not "great" literature, but a rollicking read nonetheless, giving perhaps some feel of the character of Japan at the time.
Clowes, W.L., *The Royal Navy: A History from the Earliest Times to 1900* (Chatham, 1997)	Multi-volume and extremely thorough history of the Royal Navy through this and earlier periods
Cobden, Richard, M.P., *Speech at Rochdale*, 24 November 1863	Denounces gunboat diplomacy, following Kagoshima
Continental Monthly: devoted to literature and national policy. / Volume 4, Issue 3, New York, September 1863	Article: *Japanese Foreign Relations*, by Dr MacGowan, long-term resident of Japan.

SELECT BIBLIOGRAPHY

Cortazzi, Hoare, Brailey and Hotta-Lister (authors) *The Revision of Japan's early commercial Treaties*, Four papers from symposium of Japan Society and London School of Economics and Political Science 9 July 1999	Details how the treaties came into effect; their repeated modification; Satow and the unequal treaties; their replacement in 1911
Cortazzi, Sir Hugh (Ed.), *British Envoys in Japan 1859 - 1972*, Global Oriental, Folkestone, 2004 (for the Japan Society)	Sir Hugh's essays on Alcock, Neale and Parkes are particularly illuminating and relevant to this work, as is Ian Ruxton on Satow.
Cortazzi, Sir Hugh, *Dr. Willis in Japan, 1862 - 1887, British Medical Pioneer*, Athlone Press, London, 1985	Narrative of Willis's work and remarks, including extracts from his correspondence and official documents.
Cosco, Daylan, *The Namamugi Incident*, article in Yokohama Echo, 3.3.2003	Brief article setting out the central facts of the Incident
Croydon Times 1862 and 1863 - the newspaper published where Richardson's family lived	Report of the Incident, family details
D'Almeida, Anna, *A Lady's visit to Manilla and Japan*, Hurst & Blackett, London, 1863 (e-text on Google books)	Account of an adventurous journey, with details on Japanese daily life, fashions, customs, etc, and notes on modes of travel, including reference to SS *St Louis* plying between Yokohama and Nagasaki.
de Fonblanque, Edward Barrington, *Niphon and Pe-che-li; or, Two Years in Japan and Northern China*, Saunders Otley & Co, London,1862	Dilettante / diplomat's recollection of a long visit to Japan, staying for a time with Francis Howard-Vyse
Denney, Stephen, *Interview with Asaumi Takeo* 13 August 2006 (unpublished)	Translation of notes of interview by Stephen Denney with founder/curator of the *Namamugijiken-sankohkan* - the privately-run museum in Namamugi devoted to *Namamugi jiken*
Dulles, Foster Rhea, *Yankees and Samurai: America's Role in the Emergence of Modern Japan, 1791-1900*, Harper & Row, New York, 1965.	Nineteenth century American influence in Japan; mainly concerns *bakumatsu*
Elliot, Elisabeth, *Amy Carmichael, Her Life and Legacy*, MARC, Eastbourne, 1988	Religious biography of a remarkable missionary (1867-1951)

503

RESPECT AND CONSIDERATION

Encyclopaedia Britannica, *History of Japan*	Condensed information on the period
Endo Shusako, *The Samurai*, Trans. Van C. Gessel, Harper & Row / Kodansha International, New York, 1982	Novel based on facts, esp. the voyage of Hasekura Rokuemon Tsunenaga to Europe 1613-1620 (The *keichō* Embassy)
Fortune, Robert, *Yedo and Peking: a narrative of a journey to the capitals of Japan and China*, John Murray, London, 1863 (e-text on Google books)	Notes on a visit, with detailed observation of the flora and agricultural practices.
Fox, Grace, *Britain and Japan 1858-1883*, Oxford: Clarendon Press 1969	Much scholarly information on the *bakumatsu*
Hackney Almanack & Directory, various editions between 1843 and 1855	Street directory with information about the Richardson family
Hall, Francis, *Japan Through American Eyes: The Journal of Francis Hall 1859-1866*, ed. FG Notehelfer, Westview Press, Oxford, 2001	An American resident of Yokohama: his account of the Incident
Hansard's *Parliamentary Debates*, 18 February 1859; 9 February 1864	Question re appointment of Vyse as vice-Consul in Japan; debate on propriety of Kagoshima action
Harper's New Monthly Magazine, variously *Harper's Weekly*, et al. USA	Chronicles events and has illustrations
Heco, Joseph, *The narrative of a Japanese; what he has seen and the people he has met in the course of the last forty years*, Ed. James Murdoch, Tōkyō, Maruzen, 1895	Eye witness accounts surrounding the bombardments of Shimonoseki and of Kagoshima and daily life during the *bakumatsu*.
Henderson, Philip, *The Life of Laurence Oliphant, Traveller, Diplomat and Mystic*, Robert Hale Ltd, London, 1956	Competent and thorough biography of Oliphant.
Henshall, Kenneth G., *A History of Japan: from Stone Age to Superpower*, Macmillan Press, London, 1999	Condensed and accurate history
Hillsborough, Romulus, *Samurai Sketches*, Ridgeback Press San Francisco, 2001	Mind-set, techniques and actions of the *samurai*; brief notes on earlier history; account of Richardson's murder
Hillsborough, Romulus, *Shinsengumi - the shōgun's last Samurai Corps*, Tuttle Publishing, Vermont, 2005	Latter days of the *bakumatsu*
Illustrated London News, various dates	Chronicles events with illustrations

SELECT BIBLIOGRAPHY

Ion, AH, *The Namamugi Incident and the Satsu-Ei and Bakan Wars*, in Kennedy and Neilson (editors) *Incidents and International Relations: People, Power and Personalities*, Praeger, Westport & London, 2002	Brief consideration of the incident and its consequences.
Iyenaga Toyokichi (Professor, PhD), *The Constitutional Development of Japan 1853-1881*, Tokio Senmon-Gakko, 1891	Japanese reaction to Perry and the Black Ships; British Naval supremacy; subsequent trade.
Johnston, James D., Lieutenant USN, *China and Japan, being a Narrative of the cruise of the US Steam-Frigate Powhatan in the years 1857, '58, '59, and '60 including an account of the Japanese Embassy to the United States illustrated with Life Portraits of the Embassadors and their Principal Officials*, Charles DeSilver, Philadelphia, and Cushings and Bailey, Baltimore, 1860	Much incidental detail of these events and the personalities involved.
Le Monde Illustré, (journal), Paris, various dates	Chronicles and illustrates events during the *bakumatsu*
McClain, James L., *Japan: a Modern History*, WW Norton & Co, New York, 2001	From 1600 to the present day.
Milton, Giles, *Samurai William - the adventurer who unlocked Japan*, Hodder & Stoughton, London, 2002	Early encounters between Britain and Japan, and Europe and Japan
Mitford, Algernon Bertram Freeman- (Lord Redesdale GCVO, KCB) *Tales of Old Japan* (vol. 1), London, 1871	Interesting collection of folklore, legend and factual stories. "The 47 *rōnin*" and an account of *seppuku* are relevant.
Miyazawa Shinichi, *Englishmen and Satsuma*, Takishobou-Shuppan, Kagoshima, 1988	Extracts from newspapers and other publications, with illustrations and an account of Richardson's funeral
Nitobe Inazo, AM, PhD, *Bushido, The Soul of Japan*, GP Putnam's Sons, New York, 1905	Definitive account of the foundation, culture, religion, practice and influence of *bushido*.
Noboru Koyama, *Japanese Students at Cambridge University in the Meiji Era, 1868-1912: Pioneers for the Modernization of Japan*, Translated Ian C Ruxton, Lulu Press Inc, South Carolina, 2004	Detailed account of some students who were sent to Britain for western education.

RESPECT AND CONSIDERATION

Oliphant, Laurence, *The Narrative of the Earl of Elgin's Mission to China and Japan in the years 1857, '58, '59 Vol. II,* William Blackwood and Sons, Edinburgh & London, 1859 (Google e-books)	Descriptive account by perceptive observer (esp. Chapters 1-12).
Ōno Yasumaro (attrib.) *Ko-ji-ki: Records of Ancient Matters* trans. Basil Hall Chamberlain, 1919. 1981 edition, Tuttle Publishing, Boston, Mass. Also on: http://www.sacred-texts.com/shi/kj/index.htm	Academic and too-literal translation of oldest Japanese book with unseemly passages obfuscated in Latin. Volume 1 contains the Japanese creation myth. Not an easy read.
Perkins, Dorothy, *Five Hundred Fun Facts about Japan,* Diane Publishing Co., Darby, PA), 1994. Also Google e-text.	Random notes on aspects of Japanese history, geography, governance, people, religion, etc.
Perkins, Dorothy, *Samurai of Japan: a chronology from their origin in the Heian era (794-1185) to the modern era,* Diane Publishing Co., Darby, PA), 1998.	Anecdotal history of the warrior class's activities.
Perry, Matthew Calbraith, Commodore. *Narrative of the expedition of an American squadron to the China seas and Japan : performed in the years 1852, 1853, and 1854, under the command of Commodore M.C. Perry, United States navy, by order of the government of the United States / compiled from the original notes and journals of Commodore Perry and his officers, at his request and under his supervision by Francis L. Hawks.* Vol. 1. Washington, D. C., 1856. ALSO: Perry, Matthew C., Commodore, *When we landed in Japan in 1854,* compiled from his journal and papers by Francis L. Hawks; in Eva March Tappan, ed., *The World's Story: A History of the World in Story, Song and Art,* (Boston: Houghton Mifflin, 1914), Vol. I: *China, Japan, and the Islands of the Pacific*	Official and more fulsome version of *When we landed in Japan in 1854,* below. Perry paid for this three-volume account out of the sum awarded him by a grateful Congress. Edited and annotated version of Perry's account

SELECT BIBLIOGRAPHY

Pigot, *Trades Directory*, 1839	Charles Richardson (Senior)'s London business.
Ruxton, Ian C (ed.), *The Diaries and Letters of Sir Ernest Mason Satow (1843-1929), a Scholar-Diplomat in East Asia*, Edwin Mellen Press, 1998	Contemporary account of the Incident and the Bombardment of Kagoshima, (later rewritten by Satow) some of which he witnessed.
Sabin, Burrit, *Historical Guide to Yokohama*, ed. Yurindo, Yokohama, 2002	Brief account of the Incident
Satow, Sir Ernest Mason, *A Diplomat in Japan*, ICG Muse, Inc., 2000 (originally published Seeley, Service & Co., Ltd., London, 1921)	Primary source on the *bakumatsu*. Some errors in minor detail (written up to 24 years after the events). Lively retrospective eye-witness information.
Schreiber, Mark, *The Dark Side: (infamous Japanese crimes and criminals)*, Kōdansha International, Tōkyō, 2001	Vignettes of the *bakumatsu*, and the Incident, drawn from various accounts.
Scott, JW Robertson, *The Foundations of Japan*, John Murray, London, 1922	Anecdotal survey of rural Japan between 1917 and 1922.
Shiba Ryōtarō *The Fox-horse*, from *Drunk as a Lord – Samurai Stories*, translated by Eileen Kato, Kōdansha International, Tōkyō, 2001	Factional account of the Incident.
Shiba Ryōtarō, *The Last shōgun - the life of Tokugawa Yoshinobu*, Kōdansha International, Tōkyō, 1997	Account of the *bakumatsu*, using the Japanese "factional" style.
Silver, JMW, *Sketches of Japanese Manners and Customs*, Day & Co., London, 1867	Royal Marine Lieutenant's sketches and observations of life in Japan 1864-1867.
Smith, George, D.D., *Ten Weeks in Japan*, Longman, Green, Longman and Roberts, London, 1861	Bishop of Victoria (Hong Kong) gives account of an extended visit to Japan in 1860.
Tappan, Eva March, ed., *The World's Story: A History of the World in Story, Song and Art*, Houghton Mifflin, Boston, 1914, Vol. I: *China, Japan, and the Islands of the Pacific*, pp. 427-437.	Extracted from Commodore Perry's notes and journals.
The Times, London, various dates	The Namamugi Incident and its aftermath, and various other events in and concerning Japan

RESPECT AND CONSIDERATION

Time, 11 January 1982, *Japan's Crypto-Christians*, article	The version of Christianity that survived the Tokugawa persecutions.
Toyokichi Iyenaga Ph.D., *The Constitutional Development of Japan 1863-1881*, 1891; Project Gutenberg (e-book #12355), 2004	First Professor of Political Science in Tokio Senmon-Gakko (later Waseda University) from 1882 briefly reviews impact of bombardments of Kagoshima and Shimonoseki.
Young, JML, *By Foot to China* (Mission of The Church of the East, to 1400), Assyrian International News Agency Books Online, 1984 www.aina.org	Earliest Christianity in Japan and indeed the Far East.

INDEX

Note: the following geographical names and other terms have not been indexed due to their high frequency in the text:
Britain - France - Japan - Kagoshima - London - Netherlands - Portugal - Prussia - Tōkyō - Yokohama - *shōgun* - *shōgunate*

•

· · 52, 170, 188, 200, 227, 243, 250, 266, 267, 299, 327, 331, 334, 397, 411, 429, 431, 503

A

Abe Masahiro · 17, 440
Abe Masato · 85
Aberdeen, Lord · 422
Adams, William · 11, 461
Admiralty · 50, 103, 104, 111, 136, 188, 192, 225, 237, 242, 398, 420, 436, 437, 445
Aino or Ainu · 401, 482
Aizu · 253, 286, 350, 427, 443
Akeche Mitsuhide · 347, 348
Aki · 285
Alcock, Sir Rutherford, · 36, 43, 44, 46, 50, 223, 356, 389, 398, 400, 416, 418, 423, 452, 501, 503

Alexander, John Hobhouse Inglis, Captain, RN · 196, 199, 236, 257, 260, 261, 262, 266, 292, 389
Amaterasu · 6, 87, 297, 320, 321, 322, 323, 324, 328, 329, 367
American Confederate Navy vessel *Alabama* · 154
American Navy · 152, 155, 424, 505
chartered vessel *Takiang* · 260
USS *Jamestown* · 256
USS *Mississippi* · 15, 36, 436
USS *Monitor* · 253
USS *Pembroke* · 152, 153, 154, 253
USS Steam Sloop *Wyoming* · 154, 155, 156
USS *Susquehanna* · 15
Ando Nobumasa · 56, 495
Ansei Purge · 401, 427
Applin, Lieutenant · 48, 89, 90, 95, 100, 101, 102, 115, 129, 391, 454
arahitogami, Imperial Cult · 323, 492
Arimura Jizaemon · 80, 402
Arimura Shunsei · 80, 84, 167
Armstrong, Sir William · 304
asahi (rising sun) · 337

509

RESPECT AND CONSIDERATION

Asaumi Takeo · 129, 316, 503
Ashikaga
 Yoshiaki · 347
Aspinall, William Gregson · 74, 102, 113, 114, 120, 122, 128, 391, 392
Auld Lang Syne · 294
Auslin, Michael · 501
Autopsy · 448
Avenue, the, (near Kanagawa) · 73, 119

B

Bailey, Michael Buckworth, Rev. · 68, 69, 127, 128, 129, 505
bakufu
 acceding to western demands · 19, 22
 control of country · 30, 51, 356, 427
 demand for compensation from · 140
 diminishing power · 47, 51, 52, 56, 60, 61, 86, 88, 107, 162, 253, 270, 284, 433
 for America or Britain? · 23, 25
 Ministers for Foreign Affairs · 210
 opposed · 207, 254, 279, 280, 284, 307, 402
 payment of compensation · 150, 159
 payment of indemnity · 271
 Perry's arrival · 16, 17
 policies
  open the country · 52, 402
  separate westerners from Japanese · 107
  suppress Christianity · 55
 prevarication · 143, 145, 146, 149, 163, 282
 reaction to Incident · 111
 relations with France · 147, 245, 277, 426
 security of westerners · 44
 sends students abroad · 291, 298, 299
 Shimazu Saburō's false message to · 81
 treaties · 25, 26, 28, 55, 451
bakumatsu · 2, 4, 11, 12, 298, 317, 324, 325, 329, 343, 351, 381, 492, 501, 502, 503, 504, 505, 507
Baldwin, Major George Walter · 273, 275
Bath, Most Honourable Order of the · 102, 129, 233, 410, 423
 Companion (CB) · 195, 236, 257, 270, 389, 391, 412, 417, 418
 Knight Commander (KCB) · 257, 260, 389, 412, 417, 436, 452, 505
 Knight Grand Cross (GCB) · 223, 260, 393, 416, 420
Beasley, W.G. · 501, 502
Bedford, Duke of · 426
Bird, Isabella L · 38, 502
Bird, Lieutenant Robert Nicholas · 38, 273, 275, 502
Black Ships · 11, 450, 505
Black, John Reddie · 75, 184, 413, 502
Black-eyed Susan · 82, 83
blockade · 135, 136, 137, 412
Bluff, The · 455
Bodysnatching · 482
Booth, Alan · 502
Borlase, Captain John, CB, RN · 179, 181, 235, 236, 391, 459
Borradaile, Margaret, Mrs · 66, 68, 70, 71, 72, 73, 74, 75, 76, 77, 79, 81, 94, 99, 116, 117, 118, 119, 120, 122, 128, 130, 141, 250, 252, 391, 413

INDEX

boshin War · 11, 245, 285, 286, 287, 308, 404, 406, 428, 441
Boxer, Commander Charles Richard Fox, RN · 189, 235, 236, 392, 431
Boyes, Midshipman Duncan Gordon, VC · 256, 257
Brailey, Nigel · 503
Bremer, Sir James John Gordon, Rear Admiral, RN · 412
Brine, Captain Frederic, R.E. · 165, 183, 184, 195
British Legation
    Chargé d'Affaires · 34, 75, 92, 103, 111, 129, 146, 148, 210, 229, 249, 251, 446, 452, 457
    Japanese Secretary · 140, 453, 457
    Minister Plenipotentiary · 3, 297, 302, 389, 400, 430, 432, 452, 483
    Second Assistant · 453
    Student Interpreter · 457
broadcloth · 10
Brotherhood of the New Life · 45, 297, 298
Brunet, Jules · 286
Buchanan, US President James · 17, 254, 417
Buddhism · 37, 55, 66, 295, 309, 333, 343, 345, 349, 359, 360, 367, 369, 370, 372, 373, 374, 376, 401, 493
    Amida · 360, 372, 373
    Zen · 7, 359, 360, 372, 373, 374, 376
bugyō · 25, 112, 406, 492
buke shohatto · 353, 355
Bungo Straits · 152, 253
Buruma, Ian · 502
bushidō · 7, 8, 43, 49, 84, 325, 359, 360, 361, 362, 363, 381, 428, 492
Buxton, Charles, MP · 221, 222, 223

Buys, Dutch Commodore · 97, 129

C

Calibre of guns · 240
Camus, Lieutenant · 204, 205
Canton (China) · 411, 412, 423
Capital punishment · 274
    contrast with seppuku · 497
    demanded by Britain · 135, 141, 162, 173, 174, 175, 176
    methods and practice · 275, 379
Carlist Wars · 416
Carroll, John · 502
Castella cake · 82
Casualties · 195
Chasseurs d'Afrique · 204
Chiba · 299
Chikuzen · 283, 284
cholera · 35, 392
chōnin · 307
Chōshū
    agreement · 270
    belligerence · 51, 152, 255
    Chōshū five · 291
    daimyō · 2, 152, 253, 414
    family · 56, 203, 288, 293, 427
    han · 61, 245, 285, 291
    indemnity · 271
    Mōri family · 52
    students · 292
    vessels · 152, 154, 155, 156
        Daniel Webster · 152, 155
        Lancefield, now *Koshin* · 155
        Lanrick, now *Kosei* · 152, 155
Christianity · 12, 13, 23, 24, 54, 69, 101, 127, 227, 228, 229, 295, 297, 300, 340, 342, 343, 344, 369, 372, 374, 452, 508
    Catholic · 16, 55, 69, 311, 343, 344

Earliest in Japan · 342
secret Christians · 55
Chrysanthemum Throne · 278, 323, 329, 439
Clarendon, Earl, Foreign Secretary · 393, 484, 504
Clarke, Edward, Mr., of Dent & Co · 93, 94, 131
Clarke, Woodthorpe · 66, 68, 70, 71, 72, 73, 74, 76, 77, 78, 79, 81, 91, 94, 113, 115, 116, 118, 119, 120, 122, 123, 129, 130, 131, 141, 246, 247, 248, 249, 252, 316, 392, 413, 443
Clavell, James · 502
Clowes, W.L. · 47, 502
Cobden, Richard, MP · 224, 421, 502
Cocks, Richard · 11, 19
Coercion · 2, 185, 193, 194
Commercial vessel
   SS *Fiery Cross* · 60, 61
   SS *St Louis* · 65, 68, 503
Commissioners for Foreign Affairs (Japanese) · 146
Commissions, army, purchase and sale · 395, 396
Compensation · 1, 2, 44, 45, 50, 138, 139, 140, 143, 144, 146, 162, 178, 186, 191, 246, 250, 251, 252, 281, 421, 431, 483
Confucius · 7, 291, 352, 359, 367, 374, 375, 376, 466, 498
Consulate
   American · 74, 76, 118, 120
   British · 110, 423
Continental Monthly · 502
Cornes, Frederick · 113, 114, 128, 391, 392, 393
Cornet (military rank) · 395, 396
corruption · 31, 124, 463
Cortazzi, Sir Hugh · 503
Cosco, Daylan · 503

Court, Imperial · 16, 56, 61, 203, 284, 306, 333, 354, 361, 427, 434
Crimean War · 25, 204, 257, 392, 416, 417, 422, 437
Crimp, Richard, Corporal, Royal Marines · 48, 49, 50, 105, 140, 146
Croydon Times · 503
Crystal Palace · 63
Currency
   bu · 33, 180, 360, 380, 492
   ichibu · 33, 145, 483, 492, 494
   mon · 33, 310
   rin · 310
   ryō · 33, 145, 146, 292, 340, 360, 497
   sen · 180, 310
   shu · 33, 375
   yen · 310

D

daibutsu · 37, 273, 373, 446, 493
daimyō · 1, 2, 7, 18, 19, 23, 28, 38, 45, 50, 54, 55, 56, 57, 60, 61, 71, 72, 75, 78, 84, 86, 92, 94, 102, 107, 111, 115, 121, 122, 124, 134, 135, 136, 137, 138, 143, 147, 152, 157, 163, 167, 171, 173, 174, 176, 178, 212, 215, 217, 244, 253, 254, 283, 284, 285, 287, 289, 306, 307, 325, 338, 340, 343, 349, 351, 352, 353, 354, 355, 356, 360, 361, 363, 365, 381, 401, 404, 407, 414, 432, 433, 434, 435, 438, 440, 490, 493, 494, 495, 496, 497, 500
dajokan · 218
De Bellecourt, M. Gustave Duschesne · 89, 91, 94, 392, 426
De Casembroot, *Kapitein* François · 153, 260
De Fonblanque, Edward Barrington · 400, 503

INDEX

deference · 7, 71, 86
Denney, Stephen · xii, 130, 313, 503
Derby, Earl of · 397, 422
Dulles, Foster Rhea · 32, 503
Dutch Navy
    Hr. Ms. *Amsterdam* · 260
    Hr. Ms. *Djambi* · 260, 265
    Hr. Ms. *Medusa* · 153, 253, 260
    Hr. Ms. *Metalen Kruis* · 260, 265

E

East India Company · 11, 19
East Indies and China Station · 46, 134, 234
Echizen · 253, 285
Edict, Imperial · 56, 58, 147, 152, 154
Edo period · 333, 351, 359, 407, 438, 493, 498
Elgin, Earl · 26, 45, 137, 392, 423, 463, 501, 502, 506
Elias, Ellis · 113, 114, 392, 393
Elliot, Elisabeth · 412, 503
Elswick Engine and Ordnance Works · 304
Emperor
    Go-Daigo (Southern Court) · 338
    Go-Toba · 333
    Jimmu · 6, 323
    Kammu · 358
    Kōmei · 57, 276, 278, 402, 403, 413
    Meiji · 278, 289, 302, 309, 330, 403, 413
    Ōjin · 6, 323
    Showa · 329
    Suzaku · 358
    Temmu · 319, 495
    Tenji · 332

Encyclopaedia Britannica · 504
Endo Shusako · 504
Enoshima · 42, 273
Eusden, Richard · 70, 140, 141, 143, 196, 453, 457
Evans, Lieut.-General Sir George de Lacy · 416, 418
Exchange Rates · 24, 27
Extraterritoriality · 7, 8, 18, 19, 20, 26, 121, 431, 452, 462

F

feudalism · 2, 70, 84, 309, 311, 316, 325, 332, 365, 413, 492, 493
Firearms · 185, 205, 340, 381
    ammunition · 10, 186, 247, 381
    arquebus · 185, 340, 381
    Enfield 1853 Rifled Musket · 168
    musket · 89, 168, 257, 266, 340, 416
    pistol · 44, 52, 273, 402
    revolver · 77, 144, 205
Five Nations · 2, 25, 27
Fletcher, L · 196, 457
Flowers, Marcus · 70, 279, 400, 457
Foad, Seaman Robert, RN · 278, 283
Food & drink
    Japanese
        bamboo · 39
        black beans · 39
        brown seaweed · 39
        daikon (radish) · 39
        fish Paste · 39
        lily roots · 39
        pickle · 38, 39
        raw fish · 39
        rice · 39
        sea-ear · 39

sea-slug · 39
Naval
   cocoa · 241
   pork · 167, 241, 446
   raisins · 167
   rum · 167, 241
   sugar · 86, 167, 179, 241, 310
   vegetables · 241
   vinegar · 241
Universal
   beer · 31, 38, 155, 241, 359
   eggs · 38, 39, 145
   tea · 10, 27, 31, 32, 38, 41, 64, 70, 73, 82, 84, 115, 120, 128, 206, 241, 273, 278, 283, 292, 401, 433, 450, 451
Western
   bread · 38, 241
   butter · 38
   cakes · 41
   Champagne · 34, 41, 70, 83
   coffee · 38, 41
   sandwiches · 41
   wine · 38, 241, 274, 297, 298, 322
Forts and Batteries · 183, 184, 186, 225, 226, 246, 254, 264, 269, 270, 271, 380, 461
Fortune, Robert · 504
Fortyseven *rōnin* · 360, 361, 362, 363, 364, 505
Fountaingrove Round Barn & Winery · 298
Fox, Grace · 504
French Navy
   Dupleix · 156, 260, 265, 325
   Kienchiang · 153
   Le Monge · 89, 127, 129
   Sémiramis · 260, 452
   Tancrède · 156, 260
fudai · 18, 352, 365, 493

Fujiwara · 332, 342, 380
fukoku · 277, 493
fukoku kyōhei · 277
Fukui · 56
funerals · 72, 76, 113, 114, 127, 129, 190, 205, 270, 391, 505

G

Garter, Most Noble Order of the · 410, 420
   Knight Companion (KG) · 420, 426, 435
Genghis Khan · 334
Gladstone, William Ewart · 138, 229
Glossary of Japanese terms · 492
Glover, Thomas · 245, 292, 442
Godai Tomoatsu · 181
gokenin · 366, 493, 494
gorogio · 17, 58, 105, 170, 177, 401, 493, 494
go-tairō (Five Great Elders) · 350
Gower
   Abel J · 76
   Samuel J · 76, 94, 128, 131
Gunboat diplomacy · 3, 20, 224, 232, 421, 502
   Don Pacifico Incident · 421
Gunpowder · 51, 238, 292, 336, 381
Guns
   100-pounder · 238, 240
   10-inch · 152, 187
   32-pounder · 152, 154
   40-pounder · 238, 240
   8-inch · 155, 182, 238, 264
   Ammunition · 49, 51, 155, 156, 184, 187, 188, 189, 192, 195, 198, 199, 221, 223, 232, 238, 239, 240, 244, 266, 269, 270, 411, 414, 473

INDEX

Armstrong Gun · 187, 188, 238, 240, 245, 304, 470
Coehorn Mortar · 264
Dahlgren gun · 154, 155
Field Pieces · 264
Howitzers · 264
Mortar · 182, 264
muzzle loaded · 155, 168, 188, 238, 239, 240, 340, 433
Pivot Gun · 154, 155, 156, 317, 450
Siege Gun · 183, 415
gyoretsu · 77, 81, 124, 163, 365, 402, 493

H

Hackney Almanack & Directory · 504
Hakodate · 18, 23, 26, 28, 102, 124, 301, 400, 452, 482, 484
Hall, Francis · 504
Hammond, Sir Edmund · 251, 393, 484, 485
han · 49, 54, 60, 121, 162, 217, 218, 245, 283, 286, 288, 291, 292, 306, 309, 342, 355, 401, 404, 428, 432, 434, 438, 439, 494
Hansard's *Parliamentary Debates* · 504
Harris, Thomas Lake · 45, 297, 298
Harris, Townsend · 22, 23, 25, 44, 54, 64, 119, 188, 200, 297, 401
Hasekura Rokuemon Tsunenaga · 380, 504
hatamoto · 365, 366, 493, 494
HBM Queen Victoria · 31, 35, 113, 121, 172, 221, 233, 256, 257, 393, 416, 431, 507
Heco, Joseph · 254, 504
Heian period c. 794–1185 AD · 372, 439
Henshall, Kenneth G. · 504

Hepburn, James Curtis, Dr. · 74, 75, 77, 91
romaji · 75, 491
Heusken, Henry · 44, 69
Hikone · 54, 401
Hillsborough, Romulus · 504
Hirado · 11, 19
Hiroshima · 312, 350
Hisashi Kukimura · 380
Hoare, James · 503
Hodgson, CP · 398
Hodogaya · 81, 82, 106, 107, 144
Hoey, Henry Edward · 113, 455
Hōjō Masako · 333, 338
Hokkaido, formerly Ezo · 286, 482
Hong Kong · 31, 35, 64, 66, 77, 100, 141, 234, 302, 397, 398, 413, 489, 507
Hope, Admiral of the Fleet Sir James, GCB · 46, 65, 246, 393, 411
Hotta-Lister, Ayako · 503
House, E.H. · 77
Howard-Vyse, Captain Francis · 394
  actions after Incident · 76, 90, 93, 94, 95, 98, 128
  appointment · 397, 398
  church · 70
  controversy over appointment · 398
  holds Inquest · 113, 114, 124, 128
  Inquiry into Incident · 83, 84
  Neale's complaint · 96
  rebuked · 102, 400
  resignation · 401, 485
  Richardson's father writes · 101
Hunting · 41, 45
Hutchings, Seaman John, RN · 278, 283

RESPECT AND CONSIDERATION

I

Ii Naosuke · 18, 54, 55, 56, 80, 401, 402, 433, 434, 441
Ijichi Shogi · 167, 168
IJN *fusō* · 301
Illustrated London News · 23, 223, 274, 415, 504
inada (rice fields) · 322, 494
Indemnities · 28, 144, 160, 162, 177, 184, 194, 197, 210, 211, 272, 283, 431
Inflation · 27
Inquest · 113
International Cemetery · 1
Ion, AH · 505
Iwakura Tomomi and his mission · 281, 302, 402, 403, 404, 407, 428
Iwashita Sajiemon · 207, 208
Iyenaga Toyokichi · 505
Izanagi and Inamami · 319, 320
Izumo · 313, 321

J

Japan Herald newspaper · 40, 64, 65, 68, 75, 85, 100, 132
Japonisme · 28, 312, 315, 316
Jaurès, Benjamin, French *Vice-Amiral* · 156, 260, 263, 265, 404
Jenkins, Dr. · 76, 453
Jephson, Lieutenant (later Commander) Sir Alfred, RN · 185, 188, 198, 268, 459
Johnston, James D. · 505
Josling, Captain James Stephens, RN · 185, 187, 190, 193, 196, 198, 235, 236, 404, 473

K

Kaeda Noboyushi alias Kaeda Takeji alias Arimura Shunsei · 80, 84, 167
Kagoshima
  bombardment (*satsu-ei sensō*) · 191, 197, 296, 418, 497, 507
  debate · 221, 224, 225, 230, 231
kaikin · 12
kaikoku · 18, 494
kakuro · 494
Kamakura · 37, 42, 273, 333, 372, 373, 446, 493, 502
Kamakura period (1185-1333 AD) · 372
kamikaze · 327, 337
  marching song · 331
Kanagawa
  Governor of · 108, 356, 455
  Hill · 115
Kanazawa · 42
kanji · 20, 305, 493, 494, 497
kanpaku (regent) · 332, 348, 498
Kantō · 358
karo · 494, 500
Katsu Kaishū · 19, 279, 406
Katsuro Kogyo · 287
Kawasaki · 42, 66, 68, 70, 81, 91, 106, 107, 108, 115, 116, 117, 119, 121, 128, 435
keiretsu · 292
Kido Takayoshi · 218, 254, 302, 407
Kii · 281, 438
Kikuchi Dairoku · 146, 298, 299
Kinko Bay · 164, 166, 179, 181, 190, 432, 433
kinsatsu · 495
Kirin Brewery · 292
Kobe · 23, 361
Kōbō Daishi · 342
kobu-gattai undo · 403, 408, 434, 495

INDEX

kojiki · 313, 506
koku · 11, 351, 352, 361, 365, 366, 492, 493, 494, 495
kokudaka · 495
kokugaku · 324, 495
kokushi · 495
kokushu · 432, 495
kokutai no Hongi · 328
Korea · 7, 12, 20, 46, 189, 321, 334, 335, 350, 359, 368, 372, 428, 482
Kublai Khan · 283, 311, 333, 334, 335, 336
kuge · 307, 354, 495
Kukimura Rikyū · 77, 80, 408
Kuper, Admiral Augustus Leopold, GCB RN
    arrival at Yokohama · 93, 234
    ceremonial · 129
    deaths of Josling & Wilmot · 187
    despatches · 111
    diplomacy · 103, 104, 208
    Kagoshima · 163, 167, 170, 178, 179, 186, 189, 190, 192, 193, 196
Kuper, Mrs Admiral Emma Margaret, née Bremer · 412
Kurosawa Chūsaburō · 402
kyōhei · 493
Kyōto · 30, 56, 57, 58, 60, 61, 70, 80, 87, 108, 299, 333, 342, 345, 347, 349, 351, 358, 414, 434, 435, 499
Kyūshū · 28, 152, 189, 283, 320, 334, 340, 343, 349, 432

L

Layard, Sir Austen Henry · 223
Le Monde Illustré · 160, 505
Legation, British
    attacks · 43, 44, 47, 48, 140, 161, 442
    building · 51, 455
    personnel · 76, 418, 429, 452
Liverpool, Lord · 420
Luard, Captain William Garnham, RN · 260

M

Macau · 12, 423
Madama Butterfly (Puccini opera) · 292, 313
magatama · 321
Marshall, William · 66, 68, 70, 71, 72, 74, 76, 77, 78, 79, 81, 91, 94, 113, 114, 115, 116, 117, 118, 119, 122, 123, 124, 129, 130, 141, 252, 316, 391, 413, 443
Matsudaira Yoshinaga · 58, 434, 439
McClain, James L. · 505
McDougal, Captain David, USN · 154, 155, 156
Meiji restoration · 218, 324, 403, 433, 443, 492, 501, 502
Melbourne, Viscount · 421, 435
Mexican dollars · 33, 44, 64, 145, 146, 161, 211, 425, 445, 446, 497
Miako, ancient name for Kyōto · 108, 110, 301
Milton, Giles · 505
Minamoto · 332, 333, 439
Mitford, Algernon Bertram Freeman · 505
Mitō · 45, 47, 48, 50, 52, 55, 56, 401, 402, 414, 440, 442
Mitsubishi *keiretsu* · 292
Miyazawa Shinichi · 505
Momoyama · 349
Mongols · 333, 334, 335, 336
Moore, Commander Lewis James, RN · 196, 236, 266, 414

Morgan, Surgeon David L, FRCS, RN · 236, 469, 470
Mori Goronosuke · 402
Mori Takachika · 152, 153, 253, 254, 255, 414
Morrison, George S · 44, 45, 398, 414, 443
Motoori Norinaga · 324, 325, 337
Murder · 2, 3, 6, 28, 49, 63, 87, 92, 94, 98, 104, 105, 107, 110, 121, 122, 131, 134, 135, 138, 140, 146, 161, 162, 170, 172, 174, 176, 205, 208, 210, 283, 287, 292, 333, 358, 380, 389, 407, 418, 429, 453, 504

N

Nagasaki
    attack on Charles Sutton · 203
    Castella cake · 65
    Deshima · 10, 12, 13
    Hirado (English Factory) · 11
    HMS *Icarus* murders · 278
    Perry's refusal to go there · 16
    staging post for travel · 65, 152, 153
Nagashima · 347
Namamugi
    Incident · 41, 61, 68, 71, 79, 130, 219, 280, 392, 397, 418, 435, 496, 503, 505, 507
    Incident celebrated · 87
    museum · 129, 503
    post-Incident · 91, 104
nanban · 13
Napoléon · 11, 127, 233, 285, 427
Narahara Kizaemon · 80, 81, 82, 167, 380
Neale, Edward St. John, Lieut.-Col.
    complaint against · 247, 249, 251
    diplomacy · 105, 108, 110, 112, 114, 141, 143, 144, 146, 148, 162, 163, 197, 209, 212
    Kagoshima · 167, 168, 169, 170, 171, 192, 193
    Namamugi · 75, 76, 90, 92, 93
    Namamugi aftermath · 96, 98, 100, 104, 134, 139
    receipt of apology · 161
    receipt of compensation · 159
    vindicated · 102
Nelson, Admiral Lord Horatio · 233, 234, 243, 301, 409, 424
New York Times · 36, 231, 460, 464
Newcastle-upon-Tyne · 295, 303, 304
Nichiren Daishōnin · 372
nihon shoki · 342, 424
Niigata · 23
nijō palace, Kyōto · 285
Nishino Fumitaro · 296
Nitobe Inazo AM, PhD · 505
Noboru Koyama · 505
norimon · 72, 79, 80, 83, 84, 90, 116, 124, 172, 274, 402, 408, 435, 494, 496, 499
Northern and Southern Courts · 13, 16, 313, 334, 503

O

Oath in Five Articles · 300, 403
o-bon · 309, 368
Oda Nobunaga · 345, 347, 348
Ogasawara Nagamichi · 147, 148, 150, 162, 203
Ōkano Shinsuke (false name) · 81, 491
Okinawa · 17, 60, 189
Ōkubo Toshimichi · 281, 302, 403, 407

INDEX

Oliphant, Laurence · 44, 45, 297, 443, 463, 504, 506
ometsuke · 209, 294, 361, 496
Ōno Yasumaro · 506
Opium Wars (China) · 13, 24, 64, 138, 393, 412, 423
Osaka · 145, 181, 207, 307, 351
Owari, Prince of · 56, 146, 285

P

Palmerston, Lord · 224, 420, 421, 422, 427
Parker, Master William Hennessey · 179, 181, 183, 184, 186, 187, 235, 236, 459
Parkes, Sir Harry Smith · 282, 287, 293, 294, 400, 423, 424, 426, 483, 503
Paulownia Tomentosa · 494, 496
Pearl Harbor · 181, 328
Peninsular War · 415, 416
Perkins, Dorothy · 506
Perry, Commodore
    second mission to Japan · 18, 425
Perry, Matthew Calbraith, Commodore · 7, 11, 13, 15, 16, 17, 18, 22, 24, 27, 36, 308, 311, 324, 383, 385, 386, 387, 424, 425, 440, 492, 494, 505, 506, 507
Pigot, *Trades Directory* · 507
Pinto, Fernão Mendes · 12, 311, 340, 343, 381
Platt Brothers Ltd, Oldham · 296
Poetry · 325
    haiku · 314, 450
    jisei no ku (Death Poems) · 325, 326, 497
    kyoka (mad poems) · 450
    tanka · 325, 337, 450
    waka · 313, 413, 450

Poole, Lieutenant George, RN · 196, 236, 426
Potato · 310
Poundage of guns · 240
Pride, Thomas, Captain of the After-guard, HMS *Euryalus*, VC RN · 257
Prize Money · 242
Promotions · 234, 389, 407, 490
Pruyn, Robert (American Minister in Japan) · 80, 154
Purser · 242
    14 oz to the lb. · 242

R

rangaku · 13, 497
rangakusha · 13
Red Seal Trading Rights · 11
Restaurants · 40
ri · 167, 497
rice · 10, 27, 38, 41, 58, 322, 323, 349, 351, 369, 376, 494, 495
Richardson Family
    brother-in-law, F. Searle · 63
    father, Charles · 62, 63, 251
    mother, Louisa Ann · 62
    sister, Georgihana · 63
    sister, Louisa Grace · 62, 63
    sister, Mavis Flossie · 62, 63
Richardson Residence
    Croydon · 63, 64, 101, 138, 503
    Hackney · 62, 504
    Tunbridge Wells · 63, 251
Richardson, Charles Lenox · 3, 6, 42, 52, 62, 64, 65, 68, 71, 101, 115, 121, 130, 136, 138, 167, 246, 251, 287, 312, 318, 380, 426, 448, 453, 490, 496, 507
    arrogance · 64, 75, 77, 79, 86, 87, 111

attacked · 80, 104, 117, 211, 380
autopsy · 448
compensation for murder · 139, 141, 184, 251
grave · 316
indemnity · 28
inquest · 113, 121
killed · 85, 90, 91, 95, 96, 101, 114
todome · 83
wounds · 73, 74, 81, 85, 91, 115, 118, 120
Rifle Corps · 131, 247
Robinson, Russell Brooke · 266
Roches, Léon, M. · 325, 326, 426
Rockets · 191
rōnin (masterless *samurai*) · 43, 86, 207, 274, 275, 279, 284, 307, 362, 442, 497, 498, 499
Royal Marines · 49, 156, 159, 168, 205, 212, 243, 261, 262, 266, 269, 270, 273, 404, 418, 443, 454, 470, 472, 480, 507
Royal Navy
   domestic routine · 166
   HMS *Alecto* · 237, 488
   HMS *Alligator* · 412, 488
   HMS *Argus* · 141, 163, 179, 180, 181, 189, 195, 196, 201, 236, 260, 414, 488
   HMS *Arrow* · 423, 488
   HMS *Barrosa* · 260, 267, 414, 488
   HMS *Bouncer* · 260, 267, 488
   HMS *Brazen* · 436, 488
   HMS *Centaur* · 90, 91, 141, 488
   HMS *Chesapeake* · 394, 488
   HMS *Conqueror* · 212, 213, 255, 260, 261, 267, 269, 348, 488, 489
   HMS *Coquette* · 141, 163, 179, 181, 188, 189, 195, 196, 200, 236, 260, 265, 389, 488
   HMS *Devastation* · 237, 488
   HMS *Diadem* · 436, 488
   HMS *Eclipse* · 414, 488
   HMS *Encounter* · 46, 141
   HMS *Euryalus*
      armament · 166, 182, 195, 239, 240
      Kagoshima
         action · 179, 181, 184, 185, 186, 187
         casualties · 188, 195, 198
         negotiations · 166, 167, 168
      Kuper meets Naval colleagues · 104
      Kuper meets the community · 97, 103
      Kuper's flagship · 93, 141, 160, 164, 167, 196, 234
      Officers · 235, 404, 445
      Shimonoseki
         action ashore · 261
         casualties · 266
         Flagship · 260
      Shimonoseki VC
         Boyes · 256
         Pride · 257
         Seeley · 257
      stores · 241
      Surgeon's log · 470
      takes *bakufu* indemnity on board · 160
      the ship · 237, 469
   HMS *Harlequin* · 394
   HMS *Havoc* · 140, 141, 163, 179, 180, 181, 189, 195, 236, 426, 488
   HMS *Howe* · 436, 488
   HMS *Icarus* · 278, 284, 488
   HMS *Indus* · 436, 488
   HMS *Kestrel* · 105, 488
   HMS *Leopard* · 260, 267, 488
   HMS *Moselle* · 436, 488

INDEX

HMS *Osprey* · 256, 488
HMS *Pearl* · 46, 141, 163, 166, 179, 181, 182, 188, 195, 196, 199, 236, 328, 391, 488
HMS *Pelorus* · 255, 488
HMS *Perseus* · 163, 186, 188, 191, 195, 200, 236, 260, 263, 267, 407, 488
HMS *Racehorse* · 141, 163, 179, 181, 188, 195, 201, 236, 392, 488
HMS *Rattler* · 141, 488
HMS *Rattlesnake* · 237, 488
HMS *Renard* · 49, 65, 488
HMS *Ringdove* · 93, 141, 488
HMS *Sampson* · 398, 436, 488
HMS *Scout* · 46
HMS *Tamar* · 412, 488
HMS *Tartar* · 260, 265, 267, 269, 488
HMS *Thetis* · 404, 411
HMS *Victory* · 237, 488
HMS *Winchester* · 400, 436, 446, 452, 488
HMS *Worcester* (training establishment) · 299, 301
Kagoshima · 166
uniform · 394
White, Blue and Red divisions · 234
Royal Regiment of Horse Guards (The Blues) · 234, 395, 396, 399
Russell, Lord John (later Earl) · 426
correspondence · 63, 96, 99, 100, 101, 102, 130, 134, 138, 160, 161, 193, 246, 251, 411, 445
Foreign Secretary · 50
Russia · 23, 25, 43, 219, 224, 229, 231, 295, 297, 298, 299, 301, 302, 312, 413, 417, 421, 422, 425, 430, 437, 489
Ruxton, Ian C. · 503, 505, 507
ryō · 33, 145, 146, 292, 340, 360, 497

Ryūkyū Islands · 35, 60, 179, 189, 427

S

Sabin, Burrit · 507
Saigō Takamori · 245, 282, 286, 289, 403, 406, 407, 427, 428, 429, 443
Sakai · 58, 325
Sakai *jiken* · 325
Sakamoto Ryoma · 279, 280, 281, 282
sake · 27, 73, 79, 168, 278, 279, 322, 359, 468, 497
sakoku · 7, 8, 12, 13, 18, 43, 50, 157, 291, 292, 311, 407, 451, 494, 497
sakoku rei · 12, 13, 157
sakura (cherry blossom) · 294, 299, 327, 331, 337
Sakurada Gate · 56, 401
Sakurajima · 181, 190
samurai
Chōshū · 407
Mitō · 45, 47, 48, 50, 56, 80, 402, 414, 443
Satsuma · 77, 85, 90, 362, 363, 427
Tosa · 279, 325, 326
weapons · 61, 381, 493, 494, 500
bows and arrows · 378
lances · 61, 121
spears · 378
swords · 2, 381, 408
Sanjo bridge · 205
sankin kōtai · 355, 356, 497
SatChō · 2, 212, 277, 280, 284, 285, 291, 293, 298, 308, 406, 407, 428
Satow, Sir Ernest Mason · 429
A Diplomat in Japan · 507
his teacher as conduit for diplomacy · 145
Kagoshima

captured prize · 185
re Kuper · 192
re Admiral Kuper · 411
re Dr. William Willis · 445
re Katsuro Kogyo, discussions · 287
re Kido Takayoshi · 407
re Lt. Applin · 391, 454
re Lt. Col. Neale · 415, 418
re Sir Harry Smith Parkes · 424
re Takeda Kane · 32, 429
secret report · 288
servants leave · 144
Shimonoseki
   action ashore · 256
   Chōshū determination · 254
   intelligence · 256
Satsuma
   daimyō · 2, 57, 121, 135, 138, 253, 381, 432
   rebellion · 429, 443
   Shimazu
      Nariakira · 427, 432, 433
      Narioki · 432, 433
      Saburō · 57, 60, 71, 77, 78, 79, 81, 82, 83, 84, 85, 86, 87, 103, 107, 111, 112, 135, 136, 140, 141, 163, 166, 167, 168, 169, 170, 176, 180, 182, 189, 194, 207, 208, 209, 210, 211, 212, 244, 325, 365, 382, 400, 408, 409, 419, 427, 432, 433, 434, 435, 490
      Tadayoshi · 60, 167, 380, 432, 434
      Takahisa · 340, 342
   Shimazu family · 52, 212, 316, 340, 342, 349, 352, 381, 408, 432
   Shimazu *han* · 343
   Shimazu palace · 189

Satsuma version of *Namamugi jiken* · 77, 81, 84, 87
Satsuma vessel
   Contest · 179, 180
   England · 179
   Sir George Grey · 179, 180, 181
Scandal, diplomatic, financial · 33, 124, 359, 401, 458
Schreiber, Mark · 507
Scott, JW Robertson · 507
Secret Meeting · 127
Seeley, Ordinary Seaman William, VC RN · 257, 266
Sekigahara, battle of · 11, 277, 343, 351, 352, 353, 381, 432, 437, 439, 493, 500
Sengoku, warring states era · 338, 340
sensō · 197, 285, 497, 498
seppuku · 43, 49, 80, 82, 145, 282, 283, 325, 326, 343, 347, 350, 361, 362, 363, 429, 434, 443, 497, 500, 505
Shanghai · 26, 40, 41, 46, 63, 64, 65, 66, 68, 77, 100, 131, 139, 141, 152, 153, 234, 246, 256, 292, 302, 392, 423, 452, 483, 484
Shiba Ryōtarō · 87, 507
Shikishima (poetic name for Japan) · 337
Shimoda · 18, 28
Shimonoseki
   agreement · 271
   armament · 155
   bombardment · 221, 244, 256, 404, 414, 498
   Kanmon Straits / Bungo Channel · 152, 153, 154, 157, 253, 293
   stockade · 257, 262, 270
shi-no-ko-sho, warrior-peasant-artisan-merchant castes · 288, 289, 307, 308, 350, 498

INDEX

shinpan · 18, 352, 498
shinsengumi · 280, 282, 498
shintō · 7, 55, 295, 322, 324, 329, 367, 368, 369, 372, 374, 376, 437, 494
   kami · 58, 313, 320, 337, 359, 362, 367, 368, 369, 494
   torii · 368
Ships
   1st rate · 488
   4th rate · 488
   6th rate · 488
   Corvette · 153, 255, 260, 325
   Frigate · 46, 89, 129, 237, 260, 301, 394, 398, 424, 488
   Gunboat · 267, 488
   Gunvessel · 488
   Paddle propulsion · 15, 236, 488
   Screw propulsion · 195, 236, 260, 488
   Sloop · 236, 391, 488
   Steamer · 15, 24, 60, 155, 177, 179, 181, 185, 194, 208, 226, 227, 260, 293, 452
   Troopship · 488
   Turret Ship · 488
shishi · 497, 499
Shroffing · 159
Silk · 370, 392
Smith, George, D.D., Bishop of Victoria (Hong Kong) · 35, 507
Somerset, Duke of · 50, 136, 137, 399, 435, 446
Son of Heaven (Emperor) · 87, 499
Song (musical) · 219, 281, 294, 309, 450, 464
Song dynasty (China) · 334
sonnō jōi · 8, 12, 20, 51, 52, 85, 104, 147, 203, 276, 277, 279, 280, 309, 401, 403, 441, 451, 493, 499
St Michael and St George, Most Distinguished Order of · 430
   Companion (CMG) · 430
   Knight Commander (KCMG) · 430
   Knight Grand Cross (GCMG) · 426, 429, 430
Stirling, Admiral Sir James · 25, 45, 412, 436, 437, 501
Students
   sent by *bakufu*
      Fukuzawa Einosuke · 298
      Hayashi Tadasu · 298, 299
      Ichikawa Morisaburo · 299
      Itō Shonosuke · 298
      Iwasa Genji · 299
      Kikuchi Dairoku · 298
      Mitsukuri Keigo · 298
      Nishi Amane · 291, 342
      Okukawa Ichirō · 298
      Sugi Tokujiro · 299
      supervisor
         Naruse Jogoro · 298
         Toyama Sutehachi · 298
      Tsuda Mamichi · 291
      Tsuda Omeko · 299, 300
      Yasui Shinpachirō · 298
   sent by Chōshū
      Endo Kinsuke · 293, 294
      Inoue Kaoru · 293, 294
      Inoue Masaru · 293, 294
      Itō Hirobumi · 254, 293, 300
      Mori Arinori · 295, 300
      Yamao Yozo · 293
   sent by Satsuma
      Nagasawa Kanae · 295, 298
      Sameshima Naonobu · 295, 297
      supervisor
         Godai Tomoatsu · 181, 295, 296
         Terashima Munenori · 181, 295, 296
Students, Japanese, in Britain · 457, 505

Summer Palace, Beijing · 137, 423
Susa-no-o · 313, 320, 321
Suther, Lt.-Col. William Grigor, RM · 261, 262, 270
Sutton, Charles (English merchant attacked) · 203, 204
Sweet, Able Seaman · 48, 49, 50, 105, 140, 146
Sword
    daishō · 61, 381, 493, 494, 500
    katana · 45, 80, 81, 82, 205, 279, 283, 379, 380, 381, 402, 408, 493, 494, 497, 499, 500
    tantō · 362, 494, 499, 500
    wakizashi · 80, 282, 381, 408, 493, 494, 497, 499, 500
Swordmaking technique · 378

T

Taiping rebellion, China · 246
Taira · 332, 358
Taira Masakado · 358, 359
tairō · 54, 56, 350, 401, 402, 433, 499
Takaoka, Satow's Japanese teacher · 146, 457
Takeda Kane · 32, 347, 429
Tanegashima · 311, 340
Tappan, Eva March · 507
Tariff
    Barriers · 24
    unauthorised · 31
Taxes and duties · 10, 217, 338
Tea · 241, 391
tenka fubu · 347
tennō · 30, 324, 499
Terashima Munenori · 181
The Times · 51, 130, 224, 422, 507
Thouars, Abel-Nicolas Georges Henri Bergasse Dupetit, *Capitaine*, later *Vice-Amiral* · 326

Three Sacred Treasures · 289, 321, 323
Time Magazine · 508
todome · 84, 429, 499
Tōgō Heihachirō, *gensui* (Fleet Admiral) · 299, 300
tōkaidō
    after the incident · 89, 90, 161
    excursions · 41, 70
    gyoretsu · 61
    Japanese bluster · 108
    safeguarding westerners · 107
    stations · 106
    the incident · 71, 78, 80, 84, 119
    treaty limits · 30
Tokugawa
    bakufu · 12, 272, 280, 306, 307, 308, 351, 355, 365, 376, 439, 493, 494
    by name
        Iemitsu · 61, 355, 393, 438
        Iemochi · 55, 56, 57, 58, 61, 253, 277, 401, 408, 434, 438, 441, 495
        Iesada · 54, 55, 56, 407, 433, 438, 439
        Ieyasu · 11, 19, 350, 351, 352, 353, 354, 381, 437, 438, 439, 493, 500
        Nariaki · 18, 55, 56, 440
        Tsunayoshi · 361, 438
        Yoshinobu (Hitotsubashi Keiki) · 55, 56, 86, 277, 280, 281, 284, 285, 393, 401, 428, 433, 434, 438, 440, 441, 507
    dynasty · 6, 7, 52, 277, 281, 284, 311, 351, 352, 432, 437, 439, 440
    navy · 286
    xenophobia · 337, 343

INDEX

Tories, British political party · 397, 420, 421
Tosa · 52, 245, 253, 279, 280, 282, 283, 284, 285, 288, 289, 294, 306, 325, 326
Toyokichi Iyenaga · 508
Toyotomi Hideyoshi · 348, 349, 350, 437
tozama · 18, 306, 352, 381, 432, 500
tozen-ji · 455
Trading Houses
    Japanese
        Mitsui · 305, 307
    Western
        Aspinall, Cornes & Co · 128, 391
        Augustine Heard & Co · 66, 247
        Dent & Company · 30, 93, 131, 484
        Jardine Matheson & Co · 30, 76, 119, 131, 292
        Marshall & Hart Ltd · 66
        WR Adamson & Co · 95
Treaties
    1842 Nanking (Anglo-Chinese) · 64
    1854 Anglo-Japanese Friendship · 25, 308, 437
    1854 Kanagawa (Peace & Amity) · 18, 119
    1858 Anglo-Japanese Amity and Commerce · 25
    1876 Kangwha (Japan and Korea) · 20
    1894 Anglo-Japanese Commerce and Navigation · 19, 431
    1895 Shimonoseki · 430
    Treaty limits · 42, 111
    Treaty ports · 19, 30
    Unequal · 19, 26, 55, 253, 297, 424, 462, 501
tsubo (land measure) · 455
Tsuda Omeko · 291, 299, 300

U

ukiyo-e · 28, 312
United States · 7, 15, 16, 17, 24, 25, 36, 247, 255, 295, 299, 343, 383, 385, 386, 387, 425, 434, 462, 505, 506
Universities and colleges
    Cambridge · 291, 295, 299, 501, 505
    Edinburgh · 389, 426, 442
    Glasgow, Andersonian Institute · 293
    Harvard · 501
    Heidelberg · 292
    Imperial College of Art (Japan) · 294
    Imperial College of Engineering (Japan) · 294
    Kagoshima · 443
    Kyōto Imperial · 299
    Leyden · 291
    London · 292, 295, 296, 429
    Oxford · 227, 291, 295, 452
    Royal Naval College · 301
    Stanford · 501
    Tōkyō · 443
    Tōkyō Imperial · 299
    Waseda · 508
Uraga harbour · 11, 15
US President
    Abraham Lincoln · 17
    Franklin Pierce · 16
    James Buchanan · 17, 254, 417
    Millard Fillmore · 7, 16, 18, 343, 383, 387, 440

V

van Polsbroek, Dirk de Graef, Dutch Consul-General · 153
van Reed, Eugene · 86
Victoria Cross · 256, 257
von Siebold · 196, 457
Vyse see also Howard-Vyse · 70, 83, 84, 90, 91, 93, 95, 96, 97, 100, 102, 105, 114, 115, 122, 124, 128, 391, 394, 395, 396, 397, 398, 399, 400, 401, 482, 483, 484, 485, 503, 504

W

Waterloo, battle of · 228, 416
Weigal, Mr., (Thos. Glover's Manager) · 292
Wellington, Duke of · 421
Whigs, British, also old American, political party · 16, 420, 421, 426, 435
Whitman, Walt · 37, 464
William of the Netherlands, Order of · 410
Willis, William, Dr. · 64, 90, 91, 113, 114, 116, 122, 127, 144, 196, 287, 391, 414, 418, 419, 433, 442, 443, 445, 446, 448, 453, 457, 503
Wilmot, Commander Edward, RN · 187, 190, 193, 196, 198, 235, 236, 394, 445, 446, 459, 473
Wirgman, Charles (artist) · 223

X

Xavier, Francis, Jesuit missionary · 311, 343

Y

yakunin · 356, 500
yamato (Japan as she emerged as a nation) · 337
yamazakura (mountain cherry blossom) · 337
yashiki · 500
yogaku · 13, 497, 500
yonin · 500
Yoshiwara (brothel quarter) · 31, 106

Z

Zhu Xi · 376

THE AUTHOR

John Denney is a Chartered Accountant by profession and a historian by inclination. His interest in the *bakumatsu* and the part that the United Kingdom played in it was engendered by a long holiday he spent with his wife and his oldest and Japanese-speaking son and his Japanese wife who live in the outskirts of the vast Tōkyō conurbation. They toured Japan, visiting many places off the beaten tourist track, including visits to Yokohama and Kagoshima, two of the key places for the events detailed in this book.

John is a leader of, and musician in, his thriving church, and serves other churches as a lay preacher. He is also a regular broadcaster on a local BBC Radio station. John is currently preparing three or perhaps four volumes of his contributions broadcast over many years in their *Thought for the Day* slot. He was also commissioned to write the official *History of the Chartered Accountants' Benevolent Association* published in 2011 to mark the Association's 125th Anniversary [obtainable for a donation from CABA, 8 Mitchell Court, Castle Mound Way, Rugby CV23 0UY].

www.ingramcontent.com/pod-product-compliance
Lightning Source LLC
Chambersburg PA
CBHW021132230426
43667CB00005B/83